Not Everyboday Makes It
But it's fun trying

by

Dave Thomas

Grosvenor House
Publishing Limited

All rights reserved
Copyright © Dave Thomas, 2007

Dave Thomas is hereby identified as author of this
work in accordance with Section 77 of the Copyright, Designs
and Patents Act 1988

The book cover picture is copyright to Dave Thomas

This book is published by
Grosvenor House Publishing Ltd
28-30 High Street, Guildford, Surrey, GU1 3HY.
www.grosvenorhousepublishing.co.uk

This book is sold subject to the conditions that it shall not, by way of
trade or otherwise, be lent, resold, hired out or otherwise circulated
without the author's or publisher's prior consent in any form of binding or
cover other than that in which it is published and
without a similar condition including this condition being imposed
on the subsequent purchaser.

A CIP record for this book
is available from the British Library

ISBN 978-1-906210-52-6

Dedicated

to my late brother
Tony

for all the support and encouragement
over the years

Thanks Bruv.

CHAPTER ONE

"The Early Years"
Playtime on the Bombsites

Autobiographies are usually reserved for famous people, such as politicians, sportsmen, actors and entertainers. But 'hey', not everybody makes it, and there are some interesting stories out there, I guess this maybe one of them. I always wanted to be in show business from an early age. My dream came true, I earned my living as a comedian, and even made it to the London Palladium.

I was born David Thomas McGrail on 19th June 1938, at number 1 Cloudesley Square, Islington, North London. My father was Thomas Frederick, although he did not like the name Thomas and called himself John, but I will tell you more about that later. My mother was Harriet but was always known as 'Hetty'.

It was my mother's family, the Humes that lived in Cloudesley Square. They took over two houses, numbers 1 and 2. Everybody had big families in those days and my mum's was no exception as she was the youngest of eleven children. My mum and dad lived in two rooms upstairs with my older brother Tony, who was three years older than me, until I was a year old and then we all moved to 19 Pleasant Place, Islington. It was a big house, and we had the downstairs and the first floor that had three bedrooms and it had a nice little garden. On the third floor lived an old chap on his own called Harry who was a cripple and walked with a couple of sticks. On the top of the house was another family called the Robinson's, Bill and Rosie who had a boy called William. We had two rooms downstairs and a scullery with a door that led out into the garden.

There were no inside toilets, but two outside, one either side of the garden but they were joined to the house. We had the one on the left and the other was shared between the Robinson's and Harry.

My earliest memories at Pleasant Place occurred when I was four years old. It was during the Second World War, I remember the air-raids and the bombing, but I was never afraid, as I was too young to understand, to me it was quite an adventure. We had to sleep under the table in the kitchen. It was a big square solid oak table, pulled up against the wall. A couple of mattresses were put on the floor underneath and the bed was made up. My brother Tony, mum and my aunt Flo would sleep under that table, I thought it was good fun but of course it must of been terrifying for mum and aunt Flo knowing that if a bomb had hit the house, then the whole house would have come down on top of us.

Aunt Flo by the way was our mum's sister who lived with us, she never married but she was a very special lady, and was always our favourite aunt. She had a great sense of humour and would always make us laugh. My dad during this time was away in the army, he was in the Royal Artillery, I don't remember him being around that much when we were small, but I do recall him coming home on leave in his army uniform.

Apart from aunt Flo, two of mums brothers uncle Joe and uncle Bill also lived in Pleasant Place, neither of them were in the forces as they had both served in the First World War. Uncle Joe lived with his wife and two children opposite us and uncle Bill lived down the road at number 15, he was a widower, but he was my favourite uncle. Every Sunday I used to go to get his beer from the off license, and he used to let me keep the money that I got back on the bottles and he always gave me an extra sixpence or shilling.

Uncle Bill was a good, kind man and he always made me laugh. He had a lot of sorrow in his life as he lost his wife in tragic circumstances when their baby daughter Phyllis was only a few months old.

When I used to visit him on a Sunday, Phyllis, my cousin was by then married to Eric. I remember uncle Bill had a lady friend called Polly. I thought she was a strange looking woman who always seemed to dress in black and would wear a hat. I never saw her without a hat on. He was with her for quite a number of years, but I don't think that she was too popular with the rest of the family. Anyway, the time came when he became engaged to Polly and the date was set for them to marry. I can remember him showing me his nice new wedding suit. Then before the big day came he collapsed in the street and died. It was very sad to lose uncle Bill, but somebody in the family said the thought of marrying Polly must have killed him, - maybe it did!

Lots of children were evacuated during the war, but mum wanted all the family to stay together and I'm so glad she did. We had a brick built air-raid shelter in the garden, but I can remember only spending one night in there. The V1 bombers, doodlebugs were coming over thick and fast and this particular night we were all looking up to the sky and listening to the engine sound, it was very loud and suddenly it stopped, it was quiet for a few moments and then came a terrific explosion and relief came over everybody's faces. They all knew that once you heard the explosion you were safe - until the next time. Harry from upstairs often stayed in the air-raid shelter, but we always seemed to stay under the table. I preferred being under the table, as it was much more warm and cosy.

In September 1944 our sister Maria was born. I can remember when mum first came home from the hospital with the baby in her arms. I didn't really know what was going on, but I know she sat down on a chair in our kitchen/dining room and said to me, 'David, come here and say hello to your sister.' We were now a family of five.

By the time our sister Maria arrived I was six years old and Tony was nine. I had been going to school for a year and a half, and was feeling quite a little man.

My first days at school were awful, and I hated it. My earliest memory was the day before. I was sat up on the draining board by the kitchen sink, with my legs dangling down and my mum was giving me a good wash, I remember very clearly her saying to me, 'You're going to school tomorrow.' and I wasn't to bothered about the prospect. We were Roman Catholic, and I was due start school at St Joan of Arc's R.C School at Highbury. The next morning we got on a number 19 bus in Upper Street it was about a 15-minute journey to Highbury. The stop was almost opposite the school. As soon as we got up the steps to the school I can remember that I didn't fancy this one bit. I was handed over to the teacher in tears and screaming that I did not want my mum to leave me. It was awful. When I think back now, I was coming home at teatime, what would I have been like if I had been an evacuee? - Perish the thought! What some of those poor kids must have gone through, being parted from their families, it must have been really bad.

My biggest memory of that first day in school was that I was too shy to put my hand up and ask if I could go to the toilet. In the end I could hang on no longer, it made a big puddle on the floor, and I felt so embarrassed and abandoned. Eventually I settled down, and I had a nice teacher called Miss Stephens. We also had some nuns teaching, but some of the nuns were quite spiteful, and it was not unusual to see one of them smack a kid around the face, but that was years later, not the infants. The only other clear memory I had in the infants, and this is how I know how old I was. It was my birthday, and I turned to this boy sat next to me and said, 'It's my birthday today', he said, 'Is it, how old are you?

'I'm five.' I said pushing my chest out, but I didn't tell the teacher, as I didn't want any fuss.

When we were kids Christmas was always a smashing time, and we had some great family Christmas's. We always stayed at home even up to when I was eighteen. My earliest Christmas that I remember was in 1944. There was a little paper shop and toyshop in Cross Street called 'Partridges' and my brother Tony and me would look into the shop windows and could see the Knockout and Dandy Annuals. Tony wanted the Knockout and I the Dandy. We made this known, that's what we wanted for Christmas.

It was Christmas Eve and we were in Cross Street so we looked into the shop window and there they were, as large as life staring out at us, the Knockout and Dandy annuals. At that time I thought they were the only two in the whole world. In the early hours of Christmas morning we woke up to check our stockings, and there they were, the Knockout and Dandy at the end of our beds, it was wonderful. Of course our stockings were filled with the usual orange in the toe and all the other bits and pieces.

Mum didn't have much money to spend and she used to make us rag dolls, but they weren't dolls in the sense of the word but soldiers in a uniform. She would buy these flat faces from 'Partridges' and sew them onto a head that she had made and the finished product was a soldier. I suppose the equivalent today would be an action man, but ours were soft toys, made of cloth. We had hours of fun with them and would tie them to chair legs as prisoners. When we had gone to bed at night mum and aunt Flo would go through the ritual of untying them and putting them away.

We always went to mass every Sunday morning as a family. We would go to the St John The Evangelist at the Angel, Islington. At Christmas the grown ups would go to midnight mass and mum and aunt Flo would take it in turns to look after us, and cook the turkey. When I was about eleven Tony and I went to midnight mass and I was amazed to see so many kids there, I guess I thought I'd been missing something all these years. Maria was left at home with aunt Flo. I must tell you at this point that we had a family cat called Jimmy, he was a big fluffy tortoiseshell and aunt Flo was afraid of him. For some reason I don't think he liked her, but I can't think why.

Unbekown to us at the time, while we were at midnight mass, Jimmy the cat ran into the kitchen when aunt Flo went out for something and he wouldn't let her back in. She was trying for fifteen minutes to get him out but without success. She is now concerned about the turkey in the oven and starts to roll objects along the floor to distract the cat. Eventually, she rolls an orange to one side of the cat, he goes for it and she moves into the kitchen. She rolls another orange out of the door, the cat chases it and she rushes and shuts the door behind it. She then pours herself a large brandy, before tending to the turkey. When she told us the story in more detail than I can remember she had us all in fits of laughter.

During the war years I can remember when we were issued with gas masks, mine was a red one. They called it a mickey mouse mask but thankfully we never had to use them. My other early memories of Pleasant Place was sitting on the pot in front of the fire and of course at bath time in front of the fire. We didn't have a bathroom but we did have a big long zinc bath that used to hang up on a rail in the back garden. Bath time was always in front of the fire.

When I was older I remember aunt Flo telling me that I was sat in the bath one night and there was an air raid going on. I pointed up to the ceiling and said, 'Listen to that - that's f–king old Hitler up there!' A shocked aunt Flo said, 'David you are absolutely right, but you mustn't say so.' I don't know where I'd heard that kind of language, as it was never used at home. Anyway, I guess it must have given the family a good laugh! There were lots of laughs during the war years and people were kind to each other. Of course they were dreadful times, but when the war was over I remember mum saying that everybody had their sense of humour and were good and kind to each other because they never knew if they would be there the next day.

I guess my school days at St Joan of Arc were not too bad, but in class I was always slow to put my hand up, I guess it was because I was always shy, and have been for most of my life. We have all read about entertainers being shy and most people can't understand it, but believe me it's true. Maybe it's because when you are performing in front of an audience you are a different personality and you are hiding behind that other person. When I am on stage I give all my energy to that performance, and nothing else matters. I am 100 percent focused. But when I come off I will be my quiet self again.

As a teenager I was very shy, who would have thought that I would make a career as a comedian, and one day perform on the stage of the world famous 'London Palladium' with Shirley Bassey topping the bill. I am a Gemini although I have never been one for all that stuff. When the war was over, it was great fun playing soldiers, with any lump of wood you could find to make a gun. Our playground used to be bombsites and bombed out houses. It was bang, bang here and bang, bang there. I guess all the kids must have looked like scallywags, but we all had great fun. Some of the better off kids would have toy guns, but most of them would make our own.

Eric, who was married to our cousin Phyllis, was in Burma with the RAF and he brought back for Tony and me a Japanese pilots helmet each. They were leather with flaps hanging down over the ears. They weren't very big and they fitted us two boys just right, we would go to school in them and felt it was really the business, a couple of souvenirs from the war.

When I look back and think about it today, I realise how dangerous it must have been playing in bombed out houses, some of them were falling to bits, I remember going upstairs, the banisters would give way and the floorboards would cave in. Tony and the bigger boys would get up to all sorts of daring escapades. They would walk across the planks, with a huge drop below them. Anyone who didn't do it was a sissy (I guess the word today is chicken). Tony was one of the youngest of the bigger boys, I don't know if he fancied it as he was often bringing up the rear, but I remember he always made it. Us smaller kids never did any daring stuff like that, the bigger ones told us it was too dangerous.

One day we went to Hampstead Heath and we noticed a row of bombed out houses on a road about 200 yards from the Heath. When we looked in one there were a few bits of furniture and pictures on the wall. No windows or doors, they had all been blown off, it must have been a recent bombing, although maybe not as the war was over. I couldn't see us being allowed to go to Hampstead Heath with the war still on. Anyway, I noticed this bronze Indian chief on the wall that I liked the look of, so I took it. We all took a souvenir, but I only remember the bronze Indian chief. I guess the reason I remember it so well is because it was on the wall at Pleasant Place for many years and is now on the wall of my home to this very day. A great souvenir from a great day out in a bombed house in Hampstead Heath just after the war.

We were never bombed out as such, although we had a few close calls. I remember when a block of flats were hit at the top of our road. All our windows were blown out and the plaster came down from the ceiling. Our father was at home on leave during this time and it was decided to take the family to my mums sister aunt Mary, who lived in Morden, Surrey to get away from the Blitz.

Anyway we travelled on the underground Northern line all the way to Morden and when we got there it was a site worse than in North London. On the first night the whole window, frame as well was blown out of the wall. Every ceiling in the house came down and the whole road was blitzed. I remember the next morning at the table in our pyjamas, eating our breakfast, looking out of a big hole in the wall where the window used to be, with all the passers by looking in. I think we only stayed two days and went back home again. Mum told us afterwards, that our dad joked that he would be glad to get back to the army where he was stationed up in Scotland, as it was safer.

When the war was over, it was a great joy for everybody and there were street parties everywhere. Pleasant Place was no exception. All the mums down the street helped out with the organising. They had trellis tables down the middle of the road, covered with white sheets and bunting everywhere. It was a great day with games for the kids, that the adults had arranged and plenty of food and soft drinks. Tony was ten, I was seven and our baby sister, Maria would have been one, and so I don't suppose she would remember much about the victory party. Our dad got demobbed and came home with his demob suit; I don't know that he wore it that much. He was a very smart man in his younger days and always a snappy dresser. He would always look immaculate and wore starched white collars with studs and cuff links. He would go out looking like a toff but he didn't have any money. I guess he was like the modern day Mr Micawber, from the Dickens novel.

In the winter he would wear a double-breasted camel hair coat, with football buttons over his pinstriped suit, a black bowler hat, rolled umbrella and black shiny shoes. One day dressed like this, he was walking by Buckingham Palace and as he approached the guards on duty, who were outside the gates in those days, they mistook him for a guards officer in mufti (civvies), jumped to attention and saluted him. This was quite amazing really as he was only five feet four inches tall. I guess the pencil thin moustache did it.

Father worked at John Lewis in Oxford Street, and although he went to work everyday dressed like the managing director, he actually worked in the stock room as a store man. One of the good things about working at John Lewis' was that he was able to take the family away on holiday in the late forties. We went to a small holiday camp that was owned by John Lewis and used by their employees. It was near Andover, a couple of miles from a village called Stockbridge in Hampshire. We stayed in these wooden huts that had been used by the army during the war. If I remember correctly there were about twenty of these huts, with a family in each one of them.

The dinning room was at the bottom of the camp and they had a clubroom where dances were held in the evening. It was a real smashing holiday, full of adventures. We played cricket, climbed trees, played in haystacks and explored everyday. We had coach trips about three times a week to the seaside. One day we would go apple picking in the orchard. I had never seen so many apples in my life and the weather was always fantastic. We went back there about four years on the trot. We always travelled in style. Father would arrange this big black Daimler to pull up outside the house in Pleasant Place to take us to the railway station at Victoria. Mum would wear this lovely hat with a big brim. We would all pile into the limousine with the neighbours waving us off. They must have thought we were loaded. Of course we were far from loaded, but nobody knew that.

We were coming home from one of these holidays and our luggage was being loaded into the van to the station when a man helping us picked up a suitcase and said to dad, 'Blimey John, what have you got in here? This is bloody heavy.' 'Oh just a few apples,' came the reply. Well I thought nothing more about it until we arrived back to London. Just as we were crossing a station road to the taxi rank the case that dad was carrying sprang open. It was full of apples, they rolled and scattered all over the road. There were apples everywhere. I remember us all scrambling about, trying to retrieve them. We had a good laugh but I think mum must have been really embarrassed.

It was now 1949 and almost time for me to take the eleven plus exam. My class were preparing for it. but I didn't talk about it too much; mum told me afterwards that I hadn't even mentioned it to the family at home. I told her on the evening that I had just sat for my eleven plus that day. My brother Tony had taken the exam three years earlier had done quite well and had gone on to Grammar school. Unfortunately, I didn't do as well and went on to a Secondary Modern School. I went from St Joan of Arc's at Highbury to St John the Evangelist R.C School at the Angel, Islington.

My sister, Maria was already at St John's in the infants. When she got a bit bigger, I would take her to school and take her back home. When Tony and myself were at St Joan of Arc we stayed for school dinners. Mum would give us our dinner money; I had fourpence, old money and Tony fivepence. It depended on how many kids were in the family and it went down to a penny a kid. The fifth kid only paid a penny and any with six or over had a free dinner. At St John's Junior School there was quite a lot of scallywags and I saw and heard things that really opened my eyes. The school dinners were terrible and I soon learnt that the trick was to keep your dinner money and run across the road to Chapel Market during the dinner hour to the baker's shop. You could buy a bag of stale cakes for thruppence (3d), it was quite a bag full and they tasted real good.

Of the four years I spent at St John's I enjoyed only one and that was the last year. My favourite subjects were History and English. I enjoyed doing compositions in English class. I had a great imagination and was good at putting pen to paper. The teacher would chalk up a subject on the blackboard and the class would have to write about it. My head would go down and I would begin immediately, I would look up and see some kids with blank pages when I was already on my third page. I think my teacher was impressed because one day he called me up to the front and asked me to read my story to the rest of the class. I did this and even got a few laughs from my amusing piece. I felt quite proud so I guess my schooling wasn't to bad. I couldn't wait to leave school, especially as the time grew near, as I was one of the tallest boys in the school. I always thought I looked too big to go to school anyway. Then the big day came in 1953, I left school, age fifteen.

The twelve months before that, when I turned fourteen, my mum gave me half a crown (2/6) pocket money every week. Tony was working by now otherwise I don't think she would have been able to afford it. He also gave me the odd shilling or so for doing the odd job for him. Neither of us ever got any money from our father, not a penny. He would always say that he didn't "have a farthing" and would pull the inside of his trouser pockets to show us. He looked like the lord of the manor, when he came home he would put on his smoking jacket and pour himself a glass of port from a cut glass decanter, but he never had any money. He was very big on presents, all the relatives in the family thought he was wonderful, he would never go visiting without taking a gift and would have everyone rocking with laughter. Mum's side of the family, the Humes, always called him John and that was the name he liked, but his family called him Tommy and to our cousins on that side of the family he was always uncle Tom. We always wondered where he got his money from, as he never gave it to mum, just the essential housekeeping money. Mum would ask, 'John, have you got a shilling for the boy's bus fare?' He would pull out his pockets and his answer would always be 'I haven't got a farthing'. It became a catch phrase. He often used to say 'We have got a lovely home', and I guess he was right. Mum kept the house nice, it was always clean. Like most families in those days we had a front room that was only used on Sundays. It was nicely furnished and I suppose to a stranger coming in, we looked quite well off. Father was a wonderful host, would always offer everyone a drink and serve it to them in a beautiful glass. He liked nice things and he seemed to get them.

As I have already mentioned, we didn't have a bathroom at Pleasant Place and used the big tin bath. Well one day father brought home a real bath. I don't know where he got it from but it was a big Victorian bath with legs. He carried it home and put it in the scullery. There was a low sink, about six inches high from the floor. He put one end of the bath where the plughole was with the legs in the sink so the water could drain out. He stabilized the other legs so it was firm and didn't wobble. At the other end was an old-fashioned gas copper tub that was used for doing the washing in.

We would boil the water in the copper tub and then with a saucepan, tip the hot water into the bath. It worked a treat. The first time we used the bath it was heaven, a real proper bath. It did have one drawback though, - the door from our new bathroom led out to the outside toilets. I remember a couple of times if old Bill Robinson from upstairs came down to use the toilet and mum was in the bath, he had to go through our kitchen and climb out of the window to go to the loo.

Some years later we had a gas water heater fitted and from that the hot water went straight into the bath. When I was about seventeen, I was in the bath and there was a knock at the door, Bill Robinson came through, past me to go out to the outside loo. I must say that only happened to me the once. It was our mum that really brought us up, as we didn't see a lot of dad. When we did it was not the dad I really wanted. He wasn't interested in football and stuff like that and you couldn't ask his advice on anything, it was always mum. I remember he once took Tony and myself when we were young, to the pictures. It was a gangster film with Edward G. Robinson and James Cagney, it was good and we enjoyed it. But it didn't happen too often. We would go to the pictures with mum every Friday when our sister, Maria was old enough to enjoy it. Before we went, mum would buy some sweets, a quarter of toffees and a quarter of wine gums. She would then tip them all out onto the table and shove them into three bags, one each. It was smashing, a real treat, then off we went to the pictures. We were lucky as it was only round the corner, the 'Carlton Cinema' in Essex Rd, a few minutes walk away. When I look back now, I can see that we never had any chocolates or expensive sweets, but didn't know it at the time and we really enjoyed it. Another reminder to me that money was tight was that one time I had a spell of doing the shopping. Mum would give me a note and the money and off I went to the shops with this big shopping bag. There were no supermarkets in those days so I would go to about four different shops, the butchers, grocers, bakers and sometimes the chemist. When I made the last call, I was always short of money, by either a penny or half penny, but the shopkeeper would always let me off. This happened about half a dozen different occasions, so one day before I was about to leave I said to mum 'can you give me some more money as I owe money to almost every shop down Essex Road' - that made her laugh, but of course I knew she didn't do it intentionally.

We always saw the funny side of things and there were a lot of laughs. Being part of a big family with lots of uncles, aunts and cousins, we went to a lot of weddings. There was always a row or fall out of some sort at almost all of them, I can never remember what they were over. I do remember at one such wedding, towards the end of the evening one of the uncles had a go at us kids for some reason or other and it ended up in a big row. Father got up and said to mum, 'Come on Hetty, get your things, we're going', and with that we were all gathered up and left. On the underground train home I was sat next to mum with Maria, opposite was Tony with father. He must have thought that mum didn't look to well, so he took off his bowler hat, came across to us and said, 'Hetty, if you feel sick, be sick in my bowler hat.' I thought - nice one!

I first got hooked into the entertainment business by listening to the stars of radio, on the wireless as we called it in those days. We would all listen to 'Variety Bandbox' with Frankie Howard, Max Wall, Robert Morley, Leon Cortex, Jimmy Jewell an, Ben Warris, and Arthur English to name a few. But the very best of course, had to be Max Miller. As he used to say 'There'll never be another,' and they're never has!

We would also listen to Paul Temple and Dick Barton, Special Agent with Snowy & Jock. I was a big fan of 'Educating Archie' with the ventriloquist Peter Brough and Archie Andrews. But my biggest favourite was Max Bygraves with his catch phrases - 'I've arrived and to prove it I'm 'ere,' 'Dollar Lolly' and 'Big 'ead.' I didn't know what he looked like, having only heard him on the radio. I had built up this mental picture of what I thought he looked like, a cockney workman that was rounded, balding and a cheery face - what a let down, when I did see him, it was a big disappointment to me - Max Bygraves was young!

Any way, my disappointment didn't last long and when I first saw him perform live at the Finsbury Park Empire I became a fan;

he was the entertainer that I wanted to be like. My first recollection of going to the theatre was when I was a kid, the family went to see the pantomime 'Dick Whittington and his cat' at the 'Shaftsbury Theatre' I remember, we were in the queue and that it was a magic moment to actually see a live performance on a stage. On another occasion, father took us all to the 'Collins Music Hall'. It was just ten minutes from our house and he said he had booked a box. It all sounded very grand, but when we got there it was a real tatty box - a real let down, but then again the 'Collins Music Hall' was tatty all over, really run down, but we all enjoyed the evening. There was a touch of magic about the place. I had read that it was the oldest music hall theatre in England so of course it had a wonderful history.

After hearing all these wonderful artists on radio, you wanted to go and see them perform live. Once, I went to the 'Hackney Empire' with mum, just the two of us. I don't know how this came about, the only thing I can think of is that I was about thirteen years old and Tony would have been doing his own thing, Maria would have been too young to appreciate it. Top of the bill was one of my favourites at that time Arthur English, the wide boy comic. He shared the bill with a great northern comic, Hal Monty. It was a night I have never forgotten, I even remember they did a sketch as a couple of barrow boys and at the tag, they both held up this big pair of bloomers between them from their barrow and said, 'We'll share the profits,' then ripping the bloomers in half saying, 'Half a knicker each!'

I guess it sounds a bit tame by today's standards but the theatre would rock with laughter. Not a swear word was said all night. I saw Max Miller twice at 'Finsbury Park Empire', the first time I went on my own and paid nine pence old money up in the gods, it was the top balcony, you couldn't get any higher. The theatre was packed and the audience loved him. He told so many gags but when I came out I couldn't remember any of them.

The next time I saw Max Miller I was fifteen and I went with my mate Johnny Mizon. The only thing I regret was that I wish I had been older when I saw him, as I wasn't really old enough to appreciate the master in action. His timing was superb, his facials, eye movement, he didn't have to finish a line; the look said it all, the audience knew. When I watch video film of him today he was, without a doubt, the 'guvnor'. I just feel privileged today to be able to say that I saw Max Miller live. Many years later, after I had finished my act an older pro that was on the bill said that I reminded him of Max Miller. I took it as a great compliment.

CHAPTER TWO

"The Teenage Years It's Time to Make Stage Debut."

When I left school at fifteen my first job was as a waiter at the 'Oxford and Cambridge Club' in Pall Mall. It was a gentlemen's club in swanky surroundings. I wore a uniform of black trousers and white jacket with brass buttons up to the collar; it was like a stewards tunic. We had a clean tunic each day and it was brilliant white. We used to work two shifts, early shift and late shift. The early one took us over the lunch period and finished at 2 pm. The late started at 2 pm and finished at 11 pm.

In the waiters room you would wait for the bell to ring, then an indicator would drop down on a box on the wall to let you know which room was calling for service. If you got a call to go to the morning room, you would go into this very large room with thick carpet on the floor, the decor was quite grand, paintings on the wall, a massive fireplace and leather armchairs and sofas scattered all around the room. They were what looked like, to me, at the time, a load of old men that spoke with posh accents all over the room. Some were sleeping, some were reading and others were writing at various desks around the room.

If it was afternoon, the order would usually be a pot of tea and a toasted teacake, it was served on a tray with a silver teapot, sometimes they would ask for a little pot of jam. In the evening it would often be a glass of South African Sherry or a Gin and Tonic. When I was younger my ankles used to crack and I remember one afternoon as I walked around the morning room to empty the ashtrays and tidy up the newspapers my ankles cracked with every step. There were about eight gentlemen in the room and each time I passed one of them, I would get the strangest look, because of the cracking in quietness, the silence was being broken by the noise. When I got out of the room I thought to myself - well, it could have been worse - I could have farted!

One thing I did learn about my time at the Oxford and Cambridge Club was that if you were an old bastard you were treated well. There was one such gentleman called Mr Duke. It was my second day working there and I was serving lunch in the dinning room, I was about to take a plate of soup out to one of the tables when the lady in charge behind the servery asked me which table I was going to. When I told her she told me, 'That's Mr Duke, you can't take that as it is,' she took it from me and with a clean napkin she wiped a spec of soup off the rim of the plate and gave it back to me. I took the soup out to the table and this grumpy looking man who looked in his late sixties glared at me and said, 'Thank you.'

I got to know Mr Duke quite well after that and although everyone was afraid of him he was always given the very best attention. When I had been working there for a few weeks I became used to him and I knew his likes and dislikes. I think he liked me, he called me David and at times I would even get a smile from him. I left the club after six months and on my last day Mr Duke gave me two pounds. In 1953 that was a huge tip, so the grumpy Mr Duke wasn't such a bad old boy after all.

I have often been asked why I am a Spurs supporter, being a native of Islington as it would be the natural thing to support Arsenal. Well I guess the answer to that would be that when I was at school all the kids were Arsenal fans and with not belonging to a family of great football fans anyway, I didn't get (thankfully) too carried away about the Arsenal. One day, in late 1950, when I was twelve, I was on a bus going to visit my cousins Phyllis and Eric who lived in Tottenham. There were a group of boys at the front of the bus, talking football. The conductor joined in, he said to the boys, 'Tottenham are a good team aren't they?' The boy's response was not very enthusiastic. 'They are top of the league,' he continued. 'Yeah, second division.' They replied. I don't know why, but from that moment on I became a Tottenham Hotspur supporter through and through. Of course Spurs won the 2nd division championship that year and the following season the 1st division championship 1950/51. It was the famous push and run side managed by Arthur Rowe. I can even remember the team below.

TED DITCHBURN

ALF RAMSEY CHARLIE WITHERS

RON BURGESS NOBBY CLARK BILL NICHOLSON

LES BENNETT EDDIE BAILEY

SONNY WALTERS LEN DUQUIMIN LES MEDLEY

My favourite players of that time were always Alf Ramsey and Eddie Bailey, who was known, funnily enough, as the 'Cheeky Chappie' of football, after Max Miller. Following Spurs has been quite a roller coaster, with plenty of ups and downs, White Hart Lane is a great place to be and I can't think of anywhere that I enjoy more.

My next job was at the Columbia Paper Supply in Hackney as a paper winding machine operator. I was not yet sixteen, but I soon got into the swing of things. It was a small family business with a workforce of only about thirty. I soon found out that most of them were comedians; it was a laugh a minute. All had nicknames and I guess you could liken it to the TV series 'London's Burning' Some of them were real wags and the wit was razor sharp. We had a good governor called Ernie who ran the firm with his brother in law Eric. They were the original 'Eric and Ernie', but of course this was well before Morecambe and Wise made the big time, although I do remember hearing them on 'Workers Playtime' on the radio.

The work did vary from time to time. Some weeks you would be on a winding machine, then you could be put on a bail machine making paper bails, another packing parcels and moving on to another machine. Then you would be loading the parcels onto the lorries. We had two of our own lorries, but big wagons would come into the yard throughout the day from the paper mills that had to be unloaded. I guess the work was a bit repetitive, but it was quite a joy working there when you knew you were going to have a good laugh. It was my uncle Dick who got me the job at the 'Columbia'. He was, by this time retired but he used to work for the firm as a service engineer for the machinery. Uncle Dick was a real character, he lost half of his forefinger in an accident and he would prod people with his stump. I suppose to describe what he was like would be an Alf Garnett type and he wore a bowler hat.

Just before I started work, he said to me, 'Now, don't call me Uncle Dick, call me Dick. Ok.' 'Right' I said, I was quite happy with that. After I'd been there about a fortnight he came down to the firm on a visit, when he walked through the big sliding doors everyone on the shop floor shouted 'Morning Uncle Dick!' His reply to them is unprintable. In the wintertime it could become uncomfortable, as there was no form of heating. I remember on one very cold spell that a lot of the lads were complaining bitterly about the cold. The very next day, Ernie, the governor came in with a massive box of oxos and put them on a table in the canteen, 'A mug of hot oxo would warm everybody up', he said. We all thought it was quite a laugh but the following week he bought us all a navy blue duffle coat each to wear.

At this point I must tell you about my friend Roger, we met when I joined the Tinhatters Amateur Variety Company in August 1956 when I was eighteen. I had seen Roger once before when I went to see the Tinhatters perform at the Islington Town Hall. He was already a member of the company and he did a very funny miming act. I had to audition to join the company and after successfully so, I became a fully paid member of the Tinhatters. The company was based in Islington and did variety shows for charity in town halls and various clubs all over North London. Roger and I became great mates and as time went by we became the very best of friends. He was my best friend and I was his. We had so many laughs together, didn't take anything too seriously. Life was a 'ball'.

I think I can honestly say that in the late 50's and early 60's I had more laughs with Roger than at any other time.

Although he didn't do a stand up act like myself, he would do a mime act, he was naturally a funny guy, a couple of times we did a double act with the Tinhatters.

When I met Roger he worked for a butcher, but it was not what he wanted so I got him a job up the Columbia with me. I was called up for National Service about ten months before him, when he received his papers for call up I asked him to put down for the Royal Army Ordinance Corps. He did and was posted to the same barracks as me, so we were even in the army together, we were, as they say, like blood brothers-but without the blood.

He was amazing at drawing cartoons. Everything that happened to us was put into a cartoon, I have enough for a book on it's own, but I'll tell you about that later. It was my other friend, Johnny Mizon to whom I must give credit to for my first appearance on stage. As a boy in the scouts I had before been on stage for a couple of 'Gang Shows,' but I never really counted them. Johnny and I became good mates when we were 15 and 16, but I had known him as a kid who lived in the next street to me. We both looked 18 so we would call in to the local pub for a few brown ales now and again.

We would go to the 'Finsbury Park Empire and the 'Hackney Empire' every week, no matter who was on. It was 'Finsbury Park' that we would never miss. We saw some great 'top of the bills'- Frankie Vaughan, Dickie Valentine, Max Wall, Max Bygraves, David Whitfield, Tommy Cooper and Alma Cogan to name a few. After about a year we moved onto the West End and went regularly to the London Palladium and the London Hippodrome. It was at these theatres that we saw some great revue shows with Harry Secombe and Beryl Reid, Norman Wisdom, Benny Hill, Tony Hancock and Jimmy Edwards with a very young Shirley Bassey on the bill, that was at the Adelphi Theatre. Around about that time the London Palladium was taken over by the Americans, like Frankie Laine, Johnny Ray and Guy Mitchell. I must say that during those years the best I ever saw was Danny Kaye. He was the complete entertainer and a night that I have never forgotten.

The year is now 1955 and after watching so many Variety Shows I really wanted to be a part of it. I can remember sitting in the audience in the dark, with the spot light shining down on the performer and thinking 'wow, it must be great to be up there.' The comics would come on and stand with one foot on the spotlights, one hand in pocket, looking so relaxed and when the punch lines were received with these hails of laughter I thought what a great feeling it must be to make so many people happy and help them forget any problems they may have had. Very often, many of the comics would do the same gags and I soon realised that 'it was the way you tell 'em' (before I had even heard of Frank Carson) and that the most important part of comedy, was timing.

Islington Town Hall was running a talent contest every Friday for a number of weeks with the winners going on to the final in March. I thought everyone has to start somewhere, so this could be the start for me. The more I thought about it, the more enthusiastic I became. The next time I saw Johnny I said to him, 'Johnny, we are going to enter the talent contest.' He paused for a few seconds and then, with a very surprised look on his face he replied, 'You must be joking!'

'I'm serious,' I said, 'we could enter as a double act.'

'A double act?' he said, 'I'm not a performer, and I've never been on stage in my life.' 'That doesn't matter, neither have I, it will be great.' I assured him. 'Great,' he said, 'we haven't even got an act.'

'Then we'll write one' I said.

After much discussion I eventually managed to persuade Johnny and we put our names down for the talent contest' As a comedy act we were given six minutes, we had two weeks to prepare. We wrote a piece where I would come on first to sing a song and Johnny would keep coming on with interruptions and comments about the local area, finishing with a mime to a record of Max Bygraves and Archie Andrews. We would rehearse each night in the front room of Pleasant Place and after a week we were becoming quite polished and the mime was spot on. By this time Johnny was really keen on the idea and was really enjoying it. After rehearsals we would go down to the local pub for a couple of drinks and to relax. Before we got into this talent business we used to look at the local talent and girls were high on our list of priorities but now we were so focused on getting the act together we never gave the girls a second thought, we both agreed there was plenty of time for girls later.

We were both well rehearsed and ready by the time the big night came. Friday 4th November 1955, at the Islington Town Hall. I wore a nice smart single-breasted suit complete with a white shirt and tie and it was decided to fit Johnny up in my dad's evening suit with white tie and tails. We were in my bedroom and dad brought in the suit for Johnny to try on along with white dress shirt, stiff front and double cuffs. I must say that when he was all dressed up he looked really funny, the trousers were baggy and the sleeves too long. He looked perfect, just the way I imagined he would look. Suddenly, dad came back into the room and handed Johnny a pair of gold cuff links. 'Look after these John' he said, 'as they are worth more than the suit.'

After the fitting we were soon packed up and ready to go. Father came back in again, this time to pour us a glass of whiskey each, he said, 'Good luck and down in one!' That we did and we were ready to go and perform our very first stage appearance, EVER.

At this point I must tell you that my sister Maria, who was eleven at the time had also entered the competition in the junior section that was the first half of the show, with the senior section to follow. She was going to sing a song and finish with a Spanish dance routine that she had worked out herself. It was also her first time on stage. As we were getting ready in the dressing room I could see that Johnny was becoming more nervous by the minute. In fact his nerves were helping me to forget my own. The junior section began; Maria did very well, so well that she came second. That was a big boost for us and I was ready to go.

We were announced by the compere, I walked on stage first and did a couple of quick gags before Johnny came on, but before he was supposed to, when he got to me he forgot what he was supposed to say. The audience roared with laughter and from then on all the planning and rehearsing had gone out of the window, it was ad-lib all the way and I was comfortable with that and we were getting lots of laughs. Then came the time to do our finishing number (the mime to the record). I gave the cue - a pause - and no record came on so I turned to the side of the stage and said, 'Time for the record', 'We haven't got it' came the reply from the wings. I turned to Johnny and said, 'Johnny, go and sort it out'. He turned in a spin and with coat tails flying ran as fast as he could and disappeared into the wings. Within seconds he was running back up to me and said, 'He hasn't got it.'

I said' 'Well where is it?' almost in a panic. 'It's downstairs, in the dressing room!'

The audience was rocking with laughter.

'Well don't just stand there, go and get it.' I shouted, and off he ran again.

I was on my own now and I knew it was down to me to keep the audience entertained so I was saying whatever came into my head. At one point I turned to the side of the stage and caught sight of the stage manager who said to me, 'keep it going'. I felt really proud at that remark, there was me, my first time on stage and the S.M is telling me to 'keep it going' like I was a seasoned performer. After what seemed like an age Johnny returned, the record came on and we finished our act to really great applause. In the competition, we weren't placed anywhere but the judges gave us a special mention and were invited back to try again in the next heat. Of course I didn't expect to win, on our first time out but I was really pleased with how it had all gone. All the family had been to see the show and father said how good Johnny had been, as he looked 'frightened to death' when he walked on. Well he was right! He was frightened to death and I think he was also frightened in case he lost the gold cuff links.

After our successful debut we were both all set for a follow up and even Johnny was getting enthusiastic. The next heat of the contest was four weeks away so we decided to change the act and start rehearsing. A week on and it was coming along nicely. Half way into the second, Johnny arrived at my house with a strange look on his face. 'What's up,' I said, 'you look like you've lost a pound and found a shilling.' 'I have.' he said, 'I've got 'me call up papers and I'm due to report just before the talent show in a couple of weeks.' This was a bitter blow as we both knew that we would have to pull out of the talent contest, and it had been going so well! The disappointment must have shown on my face when Johnny said to me, 'I know, it's a choker and I'm really sick about it, but it doesn't stop you, does it?' 'What do you mean?' I said. Johnny replied, 'You can enter on your own.' I guess I could, couldn't I.' I said thoughtfully. 'Of course you could, you'll be great!' enthused Johnny. Well, that was it, myself and Johnny Mizon's career as a double act on stage was over, after just one night only. I was about to embark on a solo career as a stand up comedian.

The date was 2nd December 1955, again at the Islington Town Hall, Heat 2 of the talent contest. My first time alone, I was pleased with my performance. I did not expect to win any prizes and was keen to learn from my mistakes. If it had been a disaster then I would have given up there and then, but I felt good about it. I knew I could do this on my own and felt very confident.

My next time out was on 3rd February 1956. I had worked hard on my act, written some of my own gags and would once again finish with a mime, a take off of Johnny Ray, the American singer who was at the time a big chart topper with 'Who's sorry now'. I had seen Johnny Ray live on two occasions at the London Palladium and London Hippodrome, had his movements off to a tee, but I would exaggerate his moves to make it funny. Now, for some reason, I seemed to think that the Town Hall didn't have a hand held microphone that I could use (I'm sure they did have, but I didn't like to ask) so I decided to make my own. With a long length of black cable, tapped to a black toy telephone handset I figured that it would look like the real thing from a distance.

Once again it was a packed house, as it always was on talent nights and I was really up for it. Everything went well, I felt my timing was improving all the time and the Johnny Ray impression brought the house down. I was delighted when I won 1st prize of two Guineas (£2.10 today) and a place in the Grand Final to take place on the 2nd March. After the show I went into the pub opposite the Town Hall, it was called the 'Hare and Hounds' for a celebration drink and to take a few 'bows'. I was stood at the bar when this guy came up to me and said how much he had enjoyed my performance and bought me a drink. As he walked off he said 'By the way, the telephone looked good!'

The day of the Grand Final arrived, I went down well but was not placed anywhere, I was not concerned about this, as I knew that I was still learning and was happy to be gaining more experience. Soon after the event I was invited to appear in a 'Grand Variety Concert' in aid of the Islington T.B Care Committee. I was very pleased to receive the invitation as it was not only for the winners of the Talent Contest Final, but also some of the best variety acts from across the borough. It was also staged in front of many dignitaries including the Mayor of Islington. I was still only 17 and after just five performances I just knew that it was going to be the life for me. I wanted to be in show business and be a star performer!

There had been no family holiday for a number of years, in fact not since the John Lewis Holiday Camp days in the wooden huts. Anyway, it was decided that all the family would holiday together to 'Butlins' in Clacton.

It was the middle of June 1956 and when we arrived at Clacton station, about four 'Redcoats' wearing huge smiles on their faces greeted us. They directed all the 'Butlin' holidaymakers to awaiting buses. We were well impressed, I thought, what a lovely welcome. As we were driven through the main gates of the camp it was another intake of breath as we marvelled at the size of the outdoor swimming pool just inside the gates opposite the massive reception with these giant toy soldiers along the outside wall. The water fountains were spraying high into the air, the sun was shining on the blue water, and the flowers were out in full bloom and the grass verges surrounding the pool looked magnificent. They say that first impressions are very important, and they are, I thought to myself 'If the rest of the place is as good as this then we are going to have a great holiday.'

After checking in at reception we then embarked on finding our accommodation. Outside were dozens of trolley boys with their homemade carts, made from old pram wheels fitted on to what looked like orange boxes. There were many different shapes and sizes and the boys would load the 'campers' (as they called them in those days) suitcases into their carts and off they would go taking them to their respective chalets. The boys were not paid by Butlins but made their money on tips. We were allocated two chalets, side by side. They were very basic but clean, they had no bathrooms or toilets in those days, it was just a room with a washbasin in the corner, two bunk beds and a single bed. There was no wardrobe, what served as so had no doors but a curtain pulled across the front of it. In side was a pole fitted across to hang your clothes up with wire coat hangers that were supplied.

Mum and Maria had one chalet and dad, Tony and myself had the other. There was no hot running water but each chalet had a big white tin jug. This was used to fill up with hot water found at the end of the chalet line bathhouse. Both the baths and toilets were at the end of the lines in different blocks; they were marked up as 'Lads' and 'Lasses'. I remember we all found this very amusing at first, but then agreed it was a great idea, much better than 'Ladies and Gentlemen' Well this was 'Butlins' in the fifties and you soon realised why you were called 'campers', it really was like camping but it was fun.

Father was always first one up in the mornings and he would go on the trip with the 'jug' to the hot water tap. The first morning he came back with the hot water he said, 'I was coming out of the Lads and two other lads were going in, they were both in there seventies.' He roared with laughter, he had a laugh like no other, it was very contagious and we all roared. It was non-stop laughter all the way.

The Butlins entertainment was first class, there was so much to do, so much to choose from and it was all free. The Variety and Revue shows were first class and there was a Playhouse Theatre with a Rep company who would put on four different plays each week. It was the first time I had actually seen a play and suddenly realised what I had been missing all these years. Like many from a working class background, I thought that straight theatre was a bit 'High Brow', but of course it isn't, it's for everyone. Since then, of course, I have seen many more West End plays and they're great to see. It was the Forbes Russell Theatre Company that staged there wonderful plays at Butlins and many years later I actually appeared in one of their plays at Butlins, Skegness but more of that later.

We noticed in the programme that they were running a National Talent Contest sponsored by 'Photoplay' the film magazine. I immediately decided to enter. The date was 20th June 1956, the day after my eighteenth birthday. I had given just five performances since that first time with Johnny Mizon and this was to be my biggest challenge yet! The compere was a guy called Harry Wilkes, a very good performer in his own right, I think that's why I remember his name. I was waiting in the wings, my time had come, Harry Wilkes introduced me '.....from little old Islington, Dave McGrail! The band struck up and I walked on stage to the play-on music, looking down to the pit orchestra, it was such a great feeling, one I've never forgotten. It was my first time on stage with a pit orchestra 'blasting' away. The stage lights were so bright and the spotlight at the back was shining full in my face, I couldn't see the audience, it was pitch black. It was not long however, before I could hear them. With over a thousand people in the audience, the atmosphere with the band, the lighting, the sound system everything was perfect. I felt right at home, really relaxed, I belonged there.

Within just a few seconds I got that first all-important laugh. The rest of the gags went down really well, I finished my act with a parody about Johnny Ray that I had written to the tune of Robin Hood, unfortunately I messed it up, I was not happy with it. Luckily the rest of my act had gone so well that it didn't matter. I won, 1st prize of two guineas (£2.10) and one weeks free holiday in September, and a place in the semi-finals. We all had a fantastic time on our Butlin holiday, the theatre shows, dancing in the ballroom to the sounds of the Eric Winstone Orchestra with his three front singers, and then there was the Old Tyme Ballroom, about seven bars with live musicians in each one of them. You don't see that today. Indeed Billy Butlin had it right, as there was something for everyone.

The only complaint that we had was that we couldn't fit it all in, what with rushing from one place to another, by the end of the week you were worn out, Mum said, 'We will all need another holiday when we get home, to get over it.' I guess she was right, but we all had a wonderful time, with lots of happy memories. In fact it was the last time the family had a holiday together, but it was a great one.

Family has always been important to me, I always feel, if you haven't got a family, you haven't got a life. Maybe, when you are working away and you can't see them as much as you would like to, they are always in my thoughts. I feel very close to all of them. Families grow, my brother Tony married Eve, and they have six children. Maria is married to Harry and they have two boys. When I married my wife Olivia, she already had two lovely little daughters so she presented me with a ready-made family. We were a couple for four years before marrying in 1965 so we have been together for 41 years, I can't believe it, but it's true.

Our two daughters are both married and have three children each, six grandchildren. Our eldest granddaughter, Christine is married with three little girls so now we have three great grandchildren. Yes indeed, family life is wonderful.

When we got back home to Islington after our holiday, it was back to the old routine. I was still working at the Columbia, getting up at 7.30 each morning, a quick wash, Mum would have my porridge and tea on the table, I would gulp that down and then right on time at ten minutes to eight the radio light programme would announce, 'Lift up your hearts.' That was my cue to go, I'd jump on my bike and peddle as quickly as I could all the way to the Columbia, it took exactly ten minutes. Mum would say, 'Lift up your arse, and get it on your bike.' As I rode in the yard, Roger would be coming in at the same time on his bike.

By now of course my mind was on the forthcoming semi-finals at Butlins in September. I knew that I would have to make a few changes to the act and that the Robin Hood parody was the first item to take out. I would be going over material in my head while I was at work, some of the lads would take the mickey, and they said I was talking to myself. It didn't bother me, as I knew what I was doing.

We had a few charity shows coming up with the Tinhatters Variety Company. There was one at the Civil Defence H.Q at Drayton Park, one in Stoke Newington and a couple at the Islington Town Hall so I was able to try out some new material and polish my act up.

By this time, my mate Johnny was well into his National Service and was posted to Malaya. It was just Roger and me, life was just great, and it was a laugh a minute wherever we went. Of course we had our fair share of girlfriends but most of these events were more funny than romantic. On one occasion we met two girls at a dance, I took my one home to her house, we were stood in her porch. I leaned over to kiss her when she put her arm up and said to me, 'Don't kiss me Dave, I have a cold on my lip,' I replied, 'I never noticed, I'll have a look.' With that I lit my cigarette lighter and held it up to her face, 'You're right,' I said, putting out the lighter and kissed her on the hand. Roger thought that it was priceless and drew a cartoon of it.

September soon came round and I was on my way to Clacton for the Butlin's Semi-finals. I'd already had my holidays from work but the governor Ernie gave me another week off. I think that he and all the lads up the Columbia were quite proud of my achievements so far. I went on my own and when I checked in at reception I discovered that all the contestants were to share a chalet, I didn't mind although I wouldn't like the idea today, to share with a complete stranger. I was in with a guy a bit older than me called Mike, he was a singer, and we got to know each other and became good mates for the week. As you can imagine there was a lot of talent there as they were all the winners from the whole of the summer season. They ran five heats and took two from each heat to appear in the Camp Final. I got through my heat and was in the final ten. It was September 26th 1956, the Embassy Theatre Butlins Clacton National Talent Camp Final.

Everything went well for me, the audience were great and I won through to the Grand Finals in Margate in October. I felt now that I had what it takes and was on my way.

Soon after the show I was in the bar when a chap came over to me to offer his congratulations and to buy me a drink. He introduced himself as Lionel and gave me his business card. He said he was there to see the talent and was looking for an artist to offer personal management. At the time he was working as an air steward for British Airways. He was a very friendly guy and we got on quite well. Before he left he said that it was his intention to go to Margate in October to see the Grand Final and that he would look forward to seeing me there. Back home in London I knew that I had four weeks to prepare for this next big event. I would rehearse in the front room at Pleasant Place and continue to watch and learn from performers at the Finsbury Park and Hackney Empire. One of the all-important things that I did learn was how to get on and off a stage. It may sound strange, but it is an art in itself. The way a performer walks on and the way he makes his exit is all part of the act. Some people that you see can't do it; they look embarrassed coming on and don't know which way to turn to get off. When done in time to the music, an arm movement, a bow to a drumbeat, a turn and a walk slowly in time to the music, it looks great. If it's done properly, the audience may not even notice but, if it isn't, then they will.

When I arrived at Butlins Queens Hotel at Margate, the first face I saw was Lionel the air steward that I had met at Clacton. True to his word, there he was it's always nice to see a friendly face that you know on these occasions. 'I've flown in straight from New York.' he said as we shook hands. 'I've really been looking forward to it.' He was not a pushy type and then before I had time to say anything he said, 'Look Dave, I know you will be busy with meetings and rehearsals, so I will catch up with you later.'

He wasn't wrong, as I soon learned that there were forty-five acts in all from all over the U.K. We were split into three heats and five from each heat would be picked to make up fifteen acts for the Grand Final at the end of the week. I was in heat three so I was able to watch the first two heats, they were quite mind blowing. The standard was very strong, some very outstanding singers with great voices including a female soprano and a great male tenor. Three very good comics, a vent and two vocal groups to name a few. I remember thinking 'Wow, how have I got into this company when

I have only just been performing for ten months, with only ten performances under my belt.'

My heat came, I don't remember too much about it, but I do recall how relieved I was when my name was called out and I knew I was in the Final. My confidence was now very high and even though I recognised the fact that many of the other performers were more talented than I was, with great voices and others being gifted musicians, it was me who made the audience laugh and if an audience is laughing, then that audience is happy and enjoying itself. The big night came October 15th 1956, the Grand Final sponsored by Photoplay Film Magazine. Among the judges were beautiful film star Hazel Court, actor Michael Medwin and Ted Kavanagh, a well-connected man of showbiz.

I was number eleven on the bill and my nerves were really getting to me, I couldn't talk to anyone and just kept quiet, pacing up and down, now and again I could hear the audience and the other acts before me, they were all going really well. My time came and I said a little prayer, 'Please God, help me make 'em laugh.' As I walked on, that first laugh came quickly and it was a belter. My nerves soon disappeared and I gave my best performance so far. At the end I was overwhelmed by the applause.

The Finale soon followed and we were all lined up for the announcement of the winners. '..........in third place, vocalist Charles Wilkinson. .... in second place, that classical pianist Shelagh Stamp. .... and the winner is that young man who made us all laugh, ...David McGrail! It was a really fantastic feeling to have won a competition of this magnitude and to have come on top of all this wonderful talent. I thought to myself, 'I can't sing, I can't dance and I can't act but here I am.' It was then that I realised that to make people laugh is also a gift and I guess I had it.

My prize money for winning the Photoplay Final was £25.00. It doesn't sound very much today, but in 1956 it was quite a lot. When you think in those days, if a lady wanted to go to the loo, she would say, 'Excuse me, I'm just going to spend a penny.' Today, of course even in the gents you have to put twenty pence in the slot. In old money that's four shillings. Imagine in 1956 if they said, 'Excuse me, I'm going to spend four shillings.' That's a hell of a pee!

When I arrived back home in Islington I was on a real high, but it didn't last long. I was soon to realise what it was like to 'Die a death'. I was only home two days when I did a variety show for the 'Tinhatter's Company'. We played a venue called the St Magdalene Mission. The whole show was a flop, I did my act in almost silence, it was my first experience of dying on stage and from being on cloud nine I was suddenly brought down to earth with a bump.

Over the years I have often heard of singers complain about an audience and say that they have 'died', but I could never agree with that, a singer should be able to sing the same to a good audience, as to a bad audience, the voice doesn't change (unless they have the flu).

The same as a musical act would play their instrument the same. The only act that 'die's' is that of the comedian, who has to make the audience laugh. If he doesn't, in his first two minutes on stage, then it's downhill all the way.

Of course, a singer may not get the applause he wants, or even deserves, but that would be down to the fact that the audience may not like his singing or that he is in a club and they are too busy drinking and talking, and if it is the latter, then he has a good excuse. Yes indeed, I had my fair share of 'dying a death' over the years especially in the Northern clubs. But even the experience takes years to handle properly; I learned that from watching other comics 'die'.

Many performers react differently, some comic's get aggressive and insult the audience - big mistake! That will only get their backs up and they hate you even more. You must keep calm, stay nice, smile and always be polite. If there is no way you can win the audience over, then you want them to say, 'He's not funny, but he's a helluva nice fella.' In 1964 I was in a summer show at the Pavilion Theatre, St Anne's-on Sea, near Blackpool with a Northern comedian, Duggie Clark. I remember one night we had a terrible audience and nobody could please them. At the finale with the full company on stage, Duggie stepped forward to give his curtain speech. He thanked the audience and told them how wonderful they had been and as the curtain closed on us he turned to me and said, *'Well you can't let them know they've been bastards!'*

Back to 1956, and I am still gaining experience - doing shows with the 'Tinhatters'. By this time we were preparing for the pantomime 'Cinderella' and I was delighted when they cast me as 'Buttons'. It was the best 'panto role that a comic could have, I was really looking forward to it. In between rehearsals for the pantomime we were still doing a number of Variety Shows at various venues around the Borough. It was about this time that I received a telephone call from Lionel, the air steward. Again, he said he had just flown in from New York, and could we meet up for a drink? We arranged to meet in the 'Hare and Hounds' pub in Islington. As we sat down at a table with our drinks he took a little blue box from his pocket and placed it on the table. 'What's this?' I asked. 'It's for you.' he said. 'I've brought you a gift back from New York.' I opened the box and inside was a fantastic pair of cufflinks with New York City in white pearl set on a blue background. 'I hope you like them,' he said, 'I thought they would look good on stage.' 'They sure will, Lionel,' I replied, 'and thanks, I'm really grateful, but why buy me a present?'

'Forget it, it's my pleasure, and anyway what else could I buy a 'Sinatra' fan.' he smiled. I was, of course a big 'Sinatra' fan and having New York cuff links, with two inches of cuff showing, the next time I went on stage I really looked the 'business'. I saw Lionel a couple more times after that. When I look back, even though I didn't pay much attention, I noticed that every time a pretty girl passed us I would give an admiring glance to her but he would never pass comment. Even when we were at Clacton, the bathing beauties around the swimming pool didn't even turn his head, they certainly did mine. The last time I saw him I was with a girlfriend and at the end of the evening, he drove off into the night. I never saw him again.

In the '50's nobody was 'gay', they were 'poofs, 'nancies' or 'fairies'. Or as my pal Roger put it, 'He must have been a shirtlifter!'

I was now able to put a song over quite well, I knew that I was limited and could not go too high, but I could hold a tune and was getting better all the time. The rehearsals were now complete and we had just finished dress rehearsals for 'Cinderella'. All the usual mistakes had happened as we did the 'dress run'. This was my first ever pantomime and I was really excited about it. The 'panto was booked for five performances at the 'Prince of Wales Baths' at Paddington between the 23rd and 26th January 1957.

It was a fantastic experience; I was absolutely overwhelmed by the reception. I had three numbers in the show, a duet with 'Cinderella', a front cloth duet with 'Baron Hardup', played by Max Mundy and I had a real showstopper with 'Fings 'aint 'wot they used to be'. After the matinee on the Saturday, we went out front in costume to meet all the children and were absolutely mobbed, there must have been about two hundred kids there, all pushing forward with autograph books and pieces of paper in their hands. I had never witnessed anything like it. My first pantomime was a great success, albeit an amateur production and an experience I will never forget.

It was in great contrast to a few years later during my first professional summer show in 1963 at the 'Coliseum Theatre' Rhyl. A few kids were outside the stage door after the matinee performance waiting to get autographs, apparently anyone who came out of the door was asked for their autograph. I was one of the last to leave and as I came out of the door I saw one of the stagehands signing a book. As I closed the door behind me, a boy ran up to me and asked, 'Are you anybody?' 'No', I replied. With that he spun on his heels and ran off.

It was during the run of the pantomime that I heard from Ted Kavanagh, who was one of the judges from the 'Photoplay Grand Final'. He had arranged for me to have an audition at the famous 'Windmill Theatre'. I knew that a lot of star comedians had started their careers there and that it could be a good opportunity for me. The time was arranged for 10.00am on 24th January 1957. I caught the number 38 bus from Essex Road to Piccadilly Circus, the 'Windmill' was just up a side street from there. I didn't really know what to expect, but I do know that within 10 minutes of walking through the stage door I was on.

I could see just two people sat in the stalls, one of them was the owner of the 'Windmill', Vivien Van Damm, and the other was an unknown female sat next to him.

The floor of the stage was made of glass squares, so I purposely slipped on the glass and made a comment. Van Damm who had a microphone with him in the stalls boomed out, 'Yes, you must be careful.' I continued with my routine but just after about three minutes the same voice interrupted, 'Thank you, we'll let you know.' I wasn't too put out about this knock-back as I knew I wasn't given much of a chance, what else could I expect; after all I had no professional experience It was my intention to get as much experience as I could by continuing with the 'Tinhatters' and entering as many talent contests as I could. The only way to develop as a performer was to perform in front of a live audience, no matter where. The size of the audience didn't matter, as long as you had one that was the most important factor.

After one 'Tinhatters' show at St Pancreas Town Hall in aid of the Infantile Paralysis Charity, I entered another talent contest at the Islington Town Hall and won a place in the Grand Final on 5th April 1957. It was on this night that I won the 'Islington Gazette Award' for the most original act. Soon after that on 5th May I had my first professional engagement at the Mildmay Club, a workings men club at Newington Green, Islington. It was Cup Final day at Wembley, so I wore a football scarf with a rattle to open my routine. I thought I might be topical, I was first on the bill. It wasn't great, but it was satisfactory and I was paid £3.00.

The very next day, out of the blue, I received a letter from Butlins. It was to invite me to holiday, all expenses paid, including travel, at their camp at Clacton. I could also take a friend or relative. The offer was too good to refuse and even though I wondered 'Why?' my brother, Tony and myself set off for our 'free' holiday. What I didn't know at the time was that I was to be involved in a big 'Fix'.

When we arrived, we discovered that we weren't the only ones on a free holiday. There were three other people from acts from last years Photoplay Final, the classical pianist, Shelagh Stamp who came second, Charlie Wilkinson who came third and a very strong speciality act called 'Mike'.

The next morning we were called to a meeting with the entertainments manager. He gave us a nice welcome and then began to explain why we were all there. The sponsors of the talent contest, Photoplay had now gone and the new sponsors for this year were the 'The People' Sunday newspaper, with the prize money now at £1,000. There was to be four categories, Best Comedy Act, Best Vocalist, Best Instrumental and Best Speciality. "This being the first time that the 'People' have sponsored us, we want to make a good impression," he said with a smile on his face.

"Representatives from the newspaper will be coming down this week to see the show and as, in the first week we don't get much talent, we don't want them to pull out if they don't think it's worth it." He said. As we all listened to this we knew it was a set up. He continued, "So what we would like you to do is to enter the competition in the normal way, like any other holiday maker." The following day we all did just that. With the exception of Mike, the speciality act all of us won a place in the Camp Finals in September. Unfortunately for him, the only other decent act among the holidaymakers was another exceptional speciality act. Anyway, at the end of the day the sponsors were really happy, Butlins were happy and I was happy to be having a crack at £1,000 prize money.

As I had won the same event the previous year with a different sponsor, the prize money then being £25.00, I reckoned that I must be in for a good chance. However, I was soon to find out that what started as a 'fix' was also to end as a 'fix' and I was out.

25th September 1957 Gaiety Theatre, Butlins, Clacton 'National Talent Contest, Camp Final' Heat 1.

The theatre was absolutely packed; I was in the first heat with Charlie Williamson (the vocalist from last years final). I was on top form, everything went perfectly, in fact I felt it was my best ever performance because I had given some bad performances and died a few times. But this was my night. At the end, the audience went wild and the compere had a job to calm them down again after I had left the stage.

At the end, the judges result was received with a hesitant silence, you could even hear the boo's around the auditorium. My name was not called out as a winner, neither was Charlie Wilkinsons, who had also gone down extremely well. I was very surprised with the result, especially after the performance I had given. All sorts of stories were going around and we heard through the grapevine that because of our success last year, we were never going to progress any further this year. We would have both felt better if we had been beaten by a great talent and we had performed badly. Well, as they say 'That's the way the cookie crumbles' and it was a great experience. We were used and then discarded; I guess it was a taste of the sinister side of show business.

I was in the army at this time and they were good enough to give me leave to take part in the competition. The date was 13th June 1957 and I was called up for National Service to join The Royal Army Ordinance Corps (R.A.O.C). I was to report to Hilsea Barracks at Portsmouth. My brother Tony, who had already served his National Service and was now in the Metropolitan Police, saw me off at the station with my small suitcase, the same one that he had used. As I got on the train and pulled down the window, I remember his last words to me as the train pulled out, 'Keep your nose clean, stay out of trouble and you'll be alright.'

Chapter Three

Army Days

The six weeks of basic training were very hard but after that it became quite enjoyable. If you could see the funny side of things it was a lot easier. When I arrived it was interesting to see everyone in their own clothes and with different hairstyles. We were all different shapes and sizes; there was quite a number of Teddy Boys with their draped suits, drainpipe trousers, crepe shoes, side burns and D.A haircuts (Ducks Arse). Then there were the Perry Como and Frank Sinatra look, which was the category that I put myself into. Some of the boys looked real soft, as if they wouldn't say boo to a goose. Then there were the Public School boys who spoke with a plum in their mouths. We were a real mixed bag.

Some looked real hard cases and others looked the opposite, I think many of us were thinking whom we should talk to and whom we should avoid. The first day was the best laugh; we were kitted out in our new uniforms and marched off to the barbers shop for a short back and sides - that was when we all looked the same. Nobody could remember what anybody looked like before. We were all lined up in front of the N.C.Os when the sergeant barked at us, 'You're in the army now!' He stood in front of us with his stomach in and his chest out, looking immaculate, his boots looked like glass and his pleats were creased in all the right places. He had a row of ribbons on his chest and his cap badge was sparkling in the sunshine. His voice was like a fog horn, 'There are two ways to get on in the army,' he said, 'the easy way and the hard way - the easy way is not easy and the 'ard ways bloody hard!!

NOT EVERYBODAY MAKES IT

One of the good things about the army was the fact that no matter where you came from or what your background was you were all in the same boat. It was a terrific experience and I wouldn't have missed for the world. It was hard, we were all screamed, shouted and sworn at and we thought that the discipline was over the top at times but at the end of it we came out of it as fine, fit young men who were disciplined and had a good set of values. Of course during basic training there were times that you wished you were somewhere else and there was a couple of Corporals that you felt nothing but hate towards, in fact, given the opportunity you could have shot dead, but the feelings did pass.

The morning inspections became a ritual; I was on the first floor in my Billet. It was summer time and the windows were open, each soldier would have his blankets boxed up at the top of his bed, with all the kit laid out in order. Some of the lads would lay it out the night before and sleep on the floor, but I never did that. Suddenly, the door would swing open and this frightening voice would scream out, 'Stand by your beds!' and within two seconds we were all stood to attention by our beds. As the N.C.Os began along the rows of beds you could hear the abuse and the air was blue. Nobody would dare look to see what was going on, as your eyes were to be fixed straight in front of you.

I remember one such morning that the sergeant was sounding more angry that normal. As he and the Corporal were getting nearer to me, in fact three beds away, I realised that he was picking the gear off the beds and throwing it out of the window. Boots, shirts, blankets, socks, underwear, webbing packs, nothing was missed. He came to me, some of my kit went out of the window, following everybody else's, floating down to the ground below. Nobody was left out; every single one of them had some item or another thrown out of the window.

He then marched to the top of the Billet, turned around and roared, *'this platoon is a fucking disgrace, what are 'yer?'* and in one voice we shouted, *'We're a fucking disgrace Sergeant!'* Then he said, 'I've never seen anything fucking like it in all my fucking life, if I hadn't fucking seen it with my own fucking eyes, I would never have fucking believed it! - In fact, it's *unbe-fucking-lievable*! - Now fuck off downstairs and get your kit and the last man back here will be on a charge - *MOVE IT!*'

You can imagine the scramble that followed with everybody rushing to the door, down the stairs and out onto the grass verges below. There was kit and clothes everywhere; it was sheer panic as we rummaged through it all to find our own stuff. Of course, many came back with someone else's gear, but who cared, as long as you had a full set of kit. Some of the N.C.Os had a sense of humour, one day we were doing some square bashing on the parade ground. If you were marching and you came to a wall and you had received no instruction to turn either left or right, then on arrival to that wall, you would mark time.

We were marched off the parade ground and when we came to a wall we began to mark time. The instruction from the Corporal was, 'Keep those knees up, keep those knees up!' You could hear the sound of the boots smashing down onto the tarmac. We must have continued for about ten minutes and were starting to flag. Suddenly a voice from the back yelled, 'He's pissed off.' We all turned around and indeed he had. 'What a bastard!' we laughed and then went to the Naffi for a pint.

I made some great mates in the army and there was a terrific rapport among all of us, we helped each other out, some of the things I saw were real touching. We were all excited when the post arrived and on one such day while we were reading our letters, a lad called Murphy was sat on his bed, the only person without a letter. The guy sat opposite me, who was built like a tank and was a real hard case said, 'Oh, look poor old Spud 'aint got any post.'

Then waving his letter in the air at Murphy said to him, 'Don't worry Spud, when I've read my girlfriends letter, you can have a read of it.' I thought that was a nice thing to say, but I don't think his girlfriend would have appreciated it. It was a very different matter with my mail; especially letters from my pal Roger back home. I would write to him and tell him about my army mates, what they looked like and our experiences. His replies would be filled with cartoons that he had drawn of me and the lads, the likeness of some of them was extraordinary, considering he had never met them. This caused much amusement in the barrack room and it got to the stage where the guys would shout to me, 'Hey Dave, any letters from Roger?' A well-known rule in the army was *'Never volunteer for anything'*, I can't remember any one breaking that rule but I, myself did just that.

One day, one of the Corporals asked, 'Is there anyone here who can entertain?' He had hardly got the words out when my arm shot up.

'I can Corporal, I can entertain.'

'What can you do?' he said.

'I'm a comedian.' I replied, as soon as I said the words I knew that I had fed him a line, that he would come back with a witty remark, he didn't disappoint,

'You're all bloody comedians in 'ere!' he said. He told me that the Sergeants were having a social event and they wanted entertaining and that I would be part of it.

The date was 11th July 1957.

"The sergeants social"
The Sergeants Mess Hilsea Barracks

This was my very first performance in the army; there were two other singers there as well as me. The room was packed with sergeants and their wives. I gave a good performance, it went down really well and I was very pleased with the way it went. From then on I became quite well known as my reputation as a performer began to spread and towards the end of our Basic Training I was asked to put on a show. There was quite a lot of talent in our company so we staged a variety show billed as "A Coy. Concert", we played two nights on 22nd and 23rd July 1957.

The second night was held for all the parents who had come down for the passing out parade. It was held in a little theatre in the barracks. It was a big hit, I had a wonderful time, I acted as the compere as well as having my own act. The front row was full with all the Officers with the Company Commander sat in the middle. I took the mickey out of the Officers, the R.S.M and the N.C.Os, the audience loved it. They were one of my best audiences I had ever had. The next morning as we stood by our beds waiting for the Corporal to throw us our mail, of which we would have to duly catch, he said to me, 'McGrail, you're a fucking good comedian!' before tossing my letters at me.

What with our Basic Training now completed, we felt that we were now proper soldiers, smart, well turned out, disciplined and as fit as a butchers dog. I certainly had never felt fitter in my whole life and never have since.

We were to be posted to various units; I was hoping to go abroad but unfortunately that was not to be. Instead, I went to the 1st Battalion R.A.O.C at Blackdown, Aldershot. On our last morning at the barracks as we were waiting for the army trucks to take us to our new destinations a very smart looking black soldier suddenly appeared. He looked immaculate, his backpack and front pouches were boxed exactly and blanked to perfection, as was his webbin and his brasses were sparkling. With a broad grin, showing off his perfect white teeth he said, 'I'm off to Germany, where you guys off to?' At that moment a truck pulled up, 'Say man, that's my taxi - you guys be lucky!' He climbed aboard the truck with a number of other guys and in a cloud of dust it pulled away. A moment later another soldier came up to us and asked, 'Has anybody seen my kit?' 'Isn't that it over there?' I pointed over to a shabby looking kit in a corner.

He looked over and said, 'that's not mine, my kit is immaculate, I left it here so where the fuck is it?' 'On its way to Germany' piped up a voice from behind.

I arrived at my new posting at Blackdown and soon settled in. After a couple of weeks I was given a job as a store-man in the Company Stores. It was a good number and I was lucky to get it, I worked there along side three others. We lived at the top end of the store; it was much better than sleeping in a billet with thirty or so other blokes. It was much more relaxed than at Hilsea where you were always on edge. The first time we were let out for a night out in Portsmouth we passed a cinema and one of our group smartly turned his head to the left and saluted an Officer who was standing on the steps. We all followed suit but to our horror we discovered that the 'Officer' was in fact a commissionaire for the cinema. I can't tell you what we said to the bloke who saluted in the first place!

The R.A.O.C were attached to the R.E.M.E (Royal Electrical And Mechanical Engineers) at Blackdown and lots of guys learnt a trade. There were drivers, mechanics, electricians, carpenters and even a printing and bookbinding shop. Of course there was a lot of skiving that went on, I soon learned that you could walk around the camp all day with a piece of paper in your hand and appear to be going somewhere important. One bloke, who we all knew as 'the carpenter' would do this but with a screwdriver in his hand and a couple more tools stuck in his belt, he spent more time in the stores drinking tea than doing any carpentry although I seem to recall, that he did fix some windows for us once.

There was a nice little theatre at the camp called "The Tela Theatre". I asked the guv'nor, the Quarter Master Sergeant, if we could put on a show for the boys at Christmas, he was known as 'Q'. He said he would get back to me after speaking to the Company Commander. A few days later he told me that the C.O thought it was a good idea and that I was to arrange and produce the event. I thought this was great as I had never produced a show before, and I would be able to write and cast it as well. I decided it was to be a Revue Show with comedy, music and sketches.

With a blank piece of paper I wrote down the title "Anything For A Laugh". Next job was to find the performers, I had two mates from the R.E.M.E, Russ, a great singer - Perry Como type and Arthur, a terrific mimic, and he could impersonate anyone in the whole unit. There were two Scouse lads; one a wizard on the guitar and the other had a great voice. Also, a Jock who could play the trumpet, a Welshman with an amusing mime routine and a Yorkshire comic. We were looking good.

Word soon got around that I was on the lookout for musicians and in no time at all I had a drummer, bass and sax player.

There was just a piano player to find now, which was the most important of all.

It was because I had so much trouble finding a pianist that the whole project was in danger of caving in. It got to the stage that I had to do a tour of the barrack room blocks all over the camp to find one. I did this in the evening to try and catch people in. I would stand at the door of the billet and see some of the boys on top of their beds reading or cleaning their boots, others at the table playing cards or some getting dressed for a night out. 'Can anyone play the piano?' I would shout, in the most authoritative voice I could muster. The replies would come back, 'I can play cricket', 'I can play dominos!', and another favourite, 'He can play the fool!' As I left I could still hear the laughter echoing in my ears.

It was a hard time, and some of the lads who had already agreed to do the show were losing interest. On paper, the show was looking good, but it only needed one person to drop out and another could follow. At one point, a few moans and groans were starting to creep in and I knew that I had to steady the ship or we could sink. Even Russ and Arthur, my mates were losing faith. A week passed by and a new intake arrived, news came that there was a piano player among them. I felt quite excited, but didn't want to get my hopes up, as there was no knowing how good he would be. I went to meet him and introduce myself and after explaining our predicament I took him along to the Naffi where there was a piano and asked him to play. He sat down, lifted the lid, and made fantastic music. Not only could he read well but also he was an excellent busker, he could play anything. I was delighted and "Anything For A Laugh" was back on. Or was it?

I called the first rehearsal with a band call, once they were assembled in the pit they began to play a few numbers and getting to know each other, they had a good sound together and I was pleased. The only problem was, that a part from a couple of guys that had dropped out, there was now some off sick. So there I was with a four-piece band, dead keen and raring to go, but with no one to sing with them.

I gave them some pieces of music that were to be in the show and they began to run over them a few times. I had to keep them busy so that they would not lose interest. Suddenly, a lad called Scouse Coburn, (I've never forgotten his name as he became a close pal of mine) called out to me, 'I know most of these songs, would you like me to sing them?' I thought at least it would look like we were rehearsing something, so I agreed. Within five minutes he was up on stage singing away, to my surprise he had a nice, easy on the ear voice.

After a few numbers I asked him to try the songs that Russ was to sing, as Russ was one of our sick casualties. A couple of minutes went by when Arthur, the impressionist, said to me, 'This is a waste of time.' He was sat next to me, a few rows back in the stalls.

'What do you mean,' I said, 'a waste of time? 'These songs are Russ's, how can Scouse rehearse them, when he might be in a different key?'

I knew what Arthur was saying and he was right, but I was playing a psychological game. 'I know what I'm doing Arthur, and I know what you're saying, these boys are a good little band, but if I don't keep them busy they will lose interest.' Before he had time to reply I continued, 'So I don't need your negative remarks, when Russ gets back tomorrow everything will be fine - ok.' I think he got my point, as I didn't hear another word from him. After a few days things were really beginning to take shape, and aside from the band we now had a Skiffle Group with a great guitarist as their leader, another Scouser, called Brian Grace. Scouse Coburn, who had stood in for Russ at the first rehearsal, could sing quite well, I decided to include him in the show. He was only a small chap, about five feet nothing in height and would be ideal for the part of a stooge.

I used him throughout the show as a running gag. The little man that wanted to sing but was always put down. He was like a Bobby Ball character, (of Cannon & Ball fame) but this was long before their time. He gets his chance at the end of the show - I must tell you that he brought the house down. There were three sketches in the show, but the most memorable was called "In The

Cookhouse" Before I joined the army, I remember a cheeky seaside picture postcard that I had bought, it was of an army cook who had baked a pie and was going around the pie crust edge making indentations with a set of false teeth, the caption was-

OFFICER: "Good god man, haven't you got anything better to use than that?"

COOK: "Yes sir, but I keeps it for making 'oles in the donuts!"

Well, that was to be the tag line for the cookhouse sketch, all we needed was about six minutes before it.

I mentioned this to Russ and Arthur, they thought it was a great idea, so together we sat down and kicked a few ideas around, a couple of hours later we had written the sketch "In The Cookhouse" I was to play the cook, Arthur the officer, Russ a kitchen orderly and little Scouse was to have a non-speaking part. The show was now set and we were ready to rock-n roll, but some glamour was needed. I spoke to our Q.M.S about this to see if he could book a female vocalist. He, in turn had spoken to our Officer, Captain Thompson who was quite a character and very popular with all the boys. He was very down to earth, as he had come up through the ranks. He was also a hero, he had won the Military Medal during the War, he didn't do things by the book, but everyone had a great respect for him. He was a charmer and looked like a ladies man. One day Captain Thompson MM walked into the stores, sat down, put his feet up and asked for a cup of tea. He said to me, "McGrail, I've arranged for your girl singer," at the same time throwing his cap down onto the table.

"That's great,' I said, 'What kind of stuff does she sing?"

'I don't know, I've only seen her photographs and if she can't sing I don't think the boys will notice,' he said, 'She's a cracker!'

He finished his tea, stood up put his cap back on and as he walked to the door, he said, "The cracker is called Phyllis Craig."

Looking back, we did have a lot of problems putting the show together, with the odd fall out and dropouts. I came to realise how serious it was when one day at rehearsals Russ Spender and Arthur Watkins, who were a very important part of the show, came up to me and told me that at one point they were both thinking of quitting the show as it was looking like a non-starter, that would never get off the ground. They said, 'We did it just for you, because you had so much energy and enthusiasm and confidence in the show, that we just couldn't let you down.' It was a nice feeling to hear them say that, it shows what good mates you made in the army.

Once we were demobbed and after going to Arthur's wedding I don't think I have seen any of them since. If they ever read this perhaps that will change. My next job was to arrange the publicity for the show. One of the boys in the print shop was a very good sign writer; he did two big posters for "Anything For A Laugh" with Special Guest Star Phyllis Craig.

Then there were a couple of hundred handbills to give out. Everyone's name was on the posters and mine was on twice, as on the bottom of the poster it read - Produced By Dave McGrail. It was a huge responsibility; I felt the whole success of the show was on my shoulders, as indeed it was!

**The Tela Theatre, Blackdown
"Anything For A Laugh"**

The big night came, the 20th December 1957, time for curtain up. The theatre was packed, so I guess the publicity worked, and sat in the centre of the front row was the C.O with his Officers and their wives.

We were all on a high and in good spirits but still a bit nervous, I was very nervous. The opening was received with wild enthusiastic applause. I did five minutes warm up and couldn't put a foot wrong, every gag, every ad-lib was getting howlers, then I introduced the Skiffle Group, Brian Grace and his boys, they did a set of fifties hits and from then on it was all the way up. The running gag with Scouse could not have gone better and when he at last sang at the end of the show, he tore the roof off. He was a real smash! Everyone involved in the show did really well; there was not one weakness. Our Special Guest 'Stunner' Phyllis Craig was anxious at having to follow us all, as she was going on at the end.

She walked out on stage in a tight, sexy dress with plenty of cleavage. The boys loved her. My most memorable moment of the show had to be the "Cookhouse Sketch". As the curtain opened, we were discovered on stage in different positions, doing various cookhouse duties. The dialogue was going well and all the laughs were in the right place. Suddenly, one of the cooks looks to the side of the stage and goes into a panic (Corporal Jones style, but long before Dad's Army) screaming that the Orderly Officer is coming - of course, the kitchen is in a mess, and so are our cooks whites and no where near ready for an inspection. Arthur makes his entrance, in his Officers uniform, complete with Officers stick he would have fooled anyone, he really looked the part. When he opened his mouth he took the voice of one of our younger Officers who was not very popular. It was a perfect impression; I had a struggle to keep a straight face. The audience roared and I could even see the Officers in the front row were laughing. When he finished his comments with the other two, he finally made his way up to me, where I was working on my pie crust, making indentations around the edge with a very large set of false teeth. 'Good god man,' he said in this wonderful Oxford accent, 'Haven't you got anything better than that?' To which I replied in a cockney accent, 'Yes sir, but I keeps it for making 'oles in the donuts!' Blackout.

As we hurried off stage in the darkness of the blackout, the laughter could be heard and it didn't fade, it seemed to go on and on and then it changed to thunderous applause. It was a wonderful moment, all started from a seaside postcard.

Yes indeed, it can be said that "Anything For A Laugh" was a smash hit. We staged two performances, both to full houses. It was said to be the best show that had been seen for years, in fact it was so successful that we were offered a tour of the show at various other Military establishments around the Aldershot area. This was really great news, when I thought of how it all began and now we were to take the show on tour.

Captain Thompson was in charge of the tour, but it was our C.Q.M.S who arranged the dates. The first was to be at the Naffi of 1st Battalion R.A.O.C on 10th January 1958. It was to be our worst performance. It certainly brought us all down to earth, with only a small audience and during the opening number I noticed three guys sat at a table right in front of us. One of them had his boots resting on the front of the stage and was continually shouting out snide remarks. I don't know what came over me, but I just lost it for a second. I jumped off stage and kicked his feet away then grabbed him by his lapels and with my nose close to his said to him, 'Are you taking the piss?' He and his mates looked absolutely stunned as did the rest of the cast behind me who were still singing the opening number.

'No.' He said.

'Well keep it buttoned; I don't want to hear another from you. Understand?' With that I pushed him back into his chair and jumped back on stage just in time to finish the song. All the lads thought it was great and not another peep was heard from him after that. I've never done anything like that before or since and I guess it was a dumb thing to do, but then I was only nineteen.

So, we finished the show, it wasn't a complete disaster, it was just about okay.

Twice a week at the camp, there was a mobile Naffi van that would come round. You could get tea, coffee, sandwiches, cakes and bread pudding, the usual stuff. The lady who ran it was called Mrs Dyson, she would always park outside the Company stores and us lads who worked there became regular customers. I think she used to like me, as she would give me an extra piece of bread pudding or cakes.

Anyway, it was through her that I did my first paid show while in the army. It was the day after the Naffi show on 11th January at the 'Ash Common School' for the Teachers Association. It was a good night; I enjoyed it and was paid the amazing fee of ten shillings (50p). I was happy with that of course, as I was only getting twenty-eight shillings a week as a soldier. I was invited back to do it again the following year in January 1959 and I accepted but I can recall that on the second occasion I was not so happy with my performance. We continued our tour of "Anything F or A Laugh" at the R.A.O.C, Reme Junior Leaders School, the R.M.P Establishment, Woking among others and the most rewarding of all the Military Hospital, Aldershot. We did the show in the hall; it had a fair sized stage. Showtime was 20.00hrs but before that we were asked if some of us could perform around some of the wards for the boys who were too sick to leave their beds.

We did this and it was sheer joy to see some of these boys, who were in a bad way, one was heavily bandaged and could hardly lift his head from the pillow, but I made him laugh and to hear them all laugh on the wards was so rewarding. I knew that I had made them feel better and because of that it made me feel great.

The show in the hall was a huge success, it went well and we all enjoyed it. I think that apart from the staff the entire audience were wearing pyjamas and dressing gowns.

The tour for "Anything For A Laugh" eventually came to an end when the C.Q.M.S couldn't find us any more dates. We had all had a great time with the show, it had been a great success but now it was back to our usual army duties. One day, the 'Q' called for me to go and see him and told me that the Aldershot Hippodrome were auditioning acts from all over the area for the 2nd edition of "The Army Show" and would I be interested. I guess he knew what my answer would be and before I knew it I was on the Hippodrome stage doing an audition. I was absolutely delighted to be told that I would be one of the acts to be chosen for the show.

The dates were 19th - 24th May 1958, the Hippodrome, Aldershot.

"The Army Show 2nd Edition"

This was a truly wonderful week; I made some really good friends among the other acts. My act went down really well; I felt at ease and relaxed. I was in a theatre and I knew that this is where I belonged. The fee for the week was £5.00 for twelve performances. After a couple of days the theatre stuck stickers on the posters outside stating, *"Great Success"*.

The revue in the Aldershot News:

NOT EVERYBODAY MAKES IT

"The Army Show Can Get Laughs"

'Up on the stage they enjoy themselves. The cash customers enjoy themselves. Everybody enjoys "The Army Show" this week's attraction at the Aldershot Hippodrome Forget the six chorus girls, and you can say that every member of the cast is 'in the army' all Aldershot stationed

After listing me top of the 'Outstanding Individuals' it concluded:

> The army show is nothing less than a hit. There should be a merry twinkle at the Hippodrome box office all the way until tomorrow's (Saturdays) second house.

It was just over a week after the show that something happened that was straight out off the old Hollywood showbiz movies, but his was no movie, this was real. I had a message from the Sergeant in the Company Office to telephone Ricky, the manger at the Hippodrome a.s.a.p. I remember it was a Friday afternoon. I called him straight away. 'Dave,' he said, I'm in a bit of a jam, I wonder if you could help me out?' Trying to sound as cool and calm as I could, I said, 'If I can, what's the problem?'

'I've got an act,' he explained, 'that's dropped out at the last minute and I need a replacement for Monday night. Can you do it?' 'I'll be more than happy to do it Ricky, but I will have to get permission from the C.O, I'm sure it will be okay and I'll call you back within the hour.' I sounded real cool. Once I'd put the telephone down I punched the air and shouted 'Yes'.

It was the first week of June 1958 and here I was, once again, suited and booted and make-up on, stood in the wings of the Aldershot Hippodrome just about to go on for the first house. I felt nervous, but confident. I knew that it would be different from the last time I was here, before it was packed out with servicemen and women. This time it would be the usual Hippodrome audience. It was far from a full house but they were great and I did really well. I finished my act, and then walked off the stage. As the orchestra played for me to take a final bow I walked back on. I walked off a second time and the manager Ricky was stood in the wings. Taking my arm, he said to me, 'Well done, Dave. Do the whole week and I'll pay you £10.00.' Compared to my twenty-eight shillings a week army pay I thought I was in the big time. 'Sounds good to me,' I said, 'I'd love to.' I thought it's like a scene from a movie.

It was a nude revue called "Legs, Laughter And Lovelies". Top of the bill was a stripper called Blondie Haig; she had a partner called Billie Roach who was a male impersonator. For the first two days I thought that Billie was a male, as she acted like a man all the time. They appeared throughout the show, in a number of sketches together and Blondie always ended up starkers. I remember during the second house on the Monday, I was backstage, sat on a radiator that was fixed against a wall. To my immediate left was an open doorway leading up to the dressing rooms. The number one dressing room was four steps up, and the first door that you could see. Blondie and Billie shared this.

As I was relaxing by the radiator with my own thoughts I suddenly heard the number one dressing room door open and then close. I then heard the sound of high heeled shoes, clip, clop, clip, clop coming down the steps. I slowly turned my head and caught sight of painted toenails in the shoes. 'Nice legs.' I thought, as my eyes slowly moved upwards, but I was to get the shock of my life. It was Blondie Haig wearing just high heels and a wide brimmed hat. She walked straight past me and onto the stage and sat on a swing. It was then raised a couple of feet, set swinging and then the curtains opened. There she was in her full glory.

It was strange, as most strippers and showgirls would wear a dressing gown to walk to the stage, taking it off at the last minute, but not Blondie. It became a ritual twice nightly that the dressing room door opened at the same time, spot on, each time. I became used to it after a while and didn't take much notice, but I thought it would be a nice surprise for one of my mates back at the camp. During the week, quite a number of the lads had come over to see the show, some that I didn't even know. However, there was one lad called Smith who had led a bit of a sheltered life, so I asked him if he would like to come with me to the Hippodrome on the Friday. He was delighted, so I arranged a ticket for him to see the first house and told him he could come back stage with me for the second show and afterwards go back to the barracks together.

So after the first house he came backstage and told me how much he had enjoyed the show. I explained that he could see how the show works from here and that it would be a whole new experience for him, 'But don't get in anybody's way!' I said. It was time for the show to begin, into the second half I knew it was nearly "Door Time" so I took Smithy over to the radiator. 'Sit there Smithy.' I told him, 'they will be bringing some large bits of scenery past in a minute, so it's best if you stay here until they have done it.' He sat down and I slowly moved away from him as I heard the dressing room door open, leaving him on his own. Right on cue, Blondie came down the steps in her shoes and hat and brushed passed him. Poor old Smithy, he was absolutely gob smacked, his face was a picture, he said he had never seen anything like it in all his life. When we arrived back to camp he was still talking about it and for about three weeks after. I was delighted that he had gotten so much pleasure from it. I have to say, Blondie did look gorgeous, a great body with a perfect figure, but word had it that she and Billie were a couple, she was gay.

One night an agent from London was in, his name was Mick Moran. He liked my act and took me for a drink after the show with the Theatre Manager. 'How long before you are out of the army?' He asked. 'I've got another twelve months.' I told him. With that, he gave me his card, 'Keep in touch and I'll give you a week at the Collins Music Hall' 'That would be great,' I said, 'I'm from Islington and I only live around the corner from the Collins.' Finishing his drink he said, 'Good, we can bill you as the local boy - must dash, got to get back to town.' We shook hands and he was gone, I was well pleased, a date at Collins Music Hall at this stage in my career couldn't be better.

In the end I was glad I had been posted to Aldershot instead of going abroad as being close to London I was able to go home most weekends on a 48hr pass. It was good to get back home for mum's cooking after eating army food and back into civvies to go out with my best friend, Roger. I would go to a tailor in those days, Harry

Lester at the Angel, Islington. I introduced Roger to him who also had a couple of suits made there. On one occasion we even had suits made up in the same material and would go out, dressed the same, it was a novelty, and very good for chatting up the girls. Harry was also a manager at St Josephs Dance Hall at Highgate so one weekend he gave me a date there.

It was July 1958 and my first appearance at a dance hall. It was tough going at first, the audience just didn't want to listen, they were there to dance. I eventually won them over with some visual comedy and the gags started going well. Finishing with my "Teddy Boy In A Dance Hall" routine was much appreciated and I received a great ovation. The pay was two guineas (£2.20) and luckily the manager liked it enough to give me a return booking for the following April. For my teddy boy routine I would have the record played of "Rock-a-Beating Boogie", by Bill Haley And His Comets, and many times my brother Tony would put the record on for me I had the routine down perfectly and it was received well, it became the highlight of my act and I would always close with it, I became very reluctant to leave it out.

I got an audition for "Opportunity Knocks" with Hughie Green, on Radio Luxemburg. This was before it was shown on television. It was set for a day in November 1958 so Tony and myself set off for the West End. The Auditions were staged at the Star Sound Studios in Baker Street in front of a live audience; where they did the actual recording for the show. The stage was quite small but there was a large audience. There was a control box at the back of the studio facing the stage and I could see Hughie Green through the glass with the producer and various other crew.

Hughie introduced me to the audience and I explained to him that before I could begin there were a few things that I needed to sort out, the record had to be played for my "Teddy Boy" routine on the right cue. We began to exchange words, it was like a double act and the audience loved it. It was great and I hadn't even started my act yet. I told Hughie, 'My brother is behind you at the door with the record I would like to be put on.' 'What's it for?' He asked. 'You see,' I said, 'I do this impersonation of a teddy boy going into a dance hall.' A seemingly frustrated Hughie told me, 'You do know that this is radio - they won't be able to see you!'

'I know that!' I said, 'But I thought that maybe you could have a commentator explaining to the listeners.' Waiting for the laughter to die down he replied, 'Who would you like - Raymond Glendening?' The audience roared, (Raymond Glendening was the biggest commentator of the day). I realised then that I would not be able to do the routine after all and got on with the rest of my act. It went great, what an experience. I passed the audition and was going to be on "Opportunity Knocks" on Radio Luxemburg.

By this time Roger had received his call up papers so I told him to ask for the R.A.O.C so there would be a good chance he would end up at Blackdown with me. He did this and after training he was posted there, so not only were we great mates who belonged to some amateur variety company and worked together at the same firm, we were now in the army together as well. He received a great welcome from the lads who had cartoons drawn of them by him.

It was now November and Captain Thompson asked me to put on another show for Christmas. I was really looking forward to this, as "Anything For A Laugh" had been such a huge success. Luckily, most of the old cast was still with us and now we had Roger on board.

I wanted it to be a completely new show. We all thought it was 'a right old game' being in the army so the new revue was to be called "What A Game" with new songs and sketches. Also a new female singer that was Captain Thompson's department. A few of the lads wanted me to include the "Cookhouse Sketch", even some of the new lads who hadn't seen it but had heard of it. I said no as I wanted everything to be new and it had gone so well with most of it being ad-lib, that I didn't think we could top it. Arthur Watkins who had played the officer was now demobbed, and I also felt that he could not be replaced. Anyway, I soon put the new show together on paper and with about half of the boys from the year before, and my good friend Roger along with some talented new lads. Soon we were into rehearsals for "What A Game".

We had lost a couple of musicians but new ones joined the others and once again we had two great bands, "The Skyliners" and "The Four Clovers". One day the C.Q.M.S came in and said that Captain Thompson had given us more money to spend on the show this year and that we could have a run down to London to be fitted out with costumes at a Theatrical Costumiers. We were all well pleased with this as it meant a day out to London. We travelled in an army truck to the West End and it pulled up outside that well-known Theatrical Costumier Morris Angel at Cambridge Circus. I remember they had racks and racks of costumes for every occasion.

The two bands were fixed up in band gear and the individual acts picked an outfit of their own choice, it was all very glitzy and one lad even fixed himself out in drag as he was playing a gangsters mole in a gangster sketch that we were doing. We got a policeman's uniform, everything we needed, no expense was spared. All the boys enjoyed themselves and when we were finally fixed up we jumped back into the truck and back off to Blackdown. I remember thinking to myself 'This is going to be the best dressed show they have ever seen.'

The next day I was informed that our female guest star was a singer called Judy Lane. My next thought was to get our publicity machine in action. One of our duties in the Company Stores was to take in laundry each week. The soldiers would hand in their dirty laundry, roll it up in a towel and fill in a ticket stating what was in the bundle i.e.; 2 shirts, 2 underpants, 3 socks etc. They would then tie the ticket to the bundle and hand it in to the stores. We, in turn would bag up all the bundles into sacks, throw them onto a truck, which would take them away to the laundry and bring last weeks laundry back clean. Next would be to rack them up in alphabetical order ready for when the boys would return with their tickets to collect their kit.

I thought that if we could get some small handbills made up, we could stick them into the laundry bundles. It was quite a few weeks before the show so I had some different captions run off. The first one to go into the laundry bundles read; 'Judy Is On Her Way' then the next; 'Watch Out For Judy', 'Judy Lane Is Coming Soon',

It's Almost Time For Judy', 'Don't Miss Judy Lane'. The flyers went in to the laundry every week and it was causing a lot of interest. I knew this for sure when a few weeks later one of the boys came in for his laundry, stood at the counter with his ticket and after reading the flyer said, *'Who the fuck's Judy Lane?'*

The date was 18th December 1958.

The Tela Theatre
Blackdown barracks

It was almost time for curtain up on our new revue "What A Game". We all were in high spirits and it was especially good for Roger and me as it was our first show together in the army. The whole cast looked great in their costumes and when the lights went down and the band struck up and the curtains opened on the entire company as we went into the opening number "We're Having A Ball". It looked like a first class professional show, everybody was on form and it was a smash hit. We did two performances. The only disappointment was the Top Of The Bill guest star, who did not live up to the laundry publicity - well I guess you can't win 'em all. After the show Captain Thompson said that he thought it had been my best performance that he had seen.

Christmas was soon upon us; I must say that Christmas in the army was a very nice experience. The decorations in the cookhouse looked really good, the tables were laid out in a typical Christmas manner. We had turkey with all the trimmings, Christmas pudding, wine, brandy, all the works and as is traditional in the army at Christmas time, the Officers served us and of course we all enjoyed that. The odd wag would address an Officer by saying - 'Waiter! Would you fill my glass up with some more wine.' Of course, it was all taken in good fun.

It was soon after this that we were asked to do a cabaret floorshow at the Officers Mess on New Years Eve. I arranged for six of us that could do an act and I would compere the show and include my own act at the end. When we arrived it looked like a real posh do. The Officers were in black tie and their wives and women in evening dress, it was a much more sophisticated audience to our usual army one. In fact, it was a bit daunting. We dressed in a snooker room that had two tables and we were able to spread out. A sliding door led out into the main hall and from there it was just a short walk onto the dance floor in front of a low bandstand where we would perform.

The room was decorated with Christmas decorations, the lighting was good and all the tables had candles on them, you just knew that you were in the Officers Mess as it looked like a high class night club. We were brought drinks into our changing room and all of us were knocking them back - well it was New Years Eve! I was becoming really nervous, as I didn't think that my type of comedy would go down with this kind of audience. As I looked around me I saw that I wasn't the only one, a couple of the boy's were really getting the drinks down them.

It was soon show time and we quickly found out that our earlier fears were unwarranted. The audience were fantastic and from a personal point of view I was totally overwhelmed by the applause at the end of my act. I was called back to cheers, shouts and whistles; it was indeed a great New Years Eve.

After the show was over and we were getting changed in the snooker room we were told that we could all have another drink, but were not allowed into the main room. Somebody opened the sliding doors giving us a good view of the dance floor that was full of people dancing. After a few drinks we began to move into the main hall and sat down at a table by the side of the dance floor. As we were sat there I suddenly heard a voice boom out, 'Jolly good show chaps - well done!' Looking up we saw a very tall; smart looking man with a moustache, 'Thank you sir' we all said in unison. 'Not at all,' he replied, 'It's been absolutely splendid, a wonderful evening, keep up the good work.' With that he walked away. We felt comfortable and relaxed now and knew we would be okay there, having previously been told to stay away.

A few minutes later a waiter came to the table and said, 'Oi, you lot, the major has asked me to take your order.' Our order was the first of many, I can't remember where all the drinks came from and we were the last to leave. I remember looking around and seeing one of our boy's fast asleep in a leather armchair with his feet up on a coffee table, a couple of us woke him up to go, half carrying him through to the snooker room where we found another lad flat on his back, on a snooker table. Eventually we staggered back to our Billetts. It was indeed a great night, a great New Years Eve and on the first day of 1959 I awoke with a mighty hangover.

Being on such a high after the show, it was just over a week later that I did the return date, that I mentioned earlier at the Ash Common School and I was back down to earth again as I knew that it was a mediocre performance and I was not satisfied with myself in any way. I was still learning that this was showbiz, with its highs and lows, ups and downs. It was still a business that I wanted to be part of and knew that it would not be an easy ride on this roller coaster and a few knocks would be good for me. I was still only twenty and the game plan was that I would have more ups than downs.

It was about three weeks later that I was home on leave and getting ready to make my appearance on "Opportunity Knocks". I knew what to expect as I had done my audition at the same studio, so I was feeling very confident. In those days of opportunity knocks each act had a Discoverer that Hughie Green would interview before being introduced. In my case it was going to be my brother, Tony, who incidentally was more confident than me. We knew that the winner would go on to the semi-final as well as a cash prize of £10. As we were about to leave for the studios, Tony turned to Mum and said, 'Don't worry, it's in the bag - we'll bring the tenner back as soon as we can!'

The date was 1st February 1959 and once again the venue was:

Star Sound Studios
Baker Street

This was a brand new experience for me, it being my first recording for a broadcast on Radio Luxemburg. Tony introduced me to Hughie Green, but I can't remember what he said. I soon forgot about being recorded, all my concentration was on the studio audience, and their response was great. At the end of the show the result was made by the applause of the audience. I received the loudest and I came out the winner with £10 on my person.

It was the last of the heats and the Final was to be recorded on the same night. It was because I had already done my act that Hughie Green told the audience that I would not perform again, but would be added into the Final for the actual broadcast. When we got back home, Tony took the ten pound note out of his pocket, put it on the table and said, 'Mum, what did I tell you - piece of cake,' all the family was really pleased with my Radio Luxemburg success, but it would lead to disappointment in the Final.

The "Opportunity Knocks" The Final was broadcast on the 22nd February 1959 and by this time I was back at the Barracks. It was almost time for the show so we tuned in the radio and sat on our beds in the billet at the top of the Company Stores. The radio was one of those old fashioned radios fitted into a big wooden cabinet; it was positioned on top of a steel locker. There were four of us there, listening in anticipation. Jack, another good friend of mine was sat opposite the radio. As the winners name was announced, it didn't register straight away with me, not until Jack picked up one of his size ten boots and hurled it at the radio, knocking it off the locker and smashing it to the floor. It was then that I realised that it hadn't been won by me but by a singer with a fine tenor voice. Jack obviously did not agree with the result but I guess there were a lot that did, but I appreciated his loyalty. I just wished that I could've done a different routine, as I'd just done the one recording for the two shows. Anyway, it was all good experience and I did enjoy it! The radio was wrecked but luckily we were able to find another one to replace it.

I was not the only ambitious young soldier in the Company who had set his sights on getting to the top of the tree. We had the A.B.A Welterweight Champion, Brian Nancurvis, who was the younger brother of the former British and Empire Champion, Cliff Curvis. Brian was a great prospect from Swansea who boxed for Wales and once in the British Army boxed for England. At the age of twenty-one he had the boxing world at his feet, was a southpaw with a hammer in each hand. That last season as an amateur, he had a string of twenty-three wins, seventeen of them by knockouts. He had collected the A.B.A Welsh Army and Imperial Services titles.

As any boxing fans would know, after demob from the army, he turned pro and became Brian Curvis. He went right to the top, eventually becoming the British and Empire Welterweight Champion and fought for the World Title against Emile Griffiths. Although he went the full distance, he lost on points. This was in 1964.

I recall one time when he was in training for his fight for England. It was a weekend and I was on duty, most of the camp had gone off on weekend passes and it was very quiet. Brian was left with no sparring partners so he asked our Staff Sergeant from the stores and myself if we would do it for him and of course we both agreed. He would train fifteen three-minute rounds. Three skipping, three-shadow boxing, three on the punch bag, three exercising and the final three sparing. We arrived at the gym; the Staff Sergeant was the first to put on the gloves while I acted as timekeeper with a stopwatch. Brian wanted him to keep coming at him, throwing punches so that he could keep out of our way. After the first three minutes it was my turn to spa with the future British and Empire Welterweight Champion. As I put the gloves on Brian turned to the Staff and said' 'Just two minutes will be fine, Staff.' I said, 'It's okay, I'll do three minutes.'

'Two minutes will be fine.' He repeated, and boy was he right, after two minutes I was absolutely knackered. I did as he said and kept throwing punches at him but not getting anywhere near him, suddenly I threw a right, he slipped it with his left and tapped me on the right side of my jaw. I felt a slight pain go up to my ear; I knew that if he had punched me with any power I would have been out cold. I must say that when my two minutes were up I couldn't have been more pleased. The weekend passed and things were soon back to normal with my usual duties in the Company Stores. Apart from the laundry, we would also take in boot repairs. A local contractor would collect the boots once a fortnight and bring them back repaired. I remember one day, a bloke was tying a ticket to his boots that he wanted to hand in for repair, I noticed that they were two left feet, I mentioned this to him and he looked up at me and said, 'I always wear the left one out before the right.' I asked him about the right ones. 'Don't be stupid,' he said, banging the boots down on the counter, 'The right one's don't need repairing!' With that he turned and walked out. I noticed he was wearing pumps.

My next show was on the 5th March 1959 at the W.R.A.C Camp, Guildford, Surrey. I was to do a cabaret spot at another dance. It was a tough audience and I had to work hard to win them over. I used to do a routine with various famous people playing darts. I did a Charlie Chaplin, Robert Mitcham, a female and a drunk with soft music in the background to suit each character but at this stage I was just using the drummer to give me rim-shots as the darts hit the board. As I got near to doing this routine I noticed that the drummer was not sitting by his kit. Roger, who was with me, jumped up onto the bandstand, got behind the drum kit and did the effects for me, saving the day. It went down well and I received a good ovation at the end. It was quite ironic that my very next engagement was my rebooking at St Joseph's Dance Hall at Highgate. Once again, being a dance, it was very hard going at first until I won them over; the manager, Harry Lester (my tailor) said that I was better than last time. He paid me 2gns (£2.10).

There was a venue in London called the Nuffield Centre. It was used by the Forces and used as a shop window for agents to go and see the acts. I was on leave for ten days and made my first appearance there in the middle of May. It was not quite what I had expected and I was not too happy with the performance, needless to say I did not get any offers. A few days later, I noticed that they were holding auditions for a talent competition at the "Plough Inn", Clapham Common. I went along, it was my first appearance in a pub. There was hardly anybody there and no atmosphere whatsoever and again I wasn't pleased with my performance although I passed the audition to appear again on the 16th June so I guess it hadn't been a complete wasted journey from North London.

My National Service was coming to a close and I just wanted to get cracking and get into "Show Business". When my leave was up

I headed back to Blackdown not feeling too great after giving two duff performances. That first night back at the Barracks I was feeling tired, it was about 11.15pm, and four of us were sat around the fire. I decided to get my head down and go to bed. The other boy's decided to make some toast over the old stove fire. As soon as my head hit the pillow I was away in dreamland. The next thing I know I'm being shaken awake, 'Dave, Dave, wake up, wake up!' It took me a few seconds to come round to see it was little Scouse, I thought the stores were on fire.

'What is it?' I said, to which he replied, 'd'you want some toast?' My reply to him is best left unrecorded.

Payday in the army, as I recall was always on a Thursday, where you would go on pay parade in front of the Pay Officer. You would step up to the table, salute the Officer, collect your twenty shillings (eight shillings would be sent home), take one step back from the table, salute again and about turn and march out. It became a ritual on pay night to go to a cafe and buy a slap up meal. With Roger, Jack and a couple of other boy's we would go into the village of Deepcut to do this. It was always the same meal. Steak and kidney pie, chips and beans with brown sauce, two rounds of bread and butter and to wash it down a mug of tea. After eating army food all week it was bloody fantastic, the cafe did a roaring trade on pay night as the place was always packed out.

Most of the Jocks in the Company would go to the local pub or the Naffi and come back skint and legless, rounding the night off by fighting each other, but by the next morning they would be friends again. My very last show in the army was on 4th June 1959 at H.Q Company Cookhouse, Blackdown. The entrance in my diary read: *'Last performance in the army. One of my finest moments.'* It went great and the boy's really appreciated it. It was a wonderful feeling and indeed a sad night in a way, as I knew this would be my last show here. What I didn't know at the time is that I would be back at Christmas as a paid guest star, but I will tell you about that later. On the 11th June 1959 I was demobbed from the Army R.A.O.C 4BTN. While I was pleased to leave the army it was a sad occasion saying my goodbyes to some good mates that I had made there, knowing that I would probably never see them again. On my certificate of discharge, the Battalion C.O wrote:

> 'Pte McGrail has proved himself to be a good soldier at all times during his National Service. He is sober, honest and punctual in his habits. Apart from the excellent way he has carried out his Military duties, he has been a great asset in organising unit entertainment.'

CHAPTER FOUR

Told To Get Out Of The Business, But I Face TV Cameras For First Time

It was now time for me to organise myself in 'civvie street' and to find work. I had already written to Butlins a couple of months earlier for a job as a Redcoat. A letter came back from their Director of Entertainment, Wally Goodman, who turned me down. I could not believe it, as I knew that many Redcoats were not able to entertain at all and I had my own act. Still, as they say, 'That's the way the cookie crumbles'. Five days after my demob on the 16th June it was time for the Mackesons Talent Competition that I had auditioned for months earlier. Two of my army pals, Jack and Ken came with me to give support. I wasn't feeling on top form, but it went down reasonably well but without winning any prizes.

I thought that I would contact the agent Mick Moran who had seen me at the Aldershot Hippodrome and had said that he would fix me up at the Collins Music Hall, but before I had the chance the hall caught fire and was burnt down to the ground. Next, I thought that I would call Murray Apel, an agent who had an office in Charing Cross Road. I took along some photographs. It was a tatty room with papers and files all over the place, he was smoking a cigar, his suit was covered in ash and his buttons on his waistcoat were at full stretch with his fat belly trying to free itself. It was obvious that he was Jewish from his accent. We had quite a chat, I told him what I had been doing and that I had just come out of the army. While studying my photographs he suddenly looked up and stared at me straight in the eye and said, 'Do yourself a favour - 'ged ou'da 'da business', he stubbed out his cigar into the ashtray. 'Get out of the business,' I questioned, 'I'm trying to get into the business!' He asked me, 'Wad do ya wanna do?' 'I want to do variety.' I replied. 'Variety is dead, all the halls are closing!' he told me. However, he could see that I was determined and fixed for me to do a spot at the Nuffield Centre on 28th July.

Phyllis Craig who you will remember was the Special Guest Star for "Anything For A Laugh" was at the time very impressed with my performance and she gave me her card, asking me to call when I got out of the army. I did this and we arranged to meet. At the same time I had another audition lined up at the Windmill Theatre. Phyllis invited me back to her place to go over my material. It didn't feel right to me as she gave me advice on my act and how to do things in her living room, I was uncomfortable with it but she was nice and only trying to help so I went along with it. She accompanied me to the audition and I was still feeling unsure about it and needless to say for the second time I was unsuccessful. During this time Phyllis took me to various places and sometimes lunch and introduced me to different people.

I was beginning to feel like a "Toyboy". It was a good thing that I had a steady girlfriend at the time, as people may have got the wrong impression. I met Doll soon after leaving the army. She was beautiful, tall, slim and looked like a model. I was flattered when she agreed to go out with me, she would turn heads whenever we went out. There were other girls, but Doll was special. We were together for twelve months, the longest that I had been out with a girl. Engagement was on my mind but then it all went pear shaped and we split up. She was my first love. Perhaps things may have been different if I hadn't been involved in show business, it was still my first priority.

My next engagement was at the Nuffield Centre that Murray Apel; the agent had set up for me. It was my second visit there so I knew what to expect, that's always an advantage. The act went very well and Murray was pleased. His only criticism was my cockney accent; he said that people wouldn't understand me up North. I considered elocution lessons. The next night on the 29th July I performed my first show in front of an American audience. It was held at a U.S Airforce Base in the south of England. It had been arranged by Phyllis and the agent Jack Conway, she was also on the bill along with the Playboys, an excellent vocal group.

As I was a green-horn I was to go on first, I was very nervous as it was my first time entertaining Americans, but I was not to worry as I went down tremendously well. With some gags it took a while for the Americans to catch on, but when they did it was a better. I guess my accent was okay for them. Agent Jack Conway was also pleased and asked me to see him for a chat another day, I did meet up with him, but not much came from it. As I sat in his waiting room, surrounded by other acts coming and going, the air was surrounded by calls of 'Where are you working?' Oh, I'm in Manchester tomorrow!' I've just returned from there, now I've two weeks in Sheffield!' 'I'm in Birmingham!' and so on. I'm not sure if they were doing it for my benefit as I probably looked like the new kid on the block. With no work on offer I figured that I should get a job. I decided to go back to the Columbia and fit in as many shows that I could find. It didn't take me long to get into the old routine of doing a 'proper job'. The Variety Company, the Tinhatters that I used to belong to had now finished and a new company was formed called the Starliners. It was run by more or less the same people and so I knew most of them when I joined them.

My first show with the Starliners was on the 16th September 1959. It was called "The Battle Of Britain Show" it was for a charity at the Islington Town Hall. It was my first time back there for two and a half years. I got a wonderful reception and felt on top form, it was great to be back, just like coming home. Unfortunately, the following three shows at different venues were just the opposite. There was one in particular that I thought I would do well at and I was a complete flop. It was held at the Albany Street Barracks. Nobody really stood a chance with the talking and drinking that was going on. I didn't know it at the time, but this was the type of audience that I would experience in the Northern clubs on many more occasions.

During the autumn months of that same year the Starliners performed a number of charity shows at the Islington Town Hall. On one occasion I was asked to do a routine with another boy in the company, the same routine that I used to do with Roger. We would mime in drag to the record 'Tiptoe Through The Tulips' by the American duo the Maguire Sisters. I agreed, and rehearsed with the boy, Raymond. He was never going to be a Roger, but he was okay and the show was a success. We did a repeat of the show about two weeks later at the Town Hall for "Boys Club Week". Ted Lune was the guest star; from the TV show "The Army Game". Just before curtain up we discovered that our "Tip Toe through the Tulips" record was broken. I rushed out of the Town Hall and ran along Upper Street, to the next corner, Cross Street. The record shop in Cross Street was called Al's Records. I was already known there, as I was a regular customer. I was panting and out of breath when I got there and my heart sank as I saw the 'Closed' sign on the door and the place was in darkness. I couldn't think of anything but getting hold of a replacement record, of "Tip Toe."

I repeatedly rang the doorbell and after a while a female voice shouted out of the upstairs window, 'what do you want? - We're closed.' I could see the lady from the shop leaning out and replied, 'I know, but I've got a problem and I'm desperate, I wonder if you could help me?' She asked me what the problem was and I told her, 'I'm doing a show at the town Hall tonight; it's just about to start. I'm doing a mime to "Tip Toe Through The Tulips" and the problem is the record has broken, I was wondering if you had a copy in stock, we would all be very grateful if you did!' 'Wait there,' she said, 'I'll be right down.' A great wave of relief passed over me as she closed the window. The front door of the shop was opened and I was told that the record wasn't in stock but they helped me look for an alternative. Time was not on my side, as the show must have already started. The mime was to start near the end of the first half. The lady held up "Early to Bed" by the Ponytails, 'They sound a bit like the Maguire Sisters', by now I was getting really desperate, so I took it, telling her, 'I can't thank you enough.' After paying I sped from the shop, checking my watch I saw that there was twenty minutes to go, before we were on. I ran as fast as I could, back to the Town Hall, it never dawned on me at the time, but if I had tripped or fell, the record would have smashed to bits, as of course, in those days all records were 78's.

When I arrived at the stage door I handed over the record to the stage manager and rushed to the dressing room where Raymond was waiting, already dressed in his gear. I asked him as I changed, 'Do you know the words to Early To Bed?' He didn't, but did know the tune. He was in the same position as me. 'Don't worry;' I told him, 'we'll get by. Do the same moves as in the TipToe and anticipate and mime the words as best you can, whatever happens, keep smiling!' I was just about ready when we were called. As the record came on we walked on stage. It was never going to be as good as "Tip Toe" but I was pleased that it went as well as it did. In later years I would never go on stage unrehearsed, but at the time I was young and fearless.

I had been told that before the War there was a headline act called The O'Gorman Brothers, I had never seen or heard of them but apparently they were very big in their day. Dave O'Gorman worked for A.T.V and he had seen one of my performances at the Town Hall. After seeing me a second time he gave me his card and asked me to contact him. I did and he was able to arrange a closed television circuit audition for me at the Hackney Empire for A.T.V. It was the 4th December 1959. This was a brand new experience for me, facing TV cameras. I was very nervous at first but once I had started I became quite relaxed and although there was no audience, I was quite pleased with myself. Dave O'Gorman was also pleased with my act and said to me afterwards, 'You'll just have to wait and see.' I soon learnt that the 'waiting game' was a big part of showbiz.

There were quite a number of other comics there as well as me, I stayed the whole day and it was thoroughly enjoyable. Once finished, I tried to forget about the auditions, to put it out of my mind, if it happens it happens. After a couple more shows with the Starliners, a letter arrived from Roger, who was still in the army. I was pleased to learn that he had taken over where I had left off and was organising the Christmas show. I was delighted when he invited me back to do a guest spot. It was 21st December and the show was called "Your Army Daze" and once again it was to be staged at The Tela Theatre at Blackdown Barracks. It was great seeing some of the old boys again and I was given a nice reception. A female singer had also been arranged. The show went very well. It was quite a reunion, Roger was on top form and we had a great night. I was paid £4.00 - well it was still 1959.

When I got back home the following day I noticed that a "Follow A Star Talent Competition" was being held at the Gaumont Cinema in Holloway. I filled in an entry form and was entered into the very last heat on the 30th December. As I walked into the crowded dressing room filled with other contestants, I was surprised to see a face that I knew. Her name was Lilian, a female singer from the Starliners Variety Company. 'What are you doing here?' she asked, as if I had no business being there. I told her I was in the competition. Lilian was a soprano with a lovely voice and what she said to me next surprised me.

'You're joking!'

'No I'm not, I'm on the show.' With that she stood up and announced to the rest of the room,

'Well, that's it then. We might as well all go home, he's won it!'

I wish she hadn't said that, although it was flattering, as it was unnerving for everybody, including me. As I stood in the wings waiting for my turn I was taken aback by the size of the stage, it was fabulous. I looked around the wonderful theatre, there was a packed audience and I just knew that this is where I belonged, in these kind of venues. I was relaxed and completely at home. My act went down a real treat, the applause was out of this world, Lilian was right, I won first prize and a place in the Grand Final.

It was staged a couple of days later, January 1st 1960, the first day of the swinging sixties. I was really up for the show, feeling confident, until I heard who the judges were. Two of them I knew very well, George Barnard, an Islington Councillor who was one of the directors and co founder of the Starliners Company. The other, Gilbert Dewhurst, Islington's Entertainments Officer. I thought this to be too close to home and a disadvantage for me. The best thing for me to do was to forget about them and just try my best. There were five acts on the bill.

There would be only one winner and the prize was well worth winning, a night out for four people at the glamorous Pigalle Theatre Restaurant in the West End, ten pounds worth Top Rank Long Playing Records and a winter outfit from Sharott, menswear specialist of Holloway Road. I fancied all of it so went on and gave my best ever performance. The reception I got was even better than what I received in the previous heats. I took a final bow, thanked the audience and thought to myself, it's in the bag. How wrong I was, it wasn't in the bag at all. I was convinced that if I'd not been so close to the judges it would have been a different story.

The overall winner was John Cortez, a Welsh tenor, who did have a great voice. He was already a professional singer, and nothing wrong with that and went on to do very well in the business. I often read about him over the years, but I never saw him again although he must have been near as I saw his name up at the odd working mans club that I played. The "Follow A Star" film starring Norman Wisdom followed the show; I guess that's where the name of the competition came from. Even though I was disappointed, I still enjoyed myself. You win some, you lose some. I continued to do the Starliners variety shows at various venues around North London and of course and I enjoyed my visits to the theatre every week.

It was around this time, that there was talk of the Finsbury Park Empire closing down. This was unthinkable as far as I was concerned. I saw one of my favourite comedians at the time, Jimmy Wheeler, I had seen him lots of times but this was the last time I saw him. When he finished his act, he took a bow, then came back to centre stage, holding his violin, he said, 'You have a lovely theatre here, don't let them take it away from you, otherwise we won't be able to come and see you again.' to thunderous applause. He waved his hand and walked off stage. I'm sad to say he was never seen there again, the Finsbury Park Empire did close, like many other theatres all over the country. It was the beginning of the end of variety. I wouldn't accept that and was still as ambitious as ever. "Cinders And The Beanstalk" was this years Starliners pantomime of 1960. It was two in one and written by George Barnard. Once again, I was cast as Buttons. The panto toured, playing two nights each at Islington Town Hall, Stoke Newington's Town Hall and St Pancreas T.H. It was a huge success.

Roger had been demobbed that year, in August and along with Jack, our mate from the army, we decided to have a holiday at Butlins, Clacton. We had a great time, with a lot of laughs. Roger and myself entered the Talent Show while we were there. We would not be up against each other as there were four categories, best vocalist, best comedy act, best instrumental and best speciality. Roger entered the speciality act with a mime. We both won and gained a place in the Camp Finals, two weeks hence. My next show back home with the Starliners was for the Infantile Paralysis Fellowship. Most of the audience were in wheelchairs and it was a rare treat to see them laughing and enjoying themselves. It was a small venue and the facilities weren't great, there was neither a microphone system nor a pianist. But it was rewarding to know that you could give people less fortunate than yourself a bit of enjoyment.

Roger joined the Starliners in September 1960; his first appearance was at the Islington Town Hall. I suggested that he come on during my act with a few interruptions. We were pleased with how it went down. Two nights were played, the Starliners were gaining a good reputation in Islington and we would always play to a full house when at the Town Hall. After the second show Roger and myself were due to attend the Talent Finals at Clacton, so we jumped into a taxi and dashed off to Liverpool Street Station to get the 10.40 to Clacton.

We arrived at the gates of Butlins in the wee small hours and with much amusement and laughter eventually found our chalet. Both knackered by now, we were more than happy to get our heads down, hoping that by the morning we would be feeling refreshed for the big day ahead of us. After breakfast, the next morning, we went to the usual meeting for the finalists. We were both in different heats so shows were staged both in the morning and some evenings. I did well in my heat and was selected to appear in the Final at the end of the week. Unfortunately, Roger didn't make it and was knocked out in the first heat.

The final was staged on the 15th September at the Butlins Gaiety Theatre, it was massive with big revolving stages and it could seat up to 3000 people. Did extremely well and, I was one of four acts chosen to represent Clacton in the Southern Area Finals at Margate. I won twenty guineas prize money (£21.00). In those days of the Butlins Talent Competition they would hold two area finals, one for the North, which was to be staged up in Blackpool and one for the South, in the Butlins Queens Hotel in Margate where I was to go on the 10th October.

Roger came down with me and I was glad of his support. I was relaxed but still nervous as always. There were twenty acts on the bill and I was number twenty. I would have preferred an early slot but that was the luck of the draw and I guess I was stuck with it. The competition was tough, with some excellent acts to compete with. It seemed to go on for ever and I paced up and down, trying to look as cool as I could but inside I was getting more and more nervous. I could hear the other acts getting a great response from the audience. There were a couple of other comics on the bill and I could hear some real belly laughs. It was unnerving, knowing that I had to do better than them.

The performers would go on stage looking nervous but would return to the wings smiling broadly, relieved that it was over. The tension was building up for me and with nineteen acts to follow I began to wonder if the audience and judges would get tired. I badly wanted to get into the final and thought back to what happened to me three years earlier, before my army days when I was back at Butlins for the Talent Contest for the sake of the new sponsors, The Sunday People. I was knocked out and had felt used. But that was all in the past and maybe now I could put it right.

Six were going to be chosen from the twenty for the London Final and the same at the Northern Final, to make it through to the Grand Final. Act nineteen came off stage and I was on before I knew it. I got that all-important first laugh within ten seconds and from then on the only way was up. I came off stage knowing I had done enough, but it was still nerve racking. We were all lined up at the end to await the six names to be called out. Five names were called, with just one more to go. Sweat was running down my face and dripping down to my eyebrows, the suspense was killing me, then eventually the compere announced, '...and the sixth act to go through, is the young comedian.... Dave McGrail! The relief was huge. I had made it into the Final and had a chance of winning £1,000. The six of us were well pleased with the prize money of £50.00 each for this contest.

I had a few shows to do before the final in December, three with the Starliners and a couple of paid jobs that I had fixed up through an agent. Ironically, one of those was at Butlins, Bognor Regis. I was concerned how I was going to get down there and back in the same night as I had work at the Columbia the following morning. The governor, Ernie had already given me time off from time to time and I didn't want to take liberties. My brother Tony's fiancée, Eve, offered to drive me down in her car. It was November 13th 1960.

We arrived in good time and I was told I would be doing a cabaret act in the Pig and Whistle Bar. The place was massive and absolutely packed. I was expecting it to be hard work and feared that it would be noisy. Top of the bill was a well-known name of the day, Mrs Shufflewick, a female impersonator. My performance was satisfactory, not great but at least the audience were quiet and listened. I was paid £5.00 for the night.

The drive home with Eve was quite exiting to say the least. There was torrential rain and we ran into some floods. Eve drove straight through one section and for a few seconds I thought we were going to sink. The water was almost up to the door, but we kept going and came out the other side. I was very grateful to Eve for taking me and the boat trip home was fun. My next date, a few days later was a cabaret at the Prince of Wales Baths. The venue was great, almost as good as a nightclub.

I used a hand-mic for the first time and felt the freedom of moving about on stage. I gave a far better performance than at the

Pig and Whistle. I was paid thirty shillings. I was still learning about the business and learning fast. After the show I turned down an offer by a so-called agent. There was something about him that I didn't like.

The big day came. It was to be the biggest event in my career so far. December 2nd 1960.

"People National Talent Contest"
Grand Final
The New Victoria Theatre, London

This was real class and by far the best theatre that I had played in so far, a packed audience of over 3,000, a pit orchestra, the works. It was all over very quickly and with all big occasions you can't remember much about them afterwards. The judges panel looked very impressive, with big names of the day, the band leader, Geraldo, Earl St John, Jimmy Jewel, Ben Warris and singer Carol Carr. A vocal group from Northern Ireland won the top prize and I won the second prize of £750.00, I was very pleased with that.

Sunday morning the headline in The People read:

> '*Mac the cockney mimes his way to the money*' after a nice revue, it finished with: '......*A boy with a sharp cockney humour and a hilarious mime act of an amorous Teddy-Boy.*'

Part of the revue in the trade paper, The Stage read:

> '*During his short time on stage, he proved that he not only has a ready wit but also definite talent, and a most easy, likeable personality. A highlight of his act was a mime of an amorous Teddy-Boy in a dance hall.*'

After this latest achievement I was full of confidence and knew that I had what it takes to be a performer. Rehearsals were now under way for the Starliner's pantomime "Aladdin". Roger and myself were teamed together. I was to play Wishie Washie and Roger Washie Wishie. George Bernard, who was by now the Mayor of Islington played Widow Twanky, and what a great Dame he proved to be! There is actually a park in Islington named after George called Barnard Park, positioned opposite The Anna Schur Theatre. I have often wondered whether the people of Islington have ever realised that their Mayor of Islington was once a pantomime Dame.

In early January of 1961 my tailor Harry Lester invited me once again to St Josephs Hall at Highgate. This was by now my third appearance at this venue. It had always been lucky for me and on this visit it was an Irish dance and social event. I was to work on the floor. The microphone had broken down but I was able to work around it and used it as good experience for me to get used to this kind of trouble. At the end of the night, Harry was delighted with how things had gone. It was soon after that that Harry hit upon the idea of me doing a modelling job for his tailors shop. By this time I had had about seven suits made by him. The plan was for me to be photographed in various suits and then displayed on a board with a cutting from the newspapers with the heading:

"STARS OF TOMORROW ARE DRESSED BY HARRY LESTER"

It was a real professional job and displayed in the shop window at the corner of the Angel. It stayed there for five or six weeks, I don't know if he got any extra business from it. The female Starliners singer, Lilian, that I've already mentioned also worked for a West End agent, Al Heath. She told me that he had been in the audience at the Gaumont Cinema, Holloway at the time of the Talent Contest and had asked him to come and see me at a Starliners show. I remember thinking at the time that he had already watched me in a great venue where I was a big success, why again? He came along to an O.A.P show at St Luke's Hall, Camden Sq and believe me when I say it was a night I would like to forget. The hall remained lit throughout the show, with no stage lighting. It was terrible, and I knew it, my performance went from bad to worse. I just went through the motions of my routine; if it had been my first performance I would have given up there and then, I'm not sure if I would have continued with my dream.

It was the worst performance of my life, and to make matters worse, sat in the audience, sticking out like a sore thumb, was the agent Al Heath. I was anxious to forget all about it, as the old saying goes, *"You're only as good as your last performance"*. I couldn't understand how, in a matter of weeks I had gone from by biggest high, with my success at the New Victoria Theatre in the West End to my lowest at a tiny church hall in Camden.

My next show in February was another showcase at the Nuffield Centre. I was compere for the night and also did my own spot. This time it went very well and I enjoyed it. Among the audience sat another agent from the Fosters Agency, one of the top agencies of that time. His name was Hymie Zahl, a short, fat Jewish gentleman wearing spectacles, an expensive suit and smoking his trademark cigar. He came to see me after the show and as he shook my hand, told me, 'Nice performance, can you call into the office on Friday?' Of course I could, 'What time?' He handed me his card and told me 10.30. Taking the card I told him I would be there. As he turned to go, he said, 'Good! We'll see you Friday.' And left with the other man with him.

I arrived on the dot of 10.30 at his West End offices. They were impressive, I sat on a leather couch in the waiting room where a woman sat at a desk typing and answering telephone calls. After about ten minutes a buzzer sounded, she picked up the 'phone, spoke and with replacing it, told me, 'Mr Zahl will see you now, through that door.' I knocked and entered a very large office with a thick carpet and luxurious furnishings. Hymie was sat behind an enormous desk. The man who was with him when we first met was standing by his right (I guess he was his right-hand man).

'Hello, Dave,' he said as he stood up and came over to shake my hand, 'it's nice to see you again and thank you for coming along to see me - please, take a seat.'

I sat down in the leather seat in front of his desk.

'Now, what have you been doing?' he asked. I gave him a quick run down of the army shows and what I had done since being demobbed.

'I was impressed with what you did at the Nuffield Centre,' he told me, 'you've a nice personality, the only criticism I have,' he paused, as if thinking how to say it, 'you're a bit too much Elephant and Castle - it's your cockney accent, fine in London, but if you went up North, they may not understand you,' another pause, then stretching his arms out towards me he said, 'you look very nice - doesn't he?' turning towards his right-hand man.

'Yes, quite.' The man replied.

Hymie then took a puff of his cigar and said, 'what I'd like to do Dave, is go over you're material with you- you can come here, or even better, come to my house.'

It was at that point that I thought he was more interested in me than my act. I felt like a News of the World reporter, that I should 'make my excuses and leave'. I didn't but I did tell him that I would be in touch, not that I had any intention of doing so, but it wouldn't be the last time I would see Hymie Zahl.

My family were about to have our first wedding; Tony married Eve on the 11th February 1961. The reception was held at The Prince of Wales, Brixton. I had engaged a band for the event, a four piece called The Nicki Quartet from Islington. I had seen them before at the Town Hall on a number of occasions; they had a great sound and went down very well. I remember that I also did a cabaret spot, but I don't remember much about it.

The pantomime "Aladdin" had by now opened, we did six performances and we were received very well. Roger and myself performed a duet especially written for us called "The Isling ting-Tong-Chinese Laundry Blues", a parody of George Formby's "Chinese Laundry Blues". After the panto I did a few more charity shows with the Starliners and then on the 25th June that year I had an engagement at the Pender Social Club, Stonebridge Park. I was paid thirty shillings (£1.50). It was not a very enjoyable night, with only a small audience. By now, it was beginning to occur to me that when I played to a theatre or a classy night club, anywhere with a big stage and good facilities, I would do very well, but anywhere with poor facilities and a generally lousy venue, I would always struggle. This was something I wanted to put right as the Finsbury Park Empires of this world were closing down, and there would, I didn't doubt, be an abundance of dumps to perform in, ahead of me.

It was during this time that I had been taking Lilian, the Starliners singer, out on a few dates. Roger was also taking out her best friend and we would go on a few foursomes, we had a lot of laughs, but nothing too serious. It was Lilian who suggested that I should go up North to try a few clubs. I had never given that a thought. She told me that Manchester had a mecca of clubs. I agreed that it was a good idea and that I would give it a try.

Jack, my old army pal had recently come down to London from his hometown of Sunderland and knew about the clubs in the North, we decided that he would come with me for support and act as my manger. Well, that was the plan anyway. A goal was set that we would leave about October, Jack got a job in the meantime and we began to write some fresh material. I had already done my last show for the Starliners, "The Black and White Minstrel Show" at the Town Hall.

We had quite a lot of nights out with the lads; there was Johnny, Roger and Jack. One night, Roger had a hot date, I can't remember where so Jack and me decided to go up the West End and our lads night out ended with a lot more lads than we expected. We went to the Golden Guitar Club at the side of the Palace Theatre, just off Cambridge Circus. Soon after entering, we noticed that there was a disturbing lack of women in the place. We made our way to the bar and within seconds realised that we were in a gay club. I could not believe my eyes when the first face I saw was none other than Hymie Zahl, the agent. He was sat on a bar stool with a young man who looked about twenty. He recognised me straight away, 'Dave, nice to see you again,' he shook my hand, 'Who's you're friend?' 'Er, Jack.' I told him. He shook Jack's hand and offered us a drink. We asked for a gin and tonic, as it didn't look like anybody was drinking beer.

'Raymond, give these two boys a gin and tonic.' he ordered the barman. Quick as a flash, Raymond came mincing along the bar, the biggest fairy you could imagine, 'Coming up darlings.' He said with a twinkle in his eye. He half filled two glasses with crushed ice, added two measures of gin and placed them in front of us before finally snapping off the tops of two small bottles of tonic water and pouring half into each glass. 'You two look nice.' He said before moving off to serve the next customer, 'What would you like darling?' he asked an older man sitting further down the bar.

As the night wore on, Raymond became the cabaret as he was the most camp and entertaining barman I had ever seen.

The bar filled up and Jack and me were moved further away from Hymie. Our glasses were continually being recharged by Raymond who told us that it was being sent from this person or that person, people that neither of us even knew. Looking around we could see the club was filled with young, good-looking boys in their late teens or early twenties, wearing expensive suits and shoes. They all looked immaculate, some with shaped eyebrows and appeared to be accompanied by older men. Others were sat on their own along a wall, Jack and I laughed as they reminded us of 'wallflowers' at a dance hall. It was a whole new experience for both of us as neither had seen anything like it before, remember this was still only 1961. Of course today, nobody would bat an eyelid.

The drinks kept coming, as soon as either of us would put a hand in our pocket, up popped Raymond with a fresh drink that somebody had bought us. We spent not a penny the entire night. 'Last orders, now drink up darlings it's time to go home!' Raymond yelled, mincing along the bar, clearing glasses. 'Come along now, get into your big American cars and off you go.' I don't know what time this was but in was in the wee small hours. As we stepped out into the cool night air, we remarked on our excellent nights drinking session, lit a cigarette and joked of the funny and strange characters we had seen. I'm not sure but I think we walked back home to Islington, one thing I know for sure is that our 'lads' night out at the "Golden Guitar Club" had been great, and as Jack put it, 'It cost 'nowt!'

I decided to take a few elocution lessons, as I was slightly concerned about my accent. I did the usual 'Rain in Spain' and 'Harry went to Hampstead' and 'Harry lost his hat' malarkey but I do believe that it helped and just took the edge off a bit.

The date had now been set for my trip up North, 6th September 1961 but before I left I was to experience the most thrilling night in a theatre. It is hard to put into words that are worthy enough to describe an entertainer, who was by far the best entertainer that I had ever seen and of whom the great Jack Benny introduced as "Probably the greatest entertainer in the whole wide world". I have to agree, he was right.

It was Thursday 29th August 1961; with me were Jack, Johnny and my young sister, Maria, who we were taking out as a treat. As we got off the bus at Piccadilly Circus and turned the corner towards Leicester Square we could see the Prince of Wales Theatre and the big neon sign in bright lights "An Evening With Sammy Davis Jnr". I had booked the tickets a few weeks previously for the second row of the stalls. We were so close, that when Sammy turned his head, you could see the beads of sweat cascade from his head, twinkling in the lights as they fell to the floor.

When the show was over, the four of us left the theatre and walked towards Piccadilly. Nobody spoke a word, we were all with our own thoughts. Then just before we got to Eros, somebody finally spoke, we all agreed that words were not good enough for what we had just seen. THANKS SAM. I first became a fan of Sammy Davis Jnr at the age of fifteen after hearing his impersonations of the recording of "Because Of You". He was always one of my big heroes, up until the day he died. Sammy died of throat cancer, aged sixty-four on May 16th 1990. I was in summer season at the time, at Haven's Combehaven Holiday Park, Hastings. I felt very sad and wanted to pay my own special tribute to him. Late that afternoon I went into the Conqueror Club. It was a large room with a fair sized stage. The place was deserted and in darkness apart from the cleaners lights. I walked across the stage to the disco box and put on his recording of "Candy Man". Standing centre stage, looking out into the darkness listening to Sammy's voice from the speakers I had a private moment and said a little prayer. I think Sammy would have liked it.

Frank Sinatra said;

> *'I wish the world could have known Sam as I did. Sam never gave less than 100 percent when he was on stage, and he gave even more to those of us lucky enough to call him a friend. He was a class act and I will miss him forever.'*

CHAPTER FIVE

"Manchester Here I Come"

The date was 6th September 1961. My suitcase was packed, and I was goodbyes to the family on the steps of 19 Pleasant Place. Father said, 'He'll be back in a fortnight!'

Mum was being brave and aunt Flo was crying, 'What are you crying for?' I asked her, with my hand on her shoulder. Wiping her eyes with her handkerchief she replied, 'I don't want you to go.' Mum put an arm around her, I think she was feeling pretty much the same but she knew that this was what I wanted to do and that it would do me no good to see them both crying on the doorstep. They all waved me off as I climbed into the taxi with Jack and we were on our way to Euston Station.

It was to be a big adventure as I was going into the unknown. We were going to stop off at Sunderland on the way to visit Jacks parents for a week. Once there Jack suggested that I enter a talent contest as a warm up for Manchester. It was held at the Boldon Colliery W.M Club on Monday 11th September. My first performance in the North did not go down very well, perhaps it was my accent, I certainly couldn't understand theirs, but over all I was satisfied even though I didn't get anywhere in the competition, I felt it was a useful exercise.

I had a nice week there and was made to feel very welcome at Jack's parents; they were really kind to me and made me feel at home. We arrived at Manchester Exchange Station at 5.30pm on Wednesday 13th December 1961. This was now the real unknown for both of us as this was Jacks first visit as well, neither of us knew a soul. It was a dull evening as we left the station, I remember seeing a big clock tower and lots of traffic. As we breathed in the Manchester air, our first thought was to grab a cab and find our digs that I previously arranged a few weeks before. A theatrical digs in Plymouth Grove. Apparently they were quite well known in the business, we were soon to find out why! It was situated close to the Town Centre, which we thought would suit us, down a very long road with large Victorian houses each side. It was dark by the time we arrived, the house was huge, and we were greeted by the landlady, a Mrs Stevens. I recall she was a small, woman with dyed black hair and did not look too clean in her appearance. She showed us to our room, consisting of only two single beds, two easy chairs and two wardrobes. The carpet had seen better days and there was a dusky smell in the room, it looked like Victoria was on the throne the last time it had been decorated.

Breakfast the next morning was served in the dining room at one large table with eight chairs around it, but only two places were set, presumably for us. Apparently we were the only guests. There were cornflakes, a jug of milk and a pot of tea on the table. After eating the cornflakes the landlady entered the room with eggs, bacon and beans, it didn't look to good but we forced it down. Coming back in holding the morning paper she told us that she had to go out for a while and that the evening meal was at 6.30pm.

Our first morning in Manchester we went into town for the local papers to check out the entertainment pages for the clubs, and indeed they were full of them. One stood out, The Empress Theatre Club at Stockport, I called and arranged a try out a spot there for the following night, Friday. I was pleased with myself for fixing a date so soon, albeit an unpaid job.

We arrived at the Empress Club and I was quite impressed with the set up, it was a converted cinema, as were most of the other clubs in the Manchester area. I was on in the first half; there were about eight acts in all on the bill. Feeling confident, my act started well but did slip a little towards the end, but overall I was fairly pleased with my first performance in Manchester. I was approached by a concert secretary from a nearby working men's club who offered me a date for the following Sunday night - Result!

Top of the Bill at the Empress was one of my favourites who I had seen many a time at Finsbury Park Empire, Max Wall; Jack and I naturally stayed on to watch him and we stood at the bar. He came on stage looking most uncomfortable, as the saying goes he was "Far to good for this place". Certain areas of the room were being quite noisy and the bottle collectors didn't help as they collected the glasses.

In all of these clubs the glass collectors would drop the bottles into a large basket, making a real racket, regardless of who was on stage. At one point one of them walked right in front of Max Wall who asked them in that wonderful voice of his, 'What are you doing, walking about while I'm on?' I could only imagine that it must have been his first time in a club. It was another reminder that the Moss Empires that he had had so much success in, were on the wane.

Sunday soon arrived, time for my first real engagement since turning pro. It was at Reddish North, W.M Club, Stockport. I had two spots to do, the first went well but the second died. It was too noisy and no one seemed to pay any attention although my teddy boy routine was appreciated. I was paid £3.00 and told to change my style.

A couple of days later I did a live audition at the Southern Sporting Club in Manchester. It was a nice club with nice facilities. Unfortunately, I was given a bad spot on the bill, first after the interval when the audience had just finished playing bingo. I felt good as I went on stage and gave my best performance so far, "went down a bomb" as they used to say and I received an excellent ovation at the end. Sid Elgar, the boss must have liked it as he booked me for another club the next Monday, telling me, 'To be more blue!' I did not take his advice because I didn't want to be a blue comic. Max Miller gags were fine, you could take them two ways but there were a lot of comics around that were doing material that was out and out filth, it wasn't for me. The next four days were pretty tough and Jack and me were running low on cash. I had money in the bank, the winnings from a £750.00 win that same year, but I wanted to be a good pro and to be dedicated you had to learn to go hungry, well I think I certainly did that.

We both walked the streets of Manchester, trying club after club for work. The food served at Mrs Stevens was getting worse. One morning as she brought in the breakfast we could see that her apron was covered in paint, it was on her face and hands as well, as you can imagine it wasn't exactly an incentive to eat her food. When things got even worse financially and we were almost skint we would ask her for extra bread at breakfast to make a jam or marmalade sandwich wrapped in a napkin to take out with us for lunch. I remember one morning Mrs Stevens served us breakfast that was swimming in fat and covered in black bits, the egg looked practically raw, it looked worse than ever, completely inedible. We both thought that if we didn't eat it, she may not give us much to eat in the future.

It was decided to dispose of it in the grate fire so as soon as she left the room we raced to the fireplace and scraped our plates clean. Unfortunately Mrs Stevens returned at the same time, with the sound of bacon and eggs cracking away, she threw the morning paper onto the table and walked back out. It was an embarrassing moment! One evening as we were about to sit down to our evening meal, the doorbell rang. On opening the door I discovered Gordon and Bunny Jay, a double act that I recognised from a Butlins Revue Show. They were in Manchester for a weeks work at the Southern Sporting Club. Bunny entered the house, looked around and then told us he was going to the car. We never saw them again. It was then that I figured that we must be in the wrong digs.

On the fourth day after my last performance, I was walking along Rochdale Road with Jack, when we came across the Embassy Club. Bernard Manning who was unknown at the time apart from in the Manchester area owned it. He was a fat guy with a big smile, a friendly face and a broad Manchester accent. After a short chat, he said that he could offer me a weekend spot in each club. He also owned another club at the other end of Rochdale Road, The Palladium Club.

'How much do you want?' he asked.

'For the two nights, £10.00.' I told him.

Puffing on his cigar, he told me, 'can't pay that, I'll give you eight.'

I agreed, it was a good result compared to my last wage.

It was the weekend of 23/24th September 1961. Arriving at the club I saw what a dump it was. The plan was for me to do a double, a spot in each club over the two nights. When I got there I was told not to go to the Embassy tonight but to do the two spots at this club and go to the Embassy tomorrow. I remember Colin Crompton was on the bill, at that time he was quite a name in Manchester. It was to be a hard night as the place was noisy beyond belief. None of the acts were getting any attention and I was no exception, I could hardly hear myself speak above the racket. I guess the only consolation was that at least I made the band laugh - Welcome to club land.

The following night I set off to the Embassy Club, Bernard Manning met me in the hallway and said, 'I heard it didn't go too well last night.'

'No it was a bit hard.' I replied. 'Don't worry about it.' He said as he put his hand in his pocket and handed me a fiver. "It's a hard club down there, look take the night off and enjoy yourself." I was paid off for the first time, but I must say, it was the best time. Bernard was very polite and understanding, and I was very happy with the fiver.

Many years later when I worked with Bernard Manning, I reminded him about it, and he said "you did better than Wally Harper, he didn't even turn up" (Wally Harper was another big name in the Manchester area).

After my night off, the next night on the 25th Sept I had a booking at the Palace Theatre Club at Stockport. What a fabulous club this was, it was a real treat to work there, it was my kind of club, "class". Unfortunately there were only about fifteen people in the place, so naturally I could not give of my best, I was disappointed really, but I guess that's how it goes, for my efforts I was paid £3. (I guess to a young reader that these fees must seem like a pittance, but of course in 1961 the average wage was about £15 a week.) At the end of two weeks with Mrs Stevens at Plymouth Grove, we moved out, I guess it was quite amazing that we lasted that long. We decided it would be better, if we took a flat, so we had been looking through the local papers, and fixed ourselves in a bedsit in Mayfield Road, at Prestwich.

It was a very nice Jewish area, and quite up market. It was a fair size house, and the flat was on the ground floor, it had a nice big bay window, was nicely decorated, bright and very clean. It was reasonable rent, and close to the shops. I will stop there, as I am beginning to sound like an Estate Agent.

One of the club Comperes that I had been chatting to gave me the number of an agent called Gerry Millman. I rang him up and arranged to call in and see him. His office was in Manchester's Town Centre. I recall he had a moustache and wore glasses. He was very approachable and I felt comfortable talking to him.

He offered me a try out spot that night at the Devonshire Sporting Club. I was pleased, but a little concerned how I was going to get there as by now I had a big cash flow problem. I asked him how to get there by public transport, and he told me what bus to get, and where from. I guess at that point I was desperate, and was about to ask him something that I would never do under normal circumstances, but when you are young you have a bit more front. "Could you give me a couple of quid up front for my bus fare?" I said "only I'm a bit short of cash" ——— "piss off" he said "I'm not running a charity———I'll see you tonight".

As it worked out, it wasn't too far on the bus, and I had enough money. The Devonshire Sporting Club was not the best of the Manchester Clubs. It was a big long room, with quite a big stage, and the place was packed. It was a full bill of about eight acts on, and Top of the bill was Kenny Lynch. I was the first one on to open the show. I felt very confident, and although it was a bit nosy in parts of the room, I went down a treat, and was very happy with my performance. As the night wore on, it was getting even noisier for all acts on the bill.

When Kenny Lynch was on, I thought its time to go to see the agent Gerry Millman in his office that was situated at the back of the room. In his office was a glass window through which you could see the stage. I knocked on the door before walking in. He was sat at his desk that was facing side ways as you walked in. He swivelled round on his swivel chair and said to me "It will not do Dave" "What do you mean?" I said "I know it was a bit noisy, but it's been noisy for everyone ——— listen it's even noisy for Kenny Lynch". With that he stood up and in his Jewish accent he said "ah yes——but with Kenny they can talk, and listen" he then cupped his hand over his ear, looking through the glass as Kenny Lynch was singing to the noisy throng. He then gave me £2 expenses, and offered me another date in another club.

By now we were getting very low on cash, and to make matters worse I needed to buy a small portable record player. When I did my Teddy Boy routine, I was having the Bill Haley record "Rock-A-Beatin Boogie" played. The better clubs had the equipment for me to play it through their systems, but some of the smaller clubs did not have such a facility, so I needed to get my own. We came across a shop in Great Ancoats Street that had a portable player that was ideal for the job. The guy in the shop even played it for us, and after explaining what it was for, it turned out that he was a musician, and played keyboards in one of the clubs.

We were all getting on very well, and I said to him that we definitely wanted this record player, but when we came to pay for it we found that we were £2 short. We tried to get him to knock the price down, but of course he wouldn't. In the end, we paid a deposit and told him we would be back in a day or two with the balance.

On leaving the shop, our next objective was to raise the cash to get the player. It was then that Jack suggested that we could pawn his suit. He had a brand new grey suit that he had brought to Manchester with him but had never worn it. "If you don't mind" I said "I guess we could get it out again in a couple of weeks" ——— "course I don't mind" he replied in his Geordie accent "and its brand new, I've never worn it" ———- "Great" I said "even better, we should get about four quid for it" he then paused for a few seconds before saying "only one problem. ——— I've been wearing the trousers, and I've got 'em on now." ——— It was at that point that I realised that we had to get the deal done today as it was Friday, and I needed the record player for Saturday night, and we couldn't be certain that the Pawn Shop would be open on

Saturday morning, but even if it was I have never been one to leave things to the last minute, although indeed even now we were cutting it fine. To make matters even more worse it was raining, we had now been in Manchester for three weeks and it had rained almost everyday.

We got back to the flat, Jack changed his trousers, we waved them about a bit to dry them off, and they didn't seem too bad. We then put them on the hanger with the jacket, and we had one, brand new suit. About an hour later we arrived at the Pawn Shop with the "three brass balls" hanging outside in all their glory.

Jack waited outside as I went into the shop with his suit over my arm. Before the swinging door bell had stopped ringing, I laid it on the counter. The pawnbroker then began to examine the suit, first the jacket and you could see at a glance that it had never been worn. "Its brand new" I said "good quality" he looked over his specs that were perched on the end of his nose "How much do you want to borrow on it?" ——— "Four pounds" I said, that was followed by a sharp intake of breath. He then started to examine the trousers, and I was holding my breath. He checked the waistband, and the crotch, and both looked fine, then he got to the bottom of the legs and the turn-ups. I was glad that he wasn't near a fire as they would have started steaming. "They are damp" he said, I thought for a second wondering what to say. "Course they are, it's raining, I put the trousers over the jacket to keep the jacket dry." He paused, gave the trousers a few more touches, looked up at me, and said "I'll give you two pounds." "your robbing me, ——— but I'm in a good mood so I'll take it," showing him the palm of my hand.

It was just enough, and we paid off the rest for the record player, and I must say that it served me well for many performances.

It was early in October that I walked into the College Theatre Club in the Moss Side area and fixed myself up with a live audition on a Sunday night. I remember the Compere very well, he was a chubby chap, with blonde hair, a great personality, smart, a very good singer, and very "camp". He was very friendly, easy to get on with, and he gave me a very good position on the bill. Looking back, maybe he fancied me, but it never entered my head at the time. There were quite a few acts on, and when it was my time I was really up for it, and didn't put a foot wrong, I went down very well, and the audience were great.

The owner of the College Club looked like "flying officer Kite" he dressed flamboyantly and had this big handle bar moustache. He asked me what my fee would be for a full week. I told him £35. He said that he may get me £30, but I finished up with £25. I was pleased with that as it was my best fee so far, and my first weeks booking, commencing on Sunday 22"d Oct. 1961. It was round about this time that Jack took a job in a garage, and with me now getting a few dates we were able to pay our rent without any trouble, and eat on a regular basis.

My next "walk in" was at the Princess Theatre Club at Chorlton. I just walked in and asked if they could fit me in to do a spot free, and they did. It was a real swell club, but my performance wasn't too good, and the record for my Teddy Boy routine took ages before it came on. Having said that I guess it wasn't that bad as the management offered me the next night, a Sunday, to do a Double at the Luxor Club with the Princess Club.

When I got to the Luxor Club in Manchester they had no record player, and I had not brought my portable, so I asked the band to back me for the Teddy Boy routine. I went down great and almost tore the roof off, it was a good performance all round.

When I finished the act, jumped in a cab, and was driven to the Princess Theatre Club for my next spot.

At the Princess Club, one of the best in the Manchester area, I used the band again for my Teddy Boy routine, and this was my best performance so far. The Compere introduced me —— "straight from London's West End ——— Dave McGrail", I was glad that I went down so well after that introduction. I was paid £3 and promised a weeks booking so my "walk in" was a good result.

I must say that during my early days in Manchester, I did a lot of "walk ins", and I must have covered many miles. I would get clubs from the Manchester Evening News, and even the local telephone directory. I walked the streets of Manchester to find these places. I would "walk in" then speak to the owner, or the Concert

Secretary and do my best to sell myself. I would even tell them that I had appeared, or was about to appear at several other clubs, that I hadn't. I had no agent at this stage, and it was hard, but I was young, and full of energy, and I did get a lot of work by doing this.

I often wonder if some of today's manufactured performers realise how lucky they are, all they have to do, is jump into a limousine and turn up, and then perform, it must be heaven, but having said that, it's a shame really that they haven't experienced hard times, because all the truly great performers have.

It's like being in the army, when we were doing our National Service we all had a demob chart that we ticked off everyday, but I have never met one old soldier who hasn't looked back and said "I would never have missed it," today's young men will never experience that.

My next performance I was to experience a really hard time. It was at the New Levenshulme Sporting Club. It was a dump of a place, big and tatty looking. It had a reputation of being a comedians grave yard. The owner was a fat slob pig of a man, that you took an instant dislike to.

When I got on stage, I knew it would be hard straight away. It was noisy, people were walking about, and those that were listening just stared up at you as if you were in the dock and been accused of a serious murder. When you get an audience like this, you are never going to win, and your performance just goes down hill, and you are relieved when its time to get off, and its all over. The other bad thing about these kind of nights, is that they never give you your money, and you have to go and ask for it. In the well run quality clubs they would always hand you your money in an envelope directly after the show, and on some occasions even before you have gone on.

In many of the clubs, especially some of the Working Mens Clubs, they would even pay you straight out of the till from behind the bar. I have even known them to count it out on the bar in front of everybody. Many years later, on one such occasion I had this happen to me, and a bloke sat on a bar stool next to me said "you're not fucking, worth that much"———

After coming off stage at the Levenshulme Sporting Club, I just wanted to get my £4/10 Shillings and get the hell out of the place. As I came out of the dressing room door into the main club room I could see the slob of an owner behind the bar. I then went up to him and asked for my money. He didn't say a word, he turned, opened the till, took out the money, then came over to me held the notes up and said "see this ———— for all you've been worth, I might as well stuff this down the drain" ———— my first reaction was to say "well stick it up your arse instead" but I needed the money, so I took it, said nothing, and walked away.——I then thought to myself, "well he's off my Christmas Card list for a start."

Two days later I did a live audition at the Club Monaco in Farnworth it was only a small audience, but I guess I did okay as the manager offered me a booking for November. Next was my first appearance at the Northern Sporting Club in Rochdale Road. I did two spots here, and was very pleased with both performances, they had a great band and we all had a ball, I got £5 for this night.

It was week commencing 22nd October 1961. This was my first week in Cabaret/variety at the College Theatre Club, doubling with the Alambrah Club in Manchester. It was at the College Theatre Club just three weeks earlier, that I had such a big success at my live audition, and I was really looking forward to it. Jack and I first arrived at the College for my early spot. I was in for a shock, as it was far from a walk in the park that I was expecting, in fact I had a real shaky start. It was very noisy, and hard to get attention. After the performance, we jumped into a waiting car to take us to the Alambrah Club, if I remember correctly it was up Ashton Old Road way. We got into the Alambrah Club around 10 pm and I was due on at 10.30 pm. As we walked in, my heart sank, as it looked a real rough dive. It was a smaller club, oblong shape, the stage was on the left as you walked in the door, and the bar was along the right hand wall. The place was packed, and it looked like it was full of villains, and rough necks. I noticed a few guys stood at the bar with square jaws and broken noses, it looked like a convention for punch- drunk ex-boxers. "This could be a tough one" said Jack as we entered the dressing room. "Are you trying to cheer me up, before I go on" I said as we both started laughing. Incidentally having a laugh before you go on is so important, as it puts you in the right frame of mind. I had a quick chat with the band, the Compere was on the ball and on the spot of 10.30pm I was on. As soon as I walked on the room settled down to a nice quiet and within 30 seconds, bang I got that all important first laugh. From then on the only way was up, and I came off to a great ovation, whistles, cheers, and shouts oftlinefor "more". That audience that we thought were Rough, were real Diamonds.

The rest of the week was much the same, hard work at the College, and just great at the Alambrah, it's a funny old game, you can never tell how its going to be. I enjoyed my first week, I felt like a real Pro and was paid £25.

I felt that I was now a member of the Entertainment Business, and a full time professional. I would go into the Town Centre, and on occasions would meet some of the club Comperes and musicians that I had worked with during my first few weeks in Manchester. Very often they would give me a name, or number of a local agent or club owner. It was about this time that Max Bygraves was starring in the musical "DO RE ME" at the Palace Theatre. It was Max remember who was such a big influence on me, when I first heard him on Radio in "Educating Archie" and then saw him live all those years ago at Finsbury Park Empire. I walked into this Coffee Bar, quite near the Palace Theatre, and there stood at the counter was Max Bygraves. I walked up to the counter and said "Hello", he seemed quite friendly, so I took my tea to the table he was at, and asked if I could join him, and he pointed at a chair, and asked me to take a seat. We had a little chat for a short time, I told him that I was just starting out, and that I had come up from London. When we parted, we shook hands and he wished me luck. It was the first, and last time that I saw Max Bygraves. Over the years I have met, and worked with many star names that I had admired, and I thought it was strange that the star that was my idol when I was young, I only met once in a cafe. I can remember when Max was once King of the West End. He was starring in "Meet Me On The Corner" at the Hippodrome, and a short walk up to Piccadilly Circus at the Pavilion, he was starring in the film "Out of Town", you couldn't go anywhere in the West End, or on the tube without seeing his face.

There are two other star names I can recall that I met just one time only. The first was around 1960. I went to the stage door at the Finsbury Park Empire, with comedian Max Mundy, who was going to visit a friend of his, that was in the Playboys group. The top of the bill was an American, I think it was Conway Twitty. Also on the bill was a young Des O'Connor. I had seen him on a few different occasions at the venue, and he was a great act, I can remember he used to do a routine of different people crossing the road, it was very funny. As we got to the stage door to meet the Playboy, Des O'Connor appeared, I shook hands and wished him well, and told him I was a comedian. "How are you doing"? he said, to which I replied "well" - you know - struggling —- "we're all struggling" he said, — and I've never met him again since. As we were going to a pub for a quick drink, it was in between shows, the Play boy said "they are grooming Des to be really big, he will be as big as Bruce Forsyth."-well I guess the Play Boy was spot on there.

The second time was many years later in 1985 at Thames Television Centre Teddington Loch. I had a run of about seven weeks as a Stand in for the T.V. Panel Game "What's My Line". They would record the show in the evening in front of a studio audience, and during the day for rehearsals, they would use "Stand Ins" for the celebrities that were on the show. You would take your place on the panel as one of such celebrities, and you would do the entire show. As contestants would come on and "sign in", you would ask the various questions, and it was exactly the same as doing the real thing.

One week I was "stood in" for Ernie Wise, as both Ernie and Eric were on the show. Come the evening, as they were waiting to be introduced, I was stood next to Eric Morecambe, and must say I was very surprised as he was not very tall, he looked much taller on T.V. then a moment before they went on, Eric turned to Ernie and said "this feels" strange doesn't it, - its not like doing a Proper Show".

I knew exactly what he meant, and he was absolutely right. On these kind of game shows, sat on a panel you don't even get nervous, it really is money for Jam. Anyway that was the one and only time that I met Eric and Ernie. Anyway back to November 1961, my next booking was at the Club Manaco at Farnworth, and what a lousy night that was, I just couldn't work, it was the worst performance I had given so far. Three days later I was engaged to appear at the Club Majestic, Oldham. I was keen to do well, to block out the memory of my last performance. I did quite well in my first spot, and felt very confident. I remember there was an excellent singer on the bill, you could see that he was a seasoned pro, in the first half he received a wonderful ovation, far more than myself, and the other acts on the bill.

In the second spot, I had a hard time, and it seemed that nobody was paying any attention, but I didn't let it worry me, and carried on with my act, and I thought that I worked fairly well. Shortly afterwards the singer was back on again as I was stood at the bar. In the middle of his act, he stopped and then started to talk about what a fine performance I had just given to a noisy audience. He was full of praise, and I was quite overcome and flattered, as he was such a great performer himself. He then extended his arm, and got a round of applause for me as I was standing at the bar. It was a real nice gesture and it made me feel really good.

A couple of days later I did a live audition at the Russell Club. There were 12 acts on the bill, and the Compere who was a nice guy, gave me an early spot. I did very well, and an agent called David Murray gave me his card, asked me to contact him, and said that he could use me.

The following weekend I was engaged to appear for four nights at Johnny Spots Club in Rochdale. It sounded like a Gangsters Club in Soho, but I soon found out that it was a great place to work. It was a very enjoyable four nights, and the act went down great every performance. The Friday night particularly was the best night for me. I felt it was my best performance since being in the Manchester area, and the funny thing was that I followed a Striptease Artiste. I was paid £16 and the owner was so pleased, he asked me to go back in the New Year.

I was on a high and felt that I was making real progress after my appearances at Johnny Spots Club. My next appearance was at

Outwood Working Mens Club at Radcliffe. What a crummy place this was. The stage was more or less a raised platform in one corner of the room with just a piano player, and he sounded terrible. They had no stage lighting, and the house lights were on all the time. When I walked in I spotted a bloke with cigarette ash down his suit, and a committee badge in his lapel, so I guessed he must be the Concert Secretary. I asked him where the dressing room was, and he pointed to a curtain that was covering a doorway at the back of the stage, but I seem to recall that there was another door into it. "Who's the other act on" I asked, expecting to be told it would be a male or female vocalist. "Only you"! He said "and by the way, you do four spots, —two in the first half, then after the Bingo in the second half, you do two more." Of course they had no Compere, so I had to introduce myself. My first spot went well, although the pianist missed every cue that I gave him, the second spot was okay, then after the Bingo the place started to thin out, and the place was half empty, I just knew that after my third spot it would all be over, and it was, I did three spots and that was well enough. I soon learned that at a lot of the W.M. Clubs they did expect four spots from an artiste, it was ridiculous, and far too much of one person, but so many of these concert Secretaries did not have a clue about our business, but they thought they were Lew Grade.

Week commencing 19th November 1961 I was engaged for the week at the Princess Theatre Club doubling with the Luxor Club Manchester. I enjoyed this week especially working at the Princess Club again but the Luxor? - what a dump. One of the acts on the bill was a little chubby singer with a voice like an angel, his name was Don Estelle. I remember during a band call at the Luxor Club, when Don was rehearsing the Compere saying to me and a few others that were there "He's the best Tenor that I've heard for years".

Don and I used to double together, and travel to the other club. I remember one night the Taxi hadn't turned up, so we both ended up going to the Luxor Club on the bus. I can remember both of us sitting on the long bench seat just inside the bus, with all our gear, not forgetting my portable record player, as I had remembered that the Luxor Club did not have a record player. Don was sat next to me with his legs dangling, as his feet did not reach the floor. Little did we both know then, that he would find fame many years later, but not as a singer. He was of course Lofty in the BBC Sit-Com "It Aint Half Hot Mum". I got on very well with Don Estelle, and funny enough, he is another that I have never seen since that week that we worked together in 1961.

The big clubs in Manchester always laid on a car or taxi to take you to the other club when you were doing a "double", it was a good system, as it allowed clubs to have about six acts on the bill. My next engagement was another double, and I was back at the Empress Club at Stockport, this was the very first club that I played on my arrival in Manchester. I was doubling with the Alambrah Club Manchester where I had such a big success with all the Hard Cases. On the Saturday night at the Alambrah I took the roof off the place, it was like playing at the Islington Town Hall, most of them remembered me, and it was a really great night. The Empress Club was also very good, and I enjoyed the whole weekend. My last spot at the Alambrah wasn't too good, as it was late, and there were not many people left, and during my performance I lost one of my New York Cuff-Links, and I was sorry about that, as they really looked the business. Up to now I was still without a regular agent, some of my work I had got through small local agents, but a lot of the work I had got on my own through doing "walk ins" and showcase auditions.

One such agent that was very good to me, and gave me a lot of work, was a lady who ran the ACE Agency in Manchester. Her name was Madame De Castro, but she was just known as Madame. I did all my business with her over the phone, and she never once saw me perform. I mentioned this once to another one of her acts that I was working with, and he said "she goes by reports", so I guess she must have got a lot of good ones. Having said that, I remember once talking to another lady agent, and she said to me that she never got any good reports, she only got "Bad Ones", so if you were never mentioned you were doing okay.

I did meet Madame De Castro just once. She worked from home, and I went to her house. It was a very big house, and she gave me a nice welcome as I walked in. She was a well built lady, and stood tall, her hair was up in a beehive style, she was very buxom and looked like an opera singer. I had heard that she was, but I don't know if this was true.

She told me that she had heard some good things about me, and that after meeting me, she knew that they were correct. As I was leaving she said to me, "I can tell a good performer by just speaking to them, and their attitude, they have a special something, and you have it".—— It was nice of her to say those things, and when I left, I felt really good, and even more confident. Confidence was such an important ingredient for a performer, and of course after a few bad shows, you could bare it, but when that happened you had to get it back, and quick.

It was about Christmas 1961 and Jack and I decided to go home and spend Christmas with our respective families. He got the train to Sunderland and I headed back to London. It was great to see the family after about four months, and I remember it was as always, a nice Christmas at Pleasant Place. It was also good to have a few nights out with my old mates Roger and Johnny and having a lot of laughs.

The New Year came in 1962, and after a couple of days I set off back to Manchester. My first date when I got back was 6th January at the Northern Sporting Club. I had played this venue twice before and I had done well on both occasions. This time was going to be very different. They had quite a few acts on the bill, and the Compere was a very "camp" comic that I hadn't seen before. I was due to follow a speciality act, and as he came off, I was stood waiting to be introduced as the Compere took him off. The dressing room was directly at the side of the stage, so you made your entrance from the dressing room, up a few steps. The Compere did a couple of gags, then he did a bit more comedy. Ten minutes later, and I'm still waiting to go on. By this time, the speciality act is almost changed, then he turned to me and said "he's carving you up," and I think he was right. Fifteen minutes, and I'm still there, as he is coming out with this blue material, that was so blue it can only be described as Filth. After this my act would sound like "The

Magic Roundabout". He did twenty minutes, and then he introduced me, and needless to say I went down like a lead balloon, and died a terrible death. When I came off, I had a go at the guy for stitching me up like he did. He then got his knickers in a twist and shouted —-"what are you worried about,? Everybody dies here, we had Jimmy Wheeler here last week and he died on his arse as well." I guess these kind of experiences did keep your feet on the ground.

Speaking of the material I remember the time one Sunday morning when we went to see a Stag Do at the College Theatre Club, I thought that I would be able to learn something. The bill was crammed with a load of comics and about four Strippers. When the show started I could not believe my eyes, and ears. The comics went on in between the strippers. The material they used was just unbelievable. I may have been naive at the time, but the language and the filth that was coming from the stage in the name of entertainment, did shock me. I thought, if the police arrive they will close the place down. It did not seem that long ago at the Islington Town Hall, when the Director of Entertainments called me to one side, and told me off about using the word Bloody. As we came out of the club (I had learned absolutely nothing) I remember thinking I have just witnessed the very lowest dregs of show business.

There is no talent in swearing on stage just for the sake of it, but the odd swear word at the right time in the right place during a gag can make that gag even more funny, and I have no problem with that, even though I have never used the F word on stage, and I can swear (and do) as good as the rest of 'em. Today of course its entirely different, and you have a job to see a comic who doesn't swear on stage, but to be acceptable I think it has to be funny. The man who makes me laugh out loud today who swears is Billy Conolly. He's a great performer very talented, and doesn't offend anybody, but then again, he's different class.

The next weekend, I was booked Friday, Saturday, and Sunday at the Plaza Club at Swinton, where I had two great nights, and an "iffy" one on the Sunday. I then had a run of Working Men's Clubs at Warrington, Farnworth, Eccles, Rochdale, Bury, and Manchester, before I got another full weeks engagement at the Garrick Club at Leigh, near Warrington. Week commencing 18th Feb. 1962 for a fee of £25, I doubled a couple of W.M. Clubs during this week, so the week ended up a nice little earner.

I had such a big success at the Garrick Club, that the Management held me over for a second week, doubling with Club Caroline. Everybody knows that there is a lot of jealousy in the business, and I first came into contact with it during my first week at the Garrick Club. On the Thursday the Compere was having a night off, so the Boss asked me to Compere the show for that night. I was delighted, as I fancied myself as a bit of a Bruce Forsyth. The first half was great, and I was really having a ball and I noticed that the Compere was stood at the bar on his night off. At the middle of the night it was time for Bingo, and the Boss asked me to call it, as it was part of the Compere's job. I had never even played Bingo, as the balls came flying out of the machine, I dropped one on the floor, and it bounced, and I caught it. I was then putting in comments, and getting roars of laughter, some real whoofers. Eventually, I got through the game, it was great fun, and I thoroughly enjoyed it, and so did the audience, it must have been the funniest game of Bingo, that they had ever played. After we had cleared the Bingo Machine away, I started off the second half by doing a number with the band, and we all had a swinging time. When I finished the song the Compere jumped on stage, and took another microphone off a stand. "What are you doing?" I said to him, as I switched my Mic off. "that's okay" he said "I'll take over from here and you can get off." He was the resident Compere, and I guess I was doing the job too well, he must have felt threatened. On the second week at the Garrick Club, he didn't have a day off.

It was a most enjoyable couple of weeks at the Garrick Club, and for the next few months I was left busy playing Working Mens Clubs all over the area. I also did reappearances at the Levenshulme Sporting Club, Johnny Spots Club, the Plaza Club Swinton, and the Devonshire Sporting Club, and the last one I mentioned was still as noisy as it was the first time I played it. I must say that the place was always packed, but nobody took any notice of anyone on stage. I think it was a case of just having somebody up there, the management couldn't care less, as long as the tills were ringing.

The W.M. Clubs were mainly weekends, Friday, Saturday and Sunday, and although I was keeping my head above water, and earning a living, I was keen to get some more better clubs that did full weeks. One such club was the Casino Club at Bolton. I did a "walk in" at the beginning of June. It was a quality club, great facilities, and indeed my kind of place. I had a really great night and secured myself a full weeks booking there for September. It was about a month before that, I had done even better. I had been in touch with the London agent Don Ross who was a very nice man and he booked me for a week at the famous City Varieties Theatre, Leeds in July of that year. I was delighted about this as since I turned pro this was my first booking in a variety theatre, it was where I really wanted to be. The week prior to my City Varieties date I had a week of one night stands in Doncaster. I had fixed this through a local agent, who had also arranged the digs.

About the middle of June I went home to London for a week to see the family. While I was there, I thought with a few good dates in my book I could visit a few agents and maybe fix some more. At that time there was a London Agent called R.G. Blackie, and his office was at Piccadilly Circus in the Pavilion building. I went along to see him, he was very pleasant, a smart looking man with a moustache. I told him what I had been doing, took him a few photographs, and felt that I had sold myself quite well. I then told him the date that I would be appearing at the City Varieties at Leeds. "I see and your looking for something to fill in" he said, as he started looking through a folder. "That's right" I said, he then got up, and left the room, a few minutes later he returned then said "I can offer you a week at the Huddersfield Continental to run after your date at the City Varieties, —- and the fee is £25. "Twenty five pounds?" I questioned, thinking I might get a bit more. "Its better than a kick up the arse" he said, to which I quickly replied "I'll take it".

When I got back to Manchester I had a few small club dates at Wythenshawe, Stockport, Irlam, Macclesfield, and an American Army Camp at Harrogate, that was a nice experience, and the facilities were very good. After the American Army Camp, I played a pub in Manchester. It was from one extreme to the other. I had no idea why this particular pub even booked artistes, as it had no stage and nowhere proper to perform. It was an L-shaped bar with a small rostrum about 12 inches high against the wall, with a duo of organ and drums on it. There was no room on it for anybody else, consequently you had to perform on the floor in front of the rostrum. The bar was crowded, and the punters were taking over the whole floor. I was introduced by the organist, who handed me a microphone. It was like being stood at a crowded bus stop, as I had people all round me almost rubbing shoulders. I did a couple of gags, when suddenly a bloke tapped me on the shoulder, and asked if he could get past me. It was quite unbelievable, to be performing and having people crossing past you, from the front, and the back, to go to the toilet, and they were that close they would push you forward to get by. I did the best I could, I got a few laughs, but it was mostly ad-lib, I cut it short, and I don't think the management even noticed.

My week in Doncaster was a whole new experience. When I arrived at the digs, it was absolutely crowded with people. Apart from all the club acts that were staying there, they also had some builders. The landlady crammed in as many people as she could. I could never see that sort of thing happening today, but this was 1962. When I arrived the landlady told me that a couple of the builders would be moving out the next day, and that I would spend the first night in the front lounge on the settee. "You can move into your room the very next day but you will be sharing, is that okay?" She asked. "That's fine" I said thinking one night on the settee won't be too bad. My first date that night Sunday 8th July was at the North Brierley Labour Club at Bradford. It was just about an okay night.

When I got back to the digs that night, some of the other acts were arriving about the same time. We were given drinks of tea or coffee with biscuits. The conversation was all about how well most of them had done. As a new person walked in the door, a question would be aimed at them "how did it go?" and the answer would always be the same "I went down a bomb." (going "down a bomb" was a term used if you had a great night and as I would say tore the roof of the place). I soon found out, with a lot of these pros, it became a competition, to see who could outdo the other.

We eventually got our heads down for the night, with people going upstairs to various rooms, and me getting sorted on the settee with some bedding from the landlady. I must have dropped off fairly quickly, but at 3am I was awoken by a terrible row just outside the window. I could hear a female voice and a mans voice, they were screaming and shouting at each other, 'effing and blinding, it was a hell of a disturbance. Suddenly the window started to open, and a girl climbed in, she was soon followed by a guy. As I sat up, before I could say anything she looked at me and said "Sorry, we got locked out, hope we didn't disturb you." I thought disturb me, they must have disturbed the whole street. I learned the next day, that they were a man and wife double act, and that they were always arguing. The next morning as I was going into the bathroom, they were both coming out wrapped in a towel each. "We've just shared a bath" he said with a smile on his face, "we don't keep people waiting too long that way." I must say that I was surprised after the row they had, just a few hours earlier, as it sounded to me like they were trying to kill each other.

I was eventually shown to my room. It was a large long room with two windows, and at first glance it looked like beds all over the place, more like a dormitory. There were three beds along the wall, and at the foot of the beds there were two camp beds. Two of the beds were being used by two builders, their stuff was on the beds, but they were out at work. I ended up on one of the camp beds and put my gear on that. That night I was at the Grimethorpe W.M. Club, it was quite a good night. All the other acts that were staying at these digs of course were working at different places. Before we left for work, the landlady told us to be quiet when we come back so that we did not wake the builders, who would be in bed, and had to get up for 6am.

When I got back from the club late that night, after the usual nightcap and that, we all made our way to our respective rooms. There were three of us going to my room, we were trying to be as quiet as possible, but you know what its like when you are creeping around. Every step we made, a floor board would creak. As we got to the door of our room, I was just about to open it when one of the other boys farted. It was dark, I couldn't see the others faces, and therefore did not know who the culprit was "who was that" I said "It was him" came the reply "It wasn't me, it was you." They continued to argue the toss for a few more seconds "Hang on" I said "Its only a fart, what's the matter with you two?"——— "For all we know it might have been you" came back the reply. "It wasn't me" I said "I was in front, and it came from behind"——— "you can say that again" said the lad directly behind me "anyway it could have been worse, if we had been in the room, it would have woke the builders up." With that we all laughed clamping our hand over our mouths so as not to make too much noise. As we entered the room, we could see the two builders fast asleep in their beds. When we woke the next day, late morning the beds we had seen the builders in were empty. I got to know the other two lads very well, and we had a lot of laughs. I played seven different clubs during my week in Doncaster, and it was the same routine every night and morning. We slept in the same room as the builders, but never saw them awake. On my last morning there when I awoke the builders gear was gone, and they had checked out. I never saw them again as indeed I have never seen the other two acts who were my room mates.

Speaking of farts one of the most amusing moments for me was when I was appearing in the pantomime Jack and the Beanstalk at the White Rock Pavilion, Hastings in 1973. One night I was stood back stage, the show was in full running and I was awaiting my cue. Standing next to me was the giant in his costume towering over everybody, with this massive head. Suddenly I released one, that could be described as quite objectionable, in fact if it had been in a small room, it would definitely have been a red card. Within moments two of the dancing girls that were stood near the giant gave out a stream of verbal abuse, blaming him. I slowly made my retreat, and moved away with a smile on my face, as they continued to say it was him————"Oh yes it was"————"Oh no it wasn't, I said to myself.

My next engagement was the one I had been looking forward to the most, it was the City Varieties Theatre Leeds. Jack and I thought it would be a good idea if we left Manchester as we had been there now for ten months, and moved on to Leeds. A new town with different clubs, a complete change, and who knows, it could be a whole new ball-game.

We found a flat in the Hyde Park area of Leeds, not far from the University. It was an area that was full of bed-sits, and full of students. They were all very big houses, that were converted into flats, and we had a flat in the basement. It was quite adequate for our needs, and the rent was very reasonable.

It was Monday 16th July 1962 the opening night of my week at the City Varieties Theatre. The show was called "Striptease Souffle", it was a variety show with seven acts, including a stripper. It was reminiscent of my week at the Aldershot Hippodrome when I was in the Army. It was not such a nice Theatre as the Hippodrome, in fact the city varieties looked quite run down. It was very tatty back stage, and the auditorium was in drastic need of a re-fit, but I didn't care, it was a Theatre, and it was where I wanted to be, I loved it.

I had a very good week, some nights were better than others of course, but I guess I must have done well, as the management booked me again, in fact I played the Leeds City Varieties, on three different occasions. One night stands out in my mind very well on my first visit. I had a heckler on the second balcony. I could see him as he was at the side of the stage. He had his arms through the bars, and it was one of those nights, that doesn't come very often for a performer. Every comment he made I was able to top it, and was getting great laughs out of it. After about five minutes of our double act he finally stood up, and lead the applause, it was a great moment for me. On the Friday night some of the family came up from London to see the show. Four of them came up by car, Dad, Tony, Maria and my Cousin Colin.

It was quite an expedition for them, as they travelled up at night and arrived in Leeds about 3am in the morning. I only wish that I could have seen some of the goings on that they told me about.

They eventually found the house in Hyde Park where I was staying, but didn't know that I was in the basement flat. There were four floors above, and I didn't know at the time, but some of the student rooms didn't have locks on the doors. (Either that or they left them unlocked). Anyway they approached the front door, and were surprised to find it open. Father was dressed in his usual smart attire, complete with bowler hat. He also supplied anything that was needed, it was pitch dark, so he promptly put his hand in his pocket, and if like magic produced a torch.

Leading the way with his torch, they proceeded to go up the stairs. He then started trying doors. On finding one open, he walked in where he found somebody in bed. His next move was to pull the bed cloths down off the persons head, and shine the torch in their face to see if it was me. He actually did this twice, before Tony suggested that they had better wait till morning. It must have been hilarious, you could just imagine being woke up in the middle of the night by a man wearing a bowler hat, and shining a touch in your face. You would probably think you were dreaming, and that the tax man was after you. They then went back to the car, and figured they could get a few hours sleep in the vehicle, father then produced his silk dressing gown that he put on, but he didn't take his bowler hat off.

They then noticed a night watchman a few yards away in his little hut, with a fire burning outside. They approached him to ask him something, but I don't know what. Tony told me afterwards that he could hardly contain his laughter when he saw the image of our Father walking along towards the night watchman's fire, wearing a bowler hat, a silk dressing gown that was undone and flowing in the wind, with the dressing gown chord trailing on the floor in the gutter.

The night watchman, must have wondered who they were at that time of the morning, he was certainly nervous as he said "a policeman comes round to see me every twenty minutes, and he's due any minute now."

The morning came, and we all found each other, and it was tea and toast all round for breakfast. After that Father cleaned up the kitchen, and he even cleaned the stone floor scullery just outside our door, he said "it was in a disgusting state," and I must say when he'd finished it looked real spick and span. As I have said earlier in this book our Father was a real character, and everybody that knew him, had their own particular story to tell of him. I only wish I could remember them all, as it would make a book of his own.

On the night time, they all came to the Theatre to see the show, and I think they enjoyed it. They stayed the night with Jack and me, and the six of us all bedded down in the one room, all over the floor, and we all had a good laugh.

It had been my last night at the Leeds City Varieties and it was good of the family to come up to give me support. When we woke up on the Sunday morning, after breakfast they would be getting off back home to London. I was off to Huddersfield to start my next week at the Huddersfield Continental, where I opened on the Monday. Tony said they would first drive me to Huddersfield, and drop me off.

We all drove to Huddersfield, and I remember they dropped me off near the centre of Town. It was the only time that I felt lonely, and really on my own. It was very quiet, and I could see no people about. I was stood on the pavement with my suitcase and suit, bags as I waved goodbye to the family as their car slowly pulled away with the four of them waving out of the windows. As the car pulled out of sight, I looked up at a sign that I was stood by, and it made the smile, —— it said "No Waiting"——- I picked up my gear, then headed off to find some digs. As the saying goes———"that's show business."

Monday 23rd July 1962 and I start my weeks engagement at the Huddersfield Continental. It was a cabaret style venue, with a late night supper licence. There were six acts on the bill plus dancers, and I had a most enjoyable week. It was a well run venue the type of club that was a joy to work at. About three weeks beforehand I had met a Leeds Comedian Jack Platts, who was starting up an agency of his own. Jack was a classy comic, that would smoke a cigar throughout his act, and when he finished the cigar, he would finish his act. He was very polished, and had an American style.

He fixed me a couple of club dates, including one with him at the American Army Base at Harrogate. Jack Platts called in to see me one night when I was at the Huddersfield Continental. We had a chat, and he told me that he was opening a new office premises in a couple of weeks, in Leeds Town Centre, opposite the Grand Theatre, and for me to contact him when I got back to Leeds.

When my engagement at Huddersfield came to a close, I went back to Leeds, and my first task was to do a "walk in" at the Commercial Club in Leeds, it was apparently a shop window for club acts. It was a Sunday lunchtime, and I went down very well. I remember afterwards the Compere came up to me and said "you're the best comedian, I've ever seen in a club" ———— I thought it was a wind-up "who are you kidding?" I said to him. "I'm not kidding ———— you're the only comedian I've seen in a club that gets laughs without doing any blue material". It was nice to hear, but as time went by, it became harder and harder to achieve. As the weeks went by I did a lot of W.M. Clubs in Leeds, Wakefield, Barnsley, Bradford, and Grimethorpe, to name a few. A lot of these clubs were real rough, and very hard going. Some of them were great of course, and that kept you going. These one nighters kept me going up till Sunday 16th September 1962 when I started my weeks engagement at the Casino Club Bolton. This was great, my kind of club, a touch of class, and I was there for the week. In these kind of venues I could always shine, they were the next best thing to appearing in a Theatre.

After a really great week at the Bolton Casino, I had a quiet spell for a few weeks, but I was still picking up a few W.M. Clubs at weekends. In early December I played four nights at the ACE Club at Wakefield arranged for me by the agent Jack Platts, I must have done very well as the management then booked me for Christmas week, commencing 23rd December. The ACE Club being a night club gave me the opportunity to do three W.M Clubs during that week as a double at Huntslet, Batley, and Leeds, so I ended up having a very good week. I enjoyed the ACE Club especially, and the audiences were very good.

NOT EVERYBODAY MAKES IT

One night during the week I did have a heckler, who was very abusive, and I couldn't keep him quiet, and he kept it going with threats after the show. I was having a drink at the bar with a friend of mine, when he came over to me and started aiming insults. He even said "I'll be waiting for you, when you leave". He then turned and walked away. My mate who was with me, then said he was going to the loo, and walked off in the same direction. I didn't think too much of it at the time, but I must say I was a little concerned about the guy who had threatened me. About fifteen minutes later my mate came back with a handkerchief wrapped around his hand. I said "you've been a long time, what happened to your hand?"——— "Nothing" he said as he picked up his drink off the bar. "Have you been after that guy" I said, he took a drink from his glass, put it down on the bar, turned to me and said "lets just say he won't give you trouble any more" ——— I don't know to this day exactly what happened, I can only guess, but I reckon the bully got his just deserts.

By this time I was now driving my own car. Funny enough I remember that it was Jack Platts who suggested I should "get yourself a little car" as we were driving to the show at the American Army Base in Harrogate. He said it like it was as easy as going to buy a packet of cigarettes. Jack Platts was very good to me and my mate Jack. He even invited us to his home for Sunday lunch. He had been to our flat to see me and maybe he though we needed a decent meal.

His wife was very nice, and made us feel more than welcome. She cooked a traditional Sunday Roast, it was the best meal we had had for a long time. It was also the first time that I had seen Yorkshire pudding served in the Yorkshire manner. We were given the Yorkshire pudding on a plate on its own before the main meal, and a jug of gravy that they poured over it. I enjoyed it, and it was another new experience for me, as we always had our Yorkshire pudding with the roast beef dinner.

A few weeks later, I bought my first car on the 28th November 1962, from Gallway Smiths Ltd in Domestic Street, Leeds. It was a 1958 Ford Consul Saloon, and it cost £340 of which I drew out of my bank account, and paid cash. Being my first car, it was my pride and joy. The colour was two tone blue and grey, it had a long bench seat in the front, and the gear stick was on the steering column. It looked a great car and I was pleased with it, the only problem was ———— I couldn't drive. I booked a fortnight's driving lessons, every day with the British School of Motoring in Leeds. After my second lesson, I wished that I had done this when I was eighteen, as it was a piece of cake.

When the two weeks were up, it wasn't long before I took my test, but alas I failed on my first attempt, on reversing, and a few Highway Code questions. I guess that I was lucky that I had a car, as I could practice, and Jack had a full driving licence. I was now driving to the clubs at night with my L plates on, and Jack was the navigator.

By this time we both had girlfriends, and I would drive quite often each week from Leeds to Manchester so that we could see them. The Motorways had not been built then, so I would travel over the Snakes Pass. Some of the bends were quite hair raising, especially at night, but it was that trip that I did many many times, that taught me to be a driver. Sometimes when Livvy was with me, she would say it was "like being on the Bobbs". I passed my test at the second attempt, and was now a qualified driver. Incidentally the cost of my driving lessons at that time was a £1.00 a lesson. I had booked fourteen, so it cost me £14.

For the next few months I spent my time between Leeds, and Manchester, working for a couple of agents in Leeds and a couple in Manchester. The first club I played in 1963 was the Flockton W.M. club at Flockton. This was followed by dates at Bradford, Huddersfield, Scunthorpe, Dewsbury, Macclesfield, and the Scala Club at Doncaster. One of the things that I did miss being away from home in the early sixties, was the great spurs triumphs at White Hart Lane. Bill Nicholsons team had won the double in 1960/61. The F.A. cup again in 1962, and of course this year in 1963 they were about to become the first British team to win a European Trophy when they won the European Cup Winners Cup.

I did go to quite a few games at Elland Road, Maine Road, and Old Trafford and they were always enjoyable. However for the past

22 years since I have been living back in London I am a regular fan at White Hart Lane. If I was asked of all the games I have seen over the years, who was the greatest player I have ever seen, the answer would be very easy, without a doubt - George Best.

Jack Platts was sat at his desk, in his new office in Leeds, with the window over looking the Grand Theatre. As I walked in, he greeted me with a big smile "I've just fixed you a summer season at the Coliseum Theatre, Rhyl" he said, "its for a twelve week run, plus a weeks rehearsal". The news was like music to the ears, 13 weeks in a Theatre, "that's great" I said "by the way, — where's RHYL?" "Its on the North Wales coast, it's a lovely area, you'll love it." When the contract came through the post, I signed it on the 16th Feb 1963, my very first summer season, and rehearsals commenced on Monday 10th June, and I was really looking forward to it.

Jack Platts was not my sole agent, and I was also doing club work for a couple of other agents. I was even getting return bookings at clubs that I didn't want to go back to, one such club was called the Broken Cross Institute at Macclesfield, it sounded like it would be full of Indians, and it was certainly run by a few cowboys.

A couple of weeks before I was due to go away to Rhyl, my mate Jack decided he would not be coming with me. He now had a steady girlfriend, and a job, and I guess it was now time for us to go our own separate ways. He had been a good mate to me, and we went through a lot together in our early days in Manchester, and I will always be grateful for his support. We eventually lost touch as people do, and I never saw him for a number of years. The last time I saw him, was years later when I was working at Butlins, and he was on holiday with his wife. The last I heard he was well settled with a family of his own.

CHAPTER SIX

First Summer Season, Proper Showbiz - Tour Of Scotland And Big Money From Butlins

The week before I was due to start rehearsals for the summer season, I had four W.M.Club dates. On Wednesday 5th June I was at the Bradford Hotel, in Manchester on the Thursday, it was The Farmers Arms, Stockport, (two pubs) on Friday it was the Wythenshaw Labour Club, and on Saturday Stanley Street W.M. Club at Openshaw, so I reckoned I would be in good form for when I got to Rhyl. I travelled down on the Sunday, and arrived at my prearranged digs on Sunday afternoon. I got to the address and was quite surprised to find the Boarding House that I would be staying at, on the front right opposite the Coliseum Theatre, it couldn't have been in a better location, and I was able to park my car in a side road where I could see it from my windows.

There were quite a few theatricals staying at the boarding house, the piano player, and drummer from our show were there, and a couple of acts from the Pavilion Theatre Show. The producers of our show that was called "Light Up The Town" were Jack and Bunty Billing, they had been putting in the shows at the Coliseum Theatre for quite a number of years. Jack Billing was a big man, with a squinting eye, and his hair was parted in the middle. He always wore a long black overcoat, even when it was sunny. He would stand outside the theatre doing his Spiel and enticing passers by, to buy tickets for the show. You could hear his voice from quite a distance telling the punters that there were seats in all parts and four changes of programme. It certainly paid off, as we did really wonderful business, and played to packed houses nearly every performance. Bunty Billing was an attractive lady who produced the show and did the choreography. She was very good at her job, and did not suffer fools gladly. I remember one day during rehearsals, she was working with the dancers, and somebody suggested we go outside to run some lines for a sketch we were doing. We were sat in the sunshine, going over the routine, when suddenly Bunty appeared with a face like thunder and said "what are you all doing out her? - you are not on holiday you know" and with that she promptly ordered us back into the Theatre. I remember thinking at the time "she's making a fuss" but looking back I guess she had a point.

I learned a lot from my first summer show "Light Up The Town". I was second comic to the principal comic Joe Crosbie, a Lancashire Comedian who was well known in the North of England. We did four changes of programme, and Joe supplied all the comedy sketches. I worked with him in every one. About three weeks into the season he said to me "Dave, I've been doing these sketches for quite a number of years, and worked with lots of different people but you are the best I've ever had." It was a nice compliment, and I was pleased to hear it, and of course it boosted my confidence no end. A performer must have confidence and believe in himself, because once your confidence goes, you may as well give up. The show opened to good revues, and in the Rhyl Gazette it said:

> DAVE MCGRAIL THIS YOUNG FRESH COMIC AS
> MODERN AS THE TIMES, ROCKED THE AUDIENCE
> IN THE AISLES.

The show was doing very good business, and playing to packed houses, you could even recognise faces in the audience that would come every night to see the different changes of programme. Some of the matinees would be a bit quiet especially on a hot day. One such matinee about mid season, I arrived at the Theatre to do the show, and there were about six people in the audience. Joe Crosbie peeped through the curtain, and said "This is no good," then he said to me "shall we buy the house?" I'd never heard that expression before, but who was I to argue with an old Pro. "Alright by me" I said "right" he said "well buy the house" he then walked away. Some of the other members of the company were now walking onto the stage behind the front of house curtain, and we were all wondering what was going to happen. By now we were in our opening costumes, but a few of the principals were not made-up, including me. Bunty then appeared from nowhere, asked why some of us were not made-up. "We wasn't sure if the show was on" came a reply. With that her face went white with anger, she ordered us to get made-up, stormed off and said "The Show Is On."

Within ten minutes we were all ready, the overture was playing, and we were on doing the opening. The audience by now had swelled to about thirty. As we all came off stage after the opening, Joe walked forward as the number ones closed behind him to do his usual 5 minute warm-up. As I was in my dressing room, I could hear the audience albeit a small one were all enjoying themselves. Joe came off after introducing the next item, and came into his dressing room that was next to mine. About five minutes later I heard this loud banging on Joes door. It was the boss Jack Billings, he laid into Joe and there was one almighty row. I heard Jack B say "you refused to go on" and Joe said "what are you talking about, I've been on, and I've opened the show." ——It then started to get out of hand, and I heard Jack's voice say "your fired ———- pack your stuff, and get out of my Theatre." ———- he then came into my dressing room, and said "Dave you take Joe's spot at the end of the show." It was not what I wanted, but I did a spot that I did in one of the other shows. With Joe missing we had to make quite a few changes, and the show was on at the time. The Musical Director didn't know what had been going on back stage, and he was having notes passed to him to let him know the changes.

The show wasn't as good as usual, but we got through it, and the audience enjoyed it. When the time came round to do the evening performance, I was delighted to hear that Jack Billing and Joe Crosbie had made up and settled their differences, and Joe was back on stage. I guess Jack realised that you can't sack your principal comic in the middle of a season, how could you get a replacement that late in the summer. Incidentally I never heard anybody offer to "Buy The House" after that.

My first summer season at the Coliseum Theatre Rhyl, was a great success,. And I enjoyed every minute of it. The last night was really something special. Apparently it was customary for the cast to buy each other presents. We all bought gifts, wrapped them up in gift wrapping then handed them in to the box office. That night after the final curtain, and we had taken our final bows, the usherettes came down to the stage and handed up the presents and flowers. It was endless, I had never seen so many gifts handed up onto a stage. It was the first time that I had experienced this, and it was by far the best, as I have never since ever seen so many gifts on a last night. It did prove how well we all got on with each other, and it was a really happy show, and maybe that was one of the reasons why it was so successful. They say "a happy ship is a successful ship" and I have always believed that.

In later years I learned that some pros would buy themselves presents, and gift wrap them very elaborately, to give the impression that they were popular. They would even wrap up empty boxes. The Coliseum Theatre Rhyl will always be very special to me, and I did another reason there, a couple of years later in 1965. It was thirty years on in 1995 when I next returned to Rhyl as the Entertainments Manager at Presthaven Sands Holiday Park for Haven Holidays. I walked along the front with my wife to see my beloved Coliseum Theatre, but I was not prepared to find what I saw. The Coliseum Theatre was closed, boarded up, with weeds growing around the outside of it, and bits of paper and rubbish, blowing about in the wind. It was a sad sight. I asked Livvy to take a photograph of me in front of the Theatre, as I had one taken in the same spot in 1963, when it was alive and buzzing. A similar thing happened to me in the late sixties, we were driving along Seven Sisters Road, at Finsbury Park, and I thought it would be nice to look at the old Finsbury Park Empire. I knew that it had closed, but I got such a shock when I drove up the turning to where I was expecting to see it. I just could not believe my eyes, — it wasn't even there - it had been demolished, and was flat to the ground. I thought how could they pull down such a beautiful building, it was criminal. I guess it was at that point that I realised that I was born too late. Theatres like Finsbury Park were being pulled down all over the country. I always considered myself to be a Theatre man, not a club act, and I knew that the truth of the matter was that very soon there would be no Theatres to work in. They built a block of flats on the sight of the Finsbury Park Empire, at least they named it well. Its called Vaudeville Court.

"Light Up The Town" at the Coliseum Theatre closed on Saturday 21st September 1963. My next date was on the following Friday 27th September at the Lancs Auto Club at Sale, Winterbottoms Social Club at Pendleton on the Saturday and the Ball Haye Green W.M. Club Leek. I was now back in club land, and again based in Manchester. I had a run of one night stands at Dunkinfield, Rochdale, Romily, Westhoughton, Pendlebury, and many more places all over the North West. I also played a couple of pubs along the way, the Duke of York in Manchester, what a dive that was, and unfortunately they booked me back, I was not in a position to pick and choose, so I accepted. Another pub I played was at the Royal Oak Hotel in Wythenshawe. They had about four acts on the bill, one of which was a Drag Artiste that was quite well known in the Manchester area. He was a friendly guy, and very chatty in the dressing room. After the show he asked me if I could give him a lift back into town. I said I would, and that I would wait for him outside by the bar. "Good I'll be two minutes" he said. I thought to myself, he will be longer than two minutes, to get changed back to a man, and get all that make-up off. I was stood by the bar and about to order a drink, when I felt a tap on my shoulder, and a voice said "I'm ready Darling". As I turned round, there he was in his full drag, fluttering his eye lashes, complete with high heels and hand bag. ——— My jaw dropped, as I was quite shocked to think he was going out like that, I didn't think it was legal in those days, and he was going to get into my car.————-with me! To make matters worse, I had only a couple of weeks ago changed my Ford consul car for a 1962 Red Mini, and that would put him even closer to me as we got into it.

As we walked out of the car park, these thoughts soon faded, and I could see the funny side of it. We both got into the car, and set off for the Town Centre. He was going to the Cabaret Club in Manchester, so I said I would drop him outside. As he sat in the front passenger seat of the Mini, his skirt was riding up to his thighs, and if I didn't know any different, you would have thought he was a real woman.

As we were approaching the Cabaret Club, near the Gaumont Cinema I said to him "By the way, for a guy, you've got a great pair of legs"——he giggled, pulled his skirt down a bit, fluttered his eye lashes "Thank you" he said looking really delighted with the compliment. I stopped the car opposite the club, he got out, and clip clopped with his high heels across the road, he could really walk the walk, and I think I made his day.

My last one night stand before I started a couple of full weeks, was at the "Wishing Well Club" at Swinton. On Sunday 24th November 1963 I commenced a weeks engagement at the "Milford Hall Country Club," at South Milford near Leeds. I had a very good week, with the exception of a couple of nights that were a bit iffy. The following week I was back again at the City Varieties Theatre Leeds. The show was called "Red Hot And Saucy". Top of the bill was trumpet Star Nat Gonella who had a big hit a few years earlier with "GEORGIA", he was billed as "The Red Hot Trumpet Man" and Anne Marie Ward as "Naughty But Nice." Also on the hill was the rubber faced comic Alec Pleon.

It was great to be back in a Theatre again, this was the showbiz that I really loved and wanted. It was third Division stuff compared to the Moss Empire Circuit, but I was in "the business" and making a living. I reckon a lot of the older performers were struggling to make a living, with the Theatres closing down, especially those that could not adapt to the clubs. I don't know if Nat Gonella was in that category, but he was always scrounging cigarettes off me every night. "Got any spare fags" he would say, and it was not only me he would ask everybody. Mind you I've met a lot of people like that, and some of them have been quite loaded.

I had another good week at the City Varieties, and afterwards it was back to the clubs, with trips to Fallowfield, Wythenshawe, Bolton, and Rochdale. I still did not have a sole agent, but was getting plenty of club work from small time club agents. I used to write dozens and dozens of letters sending my cv and photographs to everybody that advertised in the trade newspaper "The Stage". Sometimes for every twenty letters you may get three replies. It was sole destroying at times, but you just had to keep going. I knew that I was a much better performer now, than when I left London and came to Manchester in September 1961. And the encouragement I had been given by so many people, and the audience reaction that I was getting, I just knew that I had what it takes, so I kept writing the letters.

By now I was thinking about Pantomime, but I was having no luck with my enquiries. Some of the old pros that I would talk to would tell me, in the old days there were pages full of pantomimes advertised, and that the money would be a lot more than the summer reason. I soon realised that many pantomime producers were happy keeping the same shows together, year after year, which of course they still do today. Of course I can understand that as it saves a lot of time in re-casting, and if a show is working well, why change it? Consequently it was very hard to break into panto, but I was determined to keep trying.

Jack Platts rang me and said that Jack Billing would like me back for the 1964 Summer Season. I turned it down as I felt that I didn't want to go back to the same place twice on the trot. I was also confident that I would get fixed up somewhere else. I had written away for many Summer Seasons that were advertised in the "Stage", and I eventually got an offer for the season at the Pavilion Pier Theatre, St Anne's-on-Sea, near Blackpool. It was only for eleven weeks, but I had got it myself, and had no agent's commissions to pay.

It was a Peter Webster production, who was well known for his shows at Central Pier Blackpool. It was called "The 7-45 Show" with Helen Turner comedian Duggie Clark and Arthur Tolchar who was made a household name by Morecambe and Wise with the "Not Now Arthur" catchphrase. It was a nice little show, and did quite good business when you think the Blackpool shows were just 10 minutes up the road. Everyone in the business that knew Arthur, knew Arthur's Mum. She was a lovely old lady, that always wore a woolly hat, and looked like she was out of a Dickens Novel. She always went with Arthur, you never ever saw him without his mother. The only time I saw him without his mother was when he was playing his Harmonica on stage.

She was a great character and very Showbizzy. Some years later, when I was working with the Dallas Boys, they were telling me about the time they went round to Arthur's house for tea. It was about to get dark when Arthur's mother got up to close the curtains and said "its getting dark, I'll just close the tabs." (theatre curtains are always known as tabs). I remember she gave me a lot of encouragement one day when she said "David I've seen your performances getting better every day, and I've noticed Peter Webster has been in, watching you very closely."

She never missed one performance of the "7-45 Show", and was very knowledgeable about the Entertainment business.

I had a great season at St Anne's-on-Sea, and Peter Webster gave me a couple of Sunday Concerts at the Central Pier Blackpool. During that season the show at Central Pier was very strong. Topping the bill was Al-Reid, with the Bachelors, Johnny Hacket, and Ray Fell. Johnny Hacket was an old mate, and on one occasion when I drove over to Blackpool to see him, I remember I pulled up on the wide pavement outside the Central Pier and as I got out of the car, a group of young girls ran over to me, and two of them thrust a programme at me to sign my autograph. It was a Central Pier programme and it was opened up at a photograph of the bachelors. They had mistaken me for one of them. I did not want to disappoint them so I just signed the programmes, got back in the care and drove off.

The weeks flew by, and it was September before we knew it. The last night of "The 7-45 Show" was Saturday 12th September. It was a great last night and we all had a ball. When the final curtain came down, there were the usual presents handed up onto the stage, but it was no where near as many as the previous year at the Coliseum Rhyl. I did notice though, that one of the cast did receive a lot of gifts, many more than anybody else, and afterwards I learned that, most of them were empty box's, that the person had wrapped for himself.

After a couple of weeks rest I was back in Clubland, and doing the odd one nighters. I was now getting work from a new agency called the Anlee Theatrical Agency from Bolton. They booked me for a week at the Cabaret Club at Burnley doubling with the New 77 Club at Brierfield. It was a good week and I enjoyed both venues.

After that week the Anlee Agency asked me if I would be interested in a Tour Of Scotland. Of course I was more than interested, and agreed to do it. The tour was organised by a Scottish husband and wife double act, and would be totally self contained with organ and drums, four acts and three dancers.

The salary would be a percentage of the take, and with the venues already booked, on paper we would be on around £100 per week, and in 1964 that was almost the "big time". The rehearsals were held for two days in what looked like an old Barn in Chorley. The two musicians were good and had a nice sound. The other acts were a male singer, a female singer, a female ventriloquist that was a man awaiting a sex change, the Scottish speciality double act, and myself. They all seemed fine, but when I saw the dancers, that was a surprise ——————they couldn't dance. They were local girls from Chorley, who had never danced in their lives, and the Scottish producers wife was teaching them a couple of routines, and had made them some costumes, but their sex appeal was zero, they looked about as sexy as a Pantomime Dame.

It was Sunday 25th October 1964, when we set off for our Tour of Scotland. The convoy was four cars, a van, and two caravans, I felt quite excited, a band of performers on the road, I thought it must have been a bit like this in the old days. We headed north, and our first stop was just over the Scottish boarder at Langholm. We parked up for the night on a river bank. It was dark when we got there so we couldn't see too many surroundings. As we sat in the caravan having a mug of tea and a snack, you could hear the flow of the river just outside, it sounded very peaceful, with no traffic sounds at all.

"Listen to the sound of that river" I said to the other lads I was sharing the caravan with "I've always fancied having a wash and shave in a river, ———like they do in the cowboy films" I got a funny look from our drummer Chas "yeah right" he said "but I think it will be a bit cold for that"———"of course it will be cold" I said "but that's the whole point, it will be wonderfully refreshing, and wake you up."———"wake you up my arse" came a reply from one of the others "you wouldn't catch me having a shave in a river". As we continued talking about it, the idea appealed to me even more. "That's it, I'm gonna do it, ———in the morning, what about you Chas, with a name like yours you've gotta do it". On his business cards he had Charles Edward Gardner Hooper, and underneath was printed Drummer. "What do you say" ——— "Ok, lets do it."

We awoke the next morning to the sound of the river, a few birds singing, and also some traffic noises. I grabbed my washing bag and towel, and Chas did the same. "You ready" I said "as I'll ever be" said Chas looking at me through bleary eyes. "Lets go and do it." I opened the caravan door, and as we stepped out, and made our way down towards the river, I was surprised to see so much traffic passing by. We carefully stood on stepping stones that took us about four feet from the river bank. I started to set out my stuff, and placed my shaving mirror on a couple of rocks. I then started to lather up with my shaving brush. It was very cold water, but very refreshing. As I got a nice lather on my chin with the brush, I suddenly looked up at the bridge going over the river, the traffic had stopped and there was a double decker bus on the centre of the bridge. It was full of smiling faces peering through the windows. As the bus pulled away, they all waved, and we waved back, and took a bow. I reckon it was the only time that you would see a bus in the morning full of people going to work, with a smile on their face, its normally quite the opposite. It was indeed the one and only time that I had a wash and shave in a river, it was a good experience, and to make it even better, we had an audience of people going to work, and put a smile on their face.

Our first show was at the Bucclugh Hall at Lancholm. It was a small audience, but a great one, and I really did well. Next we did the Tait Hall at Kelso followed by the Town Hall Jedbugh and we finished the week back at the Bucclugh Hall Lancholm.

It was a great pity that the attendances were so small, because I was doing so well, but I knew after the first week that we were nowhere near to making £100. On the Saturday morning the Company Manager Don called a meeting in his caravan to give us all the bad news. As he sat down, his face looked grim as he put a bag of money down on the table. "Its bad news I'm afraid" he said. "I've just counted the weeks takings, and after the hire of the Halls and expenses have been taken out, it works out at £4.50 each. I didn't know whether to laugh or cry, but of course I laughed. "The show has been going very well, and everybody that has seen it has enjoyed it" he said in a bid to cheer everybody up. He then said "If you like I'll keep the £4.50, put it together and get food with it that will last us another week, and I'm sure next week things will pick up. ———-but of course if you would like the money now, you can have it." We all looked round at each other, but all agreed that it would be better to leave the money in the kitty for food.

Don then said that the publicity had not been good enough on the first week, and asked for a volunteer to go ahead to the next town Kinross with Posters and a pot of paste to advertise the show. I agreed to go ahead in my car with a couple of the other lads to stick up the posters. We arrived in Kinross on the Sunday, and our first show that week was at the Kinross Town Hall on the Monday.

We then began to stick the Show Posters in every possible place we could. In one road we were in, I noticed an empty house in the middle of a row of terraced houses. It had quite large windows so I decided to stick a poster over the window. I had no sooner done this when I heard a voice shouting from across the road "wa'd are ye doin', that's ma hoose." I turned and this large man came over to me with a face like thunder. "I'm very sorry" I said thinking he might be talked around to letting us do it" I didn't realise, we thought the house was empty ———we are only advertising our show that is on at the Town Hall tomorrow night ———could we have your permission?" ———"No you bloody well can't" he said "now take it down" ———"I'll give you a couple of free tickets" I said "I don't want your free tickets, I want that poster off "ma hoose yer can stick yer free tickets up yer arse".—— I took the poster down, and said no more. We did the show on the Monday night at the Town Hall and it went very well but it was only a third full.

I found the hospitality up in Scotland was fantastic, and the village pubs were great, wherever we went we were given a very warm welcome. I have always been a proud Englishman, and thank God that I was born in England of English parents, but if I wasn't English my second choice would be Scottish. My third choice would be American. I love Scotland, it's a fantastic country, the scenery is breathtaking, and the people are proud, passionate, warm, and friendly. I've never been to America, but the Americans are proud and very patriotic, I guess they have got a lot to be proud of, (not as much as us Brits of course). But I think they are a great nation. In the world of show business, their top entertainers are pure class.

The tour was very hard on our ventriloquist act, who was a female impersonator, awaiting a sex change operation. We all felt a little uncomfortable with the sleeping arrangements. The girls didn't want him with them in their caravan, and we didn't want him with us. It would not bother me today, but this was 1964, consequently she (we always called him she, as he was always dressed in women's clothes) slept in the van. She didn't seem to mind, and we had a small paraffin heater in the back of the van for her.

I felt more sorry for her during the shows, as she would more often than not, have a rough time, and die some terrible deaths. The audiences just did not like her act. Many years later she became quite a big name in Clubland, and would pull big crowds, her act was quite outrageous, with the dummy swearing like a trouper, with every other word being the F word.

After the next show at the Town Hall Pitlochry, the Company Manager Don called a meeting, and informed us that he was £5 short to pay for the hire of the venue for the next show. "They want it in advance, and if we don't pay up front ———the shows off" he said. Everybody was skint, but I had a post office book with me for emergencies, and it looked like this was one of them. "I'll put up the fiver" I said "but I can only do it this once." They were all over the moon that I had saved the show from closure. "Many thanks Dave, that's great, the first fiver in the box office is yours" said Don sounding his old enthusiastic self.

It gave me a good feeling knowing that I had saved the show, but the feeling was to be short lived. We opened at the Town Hall Blairgowrie, another small audience, but I got my fiver back. Then after another couple of shows it was obvious that we could not carry on, and that the Scottish Tour was a Financial Disaster. Our last performance was on Saturday 7th November 1964 at the Webster Memorial Hall Arbroath.

It was another great night for me with an audience two thirds full the biggest we had. Of all the performances on the tour, I only had two iffy ones. It was a great experience that I would not have missed even though we did end up driving home skint and hungry.

The Anlee Agency fixed me some club dates when I got back from Scotland, the first one being a weekend. I then had a run of one nighters that took me up to the 13th December when I started a weeks' engagement at the Cabaret Club, Broseley, Nr Bridgenorth in Shropshire. It was a great week and I enjoyed it, and I finished on a high on the Saturday night. The next night on the Sunday I was brought back down to earth with a bang, at a place called the Cronkey Shaw Social Club at Rochdale, you couldn't make it up, but I had a 'Lousy night. I was now working for a number of different agents. Apart from the Anlee Agency, Jack Platts, and Madame De Castro, I was also getting work from Peter Raistrick Entertainments from Halifax, Sonny Gross, Ray Carrot, and Dynans Agency from Manchester. Some of the clubs I was sent to were real dumps, and they were run by a Committee, with a Concert Secretary that was mad with power. Many a time I would be greeted by the Concert Secretary with his badge of office in his lapel —- "Are you any good? - you better had be, we don't take any crap in this club, what do yer do? —-"I'm a comedian" —- "a comedian, what it's a comedians' grave yard here, they all die here, — unless your good that is — if your good, they're a great audience." And that's before you've even been on.

Christmas came, and went, and it was now 1965. My first date in January was in Liverpool at The Holy Ghost Club, Netherton. I must admit that it sounded frightening before I got there, but it was ok, and I recall that they liked me. It was a Saturday night and on the Sunday I did the Rakers Club at New Brighton, overall it was a pleasant weekend on Merseyside, but the following weekend I was booked at the Top Ranks Bingo Club in Manchester at Whalley Range, now that was a new experience.

I had to perform two spots in between, the Bingo. The place was packed with keen Bingo players, and the idea was to put an act on during the Bingo Breaks. The stage was full of Bingo equipment, so there was no room for me on there, instead I had to get on to this small rostrum that was jutting out of the wall by the side of the stage. Just as I was due to go on, the Bingo caller announced "that's the end of the first session, we are now going to take a break to enable you to enjoy a drink, and recharge your glasses at the bar". As the audience stood up, and started scurrying to the bar he continued "by the way to entertain you during the break we have Dave McGrail".—-It was priceless. I got up onto the rostrum, picked up the microphone, and I could see this massive audience on the move. They were heading for the bar, the toilets, some were just going to stretch their legs. Of those that remained seated, they were talking to each other lighting cigarettes, it was just a massive movement and noise. I could see the funny side of this, and I laughed. The first words that came into my head were "Is It Something I Said"? I got some laughs from a couple of front tables that had stayed in their seats, so I figured the best plan was to play to them, and keep it short. That's exactly what I did, and I just about got away with it. I was booked for three nights, and each night it got better, as by the third and final night I had it Sussed.

Very soon after this I was back, for one night only at the Cabaret Club at Broseley where I had a very successful week. It was a Wednesday night, and I was a replacement for an act that had dropped out. Being mid-week it was a small audience, but very enjoyable as they were very good, and it was a nice venue to work. In many of the clubs that booked full weeks it was the same pattern. During the week, the attendances were small, unless there was a Big Name top of the bill that could fill a club every night.

You would become very good at working a small audience, then on the Friday night, you would walk out to a house packed to the rafters. It would be such a shock, that you almost would lose your nerve. I never did, and of course it was always far better than a small audience. I have spoken to other performers about this, and they have all agreed, they all felt the same.

My next date was a noon and night show on the Sunday, at the United Sulphuric Company at Widnes. These Noon and Night shows were very hard if they didn't like you on the lunchtime show, they would hate you in the evening. I must admit that I only did a handful of these Noon and Night Shows, it was bad enough to die once, but to die twice in a day—-that was too much.

The Noon Show would normally be all male, it was never packed, and as you walked on almost half of them would be reading a Sunday Newspaper, and you could not hear yourself above the noise from the bar, the clatter of bottles, and cries of "what time is the Bingo On!" - When you come off, a sympathetic Committee Man would say "Don't worry, they are always like that on a lunchtime, but the audience tonight are great." The night time comes, and they are not great. As you walk in you hear comments like, - "the comedian at lunchtime was CRAP - he's on again tonight, God help him."

You begin to wish it was eleven o'clock already, and you are on your way home. I then think to myself "that's no way to be, get a grip, get focused, and go out there and do your best." You then go on, your mouth is dry, the audience are hostile, you can't see a smile on anybody's face, you try to change your routine - big mistake - it goes from bad to worse. Your timing is now all over the place as you are doing a gag, you are not thinking, as you should be that this is the funniest gag in the world, no, you are beginning to have doubts, you are thinking about the next gag - but you think, that's not as strong as the one I am telling at the moment - maybe the one about the man who ties his feet to the end of the bed - that's a bit raunchy, that should get me out of trouble. By now your top lip is sticking to the top of your teeth, and the sweat is dripping off you. - Well at least they can see that I am working hard. You finish the punch line to the gag that you have been telling, but you have no confidence in it, and expect it to die, and it does. In a panic you go for the "feet to the end of the bed" gag. Its really going down hill now, like a fighter pilot that has lost control of his aircraft. All the continuity and timing from your act has gone, you are just pulling any gag out, that you think is the funniest that will turn things round, and win the audience over. - Its not gonna happen, and you know it, there is only one thing left to do. - get into the final song, and get off. I did that, and walked off to the sound of my own feet.

Of course I did learn a lot from the experience, and most importantly to never change your routine in midstream. If you have an act that is nice and polished and slick, keep it that way, even if the audience does not respond as you feel they should, keep plugging and keep smiling, and try never to lose your confidence, like a good passing football team. Keep going for goal, and eventually you will Score.

The following Thursday, Friday, and Saturday, Sonny Gross booked me at the Candlelight Club Oldham. This was a night spot, and my kind of place, with a four piece playing Jazz, there was a touch of class about the place, and I had three great nights.

That was followed by a couple of mediocre Working Mens Clubs, and in March I was booked five nights at the Bulls Head Hotel at Walkden. After my stint at the Bulls Head, I did a few more one nighters and then I had a quiet spell for a couple of weeks.

It was about his time that word was going around that there was a lot of work in the clubs in South Wales, and that they were new to it, and paying more money than anybody else. Some of the clubs were paying between £12 - £15 per night, and in 1965, that was ring-a-ding money.

I was contracted for two weeks of one night stands in South Wales for the Zodiac Agency. On the 8th May, I did the Featherstall

W.M.Club at Littleborough, a club that I had played about four different occasions, before I headed off for South Wales on the Sunday morning the 9th May 1965. I arrived at my digs in Penarth around lunchtime, and was thrilled to find that one of the other guests, was one of my boyhood heroes, Comedian Arthur English. It did not seem that long ago, when I would listen to him on the radio, then the next morning in the school playground, I would repeat his gags to the other boys. Then of course I saw him live at the Hackney and Finsbury Park Empires, and here we were now having breakfast together.

We became friends over the two weeks, and close by to the digs was a mini golf course, where we would play pitch and putt almost every day. Arthur was a great family man, and was always talking about his wife and kids. Over a beer at lunchtimes he would tell me wonderful stories about the old Variety Theatres, the Crazy Gang, and the time when Jack Hylton had a special dinner to attend after the show, and he hung his Dinner suit up in the GANGS dressing room. They took the trousers off the hanger, cut 10 inches off the bottoms, then got the wardrobe mistress to stitch them up complete with turn-ups.

He told me stories about a man who he described as "The Greatest Comedian In The World - Max Miller". I could have listened to him for hours. He was also a good listener, and was always interested in the things that I had done. He looked at me one day, and said "do you know what, you remind me so much of myself when I was your age." I took it as a great compliment.

We would drive to our respective club dates every night then meet up again when we got back to the digs. Some nights were good, some were not so good. I got the impression that Arthur did not enjoy working in Clubs but how could he, having been used to playing Theatres I remember he said to me one day "the best act that is working the clubs today, is Bob Monkhouse, he's real class and knows how to work a club audience" then he said "its so much different today to what it used to be."

Ironically many years later I worked with Bob Monkhouse on quite a number of occasions, one such time after the show he was telling me some great showbiz stories, but it was soon time for him to leave, and I recall saying to him "I could listen to you talking on the subject for hours" but alas we never had the time, and he had to leave. I must say what Arthur English said about Bob Monkhouse in 1965 still applies today - he is still "The Guvnor."

Some of the places that I played in South Wales I could hardly pronounce properly. My first date was at the Liberal Club, Pencoed, then I did the British Legion Club at Pontllotyn, Bedlinog W.M.C. The Merthyr Martyrs Club at Merthyr Trofil Galonuchaf now there's a name to put anybody off, but funny enough it wasn't too bad. The British Legion Club at Nelson, was easy for me to find, but I wish I had never found it, as it was hell, my worst ever night in South Wales. I then had ok nights at the Heolcorrig Club, Merthyr, and the British Legion at Cwmbach.

On the second week I had a couple of nights off, and one of those was the Friday. It was on this night that I was asked to sit on the Judges Panel for a Talent Competition. It had been running for a few weeks, and this was the Finals at the Marina Club in Penarth. When I got there I was very interested to learn that the Winner won a holiday at Butlins and a place in the "Sunday People National Talent Contest." Having been involved myself in this event. I was always interested in it, and would read about the winners in the "People" on a Sunday. I did notice that the same names would come up, and many of those I even knew. Once you had won it, you could not enter it again, but over the past couple of years, I noticed that there were a number of acts that had reached the Grand Final, and even got placed in the first three in previous years. It then dawned on me, that maybe I should enter it again, and win it outright, as I came second in 1960.

I did four more club dates in South Wales at Mountain Ash, Abercvynon, Pontlan, Fraith, and finished at the Miners Welfare Glyneath. I made quite a bit of money over the two weeks, but as I was driving back to Manchester, I was thinking of the good old days of the Variety Theatres that Arthur English had told me about. Of course I'd had a taste of it, at the Aldershot Hippodrome, and the City Varieties, it was real Showbiz, the clubs to me were never that. By now I was looking forward to the summer season, as before I had left for South Wales, I had been invited back to the Coliseum Theatre, Rhyl for a second term there after a years break. The 1963 season had been such a big success for me, that I could not resist going back in 1965.

My last date before I started rehearsals was at the Broadway Hotel at Morecambe, then a few days later I was off to Rhyl, and fourteen weeks in a Theatre, now that really was Showbiz. Top of the bill was Roy Rolland as Old Mother Kelly. The show was called "Carry On Kelly." Roy was an Old Mother Riley look-a-like, and in fact he had been Old Mother Riley's (Arthur Lucans) stand in for many years appearing in almost all of his films. He would often go on stage if Arthur Lucan wasn't in the mood, and the audience didn't know the difference. Roy was another of the old pros, who was full of stories, and he would have us all in fits of laughter, but if something upset him, he would walk away, and not speak to anybody for a few days. You could be on stage with him doing a sketch, and everything was normal, then he would walk off stage, his face would change from a big broad smile to dead pan, he'd storm into his dressing room, and close the door behind him. His moods didn't last long, and I must say that I liked Roy Roland, and I know that he liked me. It was always a joy for me to work with these old pros, and I learned so much from them. I had another great summer season at Rhyl, and the show was a big success, and again did wonderful business. If we had to do a matinee on a hot summer day there was no talk of "Buying The House."

During the summer I would read in the Sunday People newspaper about the winners of the Butlins Talent Competition, and as I have already mentioned some of the same names would come up. I was then thinking very seriously about going in for it again, but how could I do that when I was in the middle of a summer season at Rhyl. Lots of pro acts went in for the competition, I knew that for a fact, but a lot of them were club acts.

I was looking at a Butlin Holiday Brochure, and the last week of the season at the Clacton Camp was week commencing 18th September. That was an ideal date, as my summer season show

"Carry on Kelly" was due to finish the week before, on the same date Saturday 18th Sept. It could not be better. I knew how the competition worked. Throughout the summer they ran Heats each week, the winners would then go back on the last week of the season to compete in the Camp Finals. During that last week of the season they would run more Heats, until they got down to the Camp Grand Final, and then four acts would be selected to go on to one of the area Finals in October, and that would happen on every Butlin Site, so you can imagine what a big major Talent Competition it was.

On the last week of the season, they still run the weekly Heat, and the winner doesn't have to go back for the Camp Finals because he is already there. I figured that's what I would do, so I sent off a booking form and booked a holiday at Butlins Clacton for the last week of the season, and the one thing I had in mind was to get to the Grand Finals in London, and win the 1st prize of £1,000.

The Summer season went by very quickly, and I enjoyed every minute of it, the last night was once again another great event, but the amount of presents and flowers didn't match up to 1963 but it was still a very special night, and the audience were wonderful.

On the Sunday morning 19th September 1965, I checked out of my digs loaded my little Red Mini, and hit the road for Clacton. I arrived at Butlins Clacton around mid afternoon and checked into my chalet. I was soon in for a big shock. As I looked through the programme to check the time of the competition I discovered that the auditions for the event, that I was expecting to be on Monday morning, had been held on Sunday morning and I'd Missed It. My heart sank, but I thought there must be a way around this as the weekly Heat was to be staged on the Monday afternoon at 2pm. After making a few enquiries, I was told that the organist who played for the event was back stage in the Gaiety Theatre. I was told it was a lady musician, and that pleased me as I thought she may be sympathetic to my cause. As I went back stage I saw this lady stood at the piano on the stage. It was a grand piano painted white with a big B motif on the side of it. She was sorting out some music. She was a mature lady, quite slim with grey hair, she looked haughty, and reminded me of a music teacher. As I walked onto the stage she looked up, and with a very stern look she said "What do you want"? I was very surprised at her aggressive tone, I put on my best smile and said "Good afternoon - I'd like to enter the talent contest". - "your too late" she then put her head back down and continued sorting out the music. "look I'm very sorry that I missed the auditions, but I thought they were in the morning" I said trying to get her attention. "They were this morning, and you have missed then, you are too late, that is the rules." - "I'd be happy to do an audition now - could I audition now"? - "No" she said "and in any case, the Compere who organises the competition does the auditions, and he isn't here." - "Where will I find him"? I said, "I don't know, but he will tell you the same as I have, that you are too late." I could see that I was getting no joy from this woman, so I then set off to see if I could find the organiser of the event. I then made my way to the Entertainment Office, where I saw a couple of people and explained my predicament. They both told me that with regard to me entering the Talent Competition, it would be the Compere's decision.

All I had to do now was find him and persuade him. I was now going around the camp asking Red Coats, and various other members of staff if they knew where he was. I went in every bar, and asked musicians, but I drew a blank every time - nobody knew where this man was, I was now beginning to get despondent, to think that I had come all this way to enter a Talent Competition, and I've missed it. I remember sitting on a bench by the outside swimming pool, and lighting up a cigarette. I was collecting my thoughts, and wondering what my next move would be.

Never say die, I thought, when I was in the army I got a show on against all the odds. Then I remembered the film "Never Take No For An Answer" about a little boy with a Donkey that goes to see the Pope. Time was running out, and there wasn't much I could do until the morning. The show is tomorrow at 2pm, so I will be up early, and find the Compere, and take it from there, its not over yet.

I didn't get too much sleep that night, but the next morning I was up early and went to the first sitting breakfast. Nothing has ever put me off my food and I had the full monty, of cereal, eggs, bacon, sausage and beans, toast and marmalade, and a pot of tea. After breakfast I made my way to the Entertainment Office, it was now about 9.15am. I was told the Compere was not there yet but he's usually around about ten o'clock. "Right" I said "I'll be back at ten." I walked away and asked a few more Redcoats that I passed, but none of them had seen him. I got back to the Entertainment Office at ten minutes past 10 thinking I would give him an extra ten minutes to get there. This time I was seen by the Assistant Entertainment Manager, a medium built guy wearing a suit with collar and tie. His name was Alan Ridgway, who many years later became quite a big noise in the Butlin Organisation.

"He's probably in bed" he said "he hasn't got anything on until the show this afternoon." "Would you give me his Chalet number" I said, "and I could go round and see him" - "I don't think he would be too pleased if you woke him up to ask if you can go in for a Talent Contest" he said. I could see his point, and decided to go, and maybe come back later.

An hour later I went back to the office, it was now 11.30am, and I knew that time was really ticking away, "you've just missed him" I'm told by a girl Redcoat "he's just gone for a coffee." How can he think about coffee at a time like this, I thought. Does he not realise that I have travelled all the way from Rhyl in North Wales to enter this Talent Competition. It starts in just over two hours time, and I haven't even got my name down yet. I'm going to win this competition, go onto the Grand Finals and win the £1,000, but I haven't even put my name down yet, and nobody knows about me, and the Compere, all he does is go for a coffee. But 'Hey, how the hell can he know about me. - Lets go and find him.

I went into the nearest coffee bar but he wasn't in there, then I went in another, and another they must have had about eight different coffee bars on the camp and I went in all of them, but nobody had seen him. I checked my watch, it was now 12.30pm, I was now feeling low and almost giving up when a girl Red Coat came up to me and said that she had seen the Compere go into the Gaiety Theatre. I dashed to the Theatre, as I walked in it was now 12.50pm. I went back stage, there were a few people in there, and I noticed a couple of people talking to the woman organist. I couldn't see any sign of the Compere, I had never met him, but I was told what he looked like. Suddenly a voice behind me said "are you the lad who wants to enter the Talent Contest?" I turned round, and there he was, the man that I had been looking for. He was wearing a navy blue Blazer with white trousers, a tall guy with a friendly face. "That's me" I said "I do apologise for being late, but I made a special journey just for the competition." I then explained to him how I had offered to do an audition the day before but the woman organist had told me I was too late and that was the end of it. He then said to me "Its your lucky day, we only had four acts enter for this week, so I will put you on the end to make it five." - I was so relieved, I couldn't thank him enough, he then said "Actually she's right, I shouldn't really put you on, but she has been such a cow to me all season, that I like to put one over on her."

He then handed me an official entry form to fill in, and it was then that I used my stage name for the first time - Dave Thomas. I was always known as Dave McGrail, and my full name was David Thomas McGrail, so I thought if I knock the McGrail off and just have Dave Thomas it would be an easier name for people to remember, and I have been Dave Thomas ever since.

The other four acts were now all backstage, you could hear the sound of the audience coming in, and there was no time for me to go and get changed into my stage suit. All I had was the clothes that I was standing in, just jeans and a casual shirt, and jumper. I had no time to go back to my chalet for music or any props that I used. I was given 5 minutes so I figured the best way would be a play on and play off, and do 5 minutes of gags.

As I was introduced, I walked on to the music coming from the duo of organ and drums in the pit and as I looked down the woman on the organ was glaring up at me like a pit Bull terrier. Within 15 seconds I got that all important first laugh, the organist did not change her expression, but she did me a favour as she made me more determined to do well. My five minutes went like five seconds, and I got big 'Whoofers' (Laughs) for every gag. As I came off I knew that I had done enough to get through to the next stage of the competition, and indeed I had. I was announced as the winner, and in a funny sort of way I was grateful to the lady organist. First for being a "cow" to the Compere all season as if she hadn't I may not have got into the competition,, and secondary for the glare she gave me from the pit as it was a great motivator. I was now in the Camp Finals and my next appearance was a few hours later in Heat one in the evening. It was always a joy to perform in a Butlin Theatre, they had big revolving stages, and they had these, two giant knights on horses at either side of the stage, and for the Finals there would be the full orchestra in the pit.

On the night time show I was able to do a completely different act and I was suited and booted in my stage wear. The afternoon show had been about half full, but the evening show was absolutely packed, and the atmosphere was electric. I knew that I was one stage from the Camp Grand Final. I watched some of the other acts from the wings, and the competition was very strong, so I knew that I could not afford any slip ups, my timing had to be perfect and I was hoping that I did not forget anything. When it was my time, I walked on stage I got such a surprise, albeit a pleasant one. It was as if I had a fan club in the audience, I got this great reception from the people who were in the afternoon show.

It was a real shot in the arm for me, and I felt I was half way there before I had done anything. It was like playing at home and being two goals up in the first five minutes. I thought this is what it must be like for an established Star, the audience know you, and love you, and it's a walk in the park. I came off to a wonderful ovation, and I got through to the last night of the Camp Grand Final.

On the Final night I really felt confident and at my peak. I thought back of the times I had died a few deaths in the clubs, but here I was where I wanted to be, in a Theatre, and a couple of hours away from achieving what I had set out to do when I left Rhyl. The orchestra played my music I walked on, and everything was perfect, it was even better than the previous performance. Before I knew it all the acts were lined up for the finale, awaiting the announcement of the four winners that would go forward to the semi Finals in October. It was nail biting time again, as three names had been called out, and not mine just one more name, one final act to be announced. It seemed like an age, by now the tension was almost unbearable - and then the name came - "Dave Thomas."

With mission accomplished, I did not stay for the rest of the week. I was up early loaded up the Mini, and set off back to Manchester. After a couple of days we were back on the road again, back to London. It was my sister Maria's 21s' Birthday and she was having a party on the Saturday at the family home in Pleasant Place. Over the years we had some really swell parties at Pleasant Place, and they never finished until the milkman arrived. We all had a great night at Maria's do, it was a big success, and a good time was had by all.

Two days later we were heading back up north, and on Wednesday 29th September 1965 I traded in my little Red Mini for a 1963 yellow Mini. I had been happy with the Mini, so I thought "lets do it again." It was 18 months old, low mileage, and it looked the biz.

My next engagement was a ten day contract up in Sunderland for the Fasa Prenelle Agency. It was a town where I was to experience my very worst nights, and the greatest night ever in my career. I left for Sunderland on Friday 1st October. When I got to the digs at the back of the Royal Infirmary in Sunderland, I found it was full of club acts, and it was quite reminiscent of the digs I had stayed at in Doncaster. The landlady had packed in as many people as she could, I'm sure that it would not be legal today. My first date was at Brighams Social Club, and I recall it was what I would describe as a fair night.

The next morning I had to go to the office of the Fasa Prenelle Agency in Paley Street Sunderland. It reminded me of a chip shop. It was indeed a shop front, and as you walked in there was a long counter with one end that lifted up. They gave you a job card, there were about three guys working behind the counter. All the acts had to check in every morning, and they would write the name of the club on your Job card, and tell you where to go. They also told you "no pick ups" so you did not get any money from the club, the agency would pay you at the end of the contract.

I did not know at the time, but it was a real rip off. They would charge the club for an act, and the club would pay the agency. They would then pay the act about £5 or £10 less, then charge the act commission on what they had paid them. It was a system that quite a number of unscrupulous agents adopted, and indeed many TV Extra agencies do today. I don't know how they get away with it.

Of course I was happy with the money that I was getting at the time, and as the saying goes "what the eye don't see the heart don't grieve." My second date was on the Saturday night at Simonside Social Club, South Shields, and I had a good night. When I got back to the digs the other acts were arriving back at different times. I got quite friendly with a couple of the guys. One was comedian Dave Butler, and the other was a singer who should have been a comedian. I can't remember his name, but he was full of fun, and had a great personality.

When we had finished work we would meet up and go on to this Night Club on the sea front in Sunderland. It was the place that all the pros would go to after work to wind down. It became a regular thing, although we did try another couple of Late Nite Spots, but the one on the sea front was always the best. They would let you in when you told them who you were and showed your Equity Card. I remember one night the three of us arrived at the door, and at the same time coming up behind us on his own was the actor Richard Todd who was appearing in a play at the Theatre. As I walked in with Dave Butler behind me, our singing friend said to the man behind the reception desk "Two Comedians, a Singer, and One Actor." Richard Todd did not look amused.

On the Sunday morning I did a Noon Show at the Mile End Club. When I went on I noticed about six newspapers up that were being read. By the time I came off there must have been fifty newspapers up, I died a terrible death it was terrible, one of the most Hostile audience I had come across. One good thing came out of it though, I didn't have to go back on the night time. The night time show was at a place called Outon Manor, West, and it was quite a good night.

The next night I did the Southwich Social Club followed by the Hartlepool Supporters Club At Hartlepool. I did two spots in each so I guess I must have done ok. The Sunderland clubs were notorious for paying artistes off if they did not like them. It became quite a joke back at the digs that whoever was back early had been paid off. Even singers got paid off, it was quite unbelievable, but it happened.

My next date was in Bishop Auckland at the Belvedere Club, and it was quite a good night, then disaster struck, and I got paid off twice on the trot. Friday night in Sunderland at the Milfield W.M. Club, and it was even worse at Steels W.M.Club. It was ironic, but both of these clubs were "pick ups". You are told that they don't want you on for a second spot, then pay you half your money. On both occasions I didn't argue about it, as it had been such a bad experience, I just wanted to get out of the place.

I finished my ten day stint in Sunderland on a reasonable performance at the Ex Servicemans Club at Jarrow. After the show I loaded my Mini, and headed south for Manchester. It had been very hard, I'd had a couple of very good nights and made some new friends, and most importantly had a lot of laughs, but as I drove out of the Town I said to myself Never Again. - little did I know that I would be back sooner than I expected.

Two weeks later I was in the car heading south for Clacton, to take part in the Semi-Finals of the Butlin People National Talent Contest. I was really convinced that I was going to win the £1,000 prize. On the drive down I was going over my routines, I could not think of anything else, and I was fully focused. The event was held over the weekend of 22nd - 24th Oct 1965. It was run on very similar lines as the Camp Finals in September, but the Talent was now very strong, as I sat in the stalls watching the rehearsals and the band-calls. It was quite mind blowing, but I was still very confident.

They were going to pick six acts to join the other six acts from the Northern semi Finals, to go forward to a West End Theatre. It was very nerve racking for everybody, including me. I got through my heat to the last 12, and at the end waiting for the six names, was not so nerve racking, as my name was the first to be called out. - I was in the Grand Final, and just one more performance away from a £1,000.

My next stop was back home in Islington where I stayed with Mum and Dad for a couple of days before heading back up North. When I got back on the Thursday I was offered another week of one nighters back in Sunderland. - I thought I must be a glutton for punishment, and said yes. I guess the saying "Never Say Never" comes to mind.

I started at the Labour Club in Jarrow, and I was surprised how well I went, maybe I'm in for a good week, I was even looking forward to it. There is however another saying - "Don't Count Your Chickens." The very next night at the Elephant Club also in Jarrow I was Paid Off. My next date was at the Ivy Leaf Club in Sunderland, where I had quite a good night and on the bill working with me was a Frank Sinatra SoundA-Like singer called Johnny Garfield. He was a Londoner like myself and we got on very well and became good friends.

During the week we were booked together on two more occasions at the East End Club and the Grindon Club, both in Sunderland. I remember the East End Club very well. We were waiting in the dressing room, when Johnny was called as he was opening the show, and he went and disappeared through these double swing doors. He was an excellent singer, and a few weeks later he was appearing on the Late Night David Nixon T.V. Show. He finished his act, came off, and there was very little applause. Then it was my turn, I turned to Johnny and said "How do you get on the stage?" He said "Go through those swing doors, and you will see a bloke sat down on your right - tap him on the shoulder and say excuse me, and he gets up and you can then climb up onto the stage." I thought he was kidding, but as I went through the double swing doors the man was sat there at the side of the stage and that's exactly how it was. When I came off, and went back into the dressing room, Johnny said to me "The committee man has been in and he doesn't want any of us to go back on again, they are going to have their own people, - buts it's ok, he's coming back in a minute to buy us a drink."

He did just that, and as we were sat in a small bar next to the Concert Room we could hear these two singers they had put on, you could tell by the tone, they were pub singers that had both had a few. The audience loved them and they tore the roof off the place. We both knew that we were class acts, but did not fit in. There's no doubt about it, this showbiz is a funny old game. A few months later I went to see Johnny Garfield singing in a bar in the West End with a piano bass and drums trio. It was real class a place where he belonged, and a far cry from the East End Club in Sunderland.

When I drove out of Sunderland at the end of my week's stint I thought I had better not say "Never again," but I did think the chances of my going back would be very slim indeed. We were into November, and I just had a couple of club dates before a very big important date I had coming up. Many years earlier I remember talking to my father one day, and I don't know how it came up, or why I asked him, but we must have been talking about happy days. I said to him "what was the happiest day of your life" and without even thinking about it he answered "when I got married." It was quite a few years before I knew how he really felt. Because I felt exactly the same on the 20th November 1965 when I married Olivia at The Holy Name Roman Catholic Church in Manchester, at 11 am with the full Mass, it was also my happiest day.

We had a week's honeymoon at a London hotel, and had a great time with me showing Livvy all the sights, and taking in all the big West End shows.

I was now a married man with two little step-daughters, Sonia and Bernadette and for over thirty years they have shown me so much love like they were my very own. After the honeymoon, we moved house, just outside Manchester to Heywood.

My next big night would be the Grand Finals of the Butlins People National Talent Competition. My last club date before going to the West End was at the Brickcroft Social Club, Rochdale, and I was paid £10. I remember thinking my next performance I will put two more noughts on the end.

The date was Friday 3rd December 1965, the place was the New Victoria Theatre, London. The event was the Butlins People

National Talent Competition Grand Final. It was just after that I had qualified for this event that I knew that it would be a great shop window for people to come and see me. At that time in my opinion the top Entertainer of the day was Bruce Forsyth, and his agent was Miff Ferrie, so I figured that Miff Ferrie would be the man for me. I wrote to him sending him my CV and a photograph, and invited him to come and see me at the New Victoria Theatre London. I had a letter from him, and he said he would be happy to come and see me on the 3rd December, and I thought no need to invite anybody else as it was Miff Ferrie that I wanted to be with.

The big day came and the band call was at the New Victoria Theatre in the morning, with the Al Fried Orchestra. It had only been a couple of weeks before that, when I had been talking to my friend Johnny Garfield and asked him about my play-on music. I wanted something really big and brassy that would make people sit up. He went through some of his own arrangements, and then gave me the Count Basie arrangement for the intro of "Looking at the world through Rose coloured glasses." He gave me the parts for the full brass section and piano bass and drums. He then said to me "when you go to the band, call, give the dots to the M.D. and say just play to the sign, and repeat, make it sound like you know what you are talking about, as some of these musicians can be funny" - "Right" I said "I'll remember that."

I was sat in the stalls watching the other acts doing their band-call, when the orchestra leader Al Fried called out my name. I walked up to the orchestra rail gave Al Fried the parts and in my most confident voice I said "Just play up to the sign, and repeat." He gave me a funny look took the parts and handed them round to the orchestra. Al Fried was a small portly Jewish guy, with his hair parted in the middle. He was a man who didn't suffer fools gladly, but a great character, with his very own sense of humour. I got to know Al very well in later years when I did a couple of summer seasons with him at Butlins.

He tapped his baton on the top of his music stand, did the count, and the orchestra blasted into my introduction music, it blew me away, it was a mind blowing sound, ringa-ding ding. When it finished all the musicians looked like they had enjoyed it, and one of the trumpet players said "that was great, - can we do it gain." - "No" said Al Fried and that was the end of it.

I then gave him a couple of pieces of music for my impersonations of Robert Mitchum and Charlie Chaplin, and explained that I would finish on my Teddy Boy Routine, and at the finish to pick up again with the play-on music to play me off.

All went well, and I knew that as far as the music goes I would be in safe hands. There were twelve acts on the show, six vocalists, three comedy acts, two speciality acts, and a group of vocal instrumentalists.

The second half of the show while the Judges were "making their mind up" included the Hermanez Bernal Ballet, Teddy Johnson and Pearl Carr, and topping the bill was Dickie Henderson. The Compere for the whole of the proceedings was Tommy Trinder.

In the dressing room you could feel the tension, everybody was up tight. The boys changed in one, and the girls in another. The rooms were at the top of the building, and a lift took you down to stage level. I was thinking back to the moment when I was at Rhyl, and first decided to go in for the com petition again, and the drive down to Clacton, and when I got there, and missed the auditions. I was thinking how grateful I was to the Butlin Compere for letting me enter the event because the pianist that he worked with had been "such a cow" to him, and I could imagine what he meant. I was thinking about the £1,000 prize, and was confident that it was going to be mine - but was it, you can never be one hundred per cent sure about anything. I had come this far, it would be terrible to fall at the last fence.

Over the tannoy speakers I could hear the Al Fried Orchestra playing the overture, it sounded great, and the excitement was building. Not long afterwards you could hear Tommy Trinder doing a warm-up with the audience. The first three acts had already been called, and taken down to the stage in the lift. I had been drawn number 11 in the running order, and had a long time to wait. As the acts that had been on came back up in the lift, they all looked a lot more relaxed than they did when they went down, most of them were happy with their performance, but a couple were not so happy, and felt they could have done better, I guess we all knew how they felt, as I do not know a performer that has not experienced that feeling. I was by now more nervous than I had ever been, I was called with the other acts that were the last three on the show. We were ushered into the lift and as the gates crashed behind us, it was like going to your execution, I mentioned this to the others, and they all agreed. The lift seemed to take forever to get to the bottom. It eventually came to a halt, and the lift gates were opened with a crash.

As we walked out onto the stage level, one of the singers had just finished, and was coming off to really great applause. I can remember pacing up and down back stage, and before I knew it, I was stood in the wings looking out at Tommy Trinder who was about to introduce me. Little did I know then but a few years later the roles would be reversed, when I would be introducing him, with the AL Fried Orchestra in the pit, on a Sunday concert at Butlins.

The next thing I know the orchestra is playing my intro music, it sounds fantastic with all that brass, and I'm on. As soon as I reached the centre of the stage my nervousness left me, and I felt really relaxed and at home on this big stage. I had a really fantastic six minutes, but it seemed like six seconds, as before I knew it, I was taking my bow, to the sound of the Al Fried Orchestra.

I walked off stage, and felt really pleased the way it had gone especially as the build up to it had been the most nerve racking time I had ever experienced. It wasn't long though before I was beginning to feel anxious again. It was now the waiting game for the Result.

We were all lined up for the Finale awaiting the announcement of winners to a fan fare from the trumpeters of the Life Guards, it was well impressive as the Guards uniforms were glittering in the spotlights.

With four prizes at stake, there was to be four acts called out in reverse order. After the first two, I just new it was me. The announcer then said "The runner up, winning £750 is the show group, The Trackmarks. After the applause died down, there was another fan fare "and the winner of the £1,000 prize - is the comedian" - at that point the audience erupted, and I just heard the two words that I had been waiting for - "Dave Thomas." As I walked forward and bowed to the audience, they were going wild, so it was good to know that it was a popular result. Of course I was elated as I had achieved what I had set out to do, and won the £ 1,000. It was 1965 and a Grand in your hand was a lot of money.

On the Sunday morning my picture was on the front page of the PEOPLE newspaper and I wanted to cash in on that publicity before it cooled off. I was still desperate to get a good agent, and I was wondering if I had impressed Miff Ferrie or even if he was in the audience that night. A few days later, I had a letter from him, telling me that he had seen my performance at the New Victoria Theatre, and that he would like me to make an appointment to go to see him at his office. His headed note paper was a touch of class, real quality paper, heavily embossed with his name, well it would be wouldn't it, I thought at the time, an agent that looks after Bruce Forsyth and Tommy Cooper, must be the best.

His office was in Eaton Terrace not far from Sloane Square. It was a very expensive area, and every door along the road had highly polished brass knobs, Name Plates and letter boxes. I rang the bell it was a very nice tone. The door opened, a lady asked me in, and took me to a small waiting area. It was only a few minutes later, when Miff Ferrie appeared. He was of medium build, not very tall, had a very curly beard, and wore glasses. Then in a Scottish accent he said "nice to meet you Dave, thank you for coming." His office was not a large one, but very well furnished. After quite a discussion he then asked "why did you pick me?" I told him that because he looked after Bruce Forsyth. It was then that I noticed he did not seem all that keen on Bruce Forsyth, and spoke more of Tommy Cooper. I did not realise at the time, but he and Bruce had fallen out big time, and it even involved a High Court case, but of course that was none of my business. After my meeting with Miff Ferrie, he said he would see what he could do for me, but in the mean time to continue doing my northern club work with the agents I work for at the moment.

Mum and Dad outside No 1 Cloudsley Square, the place l was born.

Outside No 1 Cloudsley Square in 1990.

Tony, Maria and me outside the hut of The John Lewis employee's Holiday Camp.

Me and my stage partner Johnny Mizon outside the family home in Pleasant Place, Islington.

Stood by the outside toilet with my brother Tony. That's me on the left when l was seventeen.

A real family Christmas Fifties style. Back row:- Tony, Dad and me.
Front row:- Aunt Flo, Maria and Mum.

Army days. Sorting out the laundry with a pal in the company stores.

In a Butlin Bar with Roger and Terry Venables, he's on the right, and was then a Chelsea player.

PHYLLIS CRAIG

The Officer said "If she can't sing the boys won't notice— she's a cracker"! Phyllis Craig, guest singer in the Army Show.

The Tinhatters Company "Aladdin" with the Mayor of Islngton, George Barnard, playing the Dame.

The McGrail family with Sammy the dog in 1961.

With my mates Roger, in the hat, and Jack on my right.

Sir Billy Butlin giving me my first cheque, New Victoria Theatre, 1960.

Max Miller tops the London Palladium bill in 1938, the year l was born. l thought l ws born to be there. l did make it, just once.

"The Lucky Dip Show" Butlins. What about those 70's flares!

Coliseum Theatre, Rhyl. My very first summer season 1963.

Coliseum Theatre, Rhyl. Closed down, 1996.

My favourite place, on a theatre stage. New Victoria Theatre, London 1965.

"Late Night Cabaret" with my old mate, the late Ted Rogers, 1977.

CHAPTER SEVEN

From The London Paladium To The Walkden Labour Club, And Cabaret In The West End

I returned to Manchester feeling quite happy with the way my meeting had gone with Miff Ferric. My next engagement was my third visit to the City Varieties Theatre Leeds, For Don Ross. This time I was doubling with the Montpellier Club, at Harrogate. It was a strange week really, as I had a fantastic time at the Montpellier Club every night, but on a number of nights at the City Varieties I found it quite a struggle. I had never found it hard in a Theatre before, my bad nights were always in clubs. Having said that, the Montpellier was a nightclub with very good facilities, and I always did well in those kind of places. It was Christmas Eve. As I walked out of the stage door of the City Varieties and passed the dustbins in the alley, I wished that all the Theatres were still open, and I could play a Theatre every week.

A few days later out of the blue, I had a letter from Leslie Grade of the Grade Organisation. At that time I wasn't sure that I was ready for Lew and Leslie Grade, as together with their brother Bernard Delfont, they owned Showbusiness. In his letter he said that he had heard some wonderful things about me from Peggy Mount who he represented. Peggy Mount incidentally was a big name actress of the day who was on the Judges Panel, of the Peoples Talent Finals" at the New Victoria Theatre. He asked me to give him a call to arrange a meeting with him. It was Thursday 30th December. I walked into Leslie Grades office, and he greeted me with a firm hand-shake and a big smile. He was not wearing a jacket, just a white shirt, and a nice tie. He was a friendly man, and I felt at ease with him. "Peggy Mount has told me a lot about you" he said "she was very impressed, I'm sorry that I did not see you myself." He then asked me about myself, and where I had been working. After I had told him a few things, he then said "I would like to see you, could you do a warm-up spot for me at the London Palladium on Sunday?" - I almost fell off the chair, I pinched myself on the leg just to make sure that I wasn't dreaming. "I'd be happy to" I said "Good" he said, "I'll make the arrangements for you." With that he was on his feet, shaking my hand and taking me through to another office, to a man who would give me the details.

As I drove back to my parents home in Islington I was feeling very pleased indeed. I knew how proud they would be, that their son would be performing on the stage of the world famous London Palladium. It didn't matter that it was only a warm-up spot for the T.V. show "Sunday Night At The London Palladium" I was going to be there, and there were thousands of performers that would give their right arm to perform there, and many more thousands that never ever would.

It looked like the New Year of 1966 was going to be a very good year, and it began for me on Sunday 2nd January. I parked my Mini a few yards from the stage door entrance at the Palladium. Livvy was with me, and we arrived for the afternoon rehearsals at 3pm. I was given a dressing room at the top of the building, but it wouldn't have bothered me if it had been on the roof. When we got to the door, I was amazed, to see my name on the door. 'I thought I'm only here for one night, and my name is on the dressing room door, now that is a nice touch.'

We were then shown out into the auditorium, and sat at the back of the stalls to watch the rehearsals. In those days television was all black and white, but it was so much better to see it live, with the lighting and the colourful costumes. We watched the dancers going over their routines, then the various supporting acts. The atmosphere at the Palladium was magic, and I knew that I was part of it, albeit a small part.

Top of the bill was Shirley Bassey, and to watch her doing a band-call was very entertaining, especially when she wasn't happy with the tempo. I remember at one point, her little girl ran up onto the stage, and Shirley just took her hand. She stood holding her mother's hand as she finished the song, it was a real nice moment.

Before I knew it, I was suited and booted, made-up and ready for Showtime. Livvy said she was too nervous to go and watch it, and said she would stay in the dressing room, and listen to the Monitor Speaker. I knew that I was given 12 minutes, but about ten minutes before I was due to go on, I was told to make sure I did not go over the twelve minutes, as if I did I would literally have to be pulled off. "When you have one minute left, we will drop in, and close the red front of house curtains" the man said. I must say it did un-nerve me a bit, as apart from concentrating on what I was going to do, I now had this to worry about. I knew it was important, as he also said to me "and don't cut it short, and be less than 12 minutes, as we are going out live and it would leave a gap."

As I was about to be introduced, I said a quick prayer, I heard the music play, and I was on. As I walked onto that London Palladium stage, it was all I imagined it would be. I thought of all the great names that had walked that walk to the centre of the stage. Frank Sinatra, Sammy Davis Jnr, Danny Kaye, Jack Benny, Nat King Cole, Bob Hope, Max Miller, and when I thought of them, I had no business being there.

As I looked around, it was red and plush, it was Awe-Inspiring, but it felt right. I was told it was a warm up spot, and that is exactly what it was. People were still coming in and taking their seats. I was five or six minutes into my act, and I would see latecomers getting a whole row of people up to move along to their seat. I wanted to ad lib and talk to the late-comers and have some fun with them, but I was thinking about the time, and did not want to over-run. I was getting laughs, but I wasn't relaxed, I wasn't giving my usual performance. My 12 minutes felt like 12 seconds and I was off. I took my bow to good applause in that wonderful Theatre, and the next thing I know, I was making my way up to my dressing room. I had the feeling that I have mentioned before about the performers who come off, and are not satisfied, as they know that they can do so much better.

As I walked into the dressing room, Livvy greeted me with a loving smile. "I wasn't happy with that" I said "I could have done better" - "It sounded fine over the speakers, I couldn't see anything wrong with it, - trouble with you you're getting too Big Headed."

I didn't agree with her, but over the years she has always been my best critic and advisor. After I got changed, we went out into the theatre to watch the show. My confidence was again given a boost when a Canadian Comedian came on, who had made quite a few television appearances over here, and he was really struggling. I knew that I had done a lot better than him, and he was on the show, and I hadn't performed at my best.

After the show, as we walked out of the stage door, it was a great feeling to know that I had just performed at the London Palladium, and if nothing came of it, I had still done it, but I honestly felt that I would be back.

The next day I had an appointment with the Impresario Jack Fallon, who was another of the Judges at the New Victoria Theatre. He offered me a week at the "Showboat Theatre Restaurant" in the West End, for the first week in February. I was well pleased things are beginning to look up. A couple of days later back in Manchester I had a letter from Leslie Grade. It began:

> "WHILST YOU MAY INDEED HAVE LATENT TALENT, I THINK YOU NEED A LITTLE MORE EXPERIENCE WITH AUDIENCES BEFORE ONE COULD LAUNCH YOU IN TOP CLASS CABARET AND NUMBER ONE PRODUCTIONS. AS WE DEAL MOSTLY WITH THIS TYPE OF THEATRE AND PRODUCTION I DO NOT THINK THAT AT THIS STAGE WE SHOULD UNDERTAKE YOUR REPRESENTATION, BUT WOULD BE MOST INTERESTED TO SEE YOU AGAIN WHEN THE EXPERIENCE THAT WE THINK YOU NEED HAS BORNE FRUIT".

Although it was not the letter that I would have liked, it was also quite heartening, as I knew that he had not seen me at my best, and it was not a complete knock back. The only thing that did concern me was I could be picking up bad habits by working in clubs. To become a real class performer, and that was my goal, you had to work in class venues. If you are working with top quality you come up to that level, but if you play in too many low dives there is a danger that you come down to that level. It was a trap that I didn't want to get into, but the good thing was, I was aware of it.

My next date after my London Palladium appearance was at the Labour Club, Walkden, it was quite a difference, but I knew that I had the "SHOWBOAT" in London to look forward to. Very soon after that I heard from Butlins, and they offered me a summer season at Filey as a Compere for 17 weeks, of course I was more than happy to accept.

After more club dates at Fallowfield, Warrington, and Irlam, my last date before my West End Stint was on Saturday 29th January at the M.O.R Social Club at Urmston. Straight after my show I drove down to London to my parents house in Islington, as I was opening at the "Showboat Theatre Restaurant" in the Strand the very next night on the Sunday 30th January.

The "Showboat" was indeed a class place, and I felt at home there as soon as I walked in. It was lavish production show, and they had a line up of gorgeous dancers. To get onto the stage, you had to walk through the dancers dressing room. It was an oblong room that you had to walk the whole length of. The girls would always be in the state of undress, with some being topless as they sat at the mirror adjusting their make-up.

On my very first night as I walked through, I did my best not to look at anybody, but I could hear a couple of the girls talking very loudly, as they always did, about what a rat one of their boyfriends had been. Then a girl in a very posh voice said "If I were you darling I'd tell him to fuck off." I was very surprised to hear such language from a girl, but it did sound funny in a posh voice. From then on in the girls room it was effing and blinding all the time, it was like being in an army billet, but it made me feel at home, it was like being back in the army.

My first night at the "Showboat" I was not too happy with my performance, I think I tried too hard, but my second night was fantastic, and every night after that got better and better as I relaxed and got the measure of the place. My old mate Johnny Garfield that I worked with up in Sunderland came in to see me one night and he said "I thought you were good when I saw you in Sunderland, but seeing you here, you are twice as good." The revue in the "STAGE" from Peter Hepple's "Nightbeat" read:

> ANOTHER NEW FACE SHOWED ITSELF AT THE SHOWBOAT- DAVE THOMAS. A LONDON BOY WHO HAS GAINED MOST OF HIS EXPERIENCE SO FAR UP NORTH, SHOWED A PROMISE WHICH IS WELL WORTHY OF DEVELOPMENT. DAVE HAS A DECIDED GIFT FOR MIME, AS EVIDENCED BY A SERIES OF IMPRESSIONS OF CELEBRITY DARTS PLAYERS AND A FINE STUDY OF A MOD IN A DANCE HALL. HE IS THUS MORE OF A BRUCE FORSYTH IN EMBRYO THAN A JIMMY TARBUCK, AND IT WILL BE INTERESTING TO SEE HOW HE DEVELOPS ONCE HE HAS A COUPLE OF SUMMER SEASONS UNDER HIS BELT.

It was very encouraging along with Johnny Garfield's comments, but my run at the Showboat was only a short one, due to my opening night. Towards the end of the week Jack Fallon came up to me and said "I would have loved to have had you in for a long run, but after the first night the management were not too happy, and I had to go out and find a replacement."

I was disappointed, as it was really bad luck, and my last Saturday night I finished on a real Stormer, and tore the roof off. Who knows what would have happened if I had a long run at the Showboat, it would have been a great shop-widow, and my whole career could have been different. Of course I haven't been the only one, far from it, who have had missed opportunities. Some years later I was told a story about the Sheffield Comedian Bobby Dennis who I was in Pantomime with in 1977. A singer who was sharing a dressing room with Bobby at the "Showboat" recalled the time when BOBBY came off to rapturous applause. As he got back into the dressing room he lifted a chair above his head and said "Can you hear that applause, - why 'ain't I a fuckin STAR" and smashed the chair against the wall.

After my West End appearance at the Showboat Theatre Restaurant, I was back up North for my next date at the R.A.F. Club at Sale. I was now doing a few dates for the Manchester agent Harry Gunn. One weekend he fixed me a Friday, Saturday and Sunday at the "White Horse Inn" at Hutton Cranswick, near Driffield. It was a great weekend, with two other acts on the bill, and we were given food and accommodation at the venue. The Compere was a nice guy who we nicknamed 'Odd Job' as he did everything. When I arrived I noticed he was outside, washing cars. In the early evening he was behind the bar serving drinks. He then took orders for the customers' meals. At show time he introduced the show, they were a great audience, and we all had a great night.

Then come the morning we could not believe our eyes, as we sat down at the table, in comes Odd Job, who not only serves us breakfast, - he also cooked it as well.

It was a very enjoyable weekend at the "White Horse Inn" I had a really good time, the audiences were great, and we had lots of laughs with Odd Job.

Soon after this Butlins contacted me and asked me to do a couple of CABARETS over a weekend at Bognor Regis, and the Ocean Hotel at Brighton, and to do an half hour spot at each. They were both great, and it was a walk in the park to do one spot, as some W.M. clubs I had played expected four spots of 15 minutes each.

Back up North I continued doing more one nighters, mainly at weekends, then after a Sunday night at the Bury Football Club at Gigg Lane, I was given five nights at the Grosvenor Hotel Pub in Great Clowes Street Manchester.

The Monday night was okay. Tuesday was a night off, Wednesday was a "So So" night, Thursday was a night for the undertakers, I died a real death, it was terrible, and Friday they paid me off, and Saturday I was pleased that I did not have to go back. The following week I got two days work as a television Extra at Granada T.V. in a play called "The Blue In His Eyes, The Helmet He Wore", it was the first time that I had done this sort of work, and it was very interesting. It was a play about the police, and I was kitted out in a policeman's uniform.

For the next three weeks I was out of work, and then two days before I was due to start my summer season, I got two days work at Granada T.V. again, as an Extra on "Coronation Street. The first day was in a rehearsal room, and we were called for 10.00am. I remember that there were only about six extras, and everybody else in the room, were cast members, crew, and the production team. I looked around the room and it appeared to be full of faces that you knew so well having seen them all on T.V. so many times. It was all very relaxed, then suddenly the door opened and Pat Phoenix who played Elsie Tanner walked in - well she didn't exactly walk in, she made an entrance all heads turned, and she filled the room with her presence, she was made up, she looked terrific, she was wearing a beautiful coat with a fur collar, and she walked the walk.

None of the other cast members made an impact like her, and over the years I have worked on all the major soaps, and never seen anybody to match up to her. As she continued her walk, I remember thinking to myself, "Wow she's a Star.

On the Saturday 21st May 1966 I set off to Filey to start my 17 week summer season with Butlins. It was to prove to be the start of a long and happy association. To start it was quite ironic, that one of my jobs was to Compere and organise the PEOPLE National Talent Competition. I would be in the Gaiety Theatre every Monday and Tuesday morning between 10 am and 12 noon. It was a two hour stint and I enjoyed every minute of it. These two mornings were audition mornings that were held in front of an audience. A red coat would be sat at a table by the side of the stage, taking down names of contestants. A duo of organ and drums would be in the pit, and I would be in my element on the stage as Compere.

I guess that I must have been stage-struck as I would never leave the stage empty if it was a slow morning, or we had run out of contestants. I would try out new gags, adlib chat to the audience, and have a good time. My chats with the audience became quite a feature, and word would spread. The Tuesday would always have more in the audience than the Monday, and as the season got well under-way, it became clear that the audiences were coming in just to see me.

I would have to pick out, the best 10 acts to appear in the show on the Wednesday night. Then I would arrange the running order and band-call on the Wednesday afternoon. The Talent Show was always very popular, and it was guaranteed a full house for both shows. It was always twice nightly, at Butlins, and the Theatre seated 3,000 people. I would always have a wonderful time on these shows doing the links and I would do a spot at the end.

With regard to the "People National Talent Contest" I must have been unique, having been one of the first to enter it. Got knocked out of it, came second in it, won it, sat on a judges panel for it, and now I was Compere and organising it. I was given various other tasks to do on my first season at Butlins. I had to Compere competitions during the day some of which were very enjoyable to do. My favourite at the time was the Childrens Fancy Dress. It was staged at 11 o'clock in the morning, in the Princess Ballroom. There would always be dozens of entries, and the place would be packed. Some of the costumes would be stunning. It was the year that England won the world cup, and each week without fail we would have the Charlton Brothers in their England Strip, the audience would go wild, and the atmosphere would be electric.

It was on this event that I learnt the technique of interviewing kids, and getting the best out of them, they did indeed say the funniest things, and with the kids answers we would get roars of laughter.

Over the season I became very good with interviewing people on many other competitions, but I did not enjoy all of them. The event that I disliked doing the most was the "Glamorous Grandmother Competition," I just felt that I could not get any entertainment value out of it, and most of the Grannys (With The Odd Exception) would answer a question with a Yes or No, it was hard work.

As I was the new boy on the block, I did not Compere all of the events, as the workload was too much for one. There was another Compere who had been at Filey for the past two seasons, and we shared the work between us. He was very experienced, and was doing a few events that I would have liked to have done. The two events that I would most like to have done were the "Sunday Night Variety" with visiting artistes each week, and a star name topping the bill, and on the Tuesday night was the "Lucky Dip Show", it was an audience participation show. This show was reminiscent of "Beat The Clock" on "Sunday Night at the London Palladium," it was just up my street.

Working at Butlins was a great experience as they gave you so many things to do, but in my case I was never shown or told how to do them. You would be given a schedule for the week and that was it. I would be told "off you go and do the "Dad and His Lad" Competition" - "Dad and His Lad? What do I do with that? I would ask. "Oh you'll think of something" and that was how it was. I was never told a thing. I was pleased about it after a while, as I was able to do things in my own way, and I had nobody to copy from, that was a good thing.

One lunchtime event in one of the bars was Horse Racing on Film, where the punters could have a bet, and win a bit of holiday money. My first day on this I did get help, I was working with the other Compere who showed me how it was run. He used to keep a little book of all the winners, that I thought was a bit strange, but as the weeks went by, I soon found out that it was an easy game to fiddle. I'm sure that on every Butlin site many presenters must have made quite a few bob over a season.

During the week the photographic department would send a Cini-Film Cameraman round the camp everyday to film events. The film would then be edited and shown in the Playhouse Theatre on a Friday morning "Your Holiday At Butlins". It was a silent film with no sound track, and the cameraman would make up a tape of music to suit each scene. The job that I was given to do, was to sit in the front row and give a commentary of what was going on, over the microphone. It was not one of my favourite jobs, but I guess it was another string to my bow.

After my second week into the season, the Entertainment Manager asked me if I would like to do my own Late Night show on a Friday night in the Gaiety Theatre. I was delighted to do this and it was called "The Dave Thomas Hour." I would invite the four winners of the Talent Competition on the show as guests, I had the duo in the pit, and with a couple of talented redcoats I was able to do a sketch. The show would start at 10.30pm and finish at 11.30. When I look back now, I can see it was a bad time to do a late show on a Friday night, the last night of the week when most people would want to be out dancing and drinking and enjoying themselves. However it was successful, and considering the time, the audience attendance was very good.

The Tannoy P.A. System around the camp, was controlled from Radio Butlin. The operators in there would control every venue. Every time I was to go on a job, I would call into Radio Butlin where they would issue me with a microphone and long lead, you would of course have to sign a book for this equipment.

You would then go to the venue of the event, plug your microphone lead into a socket on the wall by the stage, and your microphone would be on, and ready to go. Sometimes you would be in the middle of an event, when the microphone would cut out, and the Radio Butlin operator would come in with a very important announcement. When this did happen I would mime to the girls voice that was giving the announcement, it was always good for a laugh. Of course I would never do this if it was anything serious.

My accommodation at Filey was quite adequate, I had a chalet in the middle of a line of guests. In those days the Redcoats would also be in guests lines on the end of the blocks.

I would eat in the dinning room, three meals a day, and sit with a different family every week. I got used to that, and I met some very nice people.

As the weeks went by I even had my own waiter. He became a friend, and we called him Big Time Billy. He was a Scots lad, and if he was waiting on a row that was four rows away from the row I was on, he would dash over to me and put a meal down at my table to save me waiting. He was a great character, and an excellent waiter, he would treat all of his "Punters" real special, and of course at the end of the week he would do better for tips than anybody else. When I first met him he said to me "some of these waiters in here haven't got a clue - they are Small Time - not me - I'm Big Time Billy."

The weeks would fly past, and the day that England won the World Cup the atmosphere around the camp was fantastic. During the early games watching on the T. V. screens in various venues it was like being at Wembley. We had a great team, and everybody was confident that England would win it, and we did.

The agent Miff Ferrie had been in contact with me over the weeks, and he fixed me a Sunday Concert at the Ocean Theatre down at Clacton on the 21st August. Frankie Howard would be topping the bill, and I was paid £20. My normal day off was Saturday, but I was able to change it to the Sunday, and travelled down to Clacton early on the Sunday morning.

I was asked to do a spot and Compere the show, it was not a good night for me, and at the end when I came to introduce Frankie Howard, he didn't come on the side that he said he would, and I backed right into him, it was really sloppy and I was very annoyed with myself. The following Sunday Miff Ferrie got me a booking at the Futurist Theatre Scarborough. On this occasion Matt Monro was top of the BILL, and my fee was £30. I thought great, I've got a ten pound rise in a week, and its only up the road from Filey. I enjoyed it much better then the previous Sunday, Matt Monro was a very nice man and it would not be the last time that I would work with him.

My first Butlin Summer Season was very good for me, and I felt that I was a better performer when I finished at the end of September than I was when I had started in May. My first date after the season was at the U.S.A.F. Base at Ruislip, and again it was nice to work for an American audience. By this time I had pinned my hopes on Miff Ferrie, he certainly wrote me a lot of letters, and after the sort of work that he had got for me, it really put me off working in W.M.Clubs. Consequently I stopped doing them for a while.

A week or so later I was encouraged by a letter I received from Butlins. It was from the Director of Entertainments Col Basil Brown, telling me that they had been pleased with my services, and that he had instructed their agents New Century Artists to approach me with regard to my availability for the 1967 season.

Colonel Basil Brown eventually become the number one man in the Butlin Organisation, and the next Director of Entertainment was Wally Goodman. It was always very amusing on the camps when the Colonel was paying a visit, he would drive onto the site in a Rolls Royce, and all the departmental managers would be running around like scalded cats. It reminded me of the army when a Big Wig was on a visit, everything was painted white even the stones. In the army you were told "if it doesn't move, paint it." Well this wasn't the army, this was Butlins in the sixties, and it appeared that the same rule applied.

Over the years I always got on very well with the "Big Wigs" when I met them. I would show them respect, but talk to them on the same level that I would talk to anybody else. I have never been a Creep, and these people are usually surrounded by Creeps, they know who they are, and they have no respect for them whatsoever. I remember many years earlier my mum once said to me, "always be yourself boy", and that is what I have always tried to do. It was funny, as many years later, one of my old governors at Caister Holiday Centre, Colin Wright with whom I was discussing a forthcoming event, said to me "all you, have to do, is be yourself".

It was nice to know that my summer season for 1967 was now fixed. I was going to Barry Island for 18 weeks commencing 13th May. Miff Ferrie was still writing me letters, and he fixed me a date in London on 12th December at the Lewisham Town Hall. It was a Monday night variety show, with five acts on the bill plus dancers. I was well pleased when I got there, as I found that I was topping the Bill. I had a great night and really enjoyed it. Miff Ferrie was in attendance with his wife, and after the show in the green room we shared tea and biscuits. Miff and his wife were complimentary, and he arranged for me to go and see him in his office the next day. I now even had his home phone number. As I came out of the stage door at Lewisham, I remember thinking, the only way is up" - but then I was always the complete optimist.

Miff Ferric was sat at his desk as I sat opposite him. He was giving me a few bits of advice about my performance at Lewisham. In a way I felt like a boy up in front of the Headmaster. He was telling me about where I should look and how to hold my head, and not to forget the audience up in the circle, and stuff like that.

Then he told me that he was not happy with some of my material as it was too blue. I did not agree with this, as the material that he must have been referring to were some Max Miller gags that I had been using. They were cheeky, but not offensive. "Would you do that material in front of your Mother?" He asked, and before I had time to answer he said without stopping for breath "because if you would, there's the door." At this point I was glad that I didn't have time to answer. "I put acts in at Buckingham Palace, and Windsor Castle, I've got a reputation to think of." If I had been able to answer his first question my answer would have been, yes and I already have. I was not a blue comic and I had no intention of becoming one. Many times in the clubs I was told that I was not Blue Enough.' I thought to myself, if he thinks I'm blue, he wants to go up North and see some of the Club Comics. - "What I want you to do, is write down all of your material that you are using, and send it to me, so that I can check it." When I left the meeting, and travelled back to Manchester, I thought he must see some potential in me, or else he would give me the brush off.

When I got back home in Heywood I typed up a list of every gag I had ever used, and sent the list off to Miff Ferrie.

Within a week he sent the lists back to me, and I was shocked to find that he had put a blue pencil line through two thirds of the list. He had left me with material of which I was not even using anymore. He had torn my act to pieces, some of the gags he had cut out you would hear far worse on T.V. I was quite gutted, I liked Miff Ferrie, but it was at this point that I thought "perhaps he doesn't get out much." - Miff and me, were not to be, - I never saw him again.

I was soon back working for the Manchester agent Harry Gunn, and on New Years Eve I was at Manchester City F.C. Social Club. The following weekend I was in Wales at the Miners Welfare Institute at Wfynnongroew (I can't pronounce it either). It was a

Sunday night, Monday I was off, and I travelled to Birmingham to start on Tuesday a five nights run at the Cresta Theatre Club at Solihull. I had good digs, and a great five nights, it was a good club to work.

Harry Gunn got me quite a bit more work at the Bury Football Club Gigg Lane, The Regency Club, Morecambe, then he got me a weeks booking at the Russell Club in Manchester, followed on by two nights at Worsley Civic Hall at Walkden, where I was in my element, as it was a Theatre. After a week out I was back at the White Horse Inn, at Driffield for a Friday, Saturday, and Sunday. I was looking forward to it, as I had such a great time last time I was there, and of course there was the Compere Odd Job. Unfortunately Odd Job was no longer there. I had a good weekend, but it was not the same without Odd Job, I don't know why he left, maybe he thought he was doing too much, or that he had a complaint about his breakfasts.

For the next few weeks I continued doing the Working Mens Clubs, and in late March I went up to Barrow-In-Furness for an agent called Bud Bennett of FAB Entertainments in Lancaster. I did the Vickerstown Institute at Barrow, the Engineers Club, and the Municipal and Combined Club at Ramsden Dock. I recall it was an ok weekend but nothing special. I was by now looking forward to my Summer Season at Butlins Barry Island Camp. It was anew site, having only just opened the previous year, and before I knew it, it was Saturday 13th May 1967 and I was on my way to South Wales for 18 weeks.

Unlike when I first drove through the gates at Filey the previous year, I knew exactly what to expect, and was really up for it. The Entertainment Manager was a guy called Larry Knight, he had a good reputation, and I had heard good things about him. After our first meeting, I liked him, and knew that I could work with this man, as he certainly knew what he was talking about, and he liked things to be right.

I was pleased when I received my work schedule, even though there were a lot more events on it than I had done at Filey. I was down to Compere the "Sunday Night Variety" Show in the Gaiety

Theatre, and also the "Lucky Dip Show." I knew that these were two shows that I could really make my mark on. For me doing the "Lucky Dip Show" was a piece of cake, it was an audience participation show, and I would get big belly laughs from the antics and things that I got people to say. Of course participants would vary every week, and some weeks you would be lumbered with a real "Plonker" that thought he was a "Smart arse," it would not always be easy, but you would learn to deal with that situation, and try to turn it to your advantage.

I did learn some weeks into the season from the assistant Ents Manager, who had worked for Butlins for quite a number of years that the show was an event that not many people like doing. "I can see that you really enjoy doing the Lucky Dip Show" he once said to me, "I used to hate it when I did it, in fact I've never met anybody before who liked it." I knew then that it was not an easy show to do, it was a gift, a talent to handle people. For the likes of Tommy Trinder and Bruce Forsyth, it was a walk in the park, and you could see, they enjoyed it. Well I enjoyed it as well and I guess that's why it was a walk in the park for me.

Some years later at the Bognor Camp a club comedian joined us and I was asked to show him the ropes as he was being sent to another camp as the Compere. Frank Mansell who was then the Director Of Entertainments asked him to watch me do the "Lucky Dip Show." He did this and then the following week it was suggested that I do the first house that he could watch again, and then he could do the second house. Frank Mansell would be in to watch him.

The second show started and I was looking on from the wings. He was really struggling and it was going from bad to worse, in fact it became embarrassing to watch. Twenty minutes in, and Frank Mansell came back stage "I can't watch this Dave" and he stormed out.

The performer who I will not name after such a disastrous show, went on to become quite a name in Club Land as a Bluer than Blue Comedian. Back to Barry Island, and I was doing almost every competition you could think of, and I was learning all the time. Sometimes I would make the odd slip up, like the time we did the

"Holiday Princess Competition" on a hot summers day outside on the green. One girl stepped forward wearing a loose fitting dress, after chatting to her for a few minutes, I noticed her tummy had a slight bulge. "And when are you expecting the happy event?" I asked "I'm not Pregnant" she answered indignantly, and with that the wind dropped, and the bulge went down.

Saturday would be my day off as it was the "change over" day for punters. My week would start on the Sunday. On the Sunday morning there would be church services in the chapel on the camp, and the local Roman Catholic priest would come in to celebrate Mass at the R.C. Chapel. I would always attend Mass at 11 am, as I had always done over the years. Wherever I was in the country I would always find a Catholic church, so that I could go to Mass on the Sunday I have done this up to about ten years ago, when I became disillusioned, and I have not been to Mass since. I do pop into a church sometimes when I am passing, and it is empty, and I will pray on my own - and I must say that is a nice feeling when you really want to do it, and not when the Catholic Church tells you that you have to do it.

After Sunday lunch my first job would be to Compere the "Holiday Princess Competition" at 2.30 pm. It would be staged in the Ballroom, or if it was a really nice day outside on the green near the outdoor swimming pool.

Many of the girls would wear swim suits, and if it was outside, and a breeze came up there would be lots of goose bumps on parade. It was a big competition in those days with a top prize in the final of £1,000 and a brand new car. Of course you would get the professional Beauty Queens that would come down to enter, and you could pick them out immediately, they all looked the same, with the same make-up, same hair style, and same smile.

Later in the week, I did the big fashion competition "MISS SHE" that was sponsored by She Magazine. That was a nice event to do, it was always well attended, drew a big crowd, all the ladies looked very nice in some really stunning outfits. Nine times out of ten, the winner of the "Holiday Princess" would win the "Miss She" as well.

My first "Sunday Night Variety Show" was great. It would open with 10 dancers from the resident Revue show, and when I walked out to the sound of the pit orchestra, I felt really at home, I could never feel like this in a club, this was a Theatre, where I was born to be. Topping the bill was star ventriloquist Arthur Worsley, who I got to know very well over the years "Turn Me Round Son."

It was the Entertainments Manager Larry Knight that suggested to me that I should do a children's drama in the "Lucky Dip Show." It was a thing that had been done before at Butlins, but I had never seen it. I asked him what it was exactly, and he said "get five children up on stage, one to be the Hero, one to be the Heroine, one to be the villain, and one to be the policeman." - "what about the fifth one" I asked, to which he replied "use him as a spare, in case any of the kids cries." He said to make a story up, "and you've cracked it." He didn't tell me anything else, but he had sewn the seed.

For the "Lucky Dip Show" I would have a hostess to help me with props, looking after the contestants, and handing out the prizes. It would always be the Redcoat Chief Hostess. I always remember my very first show. The Hostess was very experienced, and had done the show with various other comperes over the years. Her name was Sheila, and she was a great help to me. She guided me through the show with great ease, and it all went as smooth as velvet. Every prop I needed was in my hand before I had time to ask for it. If I had forgotten something, she would whisper and I would catch on immediately. Sheila was older than other girls that I had worked with on the show over the years, but she was the first, and I must say the Best.

Once I had started the "Kiddies Drama" that I would finish the show with, it not only became the hit of the show, but judging by the laughs it would get, it was the hit of the week.

Each week I would get four little boys, and one little girl between the ages of five and six. As they were lined up on the stage, I would interview each one, to get to know who were the best talkers, before I would cast them in their different roles.

As I would cast each one, the Hostess would then take them off to the side of the stage and dress them in their various costumes.

Of course the outfits would always be too big, and would slip over their own clothes. I would always pick the cheekiest little boy as the villain, and he would be dressed in a false nose and glasses with moustache, top hat and an old tailed coat that belonged to my father. The Hero would be dressed as a soldier. Then we would have the policeman. The little girl would be in a long dress with a hat, and the fifth little boy I would use as the scenery. He would be a tree, a door, a bench and so on. We would have appropriate music to play them on, and incidental music throughout the drama. I would give them lines to say, making up the dialogue as I went along, and they would repeat almost in parrot fashion whatever I said. The result was hilarious. As time went on and the more I did it, I got set pieces, and the whole thing became more polished, some of the kiddies each week were out of this world, and it was a sheer joy to do.

The Chief Hostess would also arrange all of the Judges for the various competitions. One such regular judge was the Manager of the News Agents and Gift Shop on the site. It was during a "Miss She" Competition that I noticed that one of the girls was carrying this fluorescent coloured carrier bag. I had seen these bags displayed in the Gift Shop. I picked up on this bag, and made a big thing of it. The next day on another event I did a similar thing with a bag that I spotted in the audience. The next day the Shop Manager came up to me and said that since I had been doing the thing with the fluorescent bags he had sold out. He then said he would pay me a few quid each week if I continued the plugging. He said it also got people into the shop, and once in, apart from the bags, they would spend money on other things. "everyone's a winner."

From then on and for the rest of the season I plugged the fluorescent bags, and they became quite a feature for me, it was a great gimmick. Everywhere I went, in the Theatre, the ballroom, and bars, I always had a fluorescent bag with me, and on the "Lucky Dip Show" we gave them to contestants to put their prizes in, and it was quite a nice little earner, but I would have done it without payment, as it became part of my repertoire and I got a lot of laughs from it.

When I was at Filey I did a spot in the "Redcoat Show," but here they asked me to do a spot, and produce the show. I was happy to do this, and having had experience of producing in the army I was looking forward to it. The only problem was getting people together, as they all worked different duties during the day, consequently we had to have late night rehearsals after midnight. We would rehearse in the Theatre until almost 2am, I don't know how we did it, but we did, and eventually we got the show on. The "Redcoat Show" would always be a revue type show with production numbers and sketches. They were always very popular with the punters as people would like to see their favourite Redcoat doing their own thing.

One night a man came up to me in the Pig an Whistle Bar, he shook my hand and introduced himself, as a Concert Secretary from a Working Mens Club in South Wales. "I've been watching you all week lad" he said "I'm very impressed, you would do really well at my club at Merther Tydfil". He took out his diary, and offered me a booking on my night off. He said he could fix me two Saturdays on the trot at £12 a show. It was quite good money in 1967, and I was pleased to accept.

The first date was Saturday 17th June at the Gellideg Social Club, Merther Tydfil, and as soon as I set foot in the place I knew it would be a tough one. - To say tough one, was putting it mildly. It was Horrendous, I had no chance at all, and I could not wait to get out of the place. It was one of the worst nights that I could remember, as I was leaving I thought to myself. "I bet that Concert Secretary wishes be never came up to me at the bar that night - I know I did.

The following Saturday I was at the Bay View Social Club at Port Talbot, and I'm happy to say that was a good night. I was getting so much adulation during my season at Barry Island Camp, but it never went to my head, as after a couple of club dates you were soon back down to earth again.

My Summer Season at Barry Island finished on 15th September. It was even more successful than the previous year at Filey, and I was doing much more. I felt each week I was learning something new, and was becoming a more polished performer by the day.

On the day that I left the Entertainment Manager Larry Knight shook me by the hand, thanked me and said "you are the best Compere that I have ever had work for me."

It was a nice compliment from a man of his experience, and he had been with the Butlin organisation for quite a number of years. As I drove out of the gates in my little Mini I felt content, relaxed, and ready for the next challenge.

After a couple of weeks break including a week in London, my next booking was a week at the Continental Casino at Burnley doubling with the 77 Club at Brierfield. It was a full bill, plus dancers, and topping was Marty Wilde. I always did very well at these kind of venues, and I had a great week at both clubs. It was a pity that I could not play these type of venues every week, but of course that was not possible. My next date was the Waterhead Conservative Club near Oldham, followed by many more one night stands in W.M. Clubs.

It was about this time that I made contact with a Midlands Agent Jimmy Haynes, he was a nice man, and everybody liked him, he would not send an act to a club if he felt it would not be right for them, and he knew all of the venues and what they were like. The first booking he gave me was an R.A.F. Camp at North Luffenham the fee was £14 and I had a terrific night.

After that he gave me four nights at the Stilton Country Club near Peterborough, it sounded like my kind of place, but unfortunately a week before the engagement he phoned me to say it had been cancelled. He did however give me two other dates.

Of course I was still working for other agents, but I found Jimmy Haynes to be the best for me. Harry Gunn fixed me at the Cala Gran Country Club in Fleetwood, and I guess I did ok, as they wanted me back again for the following Saturday. On the Sunday I was at the Leyton Institute in Blackpool, and man what a night that was I died a thousand deaths, it was very painful I remember how bad it was, as on the very bad nights I would mark in my diary a big N for "Never Again". However I was soon over that very low feeling, and back on a high after a good performance at the Glazbrook Country Club at Irlam.

Just before the season ended at Barry Island, I was given a booking by a man who I met in the bar. It was for his company Christmas Do on the 16th Dec. He sent me a letter of confirmation from his company a few days later, and the fee was for £80. I thought it would be a good idea to take a singer along with me, and make a show of it, as I could afford to pay another act out of my fee. I contacted my friend Johnny Garfield who I had worked with on a number of dates in Sunderland, and he was happy to do it.

The date was at the Abbey Hotel, Hanger Lane, on the North Circular Road. It was a Dinner and Dance, and they had engaged a very good four piece band. Both Johnny and I had a great night, and were given a nice meal afterwards.

The following morning, after staying the night at my parents house in Islington I set off once again for Manchester, as I had three nights at the Monaco Club at Farnworth. I had written lots of letters with regard to getting fixed up in a Pantomime, but without success. I guess if I had an agent enquiring about panto for me it might have been different, but I didn't so I just had to get on with it myself. I did club dates up to, and just after Christmas. We were soon about to say goodbye to 1967, the year when Spurs won the F.A. Cup for the fifth time, and it was hello to 1968.

The early part of the year was not that great, I was only doing W.M.Clubs at weekends. The only significant date I had was a week at the Cabaret Club at Peterborough, and I must say, that was very enjoyable. I had arranged for a South Coast Management to come to see me with a view for a possible Summer Season for the following year 1969, as I had already signed once again for Butlins, for the coming season at Minehead. He came down with his wife on the Thursday, and after my performance we had a chat, and he was very encouraging "of all the comics I've seen" he said "you're my cup of tea - however I still have another comedian to see." He was very pleasant, and after we had a drink, we shook hands and he went. He did not tell me who the other comedian was, but I guess he got the job, as I didn't hear from him again.

Playing the "waiting game" was never a nice experience, and I had played the game many many times. I don't know why it is, but most people in this business do not have the guts to say to somebody's face "sorry but you are not what we are looking for." I have had that a couple of times, and of course it is not what you want to hear, but it is honest, and you know where you stand, but when you are waiting for the Postman every day for that all important letter that never comes, it's a lousy game to play.

A few weeks before the summer season was due to start, work dried up, so I decided to take a job as a taxi driver for a few weeks. It was quite an experience, and one that I would not have missed. It was a private company and they had a fleet of Ford Zodiacs and Zephyrs. All the cars were radio controlled, and you would be on the road, when the girl at base control, would tell you where to go. Most of the work was in the Salford and Prestwich area of Manchester. It was quite funny on a couple of occasions when I didn't have a clue where the fare wanted to go, and I had to ask them the way, but I soon got the hang of it after a couple of days.

I remember one time I had just taken a fare to the Exchange Railway Station, and I was heading up Bury New Road, when the girl on the Radio asked me to go to the nearest Newsagent, buy a packet of 20 cigarettes, and take them to an address in Prestwich. She then told me to charge for the cigarettes, plus £5 extra. I did this, it was a young woman who had ordered it, and she was quite happy to pay. I said to her "that's an expensive packet of fags" - she said "I know, but I love em".

The thing that never happened to me, in my three week career as a cabbie, was that nobody jumped in the back, and shouted at me "Follow That Cab" I'd seen it happen, and heard the line so many times in the movies. I had always had an ambition to go to New York. I wanted to walk along Broadway to Time Square, to go to Madison Square Garden, to have a boat ride along the Hudson River, and pass the Statue of Liberty, to look at the Manhattan Sky line, and go to the top of the Empire State Building. Maybe I would one day even jump in the back of a yellow taxi and say to the driver "Follow that cab."

Yes indeed going to New York City was something that I had always wanted to do, but at the moment I can only think about it, as I stop at some traffic lights in my own cab as I drove through the centre of Manchester. I am outside a record shop with a large display of LPs in the window. The lights change to green, as I pull away, I take a glance at the window and see albums of Frank Sinatra and Sammy Davis Jr, it was as if they were looking out at me - I put my foot down, and thought to myself - Ring-A-DingDing, I'll get to New York some day.

Chapter Eight

The butlin star nights. "Never Count Your Chickens" The Touring Show, And A Naked Stripper In My Arms

Before I knew it, the date was 10th May 1968 and I was on my way to start my third Summer Season for Butlins at Minehead. It had been said that Minehead was Butlins number one site, and when I got there I could see why, as indeed it was, the facilities were first class and it was in a beautiful area. I soon got into the swing of things, and it was great to be working in a Theatre again and of course it was always a packed house of around 3,000 people. I was working hard and doing a lot of different events, but it was always the Theatre that I enjoyed the most.

Many times, some of the punters would be amazed to see me working in so many different venues. I would get comments like "I've just see you in the "pig and whistle half an hour ago, and now here you are in the Blinkin Owl Bar" Or if I had been in the Gaiety Theatre all morning doing the Talent Auditions up until 12noon, after a quick lunch I would be in the Blinkin Owl Bar at 1 pm for the horse racing on Film session. I was in the Theatre five days out of seven. The Sunday Night Variety Show. Monday was the Talent Show in the morning. Tuesday was the Lucky Dip Show", Wednesday the Talent Final, and Friday the Redcoat Show. The Resident Revue Show was only in the Theatre three nights a week, although that was my goal to be in the Resident Revue Show. Other comments I would get at Butlins on a regular basis were "what are you doing working in a place like this," and "your too good for this place, why aren't you on TV?" It was always very nice to hear these comments, but of course the people saying them didn't understand.

It was the Entertainment Manager at Minehead that first asked me to put on an "Old Time Music Hall." He gave me the format then asked me to pick the redcoats that I wanted and produce the show. I would play the chairman myself as I had already played that role when I was in Summer Season at the Coliseum Theatre Rhyl with Roy Rolland. On that occasion it was when we did four changes of programme, and one of the changes had been "Old Time Music Hall." I picked out seven Redcoats, 4 boys and 3 girls. I then chose the skinniest, wimpish looking boy to be the bouncer. The six other cast members would then be sat on chairs on stage and remain on view throughout the show. I would sit at the chairman's table at the side of the stage, and would call out each artiste in turn, who would then come forward and do their thing.

I would open the show on my own with "Lets All Go Down The Strand", and then introduce "at enormous expense, - the Entire Company," who would come on and take their places on the chairs. I would then explain to the audience, that we would like them to join in all of the songs, and if we found anybody that was not singing he or she would be "Thrown Out." This announcement was always greeted with great cheers of approval.

I would then explain that the man to do the throwing out was "our very own bouncer," as he walked on dressed in a loin cloth, this little weedy character was greeted with hails of laughter. As the show got underway, after the second artiste I would pick on a member of the audience to be thrown out. The bouncer would go to him, put him over his shoulder, and with his legs buckling, would run with him, taking the longest route, and out the door.

Halfway through the show, I would pick a second victim who would be thrown out, but this time after a few moments outside the door, they would change positions. He would pick up the bouncer, throw him over his shoulder and run back in with him, right down to the front of the stage, and dump him on the stage at my feet. It would always get an amazing reaction from the audience, and as the commotion died down, I would pull the Bouncer to his feet, glare at the man who had dumped him there, and shouted at him - "and let that be a lesson to 'yer". We would get roars of laughter throughout the show, with some great comic characters in the line up. I would use the Bouncer once more, towards the end, and this time I would pick a girl to be thrown out. As he got to the girl, she would pick him up, run with him and throw him out, and this of course would always bring the house down. When he came back in, I would call him up on stage, give him a Public Rollicking - and then sack him. - It was a very successful show, and great fun to do. I would sometimes be very wicked with the bouncer, and pick on an enormous man for him to throw out, and of course he could never lift him but if I picked on a big woman she would always pick him up like a feather, and that would go even better. The show was staged each week in the Pig and Whistle Bar, and as the weeks went by, it got better and better.

It was at Minehead that Butlins staged their first ever "Late Night Cabarets" in 1971 when I returned for my second season there. I had heard that at the end of the previous season they had done a Pilot Late Night Show to see how they would go, and it had been a big success. It was then decided by the hierarchy to programme this event, starting at Minehead.

It was staged in the Beachcomber Bar, a really wonderful setting with Palm trees, bamboo furniture, a waterfall, with a bridge going over a river, and every hour on the hour there would be a storm, and when the storm finished, a rainbow would appear in this wonderful lighting effect. Tickets were sold in advance for the "Late Night Cabaret" it was a restricted limited number of course, and they sold out very quickly, but it was staged over two nights.

On the nights of the show, the Beachcomber Bar would close at 10.00pm, and as soon as it was empty it would be cleaned, and the tables re-set. The doors would then reopen at 11.00pm. The Redcoats would be dressed in evening wear, and work as hosts and hostess to greet people as they arrived, and show them to their seats. They all looked very glamorous and it all added to the event. If made the guests feel that they were out on a truly special night, as indeed they were. Just before the doors opened a duo was playing, so they came in to the sounds of live music. The room would fill up very quickly, and they were soon being served with drinks and their chicken in the basket. It was always a joy to Compere these late Night Cabarets as it was sheer class, and I felt so at home.

Just before midnight the duo would come off, and we would soon be listening to the big band sounds of the George Birch Orchestra. They looked great, they sounded great, and in that wonderful Beachcomber bar setting it was a fantastic atmosphere.

After about fifteen minutes George Birch would introduce me, and I would come on as these great brass sounds played me on. I would do a few minutes before introducing the four dancers, who were taken from the line up of the Resident Revue Show. After the dancers I would always do a 15 minutes warm-up spot, and finish with the number "Sweet Ginger Bread Man", and with the George Birch orchestra playing for me, I always felt like I was flying. We always had a very strong supporting act before the top of the bill. The very first star to top the bill of a Butlin Late Night Cabaret, was Matt Monro.

I had worked with Matt on a Sunday Concert at the Futurist Theatre, Scarborough a couple of years earlier. He was a real nice man, and down to earth. I remember on that first visit in the dressing room when the duo came off stage they were about to get changed in what looked like a broom cupboard off the main dressing room as they went to walk into it Matt asked "what are you going in there for?" they replied "We've been told its where we have to get changed." - "you cant change in there" said Matt "Come and change in here with me, there's plenty of room." Now that's what I call "Star Quality."

The timing of the LNC was always perfect, with the big band on at midnight for 15 minutes, the dancers 3 minutes, I would do 15, the support act would do 20, with my links and plugs the star would be on by 1.00 am and be off by 2 am and the last word they heard from me was "...Goodnight and sleep warm."

I have done many "Late Night Cabarets" over the years far too many for me to remember. Not only with Butlins, but with Ladbroke Holidays, Haven Holidays, and Haven/Warner. I must say without any doubt whatsoever, Butlins were head and shoulders above the rest, they were simply the best, they were the Premier League, and the other Companies when it came to L.N.C were Division One, in fact some were Conference League.

My first season at Minehead in 1968 was a big success for me, and it finished on the 4th October. I had still been writing dozens of letters, enclosing photos and CV for pantomime, but without much luck, so it was back to the WM Clubs, and it was mostly at weekends. I had applied for a job advertised in the "Stage" for a Host, for a game show sponsored by a Cigarette Company. Ironically it was to do a tour of the Butlin Camps, and I felt that it was just up my street. I had a reply and was asked to attend an interview at Peter Prichards Office in London. A couple of weeks later I was invited to attend an audition in London and I felt really confident that I would get this job, and as my brother would always say "its in the bag." The auditions were held in a tiny arts Theatre in the West End. There were quite a number of people up for the job, but with my experience doing the "Lucky Dip Show" I really believed that the job was mine. It was a strange kind of audition really, as it was more of an interview in front of a panel of four people. The only two people I recognised were Peter Prichard, and Bob Monkhouse. It was a question and answer routine, with Bob asking the questions. It was all very friendly, and Bob put you at ease. It was all over in a few minutes, and then we were asked to wait outside. It was a long wait, but the good thing was we were going to be told who had got the job on the day. There would be no "waiting game" looking out for the Postman on this one.

As we were all waiting for the result, there was quite a jolly atmosphere in the waiting room, with the usual loud mouths and OTT types, cracking on that they couldn't care less if they got the job or not, as they had loads of work, and were in great demand. I thought to myself "yeah, if you've got that much work, what are you doing here."

I sat quiet, and didn't join in, as I didn't have a load of work, and I really wanted this job, in fact I was depending on it. I knew that I would do a great job, and it could probably lead to big and better things. It seemed an age that we were waiting, and even the cocky ones, were becoming less mouthy. Suddenly the door opened and Peter Pritchards P.A. came in holding a clip board. I remembered her very well from my first interview in the office. She thanked us all for coming, and I was absolutely certain that I would get this job, I even started to feel relaxed, as I looked around I could see some tense faces. She then announced the name of the one chosen for the job. - I had never heard that name before, all I knew was that it wasn't mine, - I was gutted.

It was the biggest disappointment I have ever suffered ever, and I have never had such a disappointment since. Of course I did learn from the experience, and that was, "never count your chickens," nothing is set until you sign a contract, and don't put all of your eggs in one basket. Afterwards I thought even the P.A. fancied me for the job, as she gave me a sympathetic look.

Time passed and I knew that I had to pick myself up and get back on track. After a couple of club dates, I had a return booking for the Company Dinner and Dance that I had done at the Abby Hotel, the previous year. On that occasion I had taken my old mate Johnny Garfield, but this time I thought I would take a female singer with me for a change, and I arranged this with a local London agent that I knew. It was once again an excellent night all round. I headed back North to Manchester, and had a wonderful Christmas with my wife and family. Before we knew it, we were bringing in the New Year 1969.

The year started slow for me, and I was now doing more TV Extra work at Granada, and Yorkshire TV Studios than I was club work. By the end of January Butlins offered me a Summer Season at Barry Island for 18 weeks, so at least I knew that I was okay for the Summer. Of course it was a lot easier doing Extra work on T.V. than doing the clubs, and I had a good run of it, in fact it became quite a "Comfort zone." I was doing quite a lot on "Coronation Street," then I had five days on the trot in a gangster series called

"Big Breadwinner Hog." I had various other bits and pieces on different shows before I was cast as a policeman in "Coronation Street." With another Policeman, I had to arrest Ena Sharples, who was involved in a "Sit Down" protest. We both approached her, took an arm each, and lifted her to her feet. The other Police Officer had one line, he said "Come along Mrs Sharples, you can't stay there." The whole scene took two days to film, and the lad who played the other Policeman, became quite a big T.V. Star. - His name was Richard Beckinsale.

On the 17th May I drove through the gates of Butlins Barry Island for the second time to start my Summer Season. I was really looking forward to it, as I had enjoyed it so much the first time. There were quite a few new faces, and they even had a change of Entertainment Manager. After the first two weeks I was really settling in, and had even produced and got the "Redcoat Show" up and running. The audiences were good, and I was even meeting people that remembered me from my last visit there, and telling me how pleased they were to see me again. Things were looking really rosy, when I was summoned to the Entertainment Managers Office, at the beginning of the third week.

As I walked in he was sat behind his desk, and asked me to take a seat. He had a serious look on his face "Dave, I've had Head Office on the phone, and they want you to go to Bognor." "Bognor?" I said "but I'm settled here now, I don't want to go to Bognor." - "1 don't want you to go to Bognor either" "but they are having a few problems down there, and have specifically asked for you." He then assured me that it would be a good move for me, and in my best interests to go. "But what about the job here?" I asked, "don't worry about that" he said they will send me a replacement." The more we talked, the better the proposition sounded, I had got Barry Island up and running, and now. I was off for a new challenge, they wanted me to go and sort it out, it was beginning to sound quite exciting. At the start of my fourth season with Butlins I was now a Trouble -Shooter. - "When do they want me to go?" I asked. He paused for a second, and I did not expect the answer that he gave, but he said it loud and clear - "Today." I went back to my chalet, packed up my gear, loaded up my mini, and I was on the road to Bognor just after lunchtime.

It was quite a long drive, but I arrived late evening. The Entertainment Manager at the Bognor Regis site was a man called Roy Markwell. He was a tall slim man, quietly spoken, and he looked older than the other Managers that I had worked for. He had a gentle approach and would leave all the shouting to his assistant manager.

In those days the position of Entertainments Manager was quite a post to hold. He would have his own Personal Secretary whose office would be adjacent to his. In the next office would be his Deputy Manager, who would share with the Assistant Manager.

It was a real chain of command, and with a staff of 38 Redcoats plus 10 Dancers who did 15 hours a week Redcoat duty for their free accommodation, various bar hosts and musicians in almost every bar, not forgetting the big band who played in the ballroom as well as the Theatre, the resident Revue Company, the actors from the Forbes Russell Theatre Company, and the visiting cabarets, it was quite a lot of people to look after and organise.

Today the job of Entertainment Manager is much less thought of, on many Holiday Centres. Nine times out of ten it would be a young girl who was a "Coat Host" for a couple of seasons, and got promoted. They have no experience whatsoever of the Entertainment business. They are all controlled from Head Office, who pull the strings and are unable to make any decisions of their own, but of course today is a different world. I must say in my early Butlin days it was good to see how different Entertainment Managers had their own ideas, and put their mark on a place, and appeared to be in control. Of course they had their Bosses too, but it did appear that they were allowed to get on with the job. At Bognor, Roy Markwell was like an elder statesman, and I was told as a young man he was a Table Tennis Champion, who played for England. He was not a well man, but he did have his finger on the pulse, and things were ticking over nicely in all areas.

At our first meeting he was telling me that he was not happy with the way the "Redcoat Show" was being produced, among other things like the "Lucky Dip Show" etc etc, and that I had been brought in to improve things. The guy that had been doing it, was not experienced enough, and was not up to the job. Consequently they were getting rid of him and moving him to another site.

I was building a reputation in my three seasons with Butlins and that the Hierarchy were hearing about it. My first task was to work on the Redcoat Show, and what they had was non-existent. That very first night I called a rehearsal after midnight in the Gaiety Theatre, and asked them to show me what they had been working on. It wasn't very much, and soon became clear to me that they were lacking leadership. One or two of the individuals were quite talented, but I knew that I had to start from scratch. I only had four night time rehearsals to get a show into shape, so I worked on the tried and trusted "If I Were Not Upon The Stage" routine that would involve every member of the cast, and I could use as the finale.

I stood on the stage, and did every character in the routine as they watched me. I then cast each one, and got them to do it, they all picked it up very quickly, we had a lot of laughs and they enjoyed themselves. I then went through the gangster sketch and picked out who I thought would be best suited for each character, after seeing them do the "If I Was Not Upon The Stage" routine.

It all went well, and it was a successful first night rehearsal. When I wrapped it up at 2 am, as we all said goodnight, a number of them shook my hand, thanked me, and said how much they had enjoyed it. I was pleased, as that was a good sign, it is always so important to enjoy what you are doing, if you want to make it a success.

After the fourth nights rehearsal, we had some kind of a show, and it was taking shape. It was not as good as I would have liked it to have been, but in the circumstances, and the time we had it was very good. I did about eighteen minutes just before the Finale to fill the time in, and after the first show the audience reaction was excellent, and I was delighted that the show was quite a hit. Of course I knew that we could improve in certain areas, and I needed to change a few things, consequently I kept the late night rehearsals up for another month, a couple of nights a week. I never got total perfection, but in the end I guess it was okay.

I soon settled in at Bognor, and the audiences were fantastic. It was at Bognor that I decided to sing on the "Lucky Dip Show." It was the last item in the show, the "Kiddies Drama." After they had taken their bows, my hostess would quickly take off their costumes. As they were stood in a line, I would thank the five children for all the laughs, and giving us all so much joy, and for making me feel like one of them, - the music would start and I would go into "You Make Me Feel So Young," the hostess would then keep handing me packets of sweets, as I went along the line giving them out to the children, as I loaded up their arms, I would finish by sticking packets of Rollo's in their mouths, got them all to turn left, and walk off stage and down the steps, I always timed it, so that as they had almost got back to their seats the song had finished. They always walked off to thunderous applause.

Many years later a young comic called Bryn Peters who was a redcoat at Bognor during that year, was doing a Cabaret Spot at Caister Holiday Centre where I was Entertainments Manager. Bryn had always been a big fan of mine, and was very open about the fact that he had nicked all my gags" he then told me, how a few years after the Bognor season, he had got a job for Butlins as a Compere, and he use to do the "Lucky Dip Show" and the "Kiddies Drama." I was then amazed when he said to me that he even sang "You Make Me Feel So Young" as he thought that was part of it, and what you had to do. Of course everybody was guilty of stealing the odd gags here and there, but it was always annoying if anybody stole a whole routine. You could always tell if somebody had nicked a routine, as they would never remember it all properly, and they would never perform it as well as the original. Even some comics could not deliver a gag properly that they had stolen. I have often seen a comic do a gag that has died, and the following week another comedian has done the same gag and brought the house down.

When I eventually became an Entertainments Manager, I found it very strange that all the comedians were doing the same gags, all the singers were singing the same songs, all the Magic acts were doing the same tricks, and even the ventriloquists were doing the same routines like blowing up a balloon, putting it in the dummy's mouth, and then the balloon would rise skywards taking the dummy up with it. Is it any surprise that variety died.

As the weeks went by at Bognor Regis, all was going well, I even had the "Old Time Music Hall" show going strong in the Pig and Whistle Bar. I do remember though that the second show we did was a complete disaster, and I really lost my temper with all the cast. I knew that the show was tried and tested, the cast did not have to be great singers, and it was always a sure fire winner.

On this particular night everything went wrong people were missing their cues, forgetting things, even certain props were left in the dressing room, nobody was smiling it was diabolical.

After the show, I called them all into one dressing room, and I guess the air turned blue. I went through every one in turn, nobody was left out. I was so mad, and with me being a part of such a crap show made me even madder. One of the girls burst into tears, "Its no good you crying" I said to her "your performance had the audience in bloody tears." After things settled down, I could tell that they all agreed with me, and that they had let themselves down.

The following week they pulled out all the stops, and the show went down fantastic. I guess my little pep talk did the trick. I was proud of all of 'em.

It was at Bognor Regis that I was asked to Compere the grand finals of the "Holiday Princess Competition." It was a swell affair, with a distinguished panel of Judges, including the popular DJ Diddy David Hamilton, and a page three girl, I can't remember her name, but I remember that she stood out on the panel. There were some big cash prizes at stake, with the winner getting a £1,000 and a brand new car. At the end of the event, the winning girl was presented with the cheque plus a set of car keys, for the car that was waiting outside for her parked on the green. You can imagine she was very excited.

The whole event went very well, and it was staged in the Ballroom, but having said that I did feel that there was something lacking, in the presentation of the whole affair. I felt that the stage setting could have been much better, and for a Butlin presentation I was disappointed.

It was ten years later that I realized what was missing when I joined Ladbroke Holidays. Now they really knew how to stage a finals for a beauty competition. It was all down to a top man they had, called John Glass. He was Mr "Razzle Dazzle" and there was no expense spared. I saw him give a presentation once at an Entertainment Manager's Seminar, and just at the right moment in what he was saying, put his hand in his jacket pocket took out a handful of sparkling confetti, and threw it in the air, it was pure showbiz. But more of that later, as we get back to 1969.

Just before the season at Bognor ended I signed up with Butlins to appear in their Winter Club Tour. It was a self contained show with six acts two dancing girls and an organist. The organist on his Hammond was one of the best keyboard players I have every worked with. I had worked with him at Minehead where he had a duo. His name was Rob Charles who now has the Rob Charles Orchestra and works for Cunard cruises.

In the press release it read:- "The production has nine artistes who are the cream of the three hundred Redcoat Entertainers and Comperes resident at Butlins Camps and Hotels throughout the Summer Season, and the show represents the finest entertainment this "Nursery of The Stars " has offered for several years. "

The show was called "Here Come The Redcoats" but out of the nine artistes only two of them were actually Redcoats. The other seven were all pros like myself. Two of them being comedians working as comperes on other camps. One was a zany comic Mike Onions, and the other a Scotsman who worked in a kilt called Justin Gregor. All three of us had very different styles, and there was no clash. Also on the show was an excellent guitarist, he was an Aussie from Adelaide, his name was Ken Taylor.

The Summer Season finished, and after a short break, we had to report at the Butlin Ocean Hotel at Brighton on the 19th October for one week's rehearsal.

The rehearsals went well, and we all got on well with each other. At the end of the week we did the show for the guests at the

Ocean Hotel, and it was very well received. For the Finale we did the "If I Was Not Upon The Stage" routine, and I must say with the line up we had it was the best that I had ever seen it done.

On the Saturday morning, we packed up the mini bus and set off North for our first date, at the Harriscott Club, Rosedale, Shrewsbury. The whole tour was booked by the Sheffield agent Len Norton. He was a great character and a performer in his own right. He was a character comedian, that did his act dressed as a vicar, in robes complete with priests Biretta, a little three cornered hat. He was also a wonderful audience, as he would often come to see the show, and laugh his head off every time.

He also had a wicked sense of humour. I remember one time a couple of us went to see him at a club on our night off. He would change into his vicars robes, and before he was due to go on, he wandered into the pool room. He stood watching for a few moments as a few guys were playing, suddenly this guy hit the queue ball, and missed his shot completely - Len in his best vicars voice, and standing proud in his regalia blurted out "You've made a right fuck up of that shot I see," the expression on the guys faces was priceless.

Our opening night at Shrewsbury was a big success, and we all felt confident that it would be a good run. We worked six nights a week, with one night off. We would stay in digs for a week or two and work from the digs as a base, before going on to the next area.

We soon had the first two weeks under our belts with dates at Liverpool, Runcorn, Oswestry, Shrewsbury, Rotherham, Leeds, and Heswall, to name a few. The show was getting a wonderful reaction at every venue, and I was amazed how well the Finale "If I were not upon the stage" routine would go, each night it brought the house down. I used to wonder how come these people have never seen this routine, as it is so old, but like I have often said, its not how old a routine is, it's the way its done, and I must say we all put a lot of energy into it.

We were well into the second week, and after each show there would be screams and shouts for more, and it began to look like we were indestructible. I remember talking to Rob Charles one night back at our digs, and I said to him "The show is going so well, it looks like we just can't die." I think that we all began to believe that. Well we did, until the night we turned up at the Walkley W.M.Club, Sheffield. I had spoken too soon, it was a Lousy night the whole show struggled and it died the death. I thought it would never happen, but it did, but as they say "That's Showbiz."

We were soon back up again, as the very next night was a real knockout at the C and C Social Club, Ashborne in Derbyshire. We then had a great run of knockout nights including three R.A.F. camps that were always excellent. The Nottingham clubs that we played were also very good, with the Gedley Miners Club at Marperley, and the Miners Welfare Club at Calverton, both having very good facilities. It was at Nottingham that we stayed in two separate digs. I was with Mike and Ken, and the others were in a house, down the road from us. It was absolutely freezing with snow on the ground, and the bedroom that we all shared had no heating at all, but it did have an open fire.

A couple of weeks before we got to Nottingham one of the girl singers had broken my Charlie Chaplin Stick and snapped it in half, I don't know how she managed it, but of course it was an accident. She was full of apologies and the very next day went out and bought me a walking stick. I accepted it gracefully, but of course it was no good to me, I couldn't use it, as it was a thick walking stick, and it wouldn't bend. Anyway I put it in the boot of my car, and that is where it stayed.

On the third night in Nottingham we came back from the club, and pulled up outside our digs, not looking forward to going into that very cold bedroom. As I got out of the Mini bus, I noticed some lumps of coal that were in the road. As I looked along the road further I could see more. It would appear that the coalman had been delivering and spilled a few lumps here and there. We then began the three of us picking up lumps of coal to take up to the bedroom and light a fire. We did find quite a few lumps even getting some from under parked cars, and we soon had enough for a fire.

We had no wood, so we got newspaper and rolled it up hard to serve as wood, but after a few tries it became evident that it was not going to work. It was then that one of the boys said "1 know, - what about your walking stick?" I said "I can't do that, it was a gift" "but you don't use it" came back the reply "you could make good use of it now." I thought for a moment, then said "what the hell - I'll go and get it." I got the walking stick, broke it into five pieces, and before we knew it we had a roaring coal fire going, it was the first time we had been warm since we had arrived in Nottingham. It was nice of the girl to buy me the stick that I couldn't use, but at least we made good use of it on that night.

We left Nottingham, and our next port of call was Cumberland, followed by four nights at the R.A.O.B. Club Whitehaven. The first night was a very small audience, the second night was Lousy, the third night was also lousy and very noisy, and our final night on the Sunday I would describe as fair. We then had two knockout nights at Newcastle and Consett Co Durham.

Our next performance was a night and an experience that I will never forget. We were at the Jubilee Club, in Newcastle. Before we arrived we had heard that it was a hard Miners Club, and it did have a reputation. I remember when we went in to unload the gear and set up, that it was a fair size club and it had a balcony. When the time came to start the show the place was absolutely packed to the rafters. As we were doing the opening number I noticed that the audience were full of black faces. As I took a closer look, they were not black people, they were miners in their working gear, and their faces were covered in coal dust. It was like we were entertaining the cast of the Black and White Minstrel Show. Apparently they had just come off the late shift, and some were ready to go on the night shift. They were sat drinking their pints of Newcastle Brown ale, and chatting and did not seem to be interested in what was going on up on the stage. Every performer, and every item was dying slowly. The show was going down hill, and it was getting worse by the minute. At the interval we were all able to have a bit of a laugh over the situation, and could see the funny side. That of course was always an advantage being part of a show, and having other performers with you. But when you were on your own in a club, and things do not go well for you, its hard to see the funny side, nobody talks to you and you really do feel alone. We started the second half, and I always followed the Australian Guitarist Ken Taylor, just before the Finale "If I were not upon the stage."

Ken came off to hardly any applause at all, and when I went on I was shocked to see that the club was almost empty. There were about 20 people left in a room that at the beginning of the show had been packed to the rafters. We were told at the end, that the place had emptied, not because they didn't like the show, but because they had to get back to work, on the night shift. Personally I felt it was a bit of both.

The first half of the tour finished on the 19th December, and after a few days break we all went on to various Butlin Camps and hotels to work over the Christmas Holiday. I was sent to Bognor, it was the first time that I had worked for Butlins at Christmas, and I must say what a fantastic time it was, and the atmosphere was terrific.

The "Touring Show" was due to start up again on the 5th January 1970, but before I linked up with the rest of the Team, I had one club date of my own, at the Churwell W.M. Club Morley Near Leeds, it was not a good night and I did not enjoy it at all.

The Tour started up again in Leicester where we were based for the next two weeks. The Leicester clubs were very good, and we had some great audiences. Of course we came across the odd venue that wasn't very good, like the Manchester W.M. Club in Leicester. It was not very well attended, with only a small audience. At half time they played bingo, and after the Bingo it was a Mass exodus, as almost everybody left the club. We did the second half to about a dozen people.

After a few dates in Staffordshire, we had an odd date at the South End Social Club, Bedford, before heading back up the M6 for a date at The Roman Bar, Trentham, Stoke-on-Trent, where we had a fantastic night. The very next night we were at the Elite Cinema, Uttoxeter. It looked like a third rate Cinema that you would expect would be owned by a family. It had no dressing rooms, so we changed at the back of the stage up against the brick wall behind the actual screen.

When the show started, it was fantastic. The audience was only half full, but they were great to work to, it may have looked a bit of a dump, but I would have swapped it for any club. It was a theatre, and I was in my element.

After a week in the Stoke-on-Trent area we moved to Warrington. After a few days Rob Charles who was also the Tour Manager said to me "In a couple of days we are in for a tough one" - "How can you be so sure?" I said. "It's in Liverpool, and its called Our Lady of Sorrows Club." As it turned out it wasn't all that bad, I would describe it as a "fair night." It was not so fair, however on our next date in Liverpool, it was St Mary's Catholic Club, and you could not hear yourself speak above the noise, we had no chance, and were all very glad to get out of the place.

The Tour continued with one night stands at dates in Leeds, Sheffield, Doncaster, Batley, Atherton Holmfirth, and many more all over Yorkshire, and we finished with one of the greatest nights we ever had at the "Blue Club" Gainsborough, before moving on to Birmingham. In Birmingham we had some excellent digs in Handsworth with a very nice landlady called Mrs Barnes, who looked after us all very well, and even did our laundry.

All went very well in the Birmingham area, but we did have one mishap at the Wednesfield Tubes Social Club. It was a very good venue, with a fair size stage with front of house curtains. The show had gone very well, and we were all on doing the Finale "If I was not upon the stage." As I have already mentioned, in this routine everybody plays a different character. I was playing the golfer. The girl next to me, a singer called Cilia Small was playing a pilot, dressed in a white boiler suit and a red crash helmet. She would sing her line, then bend forward as if touching her toes going "into a dive." I would swing my golf club over her head narrowly missing her as she went down. We were on the last chorus as I swung my club, but on this occasion she did not dive quickly enough and I caught her a terrific crack at the back of the head, just as we finished the song. She went down in a heap, and the curtain closed. As the curtains opened again for our call, the audience were going wild with applause and screams and shouts for more. I dragged

Cilia up to her feet, and held her up as we took our final curtain call. When the curtains closed again, her knees buckled her eyes rolled back into her head, and she collapsed in a heap. I was able to support her as she fell so she did not damage herself in the fall. She soon came round again and said that she was alright. Cilia was a great cockney character, and it wasn't long before she was laughing her head off. But I can tell you that after that I was much more careful with any golf club.

After a great time in Birmingham, we moved back to the Stoke-On-Trent area, and even had a return date at the Elite Cinema, Uttoxeter, and this was soon followed by three nights at the Queens Theatre, Burslem, and each night was fantastic especially for me as I was where I was born to be. - In a Theatre.

We were now approaching the end of April and we moved on to Bristol for the final week of the Tour. Once again the show received a knockout reaction, and we played four nights at the Yate Entertainment Centre in Bristol, followed by the Bristol Rovers True Blue Club. The final night of the Tour was on Sunday 3rd May 1970 at the Ringlands Club at Newport. We finished on a high, and it was a truly great night. It had been a fantastically successful tour, that had started in October of the previous year. Of course by the end we were all pleased, as it had been such a long tour, and we were tired, and looking forward to a rest before the summer season started. I had signed to go to Butlins Clacton Camp commencing 15th May for 18 weeks. This was to be my fifth season with Butlins, they had eight camps in all, so I guess I only needed to do three more, and I had done the lot.

Of course it was never my intention to be with Butlins for so long, but I was in a situation now where A: it was very rewarding, B: I was working in a Theatre, and C: it was quite a long season in comparison to the Seaside Summer Shows, and on top of all that Livvy was with me, and working as an announcer in Radio Butlin. My oldest step daughter Sonia was a dancer in the Resident Revue Show after doing a couple of seasons as Redcoat, and last year at Bognor our youngest, Bernadette worked as a Nursery Nurse, so it was quite a family affair.

I enjoyed it very much at Clacton, and the audiences were great to work for. Having just finished a long club tour, and been performing six nights a week, I felt I was really at my peak. The more you perform, the better you get, especially for a Comedian, as it can sometimes take years to get your timing to perfection. I felt really on form, and at the top of my game. Clacton was also a great season for parties, in fact once the season had got well underway, it became one round of parties, in fact I have never been to so many parties in all my life.

There were a lot of Fancy dress, and theme parties like "When The Ship Went Down." A lot of these Dos would be held in a house off the camp, and would sometimes go on until dawn the next morning. They would be organised by various members of the Entertainment Department, like one of the Musicians a member of the Revue Company or one of the Redcoats.

One of these all night affairs I remember one of the Redcoat girls from Radio Butlin, had been having a great time, and kept telling everyone that she was on early morning call the next day. She left the party about 5am and needless to say when she arrived for duty in Radio Butlin was not in the best of condition. To make her first breakfast announcement, she picked up the wrong card, as it was for second sitting. The message would read:

GOOD MORNING EVERYONE, THE TIME IS NOW 9 O'CLOCK AND ALL SECOND SITTING GUESTS YOUR BREAKFAST IS NOW AVAILABLE.

It did not come out quite like that, as the time was indeed 7.30am, and in a slurred voice she read after hitting the DING DONGS in the wrong place.

"GOOD MORNING EVERYBODY, the time is 9 o'clock and ALL SHECOND SHITTING GUESTS YOUR BREAKFASTS READY."

It did put a few smiles on peoples faces, and as far as I know there were no complaints and the girl was still there at the end of the season.

It was at Clacton that Butlins first introduced the "Donkey Derby" into their programme, and I was the very first ever commentator on this event. It was the idea of Butlins Chief Operations man Ron Hayter, who had a reputation as being the "Axe Man."

He had quite a bit of power in the organisation, and every time he would visit a site, the Entertainment Managers would be more than a little bit nervous, and very relieved when he had gone.

I got on very well with him, and I could tell that he liked me. I guess he was the right man to organise a Donkey Derby, as he was responsible for the annual "Butlin Horse of the Year Show" at Olympia. The day of the launch of the Donkey Derby came, and all the Entertainment Managers from the other seven sites came down to Clacton to watch it.

The Commentator's box was erected with scaffolding. The tote sellers boxes were set up to one side numbered 1 - 8, the track was all tapped off, an army of cashiers with cash boxes and tote tickets were in place, the crowd was gathering, and it began to look like a day at the Races. Ron Hayter sat next to me up on the Commentator's stand, and was talking me through the proceedings. The kiddie jockeys were all dressed in colours and hard hats, they were mounted on their Donkeys, and were being led out of the paddocks by their various owners.

The tote was open I was giving the run down on the owners, runners and riders as they made their way to the start. I remember looking down and seeing my Entertainment Manager, who looked on edge and was running around a lot. I was then surprised when Ron Hayter turned to me and said "Look at him, he's running about like a blue arse Fly, he hasn't got a clue, what he's doing." I didn't answer him, but then he said "as long as we know what we're doing, well be ok."

I soon got into this commentary lark, the event was a great success, and I had another string to my bow. From then on the Donkey Derby was staged right across the board on every Butlin Site. Once again the presentation was very good, and money had been spent on the sets to make it all look professional. The weeks flew by, as they did every season, there was never a dull moment, and before we knew it, the 18th September was with us and the season was over, but not before of course the traditional Entertainment Department end of season party.

Even though I always enjoyed my Summer Seasons over the years, I was always glad to get home at the end of them. I have always been a home loving man, and as the saying goes, - there is no place like home. We didn't even feel like going away on holiday, it was like we had been away on holiday all summer, and it was now just nice to relax in your own home. I was not looking forward to going back in the clubs, so for a few weeks I was quite happy to be doing extra work on T.V. At that time Granada had a lot of work on a new series called "Family at War," and I worked on that for quite a few weeks as a soldier.

I remember one day we were shooting a scene, in an old 1940s railway carriage. I was stood up with a group of other soldiers, and from the waist down we would not be in shot. A girl from the wardrobe department came up to me and started arranging the bottoms of my trousers over the web gatters. They were perfectly okay, and she had no idea what she was doing, and as I have just said, they were not even in shot.

On all TV shows the make-up and wardrobe people are constantly, running around with their little plastic boxes, touching up your make-up, combing your hair, or messing with your costume, I'm sure that they are bored out of their brains, and trying to justify their jobs. I was also doing quite a bit of work at Yorkshire T.V. on a series called "Grady," and between the two studios I wasn't doing too bad for work.

My next club date, was a Cricket Club Private Dinner, at the Wheatsheaf Hotel, Bakewell in Derbyshire. The following weekend I had a double on the Friday. It was a lunchtime show at Firth Browns Canteen in Sheffield, and I can tell you I've had better jobs. In the evening I was at the Estrilata Club, at Peterborough, and that was worth the journey as I had a really knockout night. The following night on the Saturday true to form at the United Services Club, Hadley, I died on my arse.

I was still writing bundles of letters for a Pantomime but without success. Christmas came, and went, and we were soon entering the New Year 1971. Overall I had quite a good year, and had been kept busy, but you never know what a New Year holds. My first date in January was at the Salter Gate Social Club, Chesterfield, and I had a knockout night. That was followed by another big success for me at the Friary Hotel, Friarsgate, Derby, on the Saturday night. Sunday I played the Kersley Colliery Club, Coventry, where I had a lousy night. I guess the thing about working the clubs, you could never tell what it would be like. On a great night, when the audience would be cheering, and screaming for more, you would come away feeling like a Super Star. But the next night, the audience could hate you, and you come off to the sound of your own feet, and you sometimes begin to doubt yourself. "Am I as good as I think I am?" You ask yourself. Then the next performance you tear the place apart, and as you can still hear the applause as you are in the dressing room you say "Yes I am."

I was still doing a lot of T.V. work, and I was pleased that the war was lasting so long at Granada on "Family At War." My club dates were mostly at weekends and I was doing quite a bit of travelling, to places like Nottingham, Coventry, Whitehaven, Cleatormore, (no, I'd never heard of that place until I got there). It was the Cleatormore W.M.Club, I did two spots. The first one went really well, but the second spot the audience were all pissed, and didn't even know that I was there.

It was 1971 that we had a wedding in the family at the end of February. My youngest step daughter Bernadette was getting married. She was only eighteen, and I thought she was too young, but I was only 32 myself, and here I was giving a bride away. She looked beautiful, and it was an honour to walk her down the aisle.

The very next night I was at the 28th Gunners Club, Workington, up in Cumberland, and it was a knockout night. We were into the second week in March, when I got a phone call from Butlins, and they informed me that the comic on the Touring Show, had taken ill, and would not be coming back, and could I take over for the last five weeks of the Tour. Of course I was delighted and jumped at the chance. It was so much better working the clubs as part of a show than on your own.

I joined up with the Butlin Touring Show in Birmingham. It was the 18th March and my first show with them was at the Charlemont Bowling Club, Stonecross. I had met a couple of the cast before, it was a very good show, and I soon got into it. We had a fantastic run and in the five weeks, we only had two lousy nights.

The Tour finished on 12th April at the Derbyshire Yeoman in Derby. I often wondered why I would do so well in a show, and when I would do the clubs on my own I really had to work hard. I came to the conclusion that a club audience that would go to see a Touring show, for them it was a special occasion, and they would watch and listen, a captive audience almost like a Theatre. But a normal night "When The Turn Comes On" would be taken for granted, and you would have to win their attention. My next three dates after the Tour, were at the Bass Worthington Club, Burton-On-Trent, the British Legion Club, Middlewich, and the Burma Oil Social Club, Ellesmere Port. I scored one knockout, one good, and one death, well I guess two out of three 'aint bad.

On the 21st May 1971 I commenced my Summer Season at Butlins Minehead for 19 weeks. It would be my second season there, and I was happy to return, as I had such a great time in 1968. It was at the start of this season that I was approached by the Manager of the betting shop. He was sat on the panel of judges for the fashion competition "Miss She." He asked me if I would plug his betting shop each week, and in return he would pay me a few quid. He was quite generous, and it was an offer I could not refuse. It reminded me of the time at Barry Island, when I was plugging the florescent bags. I would always start the week on the "Sunday Night Variety Show" in the Gaiety Theatre, and at the top of the show I would mention the betting shop, and its location. A few weeks into the season I was on, and for some reason it slipped my mind. I was just about to introduce the first act when the M.D. George Birch from the orchestra pit shouted up at me - "Don't Forget The Betting Shop!" I think he found it all quite amusing. About Mid-summer a fire broke out on the camp, it was a big one, and did a lot of damage, but it was not the biggest fire I ever saw at Butlins, that was to come later at Pwllheli.

I was still doing my two hour stints on the mornings of Monday and Tuesday with the auditions for the "People Talent Competition" and over the years we had some great acts. I will mention a few that you would know. At Clacton the pianist Bobby Crush who was a young lad at the time would enter every year. Stan Boardman at Pwllheli was allotted 5 minutes in the show, and he did twenty. Tommy and Bobby (who became Cannon & Ball) won a heat but said to me they were not sure if they could get back for the finals, as they may not get the time off work. The week that they were there, Hughie Green was doing the Late Night Cabaret. I remember my Entertainment Manager telling him about Tommy and Bobby, but he wasn't interested. I tried to remind Hughie Green of the time I was on "Opportunity Knocks" on Radio Luxemburg all those years earlier, and the banter that we had, but he wasn't interested in that either. In fact the man was only interested in himself, and had the cheek to do the pantomime Sticks Gag in an adult Late Night Cabaret.

Comedian Mike Reid went all the way, and won a place in the London Palladium Finals. He didn't win the Final, but of course he went on to become a household name as Frank Butcher in East Enders, and became the most successful of them all.

The season finished on the 2nd Oct, and once again I had failed in my bid to fix a Pantomime, so it was back to the clubs. My first date was a week later where they wanted me to do just one spot at the Trent Bridge Hotel, Nottingham. I did 45 minutes so I guess it was okay.

After another club date in Derby, I drove up to Scotland for a noon and night engagement. The Noon show was at the Killmarnoch Supporters Club, and I had a lousy time, but the money was good. On the night time I had a great night at the Craigs Hill Social Club at Livingston, so it was quite a pleasant journey back home to Heywood as I drove towards Manchester.

We were soon into November, and I was kept reasonably busy with club dates at weekends and T.V. Extra work. Then December came and I was offered a Saturday night at the Blue and Gold Club, Kings Lynn at a fee of £25. It was quite a drive down to Kings Lynn, and when I got there I had a bit of trouble finding the place. When I eventually did and drove onto the car park, I was absolutely Gob-Smacked to find that it was closed down, and had been boarded up. I was not a happy man, going all that way to find that it was closed. The agent that gave me the job apologised, said he had no idea, and said he would fix me another date. It was a bad situation, but I couldn't do anything about, so I just put it down to experience.

He did however give me another date on New Years Eve, at the Kingston United W.M.Club, Barnsley. Have you ever heard of a club audience sober on New Years Eve. If I hadn't been driving I would have joined them, even the Concert Secretary with his badge in his lapel was pissed, the only good thing about it was they were all too pissed to pay me off. I did two spots, and nobody noticed, the organist was pissed, the drummer was pissed, and I was sober, and pissed off. - Happy New Year. 1971 wasn't all bad though, the year ended in one, and Spurs won the Football League Cup.

1972 started for me at the Crosland Moore W.M.Club Huddersfield, on New Years day. For the next few weeks I was doing much of the same, then at the end of February I was offered three nights together in Cornwall, at the Apollo Club Perranporth for the agents Billie and Trevor George. When I got there I found that it was a small Caravan Holiday Park. It was quite a nice club and I had three great nights. It was a Friday, Saturday, and Sunday, and it was quite amazing, that the next weekend I played three different clubs at Walsall, Burton-On-Trent, and a Labour Club in Birmingham, and every one of 'em was tough.

By the middle of March after a date in Folkstone I had three nights at the New Forest Hotel, Ashurst, Near Southampton, where they also gave me accommodation. It was only a small room, but quite adequate. The opening night was quite good, and the second night was excellent. On the Saturday night it was quite difficult, as most of the audience were dining, and in the middle of their meal, I guess you cannot expect an audience to laugh too much if they have a mouth full of food.

After the performance the owner came up to me and said "Oh by the way Dave, you know that you have a show in the morning?" I said "what do you mean, a show in the morning" - "It's a Stag Show" he said "in the other bar, - we have it every Sunday with a couple of Go Go Dancers, and a Stripper." - "a stag show?" I said "the agent didn't mention to me anything about a Sunday Lunch Stag Show." I didn't get a chance to say anymore, as he came in quickly. "They all do it" he said "you've been great, - you don't have to do anything different, just do your normal act and throw in a few fucks here and there."

He then told me that the show would start about twelve noon. Sunday morning I got myself ready in my room, I was suited and booted, I checked the mirror, I looked the business, and I was ready to go to work. It was now 11.30am and I made my way down the stairs, as I got to the bottom the owner was waiting. "you didn't have to dress up," he said "they don't normally bother, most of 'em just wear jeans or something." - "That's not me" I said "I always dress for a performance, by the way, where's the stage?" He gave me a strange smile, "There's no stage" he said, "you have to work on a Table." - "Your Joking" I said "a table?" He laughed and said "Don't worry, it's a sturdy one." I could see by this time that he wasn't joking and was wondering where the door was that led into the other bar. "How do I get through to the other bar?" I asked "we haven't got a door through to it, you have to go outside, and walk round the front" he said. I then started to think about entrances "how do the girls get on to the table?" Was my next question. "They climb over the bar" - I thought great, - this is going to turn out to be some fiasco.

I went outside, and lucky for me it was not raining. There were quite a few cars parked in the car park. As I walked around the car park, I then came to a front bar entrance. As I opened the door, it was absolutely jam packed, and of course it was men only. I had to say the words "Excuse me" about ten times, as I forced my way through the crowd along the room to the top of the bar. It was an oblong room, with the bar running along the length of it on the right hand side as you walked in. At the top of the bar, it just turned about four feet on the right into a corner. Set up in the corner was a DJ with his equipment, and he was playing some music. It was the DJ that pointed out the stage to me, and it was indeed one of the bar tables, it was about a three foot square top.

It was almost 12 noon, I had been given the names of the Go Go Dancer, there was only one, and the stripper. I asked the DJ if he had some lively attention seeking music that he could put on as I went on. He said he did, and put a record on one of the turntables. I then asked him to fade out the music that was already on, give it a couple of minutes without any music, then put the music on for me to make an entrance. He did just that, and I jumped up on the Table, and was welcomed with a tremendous big cheer. The guys in the audience seemed friendly, and I hit them with a couple of quick gags and it was going very well. I then remembered what the owner had said to me about the language, and stuck in the F word at an appropriate time on the next gag. The roar of laughter that followed was out of this world, I did another, and got the same reaction. I thought this is too easy. I did about six minutes, then introduced the Go Go Dancer. She jumped up from behind the bar and stood on top of it for a few seconds, I jumped down off the table, and she then jumped across from the bar to the table. I couldn't go anywhere, so I was stuck between the DJs decks, and the table with about 12 inches each side of me. The dancer in a skimpy outfit was doing her routine, and all the lads in the audience seemed to be enjoying it. At the end of her routine in her bare feet, she just jumped back onto the bar, took a bow, and disappeared. I'm back up on the table again, and the audience are still in a good mood. I give them a couple of quick gags, and then introduce to them what they have all come to see, - the stripper. -

I jump down from the table, as she climbs up onto the bar top. She is wearing a sexy costume, and high heels, with a red Feather BOA draped around her shoulders. With her high heeled shoes, she is unable to make the step across from bar, to table, and after a few seconds she then asked me to give her a lift. Without moving very far, I put my two arms around the middle of her legs, lifted her off the bar, turned around in my own space, and put her down on the table, in one sweeping movement.

Her music was playing as she slowly began to tease her audience removing her items of clothes very slowly, and throwing them down to me, and in turn I was passing them back over the bar. She then whipped off her bra, and was wearing nothing but a tiny G-string, and the red boa around her shoulders.

The audience started to go wild, as the G-string began its slow journey towards her ankles. Before I knew it, the tiny garment was off, and heading towards me at some speed. It hit me in the chest, and I put my hand up quickly to catch it from falling to the ground. As I passed the G-string over the bar, she was now dancing with the red boa, sliding it over her body, even the feathers were standing up. The music finished, as she ended her routine by throwing the feather boa to me, and stood in a pose for a few seconds with her arms in the air Starkers.

Suddenly, the DJ put her music back on, and she had nowhere to go, I thought "how does she get off?" It didn't seem right for me to pick up a naked woman and put her over the bar. She then asked me to quickly pass her the feather boa again. She again draped it around herself and continued to do a repeat of what she had already done. Of course the audience were well pleased, if it had been today it would have been the equivalent to "Buy One, Get One Free."

When the music came to a finish, and she struck up her pose, I thought, "that's it, there's only one thing for it, she's absolutely starkers, but I've got to get her off." With that, I put my arms round the middle of her legs again, span round quickly, and put her down on the bar it got a great round of applause, and the girl looked relieved that she didn't have to do another repeat.

I was now back on to do my act and finish the show. I remembered a couple of gags that my old mate Roger would tell the lads up the Columbia Paper Works years before, they were gags that I would never dream of using in front of an audience, as they were real Barrack Room Gags. They were funny, but filthy. I could never even write them down in this book, but the tag line of one was:- .... "too late Judge, - Mind Your Eyes." After I did the gag it got one of the biggest laughs that I have ever had. I also did what the owner had said, my normal act with the odd swear word in between.

I tore the roof off, and it was a great time for me, but I had gone against all I had wanted to do. I could see how so many club comics did Stag Shows, it was so easy. But as far as I was concerned it did not require talent. Anybody can get up and 'eff and blind, it took real talent to make an audience laugh with clean material, and you could never work in a Theatre doing stuff like that. I vowed that I would never do it again, as I knew that it would be so easy to get caught up in. Lets face it, why do a clean act and die on your arse, when you could do a load of filth and tear the roof off. Anyway I stuck by my principal, and never did an act like that again.

I had done a couple of Stag Shows before this, and I knew about them in advance, I recall the first one was with two strippers and one other comic. I did my usual act, and went down very well and enjoyed it. What made it more enjoyable, was afterwards the compere said to me "you are the only clean comic that I have ever seen on a Stag Show, and you've gone down great." I thought that was a nice compliment, and I have always remembered it.

Two days after my stint at the New Forest Hotel I was booked four days, Wednesday till Saturday at the Cabaret Club, March, in Cambridgeshire. It was a nice size club, but the first night the place was empty except for a group of four people at a table near the front. There was a four piece band, so on this occasion the performers out numbered the audience.

I went on and opened up with a song, and the four people in the audience appeared very friendly. I then went into my routine, but decided to go and sit with them at their table. It worked out quite well, it was like sitting in a pub, with a few mates telling them jokes. Then I thought it would be a good idea to bring them in, and asked if they would like to tell me a joke.

One of the blokes then said " have you heard this one?" - he told me a gag that I had heard, but I didn't say so, and when he got to the tag line, I fell about laughing, along with the rest of the table.

After about fifteen minutes, I got up, walked back to the band and finished on a song, it was only a short spot, but at least I had entertained them, and I was sure that they had enjoyed it.

The Thursday and Friday were small audiences but friendly, and on the Saturday was a full house, and I finished on a great night. The following weekend was Easter, and I was booked for the five days holiday period at Butlins Bognor Regis. It was a place where I always did well and I had a fantastic five days.

When Easter was over, my first date was at the Rastrick Bowling Club, Brighouse, and it was one of the worst nights I've ever had, the audience hated me, and I wasn't too fond of them.

After a few more club dates I did an audition at Granada Studios for their T.V. Show "The Comedians." It was in front of a studio audience, and I was on with ten other comics, of which about half of them were regular faces on the show. We would all go on in turn, and do about 10 minutes each, but at the beginning we would all line up, and go on and do one quick gag, as an introduction. I was stood behind Jimmy Marshall who was one of the regulars, and he started to explain to me what was going on "We all go on and do a quick gag each" he said "have you got a quick gag ready? - if you haven't, I'll let you have one." I have always remembered that, and I thought it was real nice of him, but needless to say, I thanked him, but said I was okay, and had a quick gag ready.

The "Comedians" was a show for Club Comics, and I guess even though I worked in them I was never a club comic. I always considered myself as a Theatre Man. - I never heard anymore from the comedians.

Chapter Nine

Pantomime at Last. Tears for My Friend Johnny, and Laughter in Court, The Great Fire, and a Duck That Can't Swim

By mid May I was on my way once again to start a 19 weeks summer season at Butlins Bognor Regis for my second season there. All in all it would now be my seventh season for them. It was not what I really wanted, but they paid me, and treated me well. As a compere I was doing lots of different things, but I felt it would be better for my career if I was in Butlins Resident Revenue Company as the Principal Comic. On a number of occasions I spoke to the Director Of Entertainments Frank Mansell about it. I recall I was sat in his office one day and he said to me "What do you want to be in the revue Show for? - They only do two shows a week, and a show in the bar. - Surely you wouldn't want that, you are much better off doing what you are doing. Five days a week in the Theatre, the Late Night Cabaret two nights a week." And so he went on. I liked Frank Mansell, and after a long chat he convinced me that I was doing the right job.

On another time I was speaking to the vent act Mike Dennis who was in the revue show, and he said to me "they will never put you in the revue show, because you are too good at what you do." However I did get a taste of it, on the night before the season opened at Bognor 72.

The Revue Show would always do a dress rehearsal in front of the staff, and there were always around 1500 - 2000 of them. The principal comic could not make the dress rehearsal, so I was asked to do it. Of course I could not do the production numbers, as I had not rehearsed it, but I was able to do the warm-up at the beginning, take part in a sketch that I knew, in the middle of the show hold the front cloth, while they did a change of scenery, and do my spot at the end. All in all it was a very enjoyable experience, but it was the one and only time I ever did it.

The audiences at Butlins were out of this world, and as the week went on, and the more they got to know you, they were even better. As you walked on by the end of the week, you could feel the warmth, and knew that they were pleased to see you. I guess in a way, it was like being a star in a small town, and on sites like Minehead, Filey and Pwllheli they had 12,000 people.

The Entertainment Managers would be moved on to another site every two or three years, and I recall at the end of one season, one such Manager was moving, and he wanted me to go with him. I got on well with him but unfortunately I had to turn him down, as he was going to the site that I was at the previous year, and I wanted to go somewhere different. We were stood at the bar having a drink together, and he was thanking me for the "good work" that I had done over the season. He then said to me "you see, what puts you apart from all the other comperes at Butlins are many things. But just take the Sunday Night Variety Show. When other comperes do it, that's what it is. But when you do it - its Sunday Night at the London Palladium. I knew what he meant, as that was where I wanted to be, and when I was doing it, that's exactly where I felt I was. I was in a big packed theatre, with a pit orchestra, ten dancing girls, and Star name top of the bills, and they all treated me with a lot of respect, as I did them.

I guess with all that, every time they asked me to go back it was hard to say no, and all in all I did thirteen seasons for them, playing on every camp except Mosney in Ireland.

It is always a joy to be in a position to raise money for charity, and it was during that season at Bognor that I organised a boat race. We had a large boating lake on the camp, and I asked the Entertainers and musicians on the site if they would take part. We were all paired in crews of two in each boat. It was a knockout event, with a Final at the end. Unofficially one of the Redcoats was running a book, and a lot of bets were taken. I was amazed at the crowd that turned out to watch and all sides of the lake were packed with spectators.

I had previously told all the people that were taking part in the race, to dress up in fancy dress, but nothing good, as they may get wet. As I was stood at the edge of the Lake at the start, Mike Dennis from the Revue Show arrives wearing a Top hat, and a dress suit. "Why are you dressed in that?" I said to him "I told you to wear some old clothes." A big smile came over his face as he said "I haven't got any old clothes." It was a really wonderful afternoon, we had a few sinkings, a lot of laughs, and when it was all over the Redcoat that had been running the book, told me that he had been "bottling" as he took a bucket around the watching spectators. All in all we raised over £80 for the Children's Charity.

Towards the end of the season I had been writing my usual amount of letters for winter work, and especially Pantomime. Then at the end of the season I had a reply from one of the most well known Pantomime Producers of that time, Bunny Baron.

The Bognor season ended on the 22nd September, and after a week at home, I had one date at the Cromwell Club, Grimsby, and you could, smell the fish as soon as you drove into the town. I guess the term is "the boy done good" as I got two more dates from it, for November at the New W.M. Club, and the Excelsior Club, both in Grimsby.

Before that however I had a meeting in London with Bunny Baron. His office was in the West End, the back of Baker Street in a block of flats, where he actually lived. As I rang the bell, I knew that I had to give a good account of myself. It wasn't an audition, so I would not be giving a performance as such, but I knew that I had to sell myself, and sell myself well if I was going to get this pantomime job. It was something that I wanted real bad, I knew that I could do it, but up to now I had never been given the opportunity. I said to myself "you can do this, so don't cock it up." My mind went back to the time I went for the cigarette sponsored "Game Show," and was interviewed by Bob Monkhouse. I was absolutely certain that I had that job in the bag, but it all went pear shaped, and I took it badly. And what made that occasion even worse, was when I saw the show the following summer in a Butlin Bar, and the presenter that got the job, had no warmth, and I was much more experienced at that type of show, and could have done it so much better.

Anyway that's all in the past now, and I knew that you can never take anything for granted, and I intended to be much more relaxed this time.

The door opened, and I was greeted with a hand-shake, and a warm smile from a man who I found out to be Bunny Barons general manager, Gordon Holdom. He then took me through to the office, and introduced me To Lisa Gaye who was the Production Supervisor, and married to Bunny. She asked me to take a seat, and "would you like tea or coffee". - "coffee would be fine thank you" I said.

When Bunny Baron came into the office and introduced himself to me, I took to him straight away. He was a chirpy cockney character, was not very tall, but very down to earth, and made me feel comfortable. I gave him my CV and a few photos, that he looked through, and then began to ask me various questions. I thought the interview is going well, and I'm selling myself ok here, and I got the feeling that he liked me. We were talking for quite a long time when he said "I'm looking for somebody to play the comedy lead Pickles in "Jack and the Beanstalk" at Weymouth" - "That sounds like me" I said. He put his hand under his chin, looked at me for a few seconds, and what he said next was music to my ears, "That's just what I was thinking - Gordon" he shouted "Dave is doing Weymouth, take care of the details." With that he stood up, shook me by the hand, and he was gone.

It was a three weeks run with a weeks rehearsal, playing two weeks at the Pavilion Theatre, Weymouth, and then moving on for a week at the Queens Hall Theatre, Barnstable. It wasn't a long run, but I was well pleased, as it was a start, and could lead to better things. As I came out of the building, I punched the air, and said "Result."

I stayed with my parents for a couple more days, before I went back home, and then by mid October I had a return booking for a Saturday and Sunday, at the Cabaret Club, March. It was the club where I sat down at a table to entertain the only people that were in the room.

When I got there for my second visit, the owner said to me "I was very impressed with you, the last time you were here, especially the night you went on to just four people" I said to him "look, I was getting paid to do a job, so I did it" he then said "a lot of people would not have gone on, I have had acts in the past who have refused." I puffed out my chest with pride and said "I'm a pro."

For the next eight weeks, it was club dates of which most of them I had knock-out nights but on the occasions when it was a bad night, it was really bad, and I always felt very low afterwards, I would say to myself, "why do I put myself through this?" but when your next performance is fantastic, you know why. To have an audience in the palm of your hand, in roars of laughter, and to know that you have created that laughter, there is no better feeling in the world. And your reward for causing that fun and happiness is thunderous applause, - man I guess that's worth dying for, a few times.

On the 18th December I was in Weymouth to start rehearsals for "Jack and The Beanstalk" at the Pavilion Theatre. Also in the show was the stilt walking act Jean And Peter Barbour who I knew very well from the Butlin Revue Shows, and Len Howe who was a very well known and experienced Pantomime Dame. We also stayed at the same digs. During the rehearsals I picked up a terrible cold, and almost lost my voice. On the opening night I felt lousy, was struggling with my voice, and was disappointed with my performance. The show got an excellent revue in the local paper but of me it read:

"DAVE THOMAS AS PICKLES, GAVE A PLEASANT PERFORMANCE, BUT HE NEEDS TO KEEP HIS VOICE UP A BIT FOR THE SAKE OF THE CHILDREN.

Well at least I knew, that was due to the heavy cold, after a few performances my cold cleared up, the voice got stronger, and I really got into the part.

It was one day during my time at Weymouth, that I was just about to go into the Theatre for a matinee that I was tapped on the shoulder by my old friend Johnny Mizon. It was Johnny all those years before that had started me off on this Showbiz Lark as a double act at the Islington Town Hall. He was now married and living in the area. We only had time for a very short chat, he was on a job working in Weymouth, but he actually lived about 30 miles from there. He said that he had been following my career with bits he had read in the papers and the "Stage." I was sorry that it was such a short meeting, and that we were unable to meet up for a drink. We shook hands, then went our separate ways. I never saw Johnny Mizon again. A couple of years later I was in the middle of a Summer Season when I had a letter from his wife Chris, telling me that Johnny had died of cancer. It was a terrible shock, and I shed tears for my dear friend Johnny, who I will never forget.

After our final performance on the 6th January 1973 we moved on to Barnstable on the Sunday to open at the Queens Hall Theatre on the Monday for the final week. On the opening night, just before the Finale during the "song sheet" that I would do with the Dame Len Howe I invited some children up on stage, just as I would always do, when Len had gone off to get changed. One little boy was absolutely fantastic, he was a great little talker, he was giving all the right answers to my questions, and the audience were all in fits of laughter. The next day in the local newspaper the headline in big bold print read:

SMALL BOY STEALS A PANTO

They even named him. Mark John Lewis, I wonder whatever happened to him. We all had a great time in Barnstable, and the panto was a big success.

After my disappointing first performance on the opening night at the Pavilion Theatre Weymouth I knew that I got better and better, and I reckon I must have done okay as Bunny Baron signed me up for a second pantomime the following year at the White Rock Pavilion Hastings.

After the Panto I had about six club dates around the Yorkshire area, followed by a great night at the Galaxy Club at R.A.F. Church Fenton. I then went down to Devon for four nights at the Mermaid Inn, Paignton. That was very enjoyable, and then after a week off, I had four nights in Northampton, where I stayed with an old army pal and his family George Mitchell. I haven't seen them for many years now, but we keep in touch with Christmas cards each year. It was when I was driving home from Northampton that I was stopped by the police for speeding. Then to top that the following day I got caught in a radar trap just outside Bury. Of course I was very concerned about losing my licence. For the first speeding offence I pleaded guilty by post. I was given a fine and my licence was endorsed. As I did not appear in court, I was asked in a letter to send the fine together with my licence to the court for the endorsement to be marked up.

In the meantime I had received a summons to appear at Bury Magistrates Court for the radar trap offence, a week later. It then dawned on me, that if I sent the licence off to be endorsed, and then take it into Bury Magistrates it would not look too good, and they may even give me a ban. At the moment I had a clean driving licence, and it would look much better for my court appearance if it remained so.

I decided not to send my licence off until the second case was dealt with. I arrived at Bury Magistrates Court, and parked the car in the road along with a number of other cars. As I was waiting to be called, I looked out of a window, and could see my car below. I was due in for 10.30am, and it was now about 11 o'clock. I looked out of the window again, and could not believe my eyes, as a Traffic Warden was fixing a ticket to my windscreen, and here I was in court on a traffic offence. I could not do anything about it, but while I was thinking about it, my name was called.

As I was stood up in Court in front of the Bench, the charge was read out, and I was asked if I plead "guilty" or "not guilty." "Well your worship" I said "it's a bit of each really" - "you can't plead a bit of each Mister McGrail" said the clerk of the court, "it must be one or the other." He was smiling, and a quiet ripple went around the court. I was tempted to say "I'll have the other," but I thought better of it. I then continued to explain the situation, and found that I was getting a few laughs, even the Magistrate was smiling. I was now in full swing, and giving a performance. When I felt it was safe to do so, and I was getting them on my side, I asked the bench "Do you not think that these radar traps are not a little bit sneaky? And after all they are machines, how do we know they are accurate", to which the clerk replied "Radar was very accurate during the second world war." - "Ah yes, but they were dealing with aeroplanes - I was in a mini."

I got a few laughs on that, but it still didn't do me any good, even after I had told them what a careful driver I was, and had a "clean driving licence" as I held it up for inspection. I was fined £25 and my licence was endorsed. Just before I left the court, I said "One thing before I go your worship, as I was about to come into court today, I looked out of the window, and I saw a traffic warden put a ticket on my car, can you do something about it, after all, I am here on Court Business." - I'm afraid my appeal fell on deaf ears.

The next day, I sent my licence off to the other court, and I now had two endorsements on my licence. I have made two other court appearances on motoring offences, both of which I could have pleaded guilty by post, but I figured it better to appear in person and have a few laughs. One time I was given a fine, and on the other occasion I told the Police Officer that had stopped me, that I would plead guilty by post. I didn't of course, and I went to court. The Police Officer did not turn up in court, and the case was thrown out. - Now that was a result - Ring-A-Ding- Ding.

From the 7th April that year I was offered five weeks work at Butlins Clacton prior to my first summer season at Butlins Pwllheli for 19 weeks. I was well pleased, as I would now be working in Theatres for nearly six months. I was now a proud owner of a 12 foot touring caravan, that I would tow with my Ford Cortina, that I had traded in my mini for. Just across the road from the Pwllheli Camp was a farm, where the farmer allowed me to park the caravan in one of his fields, quite near a couple of barns.

I was always given food and accommodation on the site as part of my contract, so I decided to let my caravan off to two of the dancing girls from the resident Revue Show. They were very happy, and so was I.

The farmers' daughter had this beautiful horse called Flicker that would graze in the field. He was a very friendly horse, and would always come over to me, each time I went over to pay the farmers' wife the ground rent. I remember one day near the end of the season, when the dancers had finished their contract I had gone over to the farm to check a few things out with the caravan. I went into the van leaving the door open, when I felt a great tilt in the van. As I turned round I could see flicker the horse had followed me in. He had his front legs in and was trying to turn the corner, but his huge shoulders were stuck in the doorway. I was in a panic, as I could see this massive great horse coming at me in a 12 foot caravan. It now looked liked he could not go forward or backward, and I was scared in case he panicked. By this time the van was now beginning to rock. "Flicker Back, Back" I shouted at him, but he didn't look his friendly self. I thought maybe if I give him a carrot, it may calm him down, - but I didn't have a carrot. Then quite suddenly, he backed off, and was outside on the grass. I guess it was all over in seconds, but it seemed an age, and was pretty scary. Afterwards of course I realised that he was just a lovable horse, that was trying to be friendly.

It was at Pwllheli in 1973 that I was to witness the biggest fire that I have ever seen. I have already mentioned the fire at Minehead, and there was also a smaller one at Barry Island. It was becoming a joke that everywhere I went a fire broke out. I recall it was the night of the "Late Night Cabaret" and topping the bill was Ken Dodd. It was on the first night of the two nights event, and it was around Doddy's third visit. Ken Dodd was always a terrific success, and he would always over-run by about an hour, and the show would finish at 3am. On this particular night, after the show I came out of the Spanish Bar, where the event was staged, got into my car and drove back to my Chalet, that was on the other side of the camp.

I had just got my head down for the night, when Livvy shook me and said "I can hear a noise, something crackling, you better take a look." I got out of bed, went outside, and it looked like the whole camp was on fire. We quickly got dressed, and went to see if we could help. It was the whole centre complex containing the Gaiety Theatre, the Playhouse Theatre, the upstairs Ballroom, various bars, shops, the works, and it was all ablaze. There were rows of parked cars along the wall of the Gaiety Theatre, some owners where rushing in to drive them away from the building, and you could see other people smashing the windows of the cars to open the doors, so they could push them away to safety for fear of the petrol tanks exploding. The wind was blowing sparks as big as tennis balls over to chalet lines nearby, and the people were being evacuated and taken to the very large reception, where they had urns of soup and coffee, and piles of blankets, it looked like a scene from the Blitz.

At one point Ken Dodd came into the reception, to help cheer people up with a few gags, but on this occasion they were not in the mood. You could hear explosions as the bottles of spirits would explode in the bars from the heat. Suddenly the flames burst through the roof of the building, leaping about 40 feet into the air, the wind caught it, and with amazing speed blew the flames along the whole length of the building, it all happened so fast, and within seconds the whole building was a blazing inferno.

Many people were packing their suitcases and loading up their cars, and you could see a stream of cars heading for the exit gates. For them of course their holiday was over, but I think the biggest majority did stay to the end of the week. Eventually of course the Fire brigade brought it all under control, and thankfully nobody was hurt, but it did make me very aware of the dangers of fire, and how quickly it can spread.

The next morning you could see the damage, and the whole centre of the camp was gutted. The site was still smouldering, and the strong smell of burning was all around you in the air.

We all heard many stories the next day, and one that stands out for me, was the piano player from the Al Fried Orchestra who ran up the stairs to the ballroom, and ran across the floor to retrieve something from the dressing room at the back of the bandstand. When he came out again, he could see the flames coming up through the floor, as he dodged in between them to get out again. It was a daft thing to do, but he made it.

The very next night at the Late Night Cabaret, I was talking to Ken Dodd in the dressing room just before he was about to go on. I was telling him how I had gone to bed, and what Livvy had said to me just before we found out that the place was on fire.

It was time for him to go on, I introduced him, and he walked on to his usual rapturous welcome, dressed in his long red fur coat, and tall diddy man hat. After his opening number he would always call me back on as his "man servant, Knockers" to go on and take the hat and coat from him. After I had gone off stage with his props, he then told the audience the exact story that I had been telling him, and when he finished with the line:- "….he was in bed with his wife, and she suddenly said - I can hear something crackling." It brought the house down. He then did about 10 minutes of topical stuff all about the fire. It was hilarious, and he was a real master of his craft.

The next day was Friday and the workmen were busy boarding up the whole area where the fire had been. It was painted and the new intake of holiday makers on the Saturday could see no fire damage whatsoever. You would never know that there had been a fire. Fortunately Pwllheli was such a big site that it had another Theatre across the other side of the camp, the Empire Theatre. It also had the old Tyme ballroom, so we were able to stay open. The empire was not as big as the Gaiety Theatre, so we were doing three shows a day, instead of two. It was very hard work, and before the end of the season I was feeling quite exhausted. Very often I was feeling lousy, but I didn't have any time off, and completed the season. It was a long hard season at Pwllheli, but all in all, I did three seasons there, it was the most I had done on any Butlin Camp.

The season ended on 29th September, and after a couple of days resting at home, we decided to go on holiday to Scotland in our touring caravan. It was October but the weather was fine, and the sun was shinning almost every day. It was my second trip to Scotland, but this time I was on holiday and it was so much better. Livvy and I enjoyed every minute of it, just the two of us, away from the crowds and the hustle and bustle. As we drove through the glens, the scenery was breath-taking, the autumn leaves on the trees looked beautiful in their many different colours, and when we parked up, we would watch the sun go down, reflecting on the lakes, it really was a night to behold.

We made our way up the east side of Scotland, and stayed on some really nice little camp sites. One morning we woke up to the sound of the birds, singing, and when we looked out of the window a Robin was sat on the fence just about 2 feet away, his red breast was puffed out, and it was wonderful to see. We have never forgotten it and Livvy still talks about it even today.

Edinburgh was a great place, and the hospitality was terrific, in fact it was great wherever we went. We just had, to visit Inverness, you never know. We may even have got a glimpse of Nessie. - We never did of course, but it was great to see Loch Ness. It was a memorable holiday in Scotland, and we loved every minute of it, and vowed that we would return again one day.

By now I was really looking forward to doing my second Pantomime for Bunny Baron, and on my next trip to London I called in to see him after making an appointment. On this occasion it was a most unusual meeting, as Bunny was ill, and I was shown into his bedroom where he was conducting his business in bed. I could see that he was not a well man, and although he was very good with me, he was very grumpy to the people around him.

One of his pantomime venues was the Lewisham Concert Hall, in London, and I wanted to speak to him about maybe placing me there for the following year. A panto in London would be great for me, and an excellent shop-window. He didn't promise me anything, but I could tell that it could be on the cards for the future. He was beginning to look a bit tired, and I did not want to outstay my welcome, I stood up shook him by the hand, and left him in his bed.

I was soon heading North again, and before I was due to start panto I had quite a few club dates, and T.V. extra jobs at both

Granada and Yorkshire T.V. in Leeds. I even had a couple of noon and night shows that I said I would never do again. One was a lunchtime at the Dukinfield Central W.M.Club that was terrible, with the evening at Audenshaw Labour Club and that was a knock-out. The other was at the Bower Club Stalybridge, and the night time show at the Hyde Untied F.C.Club, both of which I would describe as fair.

The weeks passed by, and on the 16th December I was heading for Hastings, towing my caravan. I went down the day before the rehearsals were due to start, as I wanted to find a decent camp site where I could park up. After visiting a couple of places, I ended up in a field on a farm just outside Hastings. The farmers wife was very nice, I was quite near the farm house, and she charged me next to nothing. The rehearsals went well, the week flew by, and before we knew it, - it was the opening night.

It was a great show, much better than the previous year, and I was really into the character of pickles having played him now twice on the trot. We got good revues from the local press, one of which read:- Jack and the Beanstalk,

BUNNY BARONS PANTO AT THE WHITE ROCK PAVILION, HASTINGS, IS ONE OF THE BEST HE HAS EVER DONE. WITH DAVE THOMAS AS PICKLES, THERE IS A SEQUENCE OF COMEDY, IN WHICH HE AND THE DAME GET THE AUDIENCE ROCKING. WITH LAUGHTER FROM THE START, AND THE CHILDREN JOINING IN WITH INFECTION AND NOISY GOOD HUMOUR.

With each performance things got better, as they always do. On the second week, all the family came down from London to see the show, and after the performance I always remember when I went outside to meet them, and my Father shook my hand and said "David, what a lovely show, - and you've got a nice personality on stage" I have never forgotten his words, its funny how some things just stick with you forever. Mum enjoyed it of course, as did the rest of the family, and I was pleased they were able to see me in a first class show in a Theatre.

We were now into 1974, and the panto finished on the 12th January. For the next couple of months things were a bit quiet, and I did not have any club dates, but I did quite a bit of T.V. work on shows like "Emmerdale Farm," and "Coronation Street." I did a few clubs in March and April, and then the first weekend in May we had another wedding in the family. This time is was my eldest stepdaughter Sonia, who had just returned from a Caribbean Cruise where she had been working as a dancer with her fiancé Geoff, who was a member of a family vocal instrumental group the Winter Mixture. For the second time I was walking down the aisle, with a beautiful bride on my arm to give away. With both girls now married, it was just me and Livvy.

It was, I think around this time that Bunny Baron sadly died. I knew he was ill, but I didn't realise that he was that ill. I had only met him about four times, twice at his office where he lived, and a couple of times when he came to see the pantomime. I liked him, and I was sure that he liked me, but unfortunately I didn't work for the Bunny Baron Organisation again.

On the 10th May I started my 20 week summer season at Clacton, and it was a few weeks into the season that I was offered the Butlin Touring Show again, and that also expected to run for 20 weeks, so with 40 weeks work in the book I was well pleased.

I must say again, that even though I did a lot of work for Butlins, I did experience some wonderful times. It was always a joy to compere the Late Night Cabarets and to do the warm-up spot with some great Star Names. I have always said if you work with the "best" it rubs off on you, but if you are working with duff people, or you are in a bad show, there is always that danger that you would come down to their level. All of the stars that played the L.N.C would go down very well, and the audiences would be fantastic for them, so much so, that many would return year after year.

It would be difficult to say who had been the very best. Of course Bob Monkhouse would be well up there, and I have already mentioned Doddy, and Warren Mitchell who appeared as his Alf Garnett, character would be on my list of contenders.

I remember on one visit from Warren Mitchell, he was well into his Alf Garnett routine, and I could sense that he was not very happy with the noise being made from the bar staff, with the sound of empty bottles, and the like. He moved over to the side of the stage, and at the top of his voice he shouted:- "Oi, - you lot at the bar, - stop making so much Bloody noise, with those bloody bottles, I can't 'ere 'me' self bloody speak here." The audience roared with laughter, and took it as part of his routine, but I reckon he was angry, and really meant it, but it was great to see, and I laughed as loud as anybody else.

Getting back to who was the very best, for me the performer that was real class, was - Bob Monkhouse, but the all time audience favourite, the act that won the most applause, that went on, and on, was one night that I witnessed in Pwllheli. It was a singer, a female singer - it was Lulu.

The night we had Harry Worth, he made me laugh, we were in the dressing room, it was around 11.30pm and he said to me "I don't know what I'm doing here, - I'm usually in bed by this time." Harry did very well, but I don't know if he enjoyed it, as I think he was much more at home in a Theatre. I was looking forward to the night when Mike & Bernie Winters came, as I knew that they were from Islington, and with me being an Islington boy, we would have something in common. When I first met them they were not very friendly, and when I mentioned Islington, Mike Winters said "Our aunt still lives up Highbury," and that was the end of the conversation.

It was soon time for them to go on, and I introduced them. They were given a big welcome, and went down reasonably well. At the end of their act, I took the microphone out of the stand, and called them back on to take a bow. Mike came on but Bernie didn't, Mike extended an arm after he had taken a bow himself and called for Bernie to join him, but he never came back. Mike then took a final bow and went off on his own, it was a bit of an anti-climax. I then realised that they had, had a row before they went on, and they weren't speaking to each other, I guess that's why they were so hostile to me at the beginning of the evening.

By complete contrast Ted Rogers was a real gentleman, there was nothing "big time" about him, he was a great performer, and as topical as the morning papers. We became friends, and his wife Marion would invite Livvy and I for lunch on a few occasions.

Speaking of "Big Time," the acts that really did annoy me, were some of the support acts that thought they were stars and were not. Or the act that had appeared on T.V. in "Seaside Special" a couple of times, and thought they were big stars, and would talk down to you, acting real "Big Time." I've met many of them over the years, but I've never heard of them since.

Doing "False Tabs" was a thing that I never liked either. For the reader who is not sure what a "False Tab" is, I will explain - after a performer has finished his or her act, they go off and their exit music is played, they come back on, take a bow, and go off again, the music keeps playing, they then milk it for all its worth, then come back on again, and do another number, in some cases another 15 minutes. Of course its all rehearsed, and they had every intention of coming back anyway. Many a time you would see a compere come on to take the act off, and the only one shouting for more would be the compere, it would be most embarrassing. Of course I am not saying that there are not genuine False Tabs, because there are, when an audience is stood up and screaming and shouting for more, I have no problem with that. I have seen that happen many times, and the act has gone back and done another number albeit rehearsed. But throughout my career I have only ever seen one genuine false tabs that actually stopped the show, and it was fantastic to see. It was a Star Pop group that had many hits in the sixties, I had worked with them many times over the years, and we became good mates. I knew their act well, and I also knew that when they had finished their last medley, that was it, they had used up all of their material. On this particular night, they finished their act, put down their instruments, walked forward and took a bow, they then walked off and I came on and called them back to take another bow, and they did so. By this time the audience were on their feet, and the shouts for more, whistles, and screams were deafening. The play-off music had now stopped, and I just could not quieten them, - I knew the boys had used up all their material, but this audience had no intention of going home, not until they had heard one more number, - I must say I was relieved, when I saw them come back on again, and pick up their instruments. I was wondering what they were going to do, as I knew that they had nothing rehearsed. I can't remember what they did, but they did one, it was a bucking job, and the audience loved it. Now that was a real one hundred percent genuine false tab, there was nothing false about it, as it was real, and it couldn't have happened to a bunch of nicer guys. - It was Ivy League.

I am not the only one who is against false tabs, when Norman Vaughan was top of the bill, I was in the dressing room with him, and asked what he would be finishing on, then I said "Norman, will you be doing a false tab?" to which he replied "No I won't - you've got to tear the balls off them to do a false tab, - I don't do that."

Of course when I say that I am against false tabs, that does not mean that I am against the genuine article, when an audience is crying out for an encore, that's fine, even if it is rehearsed. But it is the acts that think they are in the big time, and the only one shouting for more is the Compere, even the audience think it is a farce, that is what I am against. As my season at Clacton was drawing to a close, it looked like 1974 was going to be a very good year. It had started in panto at the White Rock Pavilion Theatre, a long summer season at Clacton, and now I was looking forward to the Butlin Touring Show, for 20 weeks. It was also the year when the Spurs became the first English club to have played in three major European Finals.

After a couple of weeks off, I had one date at the Wildlife Hotel, Lincoln, before reporting to Butlins Minehead for three days rehearsals, for the Tour. We did the show on the last day for the holiday makers, and it went down very well. On this tour I took my caravan with me, and it was great, as I did not have to worry about staying in digs. I was able to put up one of the other acts, a singer called Tom, and the drummer in the show also had a touring caravan, that he shared with his girlfriend, who was the female singer on the show. When we hit the road, together with the Butlin Mini Bus, we looked like a travelling circus.

Our first date was on Monday 28th October at the Midhill W.M. Club Sheffield, and it was a good night, but there were much better nights to follow. It wasn't long before we got into winning ways, and scored "knockouts" at almost every performance. The Side Saddle Country Club, at Auckley near Doncaster, was out of this world, as was the Trent Vale Jubilee Club, Stoke-On-Trent. We were all on a high, until we got to the Buglawton Labour Club, Congleton. That really sent us back to earth, nobody did well, the whole night was lousy. We were soon over it though, as we had a great few weeks to follow, and the R.A.F. camps were exceptionally good, like the Sergeants Mess at R.A.F. Waddington.

We had a great duo backing the show, Sid Longden on keyboards, and he would sound like a ten piece orchestra, and his drummer Glen Martin, who was indeed one of the best drummers I have ever worked with, he certainly had the best kit that I had ever seen, it was his pride and joy, and he cleaned it every day, it looked magnificent.

Glen and his girlfriend, who I have already mentioned being one of the girl singers on the show, were both animal lovers. They had a dog that toured with them, and also a duck, that they had rescued, as they found it injured somewhere and nursed it back to health. We all knew that it was healthy, as it quacked louder than any duck I have heard. The only thing was it couldn't swim. When he told me, I said to him "what kind of a duck is that then? - who ever heard of a duck that can't swim." He then explained to me that it had lost its natural oil in its feathers, and when the feathers got too wet it would sink. He used to give it swimming lessons in a barrel of water, and as soon as it started to sink, he would lift it out to run around until it had dried off, and then he would lift it up and put it in the water again. I watched him a few times, and I must say that the duck seemed to enjoy it.

We were only into the tour a few weeks, when they acquired another pet, this time it was a goose. - It was when we were driving back to base, after doing the show. It was quite late, and we were going along this country lane, when suddenly the driver slammed on the breaks quickly, we came to a halt, and he said he thought that he had hit an animal or something. Glen jumped out, as he was sat in the front next to the driver, and we then saw him running up the lane. A few minutes later he came scrambling back carrying a goose. "I think its damaged its foot" he said, we must have all been thinking the same, as we all said in one voice "well what are you going to do with it?" - "I'm gonna take it back, and look after it" he said, and that's exactly what he did. The next morning when I got up and emerged from my caravan, I looked across to where their caravan was pitched, and it looked and sounded like a farm yard, the dog was barking, the duck was quacking, and the goose was eating something, and looked quite happy in his new home.

He would keep the goose tethered on a long string for a few days, until it got used to things. Then after a week it was off the leash, and would wander about freely, and always return to their caravan. We had some very good meals when we were on tour, and this was all down to the singer Tom who was staying with me in my caravan. He was an old army cook, and a very good one, the only trouble was, that he thought he was still cooking for a battalion, and always did too much. Very often we would offer some to the others, so the animals were well fed.

Chapter Ten

A letter From Frank Sinatra's Office. Pantomime Again

It was during the first half of the tour, that I was reading a newspaper one day, and I noticed a small headline "Ole Blue Eyes Is Back". I was pleased to read that Frank Sinatra was coming back to London to do two concerts at the Royal Albert Hall in May next year. A few years earlier he did a concert for Lord Mountbatten, with Princess Grace of Monaco, at the Royal Festival Hall. I then remembered on that occasion that it was announced a good six months in advance, and I had gone to the Royal Festival Hall to enquire about tickets. At the box office I was told, "we don't get Sinatra tickets, all tickets go to the Management. I remember thinking at the time, that you can buy tickets to see any performer in the world, but you just cannot get a ticket to see Sinatra.

    I thought about this for a while, and then decided to write to Sinatra himself about the situation. I put pen to paper, and in my own hand writing I wrote:

Dear Frank Sinatra,

I was delighted to read in the newspaper this morning that you are coming back to London for two concerts at the ROYAL ALBERT HALL———-I then continued the letter and explained how I was unable to get a ticket last time he was here, as all tickets had gone to the management, and how I had always said, *THAT SINATRA IS THE ONLY*

PERFORMER IN THE WHOLE WORLD, THAT YOU CANNOT GET TICKETS TO SEE.

I then thanked him for taking the time to read my letter, and wished him every success on his world tour. After I had finished the letter, I folded it, and got an envelope to address.

I then said to myself "hang on, - I don't know his address." - I then thought for one more moment, and addressed the envelope:

FRANK SINATRA
CALIFORNIA
USA

    I then posted it in a mail box, and also enclosed the news cutting.

    It was now Saturday 21st December, and it was the last night, of the first half of the Tour at Lee Moor Social Club, Walsall. It was a good night, but not a great one, and after the show we all went our separate ways to the Butlin Camps we would be working over the Christmas. I was off to Clacton, and as always I had a great five days, but it would never be as good as doing a Pantomime.

    Of course with doing the Touring Show, I was unable to do a panto anyway, but after Christmas I thought I must pull out all the stops and really try for Pantomime next year.

    With Christmas now over, the New Year was with us, and it was 1975. The Tour did not start up again until 26th January, and before that I didn't fancy doing any club dates on my own, so I did a few T.V. jobs as an extra on a couple of shows at Yorkshire T.V. I had a few days on a show called "Beryls Lot," and then a couple of days on the show "Main Chance."

    The first night back on the Tour, was at the Apollo Club, Longton, Stoke-on-Trent, it was only a small crowd, but it was a knockout night. We then had two great nights to follow, one at the Civic Hall, Brighouse, and the other at the Unity Hall, Wakefield. It was great to play two Theatres on the trot. Then after trips to Wetherby,

Leeds, and York, we had a lousy night at the Allerton Social Club, Bradford.

Most of the clubs we played, we were treated very well, and somebody would be there to meet us, and show us where everything was. But there were a lot of places, where we didn't see anybody at all. There was nobody to meet you, and we had to find out where everything was ourselves, sometimes we would be hunting for ages to find a power point. And then at the end of the evening, nobody would thank you, and we would just pack up, and leave without seeing a soul. It was quite unbelievable that this would happen, but it did, and far too often I must say. In the old style working men's club, they would have a concert chairman, who would sit in a box that was usually fixed to the wall, half way down the side of the room, and he would call for "Order" and introduce the artistes. He was quite typical of the character portrayed by Colin Crompton in the T.V. series "The Wheel Tappers and Shunters Club."

We did come across such a character, at the Lee Mount Social Club, Halifax. I recall that we had arrived in good time, as we always did when the club was still empty, and we were unloading the equipment and props. When we were almost set up, this red faced man with a boozers nose, and greased back hair came up to us in front of the stage. He was wearing a crumpled suit, with his committee badge in his lapel. "Have you got the running order?" he asked, and I told him we had. "Could I have a copy of it then" - "you can if you like" I said "but what do you want it for?" Then with a surprised look on his face, he said "I'm chairman, - I introduce the "Turns." I then said to him "that's okay, we don't need a chairman, we are a self-contained show, and for part of it we have our own compere." He looked disappointed, that he would not be doing his chairman's job for the night, then said "who is your compere then" - "as a matter of fact its me." He then put his hand on my shoulder and said "Right then, come with me, and I'll take you in the box and show you where all the switches are" I stopped him and said "look I don't do the show from the box." Then looking very puzzled he said. "Don't do the show from the box? - well where do you do it from?" - "on the stage", I said "on the stage!! - well I've never heard of anything like that before" and he turned his back, and walked away.

After a spell in the Yorkshire area, we moved back to the Stoke-On-Trent area, and played some great dates at Market Drayton, Northwich, Cannock, Crewe, and Runcorn, to name a few. One night in Chesterton, our organist Sid was taken ill, and we did the show without him, and just the drummer. We were all surprised that we went so well, and it was another knockout night.

We then went down to Northampton, and had one of the greatest nights ever at the Community Centre, Cowley Oxford, it was truly a four star performance, I didn't think the show could go much better than this. From Oxford, we hit the road up to the North East, and the first night up there was quite good at the Pallion W.M.Club, Sunderland. That was followed by a very good night at the Dragonara Hotel, Middlesbrough, it was a Ladies O.A.P. Night. I remember thinking that things were going a bit too good here, and the third night at the Catholic Club, Hartlepool, it was lousy. I was stood on the stage dying on my arse, and I thought, "what's wrong with this audience, don't they know I'm one of them."

We had a couple more 'Iffy dates in the North East, but when we got to the Fire Brigade Sports And Social Club, Lincoln, what a 'Blinding night that was, it was another four star performance, every bit as good as the one in Oxford. We played about three Fire Brigade Clubs in all, and one of them was in fact actually in the Fire Station, with the Fire Engines. They had fixed up a stage, and the area was curtained off from the engines. Seating had been put in, and they had even fitted up some lights. All the seats were taken, and I reckon it was an audience of about 300. Just before the show was about to start, the fire chief came round and said "I hope we do not get called out, but we are on call, and if you hear the bell ring, and some of the audience run out, don't worry, just carry on."

We started the show with this in mind, but the audience were fantastic, and we soon forgot about any call outs. The first half, was a knockout, and we were almost at the end of the show in the second half, when the bell went, and it seemed like all hell had broken loose. The fire engines were starting up, the big doors opened, it looked like there were firemen everywhere about a third of the audience went, the engines swept out of the station, the big doors closed behind them, we had kept going all this time, although it must have only been about 3 minutes, and it was all back to normal. - We finished the show it was a knockout night, and a great experience.

The show continued to have knockout nights, in many more clubs, but when we played the Civic Hall Royston, Near Barnsley, and the Palace Theatre, Newark, I was really in my element. Whenever we played a theatre, I would always wonder how good it must have been in the late forties and fifties, and the Heyday of the Moss Empires, yes I think I was born in the wrong era.

Unfortunately those days were long gone, and it was the clubs that were the bread and butter of the business. If you didn't work the clubs, you didn't work, especially in the winter. We have all heard many stories about the Northern Clubs, and some have been so outrageous, that you would think that the story teller was telling a "Porky", but any performer that has worked the clubs would know that most of them are absolutely true. I remember the time we were playing a W.M. Club in Bradford. We pulled up outside, and a couple of us got out, and went into the front entrance of the club, to ask if there was a back way in to unload. The dog that was a regular traveller with us by now (the duck and the goose, always stayed back at base) also jumped out of the mini bus, and followed us in. In the hallway of the club, a table was set up with a couple of committee men, ready to take tickets. As we walked in, one of the men walked into the main room. When we asked the other man if there was a back entrance he said "No, you will have to go through the club room." At that point, he then spotted the dog that had gone up to the table, and was wagging his tail.

"Who's is that dog?" he said. "Its ours" - "you can't bring that dog in here, - no dogs allowed." - "But he's one of us" - I don't care what one of you he is, he's not coming in this club." - "But he's in the show" I said. He paused for a moment, "In the show? - what does he do?" "He sings!" We both said together. "Oh in that case, I guess its alright" then he shouted in the direction of the main room

"Tommy, come and look at this, they've got a dog in the show, and it sings." His mate then appeared and said "Does he? - what time is he on? I don't wanna miss that." It was priceless.

The Tour finished on Saturday 19th April at the British Legion Club, Alrewas, nr Lichfield. I then had a restful 12 days at home before going to Butlins Bognor for two weeks, prior to my 19 weeks Summer Season at Pwllheli.

As I drove home to Heywood on the Saturday night after the show, I didn't realise what a wonderful surprise was in store for me. It was a letter from the M.A.M (Agency). As I looked at the envelope, I thought, this is the big time, how can they know about me? As I opened the letter, it was dated 9th April 1975, and it began:

Dear Mr Thomas

We have heard from Mr Sinatra's Office regarding your letter requesting tickets for the concerts in London on 29th or 30th May.

And so it went on, it had been that long ago when I had written to Sinatra, that I had forgotten all about it. I was absolutely overjoyed. To think that the biggest star in the world, had found time to arrange for a couple of tickets for a fan in England, and how I had addressed the envelope. Now that's what I call class. The letter offered me the choice of nights, and was signed by Harold Davison's Secretary.

My two Sinatra Concert Tickets were for Friday 30th May at the Royal Albert Hall. The only problem I had now, was the fact that I would be two weeks into my summer season at Pwllheli. I would have to get permission from Butlins to be released for a couple of days. I was certain that they would say yes, and it would be okay, and in fact they did, and it was, but I must say, if they had not agreed, I would have gone anyway, but I guess they knew that.

Bognor was always a favourite place of mine to work, and once again I had two great weeks there. I then travelled up to North Wales to begin my 19 week Summer Season at Pwllheli. They had done a lot of work on the place after the great fire two years earlier.

A whole new complex, and a new Theatre, the place looked new, which of course most of it was.

The biggest majority of punters at Pwllheli came from Merseyside, with a big percentage from Liverpool. It was strange, that when I played the clubs in Liverpool, some I found to be good, but most would be hard for me. But in a Butlin Theatre at Pwllheli, I would have knockout nights, and storm the place, and two thirds of the audience would be Liverpudlians. I remember one day I was in the gents toilet, washing my hands, when a voice in a broad Scouse Accent said "what are you doing in a place like this, you shouldn't be working here, you should be in the big time." I have always remembered that. I had many similar comments, as I have mentioned before, but coming from a Scouser, that was a real compliment.

The first two weeks of the season passed by, and all was going very well, and the various shows and events that I was involved in, were settling down nicely. Then the big day came, it was Friday 30th May 1975. I was already awake when the alarm clock went off, and we were up early, to get a nice early start for our trip down to London, to see Frank Sinatra at the Royal Albert Hall.

Livvy and I put our glad rags that we would be wearing for the occasion on the back seat of the car. The plan was that we would go direct to my parents house in Islington, then after a bite to eat, and a freshen up, we would get changed, and then off to the Albert Hall.

The journey was going well, and we were making good time, as we drove down the M 1 we were both feeling good and very relaxed. We were now about two miles from the end of the Motorway, when disaster strikes. My 1969 Ford Cortina grinds to a halt, and we are now at a stand-still on the hard shoulder. I was horror struck, and all I could think about, was how will I get to the Royal Albert Hall. I got out of the car, and walked along the hard shoulder to the emergency phone that I could see about a hundred yards away. We were waiting for 25 minutes when the AA man arrived. He soon had his head under the bonnet, and was doing a few checks. After a few minutes, he stood up straight and said to me "It looks like the valve" I thought to myself, that doesn't sound too bad

"The valve?" I asked - "That's right, the valve has gone" - "Is that bad news?" - "It is for you, - you'll need a Tow Job" - "A tow job?, but I've got to see Frank Sinatra." He gave me a strange look, "Frank Sinatra will have to wait" he said "I'll get a tow truck out to you" with that, he was in his van, and he was gone. There we were now, on the hard shoulder of the M1 motorway, waiting for our car to be towed into a garage, two Sinatra Tickets in my pocket, and once again, it seemed Sinatra was out of our reach.

We did not have to wait for too long, when the AA tow truck arrived, and this time it was a different patrolman. When he got out of the truck, the first words I said to him was "I've got to get to the Royal Albert Hall to see Sinatra. - Your mate said it's a valve, is that bad news?" he said "yes it is" I then asked him if he could take another look, as it was very important to me, to get going. He agreed to take a look, then had his head under the bonnet, and was doing a bit of fiddling. After a few more minutes he turned to me and said "you are the luckiest man I've seen today. - its not a valve, it's a loose tappet." - The feeling of relief that washed over me I just could not describe, and when I thought of the first patrolman who said it was a valve. What he should have said really was "I cant fix it, but I know a man who can." Anyway alls well that ends well, is what I always say, and within about five minutes we were on our way.

We arrived at my parents house in Islington safe and sound, and after a short break, a bite to eat, and a wash and brush up, we are dressed in our glad rags, its 6.30, and time to go.

We are driving through London, when disaster strikes again, we got stuck in a traffic jam. The clock keeps ticking, and eventually I decide to take a different route. I am now out of the traffic jam, and appear to be going along quite well, when I now realise, that something else is wrong. - I'm lost. I'm now in a mini panic and beginning to sweat, but as I turn into another major road, I begin to feel fine, as I can see the Royal Albert Hall in my sight, and it looks great but now of course there is nowhere to park. The time is now 7.40pm and the show starts at 8 o'clock, traffic is building up again, and it looks like many cars are looking for a parking place. There is only one thing for it, I will have to park anywhere. I take a quick turn into Kensington Gardens, and I stop on double yellow lines, before I have time to switch the engine off, a Rolls Royce pulls up directly behind me, within seconds a Jaguar XJ6, pulls up and parks in front of me, my 1969 Ford Cortina is in good company. With 15 minutes to spare we are now taking our seats in the Royal Albert Hall. We are in a balcony dead centre facing the stage. The atmosphere is electric, and you could smell Channel No.5, and the Mink was all around us.

Sinatra's performance was 1 hour, 40 minutes, and words could not describe it. He finished on "My way," he took his final bow, no "False Tabs," that wonderful orchestra played, and he was gone. I had just seen Frank Sinatra Live, and I was not disappointed, it was truly a magical night and I was there!

As we were on our way out, coming down the stairs, we heard a voice from behind us say "well that's it then, its all over, there's nobody else to see now." That really summed it up, he was right, and I felt exactly the same.

The very next day, we were on the road again back to Pwllheli to continue my summer season. Again I had an excellent season, and this was my second at this site. All the Butlin sites were good for me, and I can't say that I had a bad time in any of them. With shows like the "Sunday Night Variety," the "Lucky Dip Show," and the "Late Night Cabaret," I was always in my element. The event that I hated doing, as I could get nothing out of it regarding Entertainment value, was the "Glamorous Grandmother competition. Of course I realised that it was good for the contestants, and their families, and they no doubt enjoyed it, but I hated it. I recall one day some old guy came up to me afterwards, complaining about the result. I explained to him that it was nothing to do with me, and that it was the Judges decision. He would not leave it alone, and was beginning to get on my nerves. I then said to him "Look, do you have anybody in the competition?" He looked at me with a guilty look, then after a few moments answered "No" I then seem to remember saying to him something like - "well what you worried about?" Two days later I go into the Entertainment Managers office to see him about another matter, and he says to me, "by the way

Dave, I've had a letter of complaint about you, I'll read it to you." He then starts to read me the letter, its from the man who complained to me about the Glam Gran Competition. As he goes through the letter, he then comes to a part that reads ———

"I COMPLAINED TO THE COMPERE ABOUT THE SITUATION, AND HE SAYS TO ME, "WHAT ARE YOU WORRIED ABOUT, ITS ONLY A LOAD OF OLD BIRDS DRESSED UP FOR A LAUGH.

With that the Entertainment Manager nearly fell off his chair laughing. I don't remember saying those words, but we both had a good laugh over it.

On the "Sunday Night Variety" shows, I always looked forward to the visits of Tommy Trinder. In between shows in the green room especially at Bognor where there was a free bar, and the chief hostess would serve us all drinks. Tommy would take centre stage, and tell us all some fantastic showbiz stories, it was wonderful, and many times it was more entertaining than what he did on the show.

I worked with Tommy Trinder many times during my years with Butlins, and he was a great character. But I will never forget the first time, when the AL Fried Orchestra was in the pit, and I introduced Tommy, it was a reverse of roles when he introduced me in the "People National Talent Final" at the New Victoria Theatre with AL Fried's Orchestra in the pit on that occasion.

Sometimes the comics in the resident Revue show, would do the same gags as the visiting comedians would do. It was during the first house, Tommy did a gag, and it did not get a laugh. Tommy then looked down at AL Fried and asked "has somebody done that gag?" And AL Fried shouted back "Yeah - Dan Leno." (for the benefit of younger readers, Dan Leno was a big star comedian in the 1890s).

It was on the "Sunday Night Variety Shows" that I first worked with Bill Maynard, he would also have a good story to tell. I guess Bill liked me, I always got on very well with him, and I will always be very grateful to him, as he is the only person who really got me a break on T.V. but more of that later.

By mid-summer, I had written my usual sack load of letters, and my mind was firmly fixed on getting a pantomime fixed up.

One such letter was to the Manchester based Pantomime Producer Nelson Firth Productions. Nelson had by now retired, and handed over the business to his son Nelson Jnr.

After a couple of letters and a telephone call, I arranged for young Nelson to come to Pwllheli to see me work. It would be better than going for an audition, as he would see me perform in front of an audience, and I was very confident he would offer me a job. It was a mid-week, and the first house. I peeped through the side of the curtain, and I could see him take his seat, he actually stood out as he was wearing a light grey suit.

When I got into my act, I did not perform as well as I know that I can, I guess it was "Sods Law." It was okay, but I just wished that it had been better. After the show, I took Nelson into a quiet bar for a drink in between shows. He sat at a table, as I went to the bar to get us both a drink. I was not feeling as confident as I had been before the show. As I returned to the table, I placed the drinks down we both lifted our glasses, and said the usual "Cheers." After taking a drink from his glass, he put it back down on the table, a smile came over his face, and he said "I liked your act. - How would you like to play Billy Bones in our production of "Treasure Island" at the Forum Theatre Romily". I told him I would be delighted, and after we discussed details, it was a done deal. "I'll get the contract in the post to you in a couple of days" he said. We shook hands, and he was gone. - result.

CHAPTER ELEVEN

"Everybody that was anybody" Success In Jersey

The season was going very well, and we had some great "top of the bills on the "Late Night Cabarets." One regular on the L.N.C. was my old mate Ted Rogers. On his first visit I told him about the Sinatra Concert at the Royal Albert Hall, and he was telling me that he himself had tickets but was unable to go as he was working. He then told me that he had heard that Sinatra was coming to London again in November for a couple of concerts at the London Palladium. Ted who had recently finished a tour with the American Singer Jack Jones, then said he may be able to get some Palladium tickets from his management. "I'll see what I can do" he said "and I'll give you a ring." I remember thinking at the time 'that would be great,' but I didn't really think it would happen. In my opinion to see Sinatra once in a lifetime was out of this world, but twice in six months, that would be too much to expect.

Two weeks later Ted Rogers phoned me at Pwllheli, to let me know that he had Four Sinatra tickets for the opening Gala Night and he invited me and Livvy to join him and his wife Marian. It was for Thursday 13th November, and it was to be one of the greatest nights ever.

The summer season ended on the 26th September, and after a couple of weeks holiday, I had two very good club dates, at the British Legion Club, Meir, Stoke-on-Trent, and the Birchwood Residents Association Club, Lincoln. I then had a run of T.V. work as an Extra at Yorkshire Television in Leeds, on various shows including "Hadley," and "Selwyn Froggit" with Bill Maynard. This was followed by another good night at the Winter Gardens, Cleethorpes, and before we new it, it was time for our second time to spend an evening with Frank Sinatra. Incidentally, the first time we saw him at the Royal Albert Hall, before the show the orchestra was playing the tune "what a lovely way to spend an evening," it was very fitting.

At the London Palladium the show was billed as "The Concert" with Count Basie, Sarah Vaughan, Frank Sinatra, all on a level billing. The Gala Night was a black tie affair, and I really felt "the business" in my favourite dress suit. As the four of us got out of a taxi outside the Palladium, the crowds were outside cheering the celebrities as they arrived. I did not feel at all out of place, in fact I felt quite at home. As we walked up the steps on the red carpet, you could hear some of the crowd shouting out who they had spotted. "Look there's Dick Emery, - that's, what'er name, - you know, her from Upstairs Downstairs" - then I heard" There's Ted Rogers, - who's that with him? - with the silver hair?" - That was me, so I thought what the heck and gave them a wave.

When we got inside, the place was full of famous faces. Everybody that was anybody was there. Ted of course was no stranger to the London Palladium, as he had played there on a number of different occasions. We went into the bar, and he got served very quickly as the barmen knew him, it was strange to see these big names queuing up to get served, and some of them were looking very agitated. We even got a table, and Ted had arranged for drinks to be put out for us at the interval.

We drank up and Ted said "lets go in, and soak up the atmosphere" even he was excited, as we all were, it was great to see. We took our seats in the stalls, and they were just four rows from the front. Wherever I looked, the boxes, the circle, it was full of celebs, no wonder you could never get a ticket for a Sinatra Show, but I was just happy to be there.

The Count Basie Band, and Sarah Vaughan were fantastic, and took us up to the intermission. We then went into the bar to find our drinks at a reserved table that Ted had arranged for us, and it was great to see these Star names queuing at the bar to get served, as we were sipping our drinks in comfort. The second half started with the Count Basie Band doing an opening number, and then the American Comedian Pat Henry came on. I had heard of him, and read about him, as he had worked with Sinatra many times before, but I had never seen him live. He was indeed a great comic, and gave a really polished and class performance, he was my kind of performer.

When he finished his act, he walked off, came back to take a bow, and I noticed somebody stand up in the orchestra, and start to walk down, he was applauding Pat Henry, as if he was the Compere taking him off. The Comedian was getting a wonderful ovation from the audience when suddenly they recognised the compere that had come out of the orchestra - the place then erupted - it was the main man, it was Frank Sinatra. - His first words were "lets hear it for a wonderful performance from Pat Henry."

As the Basic Band struck up with that familiar brass sound that only Basic can do, Sinatra was into his performance, and the star studded audience were spell-bound. It was indeed a blinding night. The next morning one of the newspaper critics Roderick Gilchrist wrote:

> "CHAMPAGNE, CIGARS, PERFUME AND THE SCENT OF MONEY AND PRIVILEGE PERVADED THE LONDON PALLADIUM LAST NIGHT. SINATRA WAS ON STAGE, AND YOU HAD TO HAVE DIAMONDS OR OIL SHARES TO SWAP FOR A TICKET."

Well I didn't have these, but I had a ticket, and I was there, thanks to my old mate Ted Rogers. After the show Ted took us to a swanky little restaurant in Mayfair, to finish the evening off. At the end of the meal the waiter brought the bill, and handed it to Ted. "Let me get that Ted" I said "No that's okay, its my treat" - "Look" I said, "We've had a fantastic night, thanks to you, and I really want to pay for the meal, no arguments" He looked at the bill, then looked up at me and said "It's a lot of bread" - I could see that he didn't want me to pay, but I insisted. "Ted I want to pay and I don't mind". I took the bill from his hand, and that was the end of it. I paid. It was a "lot of bread" but after such a wonderful evening it was a snip. Of course sadly Ted Rogers is no longer with us, but I will always remember him, especially for the wonderful night he gave us, the evening we spent with Sinatra, and rubbed shoulders with the champagne set.

From watching the very best of Entertainment at the London Palladium, my next engagement was at the Miners Welfare Club, Mosborough Nr Sheffield. It was lousy, I died on my 'arse, and was paid off. As I came out and was getting into my car I thought to myself "what the hell, am I doing working in these dumps."

I soon got over it, as three days later I had two nights, Friday and Saturday at the Ideal Restaurant, Wellingborough, and both nights were a knockout. On the Saturday night I did a double with the Bingo Club, Northampton, and I could not believe it, as I had a knockout night there as well, I was surprised as normally Bingo Halls are very hard.

After a few more club dates and T.V. jobs, it was soon pantomime time, and I was really looking forward to it. Five weeks work in a Theatre including a weeks rehearsal was just what I needed, and I didn't have to worry about finding digs, as the Romiley Forum, was near Stockport, and just an hours drive from my home in Heywood, so I went home to my own bed every night.

"Treasure Island" was not really a pantomime, it was more of a musical play. It was a great little show, and had a wonderful cast. Topping the bill, and playing Long John Silver was Peter Adamson, (Coronation Streets Len Fairclough) and one of the best Pantomime Dames in the business George Bolton who played Charity Hawkins.

When I first read the script, I found that my character Billy Bones gets killed at the end of the first act. It was okay though, as in the second half I was teamed up with Tiny Ross, and we were a couple of comedy pirates. Tiny of course for many years was the dwarf in the Morton Frasers Harmonica Gang. We got on very well together, shared a dressing room, and he was great fun to work with. With me standing at six feet tall, next to Tiny we looked a great couple of comedy pirates, and after a few performances each of us knew what the other one was going to do, we just bounced off of each other.

We had a lot of laughs in the dressing room, and he used to stand on a beer crate to get to the sink. He once said to me "I enjoy a good laugh, and I don't mind anything that people say to me, but I don't like anybody tapping me on the head." I was glad he told me that, as when you are in the company of a dwarf, you don't mean any harm, but you are sometimes tempted to tap him on the head in a friendly gesture. I never did of course, but one of the cast did one night, and he went 'ballistic. It never happened gain.

I had a really great time in "Treasure Island," and it gave me a chance to do two different characters. Billy Bones was an old villain, and it was a straight acting role, and then I could be myself in the second half doing comedy with Tiny Ross. The show was a big success, and we did quite good business at the box office. The show came to a close on the 24th January, and we all went our different ways.

After a few club dates, I was getting very despondent with the club scene. In fact at one point it got that bad, that I would load my car up with my gear, and set off to go to work. As I was driving along I hadn't been going more than two minutes when I would think to myself 'I'll he glad when its 11 o'clock, and I'm on my way home again. This did happen to me on a few occasions, and I knew that this is no way to be, it was crazy. I loved this job, I loved show business, but doing these Working Mens Clubs, just wasn't show-biz as far as I was concerned.

Every time you went to work in a club, you never knew what to expect, unless of course you had been there before. It was always a journey into the unknown. Some of the venues were great of course and they had very good facilities, and I always did very well in those, but the dumps were real dumps, and the people who run them did not have a clue. Most of them did not have a stage door, and you would have to walk through the crowded club, carrying your gear, as they all stare at you like you have got two heads or something. And if you've had a bad night and died the death, you had to walk through the club again to get out, but this time it's a longer walk, and they look at you like you are something they have scraped off the bottom of their shoe. I have known a couple of acts on different occasions, that have actually climbed out through a toilet window, so they did not have to walk the walk through the club. I've never done that, but I have been tempted.

Len Norton the Sheffield agent that booked the Butlin Touring Shows, gave me quite a few club dates. I remember one time when he sent me to a club in Bradford. When I got there, in the hallway I was billed as a "Comic From Sheffield." I did two spots and it was very hard work. After my second spot the Concert Secretary came in the dressing room to pay me, and said that he wasn't very happy with the way it had gone, (I didn't need telling that as I wasn't happy either), then he said to me "you're from London, aren't you?" to which I answered "yes" - "wished I'd have known before I booked you" he said "we don't like Londoners up 'ere".

By now I was doing more T.V. Extra work between Granada T.V., and Yorkshire T.V. than I was club work. We were now into April and I was looking forward to my summer season, 23 weeks at Butlins, Bognor Regis. I arrived in Bognor two days before the season was due to start on 15th April. I was always very enthusiastic, and ready for a new challenge, although having said that I was beginning to wonder if I had been with Butlins for too long, and would I ever get the big breaks that I was looking for. Let's face it, I couldn't see any top T.V. Producers going to Butlins for their holidays. I knew that I was no good at auditions performing in front of three people, I needed an audience to work to, and ad lib, to bring the best out of me. It was the same working the clubs, nobody of any importance would see you there. I knew that it would be hard without an agent, and that is the bottom line, with a good agent, it's a walk in the park, as all you have to do in turn up, but I guess I've done okay up to now, and I'm making a living doing what I love, so looking at it like that, I guess I'm a lucky boy.

Of course over the years I worked for quite a number of small agents, including the agents that specialised in T.V. Extra work, and indeed I was very grateful to all of them for getting me the work that they did.

I guess it was ironic that the work I enjoyed the most, the summer seasons and the pantomimes I got myself with the exception of my very first summer season at the Coliseum Theatre Rhyl in 1963, that the agent Jack Platts arranged for me, but Jack wasn't big enough to take me any further. Everywhere that I worked in those two fields the management always wanted me back, and that was very encouraging.

The Bognor Season was going great, and as always I was enjoying every minute of it, I'd even managed to get out of doing the "Glam Gran Competition" I told the Entertainments Manager it would be good experience for a Redcoat to do it. He was stage struck, and he loved it.

The "Late Night Cabaret" with its name stars was still a big hit with the paying guests, and tickets would always sell out very quickly. I did notice that most of the Top of the Bills were male artistes, and we had very few female stars. One of those was Diana Dors, I remember the first time I met her, she was sat in her dressing room, eating a salad and chicken in the basket. It was many years before, that I recall I had a big colour pin up picture of her on the factory wall near my winding machine when I worked up the Columbia Paper Supply in the East End at the time she was a big movie star, and she was gorgeous.

As I walked into the dressing room, she was looking very glamorous, but of course was a few pounds heavier than she used to be. I went up to her, shook hands and introduced myself, then said "sorry for disturbing your meal" - "That's okay" she said "How are you, are you having a good season?" I told her that I was, and we had a nice little chat. I found her very friendly and a nice lady. Her performance was not great, but she did okay when she came off she caught one of the young dancers trying on her shoes, I don't think she was too pleased about that, but the girl can always say that she walked in Diana Dors shoes.

During the season at Bognor, Butlins also booked me for a few Saturday nights (my night off) at the Ocean Hotel, Brighton. I also did the Golden Hind at Portsmouth. The Ocean Hotel was always a good date, and the audiences were very good.

By mid-summer I was once again writing letters to various managements that had advertised in the "Stage" for work in the winter. One job that I applied for was for two weeks in Jersey at the Hotel De France over the Christmas period. If I got it, I would not be able to do pantomime, but I figured that it would be a good move for me, and I also knew that I was in line for the Butlin Touring Show that was going out in January for eight weeks. I had a letter back from the General Manager of the Hotel De France in Jersey, and he was quite impressed with my C.V. He requested some more information, that I sent to him. After a second letter, he then said that he would like to come over to Bognor to see me work, and asked what the best time for me would be. I wrote back to him, giving him a day and date. A couple of days later, I received another letter from him telling me that he could not make that date, but was still very interested in seeing me, and that his wife and daughter would be flying over to see me in his place. I was delighted, and it was all set up for them to come over.

At the time I did not think too much about it, but when I look back now, it was quite something for a management to fly all the way over from the Channel Islands to see an act that they had never heard of. I guess my CV and photographs were impressive, and I sold myself well. I arranged passes for them at the main gate on the day they arrived, and left details for them so they could get a meal in the restaurant, before they saw the first house in the Gaiety Theatre. I did not want to meet them before the show, as I have never been a one to suck up to people, and it did not matter if I was a nice guy, they had come to see me as a performer. I was always nervous before I went on, and on this occasion I felt more nervous than usual, as I knew it was important that I did well. I walked on, and as normal my nerves fell away from me, and all went more than well, I was very happy with my performance, and felt confident. After the show it was now time for me to go and meet the ladies. They were both dressed very smartly, and spoke well. As I sat down and joined them the General Manager's wife came straight to the point. "You are just what we are looking for" She said. With that she continued to tell me about the terms and details. Apart from my salary it was all expenses paid plus food and accommodation in the Hotel "for both you and your wife." It was a very good deal, and a great result.

It was only a couple of weeks later that I signed a contract to do the Butlin Touring Show, and I felt very contented. Over the years I had so many wonderful nights at Butlins, too many in fact to even remember, but of course some performances you just never forget both good and bad. One such performance at Bognor in the Gaiety Theatre was a night when I was coming to the end of my act, when the heavens opened with the biggest down pour of rain that you could imagine. The noise as the rain bounced off the roof was so loud I could hardly hear myself speak. I stopped for a few seconds, then signalled to the M.D. to go into my finishing number that just happened to be the song from the show "Half A Six Pence" - "If The Rains Got To Fall". The place erupted, and the audience went wild, they thought that I had just put the song in for the weather, it was perfect timing, but what they didn't realise was, I was going to sing it anyway, even if it had been a heat wave, but I must say it was a memorable moment.

Working very close with Butlins Chief Entertainments Executive Frank Mansell, as his right hand man was Ken Hopson. I had known Ken since 1966 when I first started with Butlins up at Filey. It was Ken who gave me the hotel work during the summer, and he also took over the Touring Show. The season ended on Friday 24th September, and Ken fixed me the Saturday and Sunday at the Ocean Hotel, Brighton, and the Norfolk Hotel, Margate, both nights were great and it topped off the season nicely. Five days later I was back at Yorkshire T.V. working once again on "Selwyn Froggitt" as a walk-on. For the next few weeks I did quite a few days on the show, and also other shows like "Beryls Lot" "Raffles" and "Emmerdale Farm" as it was called then.

I was doing club work at weekends at places like the New Reform Club, Grimsby, and the Garden Centre Restaurant, Windermere. Two weeks before I was due to go to Jersey I had three separate days over the two weeks on a show called "Hard Times." It was a Dickens story being produced by Granada T.V. In

Manchester. It was certainly "hard times" over the three days that I worked on it. Granada had found an excellent location at a couple of disused warehouses apposite some tiny houses in these cobbled streets. The smoke machines were working overtime, and once you were dressed in your Victorian style costume, you really felt that you were transported back in time to those Victorian days that Dickens would write about and describe so beautifully. The sound of the horses hoofs, and the carriage wheels on the cobbles as they rode through the smoke past the tiny houses on the dimly lit street. They were dark clouds above, it was drizzling with rain, and it all looked very grey and authentic.

The people from the make-up and wardrobe department would spend their day rubbing mud over all the extras, and dirtying their faces, and hands, we were all beginning to look like coal miners after being down the pit for twelve hours. It was a big call, and they must have had about two hundred extras on the show. You would hear comments like "I'm sure everybody wasn't this filthy in Victorian Times," but they were as far as the make-up girls were concerned. You could stand around for hours on these jobs doing nothing, when suddenly one of the make-up girls would come up to you, and scrape some mud off the floor with a piece of wood, and then wipe it all over your trousers - well I guess they got bored too. People would be falling asleep all over the place, as was quite normal on all early calls, as you would be up for 5am to get to a location for 1am. I must say that "Hard Times" was not a good job to be on. We would all be cold, wet, and hungry. The callboy would normally be some arse -hole of an up-start, going around with his walky-talky radio, and his clip board. He would call groups of people about two hours before they were required, and leave them standing in the rain.

On the second day it was still raining, and about six of us decided to go up into the warehouse where the costumes were, and it was dry and warm. We did tell the callboy where we were going, and he could call us when needed. It was about 7.45am and on the first floor of the warehouse where all the costumes were on racks, there was also some furniture up there including some old leather chairs. Six of us went up there, and we promptly made ourselves comfortable. The next thing that I remember was hearing a voice saying "Its Lunch Time." I got up from my chair, and saw another bloke spark out in a chair opposite me, we were the only two left from the six. Apparently the call boy called us, the other four went, and left us two fast asleep. I was glad that they did, we went down for lunch, and nobody knew any difference - it was a nice mornings work.

It was Thursday December 16th, when we flew out of Manchester airport, and in no time at all we were landing in Jersey a car was waiting to greet us, and take us to the Hotel de France St Helier. We were certainly given five star treatment, and I remember thinking I could certainly get used to this. After we had settled in, I had a short meeting with the General Manager, and was surprised when he told me that I would only be doing one show the first week at the Hotel de France. I had signed a contract to do 17 performances, and I was beginning to wonder how I would fit them all in. However not to worry, with a few days off it will be like a holiday. He also said that they would give me a car for the time that I was there so that I could get round the Island. We took advantage of my time off, and drove all over the Island. It didn't take too long to do that, as I was told that it was only 12 miles long, and six miles wide. Jersey was a wonderful place, and we both loved it.

The Hotel was first class, the food was wonderful, and when I did my first show on the Monday, it was not such a great night, it was fair. Maybe it was down to the fact that a lot of the guests were French, German, and Belgium, I don't know. However I was soon to find out how I was going to get my 17 performances in. I was about to embark on a run of Hotels doing three a night. An Assistant Manager from the Hotel was to be my driver, and he would drive me to each gig. I was told that it would be such a tight schedule, that I would not have time to change. Once I was in my working gear, I would come off stage, jump in the car, and then off to the next hotel. I decided to get my dress suit on in my hotel room, and then I would be ready for the whole night. I was down to do 25 minutes at each show.

The first show was at the Pomme d'Or Hotel, and it was okay. I took my bow, was in the car and 15 minutes later I was at the Hotel De La Plage, and it was a Knockout, by now I am drenched in sweat, and feeling uncomfortable but there is no time for a shower or to freshen up, its back in the car, and off to the next gig at the Grouville Bay Hotel. Once again the audience are great, I give a good performance and its another Knockout night. The next day is Christmas Day, and I have three more shows. The first one was the Jersey Holiday Village, and a band - call had been arranged for the afternoon. When we arrived the first thing we saw was a big bronze bust of Billy Butlin. I did not know until then that he even had a site on Jersey, but apparently he kept it separate from his main Holiday Camps. It was a great little Holiday Village in wonderful surroundings. The General Manager was a man that I knew very well, as he used to be the G.M. at Butlins Bognor. His name was Terry Divine.

At the band-call it was a duo, of organ and drums. I was soon to find out that the keyboard player was not a very good reader. One of the numbers that I would usually open with was "Sweet Gingerbread Man." I had a fantastic arrangement for a ten piece band that was written for me by a very talented arranger Chris Winter. I took out from my pad just the two parts keyboard and drums, and gave them to them. They played the intro, and I did not even recognise it. I told him it was not right and to try it again, it got from bad to worse, then he had the nerve to turn to me and say "who wrote this - its all wrong." After a few words, I then gave him a printed piano copy of "The Bird On The Second Floor," and he was struggling with that. "Look " I said, "you can't read can you, why don't you own up, that you can't read music?" He didn't answer me, he looked, but he never said a word. With that I took the music off his stand, and said "Forget the numbers, just play me on with something lively, and play me off when I say good night." I went on at 8pm to a packed house, and the audience were fantastic I couldn't do anything wrong, I was at the top of my game, it was my best performance so far. At the end of my 25 minutes I was in the car, and as my driver pulled away, the applause was ringing in my ears.

I was due on at 9pm at the Hotel De La Plage, the venue that I had a knockout, the previous night. Once again it was a knockout, and I was back in the car with my driver speeding along the narrow roads to get me to the Pomme d'Or Hotel for 10.15 pm. As we arrived the compere was waiting to introduce me straight away. I got out of the car and within a couple of minutes I was on the cabaret floor. The audience were quite hard, and I would say I gave an okay performance, but I didn't enjoy it. The next day I had two performances, the early show was at the hotel that I was staying, the de France, and the late show was back at the Hotel de la Plage, and I scored a hat trick of Knockouts. On the other hand the Hotel de France I would only rate as fair.

During our stay on Jersey we met an old pal that was working on the Island. His name was Colin and I first met him a few years earlier when he was the piano player in the AL Fried Orchestra, and he would take charge of the band on many occasions when AL was having that extra drink at the bar. The last time I saw him was on the Butlin Late Night Cabarets when he was working as M.D. for the Liverpool Entertainer Johnny Hackett. I've worked with some great keyboard players over the years, but I would rate Colin as the best, he really was a great musician, and here he was doing the odd gigs in Jersey. We would all have some late night drinking sessions after the shows, and it was very enjoyable. The booze on the Island was very cheap compared to back home, and I remember Colin would say that "Jersey is full of drunks clinging to a rock."

The next day I had four shows to do, the first one being at 3pm at Fort Regent. There were three other acts on the show, and I was delighted to hear that Colin would be playing for the show together with a drummer. When we got to Fort Regent I was disappointed to find that it was a giant concrete shopping centre. The area where we would be performing, was a high stage with a few rows of seats in front of it. There were no curtains, it was all very cold and bare, and on either side there would be various other activities going on. It was all open plan, and crowds of people would be constantly walking about the whole time. It was quite sole destroying, as it was impossible to get any attention. One good thing came out of it however, and as far as I was concerned made it all worthwhile. When Colin played "Sweet Gingerbread Man" it was like I was flying. It was the best that any keyboard player had ever played it for me. He was a truly fantastic musician, and he was the reason that I was even looking forward to our second show at Fort Regent the following day. I often wander what happened to Colin, as indeed he was a great talent, but as we all know, - not everybody makes it.

After the Fort Regent Show, I had a very good performance at the Pomme d'Or, another really knockout night at the Mayfair, and then had another lousy night at the hotel where I was staying the de France. It was unfortunate that the man who brought me over to Jersey was the General Manager of the Hotel de France, and he only saw me perform at that venue. The next day we were back for the afternoon show at Fort Regent, and it can only be described as a joke, as it was never a venue in its present form to put on a show, it was more of an exhibition centre. I didn't do many gags on this occasion as there was no point, so I gave Colin three numbers to play, and we had a ball with all of 'em. On Friday the 31St Dec I played my last three Hotels, and they were all satisfactory. Over all it was a successful trip, and I enjoyed it, I was only sorry that it didn't work out for me at the Hotel De France. We flew out of Jersey on New Years day 1977, back to Manchester via Heathrow. When we got back home to Heywood I had nine days rest before I started the Butlins Touring Show.

It was to be a year where I suffered a big disappointment, and experienced what in my opinion was the greatest night of my career. The disappointment was nothing to do with my career. At the end of the 1977 football season Spurs were relegated to the Second Division. It was a bitter pill to take, especially from Arsenal fans. However I guess we needed a kick up the backside, and I was confident that we would bounce back to the First Division the next season.

CHAPTER TWELVE

My Greatest Night Ever, The Sunderland Empire, Disaster on the M62, Debut In A Stage Play

When I met up with the rest of the cast for the touring Show, and was given the itinerary, it was nice to see that for the first two weeks we would be playing clubs down South. It would make a nice change from doing the Northern Clubs. The third week would be in Yorkshire, then two weeks after that, we would be in the Midlands for a couple of weeks. I turned a couple more pages, and then noticed that we would be finishing the "tour" up in the North East, and then jumping out at the page at me I saw Sunderland. It was not my favourite town, and most of the clubs that I had played up there hated me. I had never forgotten the time that I was paid off, three times in one week. I didn't read the venue I just saw the town Sunderland. Ah well, I guess if 'yah 'gotta go, 'yah 'gotta go.

The show opened to a fabulous night at the Embassy Suite, Colchester on Monday 10th January, it was a real knockout, and we continued with knockout performances at Southend, and Bishop's Stortford. We then went to the Picketts Lock Centre, Edmonton, and although it was very good, the venue was far too big. The show continued its successful run of knockout performances at the Town Hall Ilford, followed by dates at Stevenage, Wisbech and our final date down south was in London's East End at the Assembly Hall in Leytonstone. We then had the weekend off, to travel up to Yorkshire, and our first gig up there was at Tiffanys in the City Centre of Hull. We had some nice venues that week including the

Cats Whiskers, York, the Unity Hall, Wakefield, and the Cats Whiskers, Leeds. After our final date at Doncaster, we were all packed up and our vehicles and caravans were heading back down the Motorway to Stoke-On-Trent. Once again we all enjoyed some knockout nights at places like Burslem, Middlewich, and especially the Charter Theatre, Preston, and the Civic Hall, Wallasey. Things were all going extremely well, until we played the Berry Hill W.M.Club, Stoke-On-Trent, and everybody died on their arse. It was a really lousy night, and when we left, even the Mini Bus wouldn't start.

We got it going in the end of course, and after that we had five knockout nights on the trot. I was pleased about that, as I knew our next port of call would be Sunderland, and I must admit that I wasn't looking forward to it. Out last show in the Midlands was at the Town Hall, Dudley. It was during the interval in the dressing room that I took another look at the Itinerary to check out the North East dates, it was only then that I noticed the Sunderland date properly. I got a very pleasant surprise as I read Sunderland Empire. It was now a Civic Theatre, but it used to be one of the great Moss Empire chain. I was now beginning to look forward to the trip, it may well be Sunderland, but it is a Theatre, and one of the finest in the North East.

After the Dudley date we had a day off, and I returned home for a night before setting off the following day for the North East. I hitched up the caravan onto the tow-bar of my car, and we set off. With Livvy sat next to me in the passenger seat, and some cool Jazz playing on the radio we were going along fine, and I felt very relaxed. We were soon onto the M62 Motorway, with both car and caravan under my control, and we were doing a steady safe speed. It was getting rather windy as it always seemed to be on the M62, but on this day it appeared to be worse than normal. Suddenly I could feel the caravan was bumping with the wind, and as I looked in my rear view mirror, I could see it was beginning to swing from side to side. I felt that if I were to accelerate it would pull the caravan back into a straight line. - It didn't work, and was now out of control. The caravan now began to jack-knife, and was crashing from side to side into the back end of the car. It was now like a mad run away horse that I was trying to bring under control. At one time the position of the car was across the motorway, and I was facing the hard shoulder. As I looked out of the passenger window on my left, I could see all three lanes with traffic coming to a stand still. I was keeping as calm as I possibly could, but by now it was beginning to get really hair raising. At that very moment I did not realise the real danger that we were really in. As I fought with the steering wheel, at one point I could not even tell which way the front wheels were locked. It was now getting very scary as I was struggling to get both car and caravan back on track. The fight seemed to go on, and on, and I was now breaking out in a terrible sweat, as I turned the steering wheel from side to side to get it straight. We now seemed to be in slow motion, and I could feel calm coming over this wild beast that was out of control. I was now going slowly along the hard shoulder, and as I pushed my foot slowly down on the break pedal, we gently came to a stop. I just looked up at the sky and thought 'somebody up there likes me.'

As I got out of the car, a lorry pulled up in front of me, the driver jumped out of his cab and came walking back to us. "Are you alright?" he said - "Thanks, we're fine." He came right up to me "you had me worried there" he said "I thought the caravan was going to turn over it left the floor by at least twelve inches." I assured him that we were both okay, he then got back in his truck and drove off. We were quite shocked when we saw the damage. Both sides of the back end of the car were dented in where the caravan had jack knifed crashing in to each side. The front section of the caravan where the gas bottles are stored had completely disintegrated, it looked a real mess. I was dreading looking in the caravan, I just could not imagine what it would be like.

I opened the door and as I looked in, it was almost unrecognisable. The only way that I could describe it, is if you could imagine King Kong picking up the caravan and swinging it around before throwing it to the ground, that was what it looked like inside. I closed the door, we got back in the car, and we continued our journey. We arrived in Sunderland in good time, and met up with the rest of the cast at a pre-arranged camp site. They were all shocked when they heard what had happened, and saw the state of the caravan. We soon tidied things up got ourselves sorted out, and I knew that we had to put it behind us quickly, as that very night we had a show to do at the Sunderland Empire. As soon as we got to the Theatre I knew that this was my kind of place. A few years before there used to be hundreds of Theatres like this all over the country, but now of course most of them are car-parks and Supermarkets. The theatre management must have done a good job on publicity, as the theatre was just over two thirds full. At the back of my mind I was still not too sure how the Sunderland locals would react to me, as I had experienced some really bad times in the working Mens Clubs here. But whatever the audience would be like, I was determined to enjoy every minute of this wonderful Theatre.

After the show opening, and I walked forward in front of the front cloth all my doubts were gone in seconds. I always did a five minute warm-up spot at the beginning of the show, and on this night in what can only be described as perfect surroundings, the audience were out of this world. As I was coming to the close of my warm-up I remember thinking to myself 'I can't wait to get back out here at the end of the show to do my act. The whole show was a knockout, and everybody went well. My turn came, and I was on, I could feel the warmth from the audience, and I knew they were pleased to see me back on again. I knew that this would be my best performance ever, the roars of laughter were loud and long I would stand for ages just waiting for the laughter to die down, (I now knew how Jack Benny must have felt) when I did my act at the London Palladium it was a great thrill, and a tremendous experience, but on that occasion I was on trial. Here at the Sunderland Empire I already had the job, and I could relax entertain and enjoy. I guess over the years I have given performances as good as this, and even had audiences as good as this, but in my opinion my night at the Sunderland Empire will always remain the Greatest Night of My Career. The funny thing was, they were the same people that hated me in the clubs. I now knew that there was no doubt about it. I was born to be in Theatres, - trouble was the theatre days were long gone.

The next night we had a good show at the Centre Hotel in Newcastle, followed by a fair night in Hartlepool, then an 'iffy night in Middlesbrough. The Tour then finished its run with a knockout night at the Phoenix Theatre, Blyth, on Friday 18th February. I then had a couple of weeks "resting", before I contacted the local agents, who gave me a few club dates. I then had a very good run of T.V. work, and did a lot of days on "Crown Court" for Granada T.V. Sometimes I would be on the Jury, others I would be in the public gallery, and a couple of times I played a Policeman. It was nice work, and interesting as you didn't know the outcome of the case until the Jury delivered its verdict. It was like watching a case in a real court of law with stoppages. Other Granada Shows that I had quite a lot of work on were "The XYY Man," "This Year, Next Year" "Caledonian Cascade," and I even had another day on "Hard Times." For Yorkshire T.V. in Leeds, I did a number of days on "Cost Of Loving," "Sister Dora" and "Flambards."

We were now into May, and I was offered two days on "The Liverbirds" for the B.B.C. that was being filmed at the Adelphi Hotel in Liverpool. After the second day I was called back to do a third day the following week. I was now looking forward to starting my Summer Season at Butlins Skegness for 17 weeks commencing on 20th May. My last club date before that was at the Golden Hill British Legion Club, Stoke-On-Trent. I did 40 minutes, was paid £35, and died on my arse. I did enjoy one thing though. - The drive home.

The Gaiety Theatre at Butlins Skegness is the biggest air conditioned Theatre in Europe, it seated 3,000 people, was always packed for two houses every night, and I had some wonderful nights there. It was a great season once again, and it was to be the season that I played my first acting role. It came about by accident and I guess I was in the right place at the right time, but more of that later.

It was at Skegness that I first met Vince Earle, who went on to being a big success in the TV Soap "Brookside." In those days Vince was fronting a band in one of the bars as The Vince Earle Attraction. He had a great sound, and indeed he was a big attraction. We became mates, and would play golf together. As the season went on Vince would do more and more gags, and he proved to be a very good comedian, as well as a good singer. I do not know if he ever realised it, but his gags would be a constant annoyance to his band. We were on the golf course one day with his drummer and he started to tell me of his frustration. "We are standing there every night like a load of Prats" he said "waiting for him to sing, sometimes he only sings three songs the whole set, - its like backing a fucking Comic."

Another regular golfer that would often join us, was the actor John Gordon-Ash who was also the Company Manager of the Albany Players, who were the resident rep company at the Butlin Playhouse Theatre. The company would put on some excellent plays, and I had seen about three of them. One tea time about 5pm John came round to my chalet and told me that one of the actors had fallen and broken his leg, and would I do him a favour and stand in for him. "When for?" I said - "tonight." - but don't worry" he said "the curtain does not go up until 9.30 and you won't be on until the very end of the last act." He then fully explained what it was, and I agreed. He then gave me the book to look over the lines. The play happened to be my favourite, it was the comedy "Rogers Last Stand," and I was thrilled to be part of it. Although it was only a small part, it was indeed a key one to the denouncement of the comedy.

John said that if I wanted, I could take the book on with me, but I didn't want to do that, and I was sure that I could get through it. Fortunately there was not a lot of dialogue for me to learn, but of course it was important that I got it right. I then went with John to the Playhouse Theatre, where we met up with the other actors, and rehearsed the last scene. They were al I very professional, and I knew that I was in good company. I now knew where to make my entrance, and where all the furniture was. All I had to do now was learn the lines. I had two shows of my own to do in the Gaiety Theatre, and when the second show was finished at 9pm, I was straight over to the Playhouse for "Rogers Last Stand."

As the curtain went up at 9.30. I was in the dressing room going over my lines. It was now into the last act, and I was in position to make my entrance waiting for my cue. I knew the dialogue but then it went from my mind, I took another quick look at the book, and it came back to me again. The next thing I know, I'm on stage and speaking to the other actors. It's a joy to be working with these excellent pro's, I forget one of my lines but one of the actors picks it up straight away, and nobody notices. I'm back on track, its time for the Tag, I deliver the last line of the play, and a mighty roar of laughter erupts from the audience. The curtain falls, I'm in a line up of actors as the curtain goes up again, and we take three curtain calls. - Well what do 'yah know, - I'm an Actor. I was only on for a short time, but it was a great experience and I enjoyed every minute of it. The next day the actor who had broken his leg Russell Wootten, was back on stage complete with crutches in the company's next production "Party To Murder."

I was now bitten by the acting bug, and one day on the golf course with John Gordon - Ash, I was talking to him about it, and he said to me "there's no money in it, - you're better off doing what you do." After we had quite a long chat about it, he then said to me "Why don't you contact Bill Maynard." I never did, but as time went by Bill Maynard through an agent contacted me, and that proved to be the best break that anybody gave me.

Many things happened on the Butlin sites in 1977, and one such event that came through the grape vine from Filey, and it was later reported in the "Butlin News," was that they had just staged the longest Conga line in the world - 5,850 holiday makers and eight donkeys. The world record conga took place on August 25th only days after former British Heavy Weight Boxing Champion, Richard Dunn had led a line of 4743 holiday makers at Filey and claimed the world record. But at the same time a similar event was being staged at Sidmouth in Devon with a line up of 5662 people. Not to be upstaged Entertainment Manager Rocky Mason, organised a marathon conga to end all congas and won by a clear 188 assorted holiday makers and eight donkeys.

The Skegness season was going along nicely, and by mid summer my mind turned once again to pantomime. I contacted Nelson Firth to let him know of my availability, and a few days later he got back to me and offered me "Aladdin" at the Forum Theatre, Billingham. The best part was that it was for the role of the Villain, Abanazar. I was delighted as it was more of an acting role, and a strong part that I could get my teeth into. It was a three week run, and I would be teamed up with that experienced Sheffield comedian Bobby Dennis, who would play Wishee Washee. The summer season ended on the 16th September, and even though you enjoy every minute of it, you are always pleased at the end, and ready for a break and a change of scenery, I'm sure that most performers would tell you the same.

I had a month out of work, but I wasn't too concerned, as I knew that something always turned up. I remember once at the end of a summer season my brother Tony asked me what I had lined up next. When I told him that I didn't know, he was aghast, - but I guess I have always sailed close to the wind. I have always been a complete optimist, no matter how bad things look, always look on the bright side, nothing ever turns out as bad as you think.

It was the middle of the third week after the summer season when one of my agents for T.V. work rang me "Granada are looking for somebody to play a hotel porter in an episode of Coronation Street" she said "I think you would be right for it, are you available on Monday 17th October?" - "I'll just check my diary" I said, as I flicked through the empty pages, that were all blank "the 17th of October you say" I said "that's right" - "actually I do have a job pencilled in for that date," I then thought to myself don't push your luck but its not a problem I can cancel it" I said. "Fine, I'll put you in, and let you know the call time in a couple of days." I was called for 8.30am at Granada Studios where I was soon changed into my hotel porters uniform and we were in the Mini Bus and transported to the Piccadilly Hotel in Manchester, where the scene would be filmed. It was the time when Stan and Hilda Ogden had won a weekend in a Posh Hotel. It was only a very small part for me, but I did have a cough, and one line to deliver. I took the Ogdens up in the lift, then carried their bags and took them into the room. While I am waiting for a tip, Stan ignores me, and I give a little cough. Hilda then gives Stanley a nudge, he then puts his hand in his pocket, and gives me a tiny tip. I look at it, then look up at Stan and say "Thank you very much Sir." It was my biggest part on "Coronation Street." I honestly did not think it was much of a thing to do, but it did lead to something else, and that did surprise me.

After that I was very lucky with the T.V. work, and managed to fix something every week right up to when I started rehearsals for the pantomime. Granada were still doing "Crown Court," and I had quite a few days on that, I also worked on a show called "Girls," and played a waiter for a couple of days on a show called "Mirage." I did lots of other various days here and there, and then I did two days at Yorkshire T.V. Leeds on "Selwyn Froggitt" with Bill Maynard. It was always nice to work on this show as Bill was always very friendly towards me, as he remembered me from the times he appeared on the "Sunday Night Variety" shows for Butlins. Speaking of Butlins by this time I had already signed another contract with them for the 1978 season at Pwllheli for 17 weeks. It would be my thirteenth season for them, and my third at Pwllheli. I was beginning to think that I was treading water, and had possibly made a mistake by staying with them for so long. Of course I knew that Butlins had been very good for me, had taught me a lot, and I was grateful to them for their continued confidence in me. But then of course on the other hand if I had not been any good, they would have dropped me like a brick. I was getting itchy feet, and fancied a change, I was in a "comfort zone" and maybe I should make next season my last, and look elsewhere.

It was now Thursday 15th December and the first day of rehearsals for "Aladdin" at the Forum Theatre, Billingham. I was absolutely word perfect for my role of Abanazar, and I was surprised that I was the only one working off the book. I was determined to be a big success, and had worked very hard. The weeks rehearsal went by very quickly and before we had time to say "He's behind you" it was the opening night. I was very satisfied with my performance, but the local press gave the show mixed revues, but both Bobby Dennis and myself came out very well. Theatre critic Keith Newton of the Evening Gazette wrote:

"TWO SIDES OF PANTOMIME STEAL THIS SEASONS SHOW AT BILLINGHAM FORUM. ON ONE SIDE IS BOBBY DENNIS AS WISHEE WASHEE, ON THE OTHER IS DAVE THOMAS AS THE EVIL ABANAZAR. THEIRS IS A BATTLE OF READY WIT THAT LIFTS THE ACTION DURING THE 100 MINUTES OF A TYPICALLY TRADITIONAL ALADDIN. BOBBY DENNIS WORKS HIS AUDIENCE BEAUTIFULLY, PICKING UP CHANCE REMARKS, EVEN USING INSULTS TO THE ADVANTAGE OF STORY LINE. IT'S A MASTERLY PERFORMANCE FULL OF PANTO'S COMIC SPIRIT THAT IS APPROACHED ONLY BY DAVE THOMAS'S VILLAINOUS BRAND OF MAGIC AS THE WICKED UNCLE. A PRODUCTION WITH A PAIR LIKE THESE KNOWS IT IS ON SAFE GROUND NO MATTER WHAT HAPPENS ELSEWHERE".

We had similar revues in three other papers, and I was very pleased. As the days went on the show got better with each performance, the business was good, and overall it was a great success.

I enjoyed working with Bobby Dennis, and we became good mates. He was a great character, I remember one day we were in the town looking around the shops, and in one store was a grand piano in the window. After walking around the shop, as we were about to go out Bobby climbed into the shop window sat at the piano and started to play. He was a very good piano player, and after a few minutes a crowd started to gather on the pavement outside looking in at him in the shop window. He then looked over his shoulder saw the crowd outside, pulled a funny face, slammed the lid down and promptly walked off, it was hilarious to see. The best laugh of the lot though was when the crowd on the pavement burst into a round of applause.

The old year went out, and it was the New Year of 1978. It was the year that Spurs got promoted back into Division one at the first attempt and that really pleased me. The pantomime had now finished its run, and the first work I got after that was a couple of Photographic jobs for Tetley Bitter at the Atlantic Tower Hotel in Liverpool.

I then did a weeks cabaret at the Aquaris Club, Chesterfield. I had a really knockout week, and I knew I would as soon as I arrived for the Band-Call, on the Sunday. It was such a well run club, and very professional in every way. On my last night of the week, I did a double with the Red Lion Restaurant, and I scored a knockout there. It was a fantastic week, and once again I wished that I could play these kind of venues every week.

At the beginning of February Thames T.V. were doing "The Life of Phyllis Dixie," and they were filming up in Blackpool at the Opera House. I was given four days on the trot on the show, Monday to Thursday. It was one of those shows with a cast of hundreds, and after the first two days it was getting boring. In the lunch break on the Tuesday I rang one of my agents to see if there was any work for next week, and she asked me if I could do a day for Granada the next day (Wednesday), I thought 'why not, they will never miss me.' The next day I went to the Granada Studios and worked the day on a show called "The Intervener's." The next day I went back to the Blackpool Opera House, and nobody had even missed me. I knew it was not the right thing to do, but there was no harm done, and, hey -'all's fair in love and war - and Phyllis Dixie.

On the Friday I was over to Leeds on a show called "Wild Alliance" for Yorkshire T.V., and in the end it was a great result as the week turned out to be a nice little earner. I then had a good run on doing some photographic work advertising Tools, Overalls, Beer, and various other products. It was good money, and compared to doing the W.M.Clubs it was a piece of cake. With doing this type of work, and T.V. Extra work almost every week, I had money coming in, and thought why bother with working Mens Clubs. I was now only interested in playing in decent venues.

For Yorkshire T.V. I worked on shows like "How We Used To Live" and "The Racing Game," and on Granada "Strangers," "Me Lord," and of course "Crown Court seemed to go on forever, I was even promoted to police Sergeant on that one.

Before I knew it, the date was 17th May 1978 and I was heading for Butlins Pwllheli for 17 weeks on what was to be my very last season with Butlins.

Pwllheli was always very good for me, and I enjoyed every season there, and the biggest majority of the punters were from Scouse Land. Once again there was a great line up of Star names on the "Late Night Cabaret," and the season soon got into full swing. All the events that I was involved in were going very well, and once again it was proving to be a knockout season. On one occasion that I recall, one of the musicians, a bass player in the band was literally knocked out in one of the toilets. As he pulled the chain, the whole system fell down on him smashing him on the head, and cutting his arm. He reported it to the Security, and was told to go to the Security Office to make a full statement. Now in those days the Butlin Security were dressed in blue uniforms with a Gestapo style peek cap. It was like the Butlin Police, and some of them thought that they were in the Police Force. By this time the musician had his head bandaged and his arm was in a sling. He was sat waiting in the security office, when a security officer came in and sat at a desk in front of him complete with the necessary documents. He then asked the lad to explain to him exactly what happened as he was writing it down. He told him "I had just used the toilet, and I stood up and pulled the chain, the whole system above just disintegrated, collapsed and fell down on top of me." The security man then stopped writing, looked up at him and said "Was There Any Witnesses."!!

Chapter Thirteen

'Oh no - I'm On Selwyn Froggitt' I Join Ladbrokes But Not The Bookmakers, Back where I belong.

We were now at the end of July, and I got a message from the Entertainment Office to telephone my T.V. agent in Manchester. I rang her back and she told me Yorkshire T.V. had been in touch and they wanted me to play a telephone engineer in "Oh no, Its Selwyn Froggitt." Its five days, Monday to Friday starting on Monday 7th August" she said "will you be able to get away?" - "yes, that will be fine." I said "I'll do it." I didn't really have time to think, it would mean I would have to have the week off. Well they let me have time off for Frank Sinatra, so why not Selwyn Froggitt. I went to see my Entertainment Manager right away, and even though he felt it was a long time to have off, he agreed to it, as he could see, it could be a break for me. I signed the contract with Yorkshire T.V., and the script was sent to me a couple of days later. I had about five lines of dialogue, and a couple of good laugh lines at that.

On the second day of rehearsal I was wondering how I had got the job, as I knew that there were thousands of actors out of work. I was sat in the canteen having lunch with Bill Maynard and a couple of the other cast members when I turned to Bill and asked "how did I get this job?" - "I asked for you" he said "I saw you do a thing with the Ogdens on Coronation Street, and told the producer that you would be right for the part." He then told me that in the story Selwyn would be going in for these telephone quizzes, and the Froggitt household did not have a telephone, so an engineer would fit one in.

The rehearsals went well, and on the Thursday we were in the Studio, and the show was to be filmed in front of a studio audience on the Friday. When the recording started I was hoping that I would not have to do too many takes. Whenever I have done a sit-com that has been filmed in front of a live audience, it has always amazed me how the audience continued to laugh no matter how many times they do another take, but they always do.

I did my first scene and it all went well, then I made my exit, and was stood waiting just behind the set. A few minutes later, Bill Maynard came off the same exit then said to me "Well done Dave, you only had two laughs, and got both of 'em." - It was nice to hear that from the Main Man , and he gave me a lot of confidence. I remember once when he said to me, "Look, if I didn't think you could do it, you wouldn't be here." After the show we all had a few drinks in the studio bar to unwind, then Bill said "would you like to taste some Real Ale?" We didn't need asking twice, and he took three of us to a pub that he knew in Leeds, and it rounded off a truly wonderful day.

On the Saturday morning I drove back to North Wales to continue my season at Pwllheli, and there were about six weeks to go. By this time I had already fixed pantomime once again for Nelson Firth. After playing Abanazar I was keen to play some more bad guys, and this time I was to play the Bad Robber in "Babes In The Wood" at the Lancastrian Hall, Swinton. It is always a nice feeling when you have work in the book, and I was feeling good and very relaxed.

I had another excellent season at Pwllheli, and then on the 15th September 1978 I did my very last performance for Butlins. As I drove out of the gates, my mind was made up, and I was determined to find something new. I had always maintained and promised myself, that if I did not make the big time by a certain age, I would pack it in. I would never become an "old pro". Over the years I had seen many old pro's some of which I even remembered seeing in the Moss Empire days. It was a sad night to see some of them. They were well past their sell by date, and were just not funny anymore. The sad thing was, they did not even know it. They would die on their arse, come off, and think they had done well, it was pathetic. Not for me, I would make sure that did not happen to me.

I was now 40, and still had what it takes, and as many people know a comedian is not in his prime until he is in his forties. Unfortunately for me, I was loosing interest in working the clubs, and there were no theatres to speak of.

It would be nice to get into acting, and I knew I could do it, if I was given the chance. I continued doing T.V. Extra work, but I was finding that very frustrating especially after working on "Oh No Its Selwyn Froggit" and Coronation Street, where I had played small parts. I worked on shows like "Take My Wife," "Barmitzvah Boy" and "Fallen Hero," then I played a security guard on "the Racing Game" for Yorkshire T.V. followed by four days at Granada on "Collision Course."

I then took a one night stand at Tiffanys, Hull in an "Old Time Music Hall" show, it wasn't a knockout night, but it wasn't bad. The next day I was back at Granada T.V. playing a policeman on "Strangers," followed by a couple of photographic jobs.

The following week I had two more days on "Strangers," and this time I was asked to be one of the drivers of a police van. It was filmed outside an old warehouse, and on the first rehearsal we were asked to drive at high speed up to the wall of the warehouse, come to a stop, the back doors would fly open, and half a dozen extras dressed as coppers would jump out and run into the warehouse to catch the villain inside.

On the first run I did just that, stopped at the wall, and the guys in the back jumped out. The director then said it was not fast enough, and would I drive faster up to the wall. On the next take I drove up to the wall at quite high speed, as fast as I dare, I slammed on the breaks, skidded to a halt about four inches from the wall. As the back doors flew open the first guy fell out, and as I looked in the rear view mirror I could see the rest of them on their backs rolling all over the floor of the van, - take three - in actual fact we had about ten takes before it was right.

The night when one of Ken Barlow's wives died in a fire on "Coronation Street" I played a fireman. There were about four of us dressed in full fire fighters gear, complete with the oxygen cylinders on our backs, the full works. The call boy asked us to get all the equipment on about an hour before they were going to do the take. It was very heavy, and after standing up in it for about 20 minutes, we were all completely knackered.

We were eventually told to run into this smoke filled building, and to keep walking through the thick smoke until we saw one of the assistants at the other end. The smoke was so thick that you could not see a hand in front of your face. Suddenly we saw a torch flashing, and a voice was shouting "Keep coming this way" the voice then said "grab my hand," I put my hand forward, but could still only see the torch I then felt a hand take mine, and I was led outside back into the fresh air. We were then asked to climb up a ladder, when we came back down again, our legs were buckling under the weight of all the equipment. The Director then came up to us and said - "Look lads, you're not a bit like fireman, could you put a bit more effort into it?" to which one of the other fireman said "How can we put more effort into it, - we've had this fucking gear on for nearly two hours, and we're knackered."

We were then given a break before we did the scene again, and all went well.

We were soon into December, and the pantomime rehearsals began on Friday the 15th. As I have already mentioned I was cast as the bad robber, and I was teamed up with the good robber who was played by the old comic Jimmy Page. Jimmy was quite small around 5 feet tall and was in the Norman Wisdom mould. He was very experienced, very funny, and we hit it off straight away. He did have a reputation for being a heavy drinker, and if that were true it did not affect his work.

We made a very good team, and the more performances we did, the better we got to know and understand what the other would be doing. He would pull some strokes that only an old pro of his calibre would get away with. We would be doing a scene with the Sheffiff, and as we made our way up stage Jimmy under his breath would be 'effing and blinding, and calling the Sherriff terrible names as he would be into a long speech. Of course the audience could not hear him, only me and the Sherriff could. Fortunately for the Sherriff he was a very good actor, and it did not crack him up, but when we came off he would give Jimmy some stick..

I must say that the Pantomime had a very slow start, and the two robbers did not make their entrance until about eighteen minutes into the show. We would both be stood in the wings waiting to make our entrance, and Jimmy would always turn to me and say "The Pantomime Starts Here." - After a couple of performances I knew what he meant, and he was right. The kids loved him, and they loved to hate me, and every time we were on we had a ball.

At that time I had a long fur coat that I wore in the winter. I later wore it as a prop doing a Flanagan and Allen routine. Anyway one night I arrived at the theatre, hung my fur coat in the dressing room, and got changed into my panto costume.

During one of our scenes in "Babes In The Wood" we make an entrance into the babes bedroom. Jimmy would open the window at the back of the set and climb in, I would walk on from the side. On this particular night I made my entrance in the usual way sneaking into the Babes bedroom, but there is no Jimmy. I knew we had left the dressing room together, so he could not be far. I continued to creep around the bedroom when suddenly the window opened, Jimmy climbs in, and he is wearing a flat cap and my fur coat. He looked so funny as it was miles too big for him. The audience were roaring with laughter, and must have thought that he always dressed like that.

I did have a great time working with Jimmy Page, we had a lot of laughs, and that's always been the way I like it. The curtain came down for the last time on Saturday 20th January, and once again we all went out own ways.

It was now 1979, I had finished with Butlins (on good terms I must ad.) and now I was wondering about getting fixed up with a summer season elsewhere. I wrote letters to everybody that I could think of, and answered about every advertisement in the "Stage" newspaper. I even arranged for an audition at the Theatre Royal Stratford East, and for the Albany Players Rep Company. I travelled down to London, and I don't know why, but I didn't audition for any of them. With regard to the Albany Players, I met up with John Gordon-Ash in the West End, we had a nice pub lunch, a good talk, and that was it. John really talked me out of it, as he said the money would be an insult after what I had probably been used to. I honestly was not bothered about the money, but nothing came of it.

One of the people that I had written to was Terry Devine the former G.M. at Butlins Bognor, but was now the Managing Director of the Jersey Holiday Village. I had such a great success there when I was over in Jersey, and I felt it would be a great place to do a season.

He wrote back to me a very nice letter, but offered me a job as Entertainments Manager. I would also be able to do my own thing, and the season was from 16th February to the end of October. He said that if I was interested to let him know and we could discuss salary.

It sounded like a great offer, and was a hell of a long season but I didn't have to think about it too long before I turned it down. I was first and foremost a performer, and felt that I still had quite a bit to offer before I thought about going into management.

I guess I did turn down a plumb job, and I know lots of people that would have given their right arm for the opportunity, but I had no regrets and knew that I had made the right decision at the time. I was still doing quite a bit of T.V. extra work, and the odd photographic job came in every now and again. For every 20 letters I would write I may get six answers. One of the answers I got, was from the Entertainment Executive of Ladbroke Holidays, Jack Pound. I had never heard of Ladbroke Holidays before this time, when you think of Ladbrokes, you think of betting shops and gambling, not Holiday Centres.

Anyway it was arranged for me to go down to Watford for a meeting with Jack Pound and Gary Brown of the Gary Brown Organisation who apart from being the main Booker for the Cunard Cruise Line also did Ladbrokes bookings.

It was the middle of March and I recall it was terrible weather. The day before I was due to go to Watford, we were all snowed in and a lot of roads were closed. I was about to phone Jack Pound, when he rang me to postpone our meeting until the following week, as he was snowed in as well.

The meeting was set up for Monday 26th March at Ladbrokes Mercury Hotel, near Watford, for 2pm. I drove down to London on the Sunday and stayed at my parents' house. It was always a joy to go home to Islington and to see the family. On the Monday I set off for Watford, and arrived at the Mercury Hotel about 1.30pm.

I was shown to a waiting area in the foyer, and was surprised to see how many other guys there were after the same job. There must have been about a dozen of them. We were all sat on various sofas and arm chairs. They were quite a mixed bunch, some looked very smart in suits, and carrying brief cases, others were more casual, and a couple looked scruffy.

A couple of them, were the usual loud types trying to impress anybody that would listen, and I had met many of those over the years. It was usually the young inexperienced that would hang on to there every word. I have never had any time whatsoever for bullshiter's.

Anyway as I looked around me, I knew that this would not be the walk in the park that I had expected it to be. I was going to have to pull out all the stops at this interview, and sell myself really well. I was feeling confident, I had a good C.V. and photographs, and even took a couple of action shots of myself doing the "Lucky Dip Show."

People were being called up in turn about every 15 minutes. Eventually there were just four of us left and I was called. I was shown into one of the bedrooms where they were conducting the interviews. Jack Pound greeted me with a smile and a handshake, and introduced me to Gary Brown. It looked like they had been busy, as there were photos and cvs all over one of the beds.

They both fired questions at me that I was able to give a good answer to. Jack Pound then explained the job to me. It was for a compere/host in an adult only club, with a nightly Cabaret. The compere would be responsible for running the whole evening from 7.30 till midnight six nights a week, with one day off. It was a nice size venue of 600 seats. The interview went very well, and I could tell that I had impressed both of them. However I knew that they still had about three more applicants to see.

Gary Brown then said that he could let me know by tomorrow. I then told him that I was staying at my mothers house, but would be leaving London to go back up North by mid-day. "I'll phone you in the morning by 10.30" he said I then gave him my mums phone number, we all shook hands, and away I went. I was now back in the old routine of playing the "Waiting Game," although it wouldn't be that bad, as I knew I would know by 10.30, the following morning.

After spending a very pleasant evening with the family at Pleasant Place, I had a good night's sleep. The next morning after I had breakfast we were all trying to keep nice and relaxed, as we were waiting for the phone to ring. It then began to go through my mind, 'what if I didn't get the job' - 'maybe the other guys were on top of their game' - 'what would be my next move' - 'Nah, I'm sure its in the bag' - 'but you can never be certain I'd been to other auditions and interviews before that I was certain of, and they went pear shaped. - They had seen a lot of people, and they would only pick one. I looked at the clock and it was now 10.15, I was so confident when I came out of the interview, maybe I was over confident. But then you have to be confident or you never get anywhere. - Come to think of it one of those mouthy guys, who was full of himself, he was confident, he might get it the flash 'git - 'Ring' 'Ring' the phone 'Ring Ring', don't pick it up too quick I thought, don't want to sound too keen.

"Hello, Dave Thomas" - "Dave, its Gary Brown, how are you" "I'm fine thanks, how are you" - "I'm very well, and I'd like to say congratulations, you've got the job." After a bit more small talk, I thanked him and put the phone down. - result.

It was a very pleasant journey back up to Manchester. I had just fixed myself a 21 weeks summer season at Ladbrokes Caister Holiday Centre, as compere in the Holiday Inn, and the salary was £40 more than I had been getting at Butlins plus food and accommodation.

I had about six weeks to fill in before the season started, and after a couple of club dates in what can only be described as a couple of dumps, I decided not to take anymore club work, and continued with my T.V. work on shows like "A Case of Spirits," "Dandyke" "Love Among The Artists" and "Fallen Hero" to name a few.

Time past by and on the 14th May I set off for Great Yarmouth to start my season at Ladbrokes Caister Holiday Centre.

As I drove in the gates it struck me as a very small place to what I had been used to. At Butlins they could take 12,000 people, it was like a small town, but Caister looked like it would take maybe two-three thousand. I checked in at the reception and was given a nice welcome by the lady receptionist. She gave me my chalet keys and directed me to the dinning room where I could have a meal. I did not realise it at the time but I arrived during the Entertainment Managers Seminar. Jack Pound was there and he invited me to attend with the rest of the Ents Managers.

I tagged along and found it quite interesting. At one point a few cases of whiskey were produced, and everybody was given a bottle including me. I must say that I was very impressed as I had not experienced anything like this before. I was the only one in attendance that was not an Entertainments Manager, and as I looked around, I could see that they were not in the same league as the Butlin Managers. Anyway it was all very friendly and I got to know many of them very well.

As the days went on they would all be given various bags of "Goodies" from different sponsor's and I was always included. It was at this Seminar that I first met John Glass who was the master of Showbiz Razzamataz, that I mentioned earlier. John was also a very good speaker and got lots of laughs with his camp style. Caister Holiday Centre was a very nice site, it was well laid out, it had three clubs, and I soon found out that it was Ladbrokes Flagship. The main club was Neptune's Palace, it was a great room with excellent facilities. Then there was the Stardust nightspot that overlooked the outdoor swimming pool, it was a small room but had a very nice atmosphere and was for adults only. Finally at the end of the site by the beach was the Holiday Inn. This was the club that I would be working in and once again it was adults only. It was a great room, especially for a comic, and it was a venue that was to prove to be where I would experience some of my greatest nights ever.

My accommodation was situated at the back of the Holiday Inn, in fact it could not have been in a better location. It was on its own very quiet, and opposite the main Food Stores. There was always a very pleasant smell coming from the stores, in fact it was almost like living next to Sainsbury's.

As the weeks went by I became very friendly with the Store Manager, and he would look after me with regard to provisions. Of course I could eat in the dinning room, but my chalet was self catering so I had the best of both worlds.

After I had settled in for the first week Livvy came down, and I was able to fix her a job in reception. We had always been together on all of my seasons since 1969, and I didn't want that to change.

The compere that worked in the Holiday Inn the year before me was very popular, and for the first couple of weeks many of the punters would ask me where he was. This would always happen on the Saturday Night, being the first night of the week. His name was Stevie York, and I'm pleased to say that after my first appearance nobody ever mentioned him again. I remember one Saturday night about a month into the season, this mouthy girl came up to me and said in a loud voice "Where's Stevie? I knew who she meant of course, but I answered "Stevie Who" - "Stevie York" she shouted "he's the compere here." - "Not anymore he isn't" I said "well who's the compere then" - "I am" she looked at me for a few seconds before saying "you better be good." By the end of the week the same girl came up to me again and said "you're great, even better than Stevie York."

I must say that I was having a really wonderful time as compere of the Holiday Inn, and I would get the same faces coming in every night, they even had their own seats. I had a great four piece band working with me, they were excellent readers, and I had no complaints from any of the visiting cabaret artistes, quite the opposite in fact. Every act would comment on how good the band had been.

The keyboard player was a real jazz man and working with him was always a joy. I remember one night when I was doing "If The Rains Got To Fall," he played every rain song that you could think of. "Raindrops Keep Falling On My Head" "Pennies From Heaven" "Blue Skies, he did the lot, and then would come back to "If The Rains Got To Fall," I would just keep singing, and it was pure jazz. You don't have to be a great singer, if you have a great band, you just go with the flow.

As the weeks went on it would get better and better, and the Holiday Inn became my very own room, in fact I was Mr Holiday Inn. I arranged all the running orders and schedules for the week, and I was very conscientious about the room. I also had a girl organist that would play in the band breaks, and I always had her start at 7.00pm as people were coming in. The place would always be pretty full by 7.30, and by 8 o'clock you could not get a seat.

At 7.30 each night I would go on and make my first appearance, and just chat to the audience and welcome them in. It was a small dance floor in front of the band-stand, and it was nice and easy for me to do "Table Talk" to the front ring siders.

The main entrance doors were to the right of the stage, and as people came in I would welcome them, and talk to them as they made their way to their seats. It was all very intimate, and it made them feel part of it. After a couple of nights at the start of a new week, I would even get to know their names, and if a new face arrived and went to sit at a certain table I would say "sorry you can't sit there" and if they were to answer "why?" The whole audience would shout "because its Fred's seat." It became quite a feature. I must say at first I was quite amazed by this, and some of the regulars would come two or even three times a year, and each time they would sit at the same table. I would get really great laughs by just chatting to them about ordinary things.

Another great feature that I had happened by accident as many things do. One night before I went out to work, I was watching an episode of "Crossroads" on T.V. I cannot remember what it was about, but it must have been fairly interesting as it stuck in my mind. At 7.30pm I was on and after about 15 minutes of my "Table

Talk" I suddenly asked the audience "Did anybody watch Crossroads tonight?" to which about half a dozen replied "Yes" as they put their hands up. Then a couple of people said "No we missed it, - what happened?"

I then started to tell them, and of course I dressed it up a bit, and I was getting lots of laughs. Anyway I went through the whole episode in about 5 minutes, and although I say it myself, it went really well.

The next night I was on, then after about 15 minutes or so somebody in the audience shouted out "what happened in Crossroads tonight?" So I went through that episode with the same success. From then on I did "Crossroads" every night until the end of the season. It was great fun, the only drawback was the fact that I had to watch it every night. I did get through a lot of material over the course of a week, but I would spread it out evenly, and would only do a ten minute warm-up spot before each cabaret act went on, unless it was a comic, then I would do a song. I always remember one act that was a regular every other week liked my warm-up before his act, and said to me "going on after you have warmed the audience up, is like walking on velvet - I liked that. My "table talk" at the beginning of the evening would always be about 25 minutes before I introduced the band, and I never knew what I was going to do until I got on, except the Crossroads routine of course.

In the middle of the week I did a "Lucky Dip Show," and that was a great success, and Ladbrokes were never stingy with their prizes. As the night went on, the room would really be buzzing, and they would be stood three deep at the bar.

It got to a stage that when I was off, and stood at the bar, I couldn't wait to get back on again, the audiences were so warm and friendly, and I must have still been "stage struck". I was constantly having drinks bought for me, and it was difficult to keep up. Many times one of the Punters would be walking away from the bar with a tray of drinks and shout to me "Dave, I've put you one in behind the bar." Sometimes I would lose count of how many drinks were in the till for me, but when I would go to the bar when I arrived early evening, and went to pay for my drink the bar supervisor would say "you've still got about six drinks in from last night."

Of course I didn't over do it, as I needed to keep a clear head, but on Friday the last night of the week I must admit I did have quite a few. It was difficult not to, as I would have glasses of whisky lined up on the bar, and of course I did not want to offend anybody, but those Friday nights were some of the greatest memories of my career. Fortunately I did not have to go far to get back to my chalet, as the back exit doors were just about thirty yards from my front door, - and I always made it.

It was during the season at Caister that I realised the Entertainment Managers were not like the Butlin Ents Managers that I had been used to. They had no assistant, and no secretary, and many of them no class. I used to do two lunchtime sessions in the Holiday Inn, a midweek talent auditions, and a Sunday Lunchtime sing-a-long. It was on one of these lunchtimes that I went into the club early one morning to check on something when I saw the Entertainments Manager sat at one of the tables running a Dominoes Competition, I don't know if he was short of staff, but it didn't look right to me for the Boss to be doing that, I just couldn't get my head round it.

The resident Director at Caister was a man called Colin Wright, and he was the Gov'nor in every sense of the word. He was a big man with quite long grey hair, and horn rimmed glasses. He always looked immaculate and would have a big silk handkerchief tucked in his breast suit pocket. He was very "hands on" and spoke to all the guests, he was very fair to his staff, but when he said "jump" they would say "How high."

However he did have his critics, and some were in high places, but he got things done, I liked him very much, and he was a touch of class.

Word soon got around about the success of the Holiday Inn, and I guess that was the reason why we were packed out every night. I was so involved with the room, and focused on its success that I was completely oblivious as to what was going on elsewhere on the rest of the site. The Premier Room was Neptune's Palace, where they staged the big events, and the "Late Night Cabarets," and the Stardust Night Spot was an adult club like the Holiday Inn only smaller. I would never go out of my own room, as I was just not interested in anything that I wasn't involved in, and I could give one hundred per cent and focus fully on my own job.

I guess it sounds strange, but at that time I knew nothing about what was going on elsewhere. A few times I did go up to see the L.N.C. but it was always a pop group, and you couldn't hear yourself think. I did hear a story of a big T.V. Star who played a few dates at Neptune's Palace for free. Apparently he was paying back his gambling debts for Ladbrokes. I don't know if it was true, it could be, as he was well known for his love of horses.

The season was going along nicely, and the punters were now beginning to buy me presents on a Friday night, and I had to open them on stage. After a while the gifts started to get a bit saucy. Of course this only had to happen once, and then it snowballed. One lady knitted me a Willy Warmer, you can imagine the response that got. Then another occasion this old boy gave me a package all nicely wrapped up, and when I opened it, it was a Vibrator. I just said "Thanks that will come in handy when I am mixing my cocktails."

At the end of the night I took it back to my chalet, and put it on a table in the kitchen. About 3am we were woken up by a strange noise coming from the kitchen, I thought it was something to do with the fridge. I got out of bed to investigate, and was shocked when I saw the vibrator moving about all over the table, and it was still in its box. It had come complete with batteries, and it must have just triggered off on its own.

The next night I told the audience about it, and the old boy who had bought it for me shouted out "Them vibrators have got a mind of their own," he got a bigger laugh than me.

Up to now in my career I had never gone back to the same place twice on the trot. I always felt it was better to go to a different place every season. I had gone back to a place after I had a break from it, but never twice on the trot, but life was so good at Caister and the Holiday Inn, that I was beginning to think to myself 'I could do this again.' By now of course I was really feeling part of the Holiday Inn. I had even turned the dressing room from what could only have been described as a "shit-tip" when I first arrived into a very nice dressing room. I had acquired some new carpet for the floor, got a decent bit of furniture in, and would even go in, on the odd morning with some spray polish, empty the ash tray, and hoover the floor, it was spick and span and it looked a treat.

One day even Colin Wright came in and said to me "I've come to look at this dressing room that everybody is talking about." I then explained to him that when a cabaret artiste arrives if it's a nice room, and he has somewhere to hang up his gear, then he or she are in a good frame of mind, they are happy, and when they go on, they give a good performance. On the other hand if they turn up to find a "shit-tip" with nowhere to hang their clothes, they are in a bad mood before they start, and it can affect their performance.

The Governor was impressed, and it was then that he dropped a hint about me returning again next season. "Why not," I said "I'd love to come back" - "Good" he said "I'll get on to Jack Pound right away." A few minutes later he was gone, and I knew that I would be back next year in 1980.

As we came to the last week of the season, it was Finals week, when all the winners of the sponsored competitions come back. I was not involved in any of this, although I did run the adult Talent Competition that was staged in the Holiday Inn, but the Site Finals would all be staged in Neptune's Palace.

When I looked in at Neptunes and saw the stage sets, it was quite breathtaking, especially on the last night for the "Miss Ladbroke" Final. They had built out a cat-walk with red carpet, and in the centre of it all was this amazing water fountain. There were plants and flowers at the back of the stage, and also along the sides of the cat-walk. A new archway at the back of the stage had been built, it looked like no expense had been spared. The ten piece band had been moved on rostrums to the side of the stage, and when the Neptune's Palace first class lighting system was switched on, the whole set looked magnificent. I must say that this even put Butlins Final in the shade.

On the night of the Miss Ladbroke Final, Colin Wright invited Livvy and I to watch the event in the VIP enclosure. It was a section at the front of the stage of about 50 seats that had been roped off for specially invited guests all of which were in black tie and evening wear.

It was a grand night, and a swell affair, but as I watched it I felt that there was something missing, and that there was room for improvement. Little did I know at the time, that in two years time, I would be the one to make those improvements.

By this time I had already fixed pantomime once again with Nelson Firth. He had offered me the part of Abanazar once again in Aladdin back at the Lancastrian Hall Theatre Swinton. I was well pleased with that of course as it meant that I could work from home.

The season at Caister ended on the 6th October and I had enjoyed every minute of it. When I looked back over the season, I knew that I had stayed with Butlins for far too long. I had no idea what was going on in the Great Yarmouth area. There was an abundance of small holiday parks all over the area, and clubs in everyone of them. The area provided work for an act seven nights a week for twenty five weeks or more. Had I known about it a few years earlier, I would have been down there like a shot, still I guess it was no good thinking about what might have been. I had just finished a great season, had a panto lined up, I was fit and well, what more could I ask.

In the ten weeks before the Pantomime season I spent two weeks in London, did a couple of club dates, was out of work for a while, did some T.V. work for Thames TV on a show called "The Coo," a few days for Granada on a series called "Silk Drawers" and also "Fallen Hero."

In November we moved house from Heywood to a flat in Ramsbottom in Lancashire. It was a beautiful area, and very quiet. I liked it, but deep down, I was never a country boy. In early December I landed a role of a cabbie in one episode of the Granada series "Cribb" driving a horse drawn hansom cab. I had one line, the horse didn't move, and I got a credit in the T.V. Times. This acting lark is so much better than working the clubs!

The rehearsals for the Panto started on 21st December and I was delighted to be working with my old mate comedian Tony

Peers. We had known each other for a number of years from his days in the Butlin Revue Shows and we had also worked together on the Butlin Touring Shows.

Tony was playing Wishee Washee, and with me playing Abanazar we could have done some great things together, but unfortunately the script only had us on stage together on our own only once, but that one time it was a magic moment. After five great weeks the panto closed on Saturday 19th January, and we were now into 1980.

I was soon doing more T.V. work on shows like "Lives Of Our Own" and "Live from 2" for Granada "Good Companions" for Yorkshire T.V., and a couple of Commercials that were shot in Liverpool.

Six weeks after the Pantomime had finished, we were moving house again. It was Saturday 1st March 1980, St David's Day, we upped sticks once more and moved from Ramsbottom to London, to where I was born in Islington I was going home. - But was I making the right move?

Chapter Fourteen

From Performer to Entertainment Manager, To Actor in "the Gaffer"

I had been away from London, and living in Manchester since 1961, and nineteen years is a long time. It all looked different to me, and I figured it would take a bit of time to get used to. - By the next day, I was used to it alright, it was like I had never been away, Islington was in my blood, it was part of me, and I felt that I was back where I belong.

Of course I knew that I had left all of my contacts up north, and that it would be like starting all over again, but I had always sailed close to the wind, and was certain that things would work out. For a few weeks I had no work at all, and I was doing my best to make contact with a few London T.V. agents. I was eventually offered a days work at London Weekend T.V. on a show called "End of Part One," it wasn't much but it was a start. It was ironic I guess, but on our first trip back to Rochdale to see the family, I got two days work at Granada T.V. on "Strangers." Time past by and before I knew it we were into May and I was packed up and heading for Great Yarmouth, and my second season at Ladbrokes Caister Holiday Centre.

I was excited and looking forward to it, although at the same time, I was apprehensive I had no new material to speak of, and I knew that the Holiday Inn punters were a bit like homing pigeons, and came back year after year. I was asking myself 'would they laugh at my stuff for a second time?' Well I guess that I will soon find out. I will never forget the very first opening Saturday night, I walked into the club about 7.00pm, and the place was packed not an empty seat in sight. When I took a closer look at the faces I was stunned, as I recognised almost every face, and many of them were in the seats that they sat in the previous year. It was unbelievable, and it did knock me back a bit. I was due on for my first appearance at 7.30, and for the first five or six minutes I have a set routine, before I go into my "Table Talk." I was concerned as I knew they had all seen me do this routine before, last year. I heard a drum roll, and a cymbal crash, then the band leader introduced me. As I walked out into the spotlight, I was given a welcome that was out of this world. The applause went on and on, and it was quite a few seconds before I even said a word. I then went into the routine as if it was the first time that I had done it, and the response was fantastic, every gag was getting a 'whoofer. (a big belly laugh). In fact it was even better than the first year. It was then that I realised that if an audience know you, and like you its so much easier. And for a star name with a room full of fans, it's a walk in the park. Each night became better than ever, and I could do no wrong. A couple of weeks into the season, I was in the middle of my "Table Talk" when a voice shouted out "What happened on Crossroads tonight?" within seconds many other members of the audience also wanted to know. It had not been my intention to do it again, and I hadn't watched the episode that night. I just said "I don't know, it was doing my 'cad in, so I stopped watching it - but if you really want to know I'll start watching it again." - "Yes" came back the yells "start watching it again," then a bloke at a front table said "I can't stand it me'self, but I like it when you talk about it," and I can tell you he got a big laugh for that. Of course from then on I was back on to the Crossroads routine again until the end of the season.

 As the weeks went by it was like one big happy family. If ever I was on and anybody came in the front door at the side, I would always stop and let on to them whoever it was, sometimes I would recognise them and know their names, and ask them why they were late. Some of the answers I got would get roars of laughter. It didn't matter who got the laughs, if I was on stage at the time, half of that laugh was mine. I remember one night towards the end of the week, a bloke came in late, I said hello to him and had a few words as he made his way to the bar. I didn't think anymore of it, until I came off and went up to the bar. This guy then came up to me and bought me a drink, he then said "you know what Dave, I've not been in for a couple of nights, I thought I'd give the other clubs a try, but when I came in tonight, and you let on to me, it was great, it felt like I was coming home" "that's nice" I said as I picked up my glass "cheers, nice to have you back." - He then said "I tell you what, I've just come out of that Stardust Club, they had a comic on, and talk about blue, my wife and I couldn't stand it, we had to walk out. You should have heard the language, every other word, I don't wanna go on holiday and hear language like that, it was "fucking disgusting."

My second season in the Holiday Inn was proving to be an even bigger success than the first. The room was buzzing, and it was swinging every night. It was fun and laughs all the way. A couple of times during the season, a week at the beginning and a week at the end, we had quite a number of parties of handicapped people, and a lot were downs syndrome. They were always a joy to entertain, and I have never felt so humble.

They always had a wonderful time, and would be a wonderful audience. I was never sure if they understood all the gags, as very often they would laugh in all the wrong places, but I didn't mind that, as I could see they were all enjoying themselves.

I would always try to adapt to suit them, and I soon found out that their favourite word was knickers. If ever I said that word it would be greeted with howls of laughter. It was wonderful to see them, and I always felt that it was a great honour, to be able to bring a little bit of joy into their lives. They really were wonderful people, and were full of love.

Caister had a new Entertainments Manager for my second year, he was a nice enough guy, but did not appear to be up for the job. I think he was inexperienced, and it was getting a bit much for him.

I was in his office one day when he said to me "This job's not what I expected it to be, I was expecting to run all the Stage Entertainment, I don't know nothing about darts, and pool, and bingo, and all that stuff' he then told me how he depended on one of his Bluecoats Harvey, who did all the bingo sessions. "If it wasn't for Harvey" he said "I'd be in a right mess, he does all the bingo sessions, and he's keen to do them, I'm sure the little bastard is fiddling, but I don't care as long as the job gets done."

Harvey was in his second year, and an ex. Redcoat, he had ambitions of his own, and as the weeks went by I could see that far from being helpful, he was making things difficult for his boss.

In the peak weeks they had a "Donkey Derby," and seeing I was a pioneer of the Butlin Donkey Derby, I thought I would take a look, and see how it was run. It was staged on the football field at 10.30am on a Sunday morning, and I remember thinking at the time before I even got there 'that's not a good time for this event.'

When I got to the football field, it was a complete shambles. They had no proper tote facilities, and were selling tote tickets from the back of the donkey truck. The Entertainment staff had no interest, there was only a small crowd, there was no fun in it, in fact it looked like a complete waste of time. I watched a couple of races and left.

I guess it's the Ents Managers job to make sure that everything ticks, and there were quite a number of events that were not ticking. I had not even noticed anything on my first year at the site, as I was only interested in what was going on in my room. However on this second season I did take in a few events, and by what I saw, Harvey wasn't helping at all.

As the weeks went by, we got to about mid-season and the Entertainment Manager was removed from his position, and surprise, surprise the man who took over his job was none other than Harvey. It was only just over a week later, that the Resident Director Colin Wright spoke to me, and asked if I would be interested in the Entertainment Manager's job. I told him no, that I would not be interested in taking over in the middle of a season, but I may be interested in talking about it for next year.

By this time I was 42, and with the performances I was giving I knew that I was at my peak. If I did decide to go into management, now was the time. Like I said, I never wanted to become on "Old

Pro," and while I was still a good performer this may be the ideal opportunity for me to change direction in the business.

I then let Colin Wright know that I would be interested in doing the Ents Manager's job for next year. "splendid" he said in that rich deep voice of his "I'll arrange a meeting with Jack Pound, and let you know when." In the meantime Harvey was Caretaker Manager for the rest of the season. I must say that he was a cocky little sod, and did get too big for his boots.

One night he came into the dressing room in the Holiday Inn and said "Well done lads, you are all doing a good job in here. - one thing though, when the cabaret was on the band played a couple of flat notes on her second number," to which the keyboard player replied - "Harvey, - piss off." He didn't come back in a hurry, it was obvious that because he was the Ents Manager, he felt that it was his job to make a comment and he couldn't think of anything to say so he made something up about the "flat note."

A short time after that he even began telling people of his plans for the site next year, and he was very confident that the job was his. Of course I did not tell him that I had been offered the job, I figured that he would find that out sooner or later. After my meeting with Jack Pound, it was a done deal for me to take up the position of Entertainments Manager for the next summer, and I did not expect it, but I doubled my salary at Ladbrokes in just two years. The only draw back was that I had to do the Christmas week, and that meant of course that I would not be able to do Pantomime. I loved doing panto, and working in a theatre, as I suppose you could call it proper showbusiness, but there was nothing I could do about it.

I soon got used to the idea of working the Christmas period, and then began looking forward to it. I would be working in the main room Neptune's Palace, and that would be a new challenge for me. Neptune's Palace would always have a big band playing there, and on that second season was Ivy Benson and her all girl band. Ivy was quite a character, and used to spend all of her band break time playing the slot machines. She must have put a fortune in them. If she had been on a machine for a long time without it paying out, and was called back on the band-stand, she would then bend down and pull the plug out from the back, so that nobody else would be able to play in case the Jackpot came up. I don't know if it ever came up for her, I know that it never came up for most of her girl band, but that's another story.

1980 was one of my most memorable seasons in the Holiday Inn. It was a great success for me work wise, I made a lot of new friends. The Chef and the Stores Manager looked after me even better than the first year, and I would even see from my chalet window other departmental managers call in at the Stores, and load up their cars with a few groceries for the weekend, and why not, it was one big happy family at Caister, and I was glad to be part of it.

The season ended on the 3rd October, and that last Friday night was more than special in fact there is not a word good enough to describe it, the only word I have in mind, is the one I will have to use, I wish I could think of a better one, but I can't, - the only word is - fantastic.

We drove back home to London, and for the next three weeks or so I had no work, but was kept very busy painting and decorating our new home. I was of course making lots of calls and enquiries about getting some T.V. extra work in London. I was soon put in touch with a number of different agents, one of which was Johnny Lynn of the Alander Agency. Johnny had an office in Leicester Square, we had a meeting, he was quite easy to talk to, and he said that he would be able to offer me some work possibly the following week.

A couple of days later, he called me, and got me a days filming on the ATV series "Nelson" at Elstree Studios. Three days later I was booked for six days on the trot on the show, as a sailor on Nelsons Flagship.

It was a great show to work on, and I was one of the gun crews in a big battle. Some of the stunts were excellent, and one stunt man was set on fire, just before an explosion, and then throws himself across the deck in flames screaming in agony before the Director shouts "cut," and two crew men come and spray him with a fire extinguisher to put him out. He is then cleaned up again and put on his mark for the opening positions for another take. We did about four takes and it would amuse me when I heard the instructions. - "Quiet in the studio everywhere" - "running" - "mark it" - "set Jeremy on fire" - "and action."

It was a good week, and not a bad little earner, but of course I knew that it wouldn't last forever, and I soon had to find myself some more agents. Eventually I had four different agents that I was working for, and the best for me was Ivor Kimmel Casting. The first job he sent me on was for the BBC at Shepherds Bush as a stand-in on the "Generation Game" with Larry Grayson.

During rehearsals on the show, actors are used in place of the contestants, and they go through the whole show, and all the games. Even the interviews are rehearsed, and I must say that it did surprise me, when Larry Grayson came up to interview me, all the gags were written on the cards.

Anyway it was great fun, especially doing the games, one of which was plate juggling like they do down Petticoat Lane with all the jargon. I enjoyed that, did the jargon, didn't break too many plates, and thought I did okay.

The following week I did a training film at St Johns Wood Studio's with John Cleese for Video Art Films. I was now getting lucky with the London agents, and was getting a few days work every week. I worked on shows like "Westend Tales" at I.T.V. Studios Elstree. A show called "Bognor" for Thames T.V. at Teddington, and many others. I was called back a couple of times to work on Larry Grayson's "Generation Game," and I must say, that I enjoyed that the most as I was more involved.

I was not doing any club work now, but a week before I was due to start back at Caister for the Christmas week I had a cabaret date for the Norwich Brewery Social Club. I had this date in the book for quite a long time, as I was booked by a guy from the Brewery who was on holiday and had seen me at Caister in the Holiday Inn.

The very next night on the Saturday I was booked to do one spot at the "Hotel Norwich," in Norwich, for which I was paid £100, so I was quite happy to do selected cabarets, but I felt my Working Mens Club days were now over. We arrived at Ladbrokes

Caister Holiday Centre on the 22nd December for a weeks engagement, and apart from being the host and compere in Neptune's Palace I would also be the Entertainments Manager.

Christmas at Caister would always be a limited number of guests, with Neptune's Palace being the only venue open. By keeping the numbers down of course, all guests were guaranteed a seat and table. One of the first people I saw when I drove in the main gate, was Harvey. I don't think he realised what the score was, but he was very soon to find out. I was called to a meeting with Jack Pound in his office that was situated across the main road opposite the entrance to the site. Harvey was also in attendance, and when Jack told him that I would be in charge his face was a picture, I thought he was going to cry. Anyway he soon got used to the idea, well at least he looked like he had, and the meeting went well.

Of course there were lots of things to organise, and top priority had to be the arrival of Father Christmas on his sleigh in Neptune's Palace at 11 am on Christmas morning. All of the children would be given a present and you can imagine there were sacks full of presents for boys and girls in different age groups.

My opening night for the Christmas period in Neptune's Palace was a great success. The Christmas decorations in the venue were breath taking, and looked better than Regent Street. It was entirely different from working in the Holiday Inn, it was a far bigger venue, with much better facilities, but I soon got the measure of it, and early evening I had such good attention, that I decided to try some "Table Talk" with the ringsiders and its worked a treat.

Each night was better than the previous one, and on Boxing Night I noticed a lady in the front, take out a mince pie from her bag. She had obviously brought it out from the Dinning Room. "What's this?" I said "there's a lady here with a mince pie in her bag, - we 'can't have this, nicking the mince pies, I'll have to have a hand bag check." By this time I was getting a great reaction, with some members of the audience "grassing up" their mates, - "she's got some in her bag" a voice shouted out, - "and this ones got some Christmas cake" shouted another I said "I bet they've got more pies in here than Mr Kipling's factory."

I had a wonderful ten minutes with it, and continued my "Hand Bag Checks" for the remaining two nights. It had gone down that well that I thought I could improve on it. When I was asked back the following year to do my second Christmas, I arranged a plant in the audience. It was a lady who was a big fan of mine, and a regular punter in the Holiday Inn. She was a really big lady with a great sense of humour, and was known as Big Jean because of her size. She was always game for a laugh, and I asked her if she would pack some food from the dinning room into her bag. She was happy to do so, and when the night time came, she was even better than I expected.

When I did the handbag check, I went up to her table (she always got a seat in the front) and asked her to turn her bag out. She then produced two mince pies, a piece of Christmas cake, a sausage roll, a chicken leg, cheese and biscuits, the works, then I said to her "Is that it?" and she said "No I've got a banana and two apples for tonight"!! - You can imagine the laugh that got.

Anyway back to my first Christmas of 1980, It really was a wonderful experience, and I learned a lot from it. Father Christmas went down a treat on Christmas morning, and it was a joy to see the very tiny tots getting their presents from him. I had enjoyed it all so much I just knew that I would be back again for the next Christmas, as indeed I was, as I have already mentioned. I was even thinking ahead of what I would do to make things even better.

The week went by so quickly, that we were back home before we knew it, and bringing in the New Year of 1981. For all of us long suffering Spurs Fans we are always pleased to see a year that ends in one, as we always feel confident that our team will win a trophy having done so in 1901, 1921, 1951, 1961 and 1971. Well the Spurs did not let us down, and in 1981 we won the F.A. Cup for the sixth time.

I had no work for the first two weeks of the year, then I had a days filming on a show called "Strangers" for London Weekend T.V. Then the following day on Friday 16th January I had a meeting with Jack Pound in Watford. It was to tie up a few loose ends, and a briefing on the coming summer season, that would be my first season as an Entertainments Manager.

It was a good meeting and I was pleased with the outcome. I would still be able to keep my hand in as a performer, but I was happy to phase it out slowly. With three clubs to run at Caister I would have a resident compere in each, who in turn would have a day off each week, and I would cover their nights off. It would also be a nice change, as I would work a night in all three different venues.

The terms were agreed, the contracts were signed, and I was really looking forward to a new chapter about to start in my career. The season would start on 1st May and run for 23 weeks. At the end of January I had three days work on a beer commercial at the Lees International Studios Wembley. This was followed by a day on the "Bracks Report" for Thames T.V. at Teddington. Soon afterwards I did an audition for a "Double Diamond" beer commercial at Lexington Street, and I got it, and once again I was back at the Lee International Studios. I then went for another audition for a Stones Bitter Advert. I don't know why they call them auditions as all they do is take a Polaroid picture of you. Anyway I got that job as well, and it was filmed at the Halifords Studios at Shepperton.

I was kept quite busy with the T.V. Extra work, and the odd commercials, and I only had about four weeks when I had no work at all. It took me up to the start of the summer season, and on the 1st May we set off for Great Yarmouth and Ladbrokes Caister Holiday Centre. Being an Entertainments Manager was a whole new ball game to what I had been used to, but I was certainly up for the challenge.

I guess it was quite a big responsibility to run a site as big as Caister, and indeed it was Ladbrokes flag-ship site. Of course compared to Butlins it was small, but it could take 4,000 punters so I guess it wasn't too small. I had a staff of fourteen Blue-coats, four life guards, and three games room attendants. The life guards would do Blue Coat duties in Neptune's Palace in the evenings when the pool was closed. They were not particularly interested in the job, but they liked the Blue Jacket as it was good for pulling the crumpet.

I remember one day, it was only the second week of the season I was having a walk about around the site, and I walked in to check out the swimming pool. This lifeguard came straight up to me and started to talk, but in all fairness to him, he did not take his eyes off the pool. I was also looking in at the pool, and could see no problems. Then suddenly, he dived in, and pulled out a bemused looking boy. As soon as he got him out onto the side of the pool, the boy jumped back in again. I then said to the life guard "what did you pull that boy out for? - he didn't look like he wanted to come out" to which he replied "I thought he was drowning." It was so obvious that he was trying to impress me.

Of the three comperes that I had, one was really outstanding. He was a Welsh comic called Phil Jones, and I was pleased that he was in the Holiday Inn. Like me he was a former winner of the £1,000 People Butlin Talent Contest. His style was completely the opposite to mine, and he would get away with murder, and use material that I wouldn't dare use.

He once said to me "every week people talk to me about Dave Thomas, so I 'ave to use strong material or I would die on my 'arse." He never did die of course, and he even made me laugh.

In Neptune's Palace I had the best band that I have seen on any holiday site, it was the Christy Lee Band. Christy Lee was Britain's No. I girl drummer, with a ten piece band including three front singers. I was delighted that she was with me, as I knew her very well having done a couple of season with her before, when we were both at Butlins.

In the three clubs we had different Cabaret every night, and Thursday was the Late Night Star Cabaret. I always compered the L.N.C. myself, and did the warm-ups I would then introduce the Neptunes Compere to do a short spot before the star attraction.

I wanted to make the L.N.C. a special evening as it always was at Butlins, and was fortunate enough to have three girl dancers that would open the show. I would do a fifteen minute warm-up, then introduce the dancers followed by the singer doing three numbers and then the Top of the bill, and it worked very well. I had heard through the grape vine that the LNC on the other Ladbroke sites, had no warm-ups, no dancers, no support act, it was straight into the top of the bill. I drew upon my experiences from working at

Butlins on how to run many events that were in the programme. I also knew that I would need an assistant and somebody that I could trust, and who is better than my wife Livvy.

I fixed it so that she would be my assistant manager, and we became the perfect team. Livvy would look after the Bluecoats and organise all the daily details, and do the paper work, and I would organise all the evening entertainment taking care of all the cabaret acts, comperes, bands and musicians DJs, various artistes in visiting touring shows, wrestling and sports personalities. I would always do my best to meet every cabaret act that arrived, and after their performance to go backstage to the dressing room to thank them. Being a performer I knew how they felt, and that they would appreciate that. Of course it would take me about four weeks before I could get round to see everybody perform in three different clubs. I would not take a day off for the first three weeks, so that every act would see the Entertainments Manager, and not feel ignored.

I have always admired and had great respect for musicians, it must be really wonderful to sit down at an instrument especially a piano and make beautiful music. For the truly great musicians it's a gift from God. But as the saying goes "where there's talent, there's temperament", and most of them are indeed a lot of temperamental buggers. Musicians are a special breed, and I love 'em, but you have to know how to handle them, and treat them with respect. I think I had the knack and over the years I have always got on well with them, and been able to sort out any problems that they had.

During my years as an Entertainments Manager I only had to sack two bands. One of those was a Hi Tech Band that I did not consider being musicians anyway as their instruments were like computers and played themselves. The other band were good musicians but had no discipline they were continually late on stage, and would come off early. I gave them so many warnings I lost count of how many. In the end it was clear to me that they were "taking the P," - and they had to go.

The Donkey Derby was an event that I knew I had to sort out after seeing what a disaster it had been when I had watched it the previous year, with a hand-full of people watching. I had a meeting with the resident Director Colin Wright, and he agreed to spend some money on making up some sets and Tote Board numbers. I changed the lay out of the track to a half circle, we had bunting put up to make it look like a real event. The accountant was in attendance to organise the tote sellers, I was up on the rostrum to do the commentary, and as the Donkeys paraded round the track just before the first race a big crowd had gathered, and it was a great success. A lot of money was taken over the tote, and it looked like everyone was a winner - well maybe not everyone, but I'm sure that everyone had a good time.

In between races we organised a few fun sporting events with the Bluecoats so that something was always going on. As the season went on I was learning all the time, and although I say it myself I think I was getting quite good at man management. If a member of the staff were to come into my office about a problem that they had, nine times out of ten they would leave the office with a smile on their face and feeling a lot better than when they came in.

We would run the department firm but fair, and it is most important to have discipline. Of course it is also important to have laughs, and be happy in the job, as I would always say "a happy ship is a successful ship." It would always please me when I would see how the Entertainment Team would shape up, work as a team, be proud, and want to be the best

Of course over the years there would always be the odd slackers that were not cut out for the job. If you had a bad apple that could be bad news for the rest of the team, I have never suffered fools gladly, and I would always get rid of any Bluecoat that I thought would upset the apple cart. It was never a nice experience to sack anybody, but as the saying goes "it's a dirty job, but somebody has got to do it."

It was an awful experience especially if they would not accept it, and if it was a girl who had burst into tears. The boys would normally know why they had been carpeted, but I remember one girl once, who was in tears and pleaded with me to let her keep her job. She even said to me that if she was sent home her mother would kill her for being a failure. I very nearly weakened, and thought of giving her another chance, but when I thought of how she had conducted herself, and been given two written warnings, I knew that she was bad news and would never change, - No - I thought she's got to go, - if her mother doesn't want her why should I.

One night I was in the Stardust Nightspot and a comedian was on doing his act. He was not going too well, a group of about four lads who had quite a bit to drink, were giving him a bit of stick. They were heckling, but he was doing ok with his comments back to them. I could see that he wasn't too happy with the situation, but as far as I was concerned it was not out of control, and of course I had been in the same situation myself. The heckling continued, and by now the lads were laughing at their own remarks, and so were the audience, in fact it looked like everybody was enjoying themselves except the Comedian on stage. He finished his act, and got quite good applause, with the loudest cheers coming from the hecklers.

Soon afterwards he came up to me with a face like thunder to complain about the hecklers. I took him over to a quiet corner, and listened to what he had to say. He felt that the hecklers should have been asked to leave by the security, the actual words that he used were "they should have been chucked out." He was a young comic, and was of course still learning the business. I then explained to him that he should be proud of himself as his performance had played the major part in what was a very entertaining evening.

"If I had got security to chuck those guys out, it would have caused a massive disturbance, and you would have lost the audience all together." I said "When those guys go back to their accommodation tonight they will be saying what a great night they have had, and its all down to you. If you had not been on they wouldn't have had such a good time, they may have got laughs from the audience, and your act may not have gone the way you had planned it, but they would not have got any laughs if it had not been for you. - Don't you forget it, they were your laughs, as you created them."

He thought for a moment, then a smile broke out over his face. "You know, I never looked at it like that, - your right, I'll remember that in future, - Dave, let me buy you a drink." A smile then broke over my face as I said "Thanks, I'll have a pint of Guinness."

During the summer my brother Tony would pop over to Islington every couple of weeks to see our mum and take her out for a walk. They would always go round to my basement flat to check that everything was ok, and send on the mail.

It was one such visit, when mum and Tony were having a cup of tea, when the phone rang. Tony picked up the phone to find that it was one of the Manchester T.V. Agents that I had worked for. He explained to her that I was away for the summer season, so she asked him to contact me, and get me to give her a call asap and it was urgent.

He got in touch with me that same day, and when I rang the agent back she told me that Yorkshire Television had been on to her, and they wanted me to play the electrician Sparky Bright in "The Gaffer" with Bill Maynard. It was for a week commencing Sunday 29th November.

Of course I was delighted, but I realised how lucky I was that Mum and Tony had been in my flat at the very moment that the phone rang, being in the right place at the right time, was never more appropriate. If they had not been there, the agent would not have known where I was as she was not my sole agent, I would have lost the part, and it would have gone to somebody else.

As the weeks went by, I must say that my first season as an Entertainments Manager was most enjoyable. Of course there were ups and downs, but that was all part of the job. It was so close to the TV Show "Hi De Hi" that you would not believe it, but all in all it was a real ball.

When the finals came at the end of the season, I really wanted it to be a great spectacle, especially the last night with the site Final of the "Miss Ladbroke Holidays." I wanted to do a curtain raiser. The carpenters built another great set, and I got them to make me an old victorian lamp post, that would be set at one side of the stage, with a dimmer switch so that the lamp would light up slowly.

The idea was for me with two other boy singers to stand under the Lamp post and sing "Standing on the corner, watching all the girls go by." As we sang the song the girls would walk past us, and down the rostrum and inter-change with choreographed movements. At the rehearsals in the afternoon, you could see that this was going to be a bit special. It took quite a bit of time to get the girls going in the right places, but we got there in the end.

The room was full of noise and activity before I could start working with the girls. The carpenters were banging nails in here and there, the gardeners were putting the plants and flowers in place, the judges tables was being set up with a green baize flowers, water jugs, glasses, ash trays, and everything you would expect to find at a Judges Table, not forgetting printed name plates.

At one point everybody was asking me questions, and I guess as the boss I had to expect that. Fortunately I was able to give them all the right answers. As happens on these sort of occasions, tempers sometimes got a bit frayed, and its funny how people always want to put their two-penneth in.

Eventually I was working with the girls on stage, and things began to take shape, when the Guvnor Colin Wright walked down to the front of the stage and started putting his two penneth in, I looked down at him, stopped him in his tracks and said "Excuse me, but who's In charge here?" - For a split second the whole place went quiet, and a few close by stood with their mouths wide open, as their jaws dropped to the floor - "I'm so sorry David, your absolutely right, I won't say another word." - He backed away, and everybody carried on with what they were doing.

I guess everybody looked shocked, as nobody had ever spoken to him like that before. Colin Wright was the Guvnor, the main man, and I had a lot of respect for him, and on that occasion he confirmed what I always thought, that he had a lot of respect for me. The band were well rehearsed and sounded great, and we rehearsed an appropriate tune to play on each of the five judges.

The night time came, and it was a fantastic success as were all the other finals. Colin Wright was over the moon, and I could see that he was as proud as I was. He was a wonderful host at the after show party, and the champagne was flowing. It was a swell affair and I enjoyed all the bouquets. On the last night of the season Colin Wright was talking to me about his plans for next year. - Could I do another year as Entertainments Manager here.- It was a nice feeling, I had next summer sorted, and before that, I had some acting to do.

After about ten days break, I got two days work on "The Gentle Touch" for London Weekend T.V. playing a policeman. I then worked on "Murphys Mob" at ATV Elstree, "Nancy Astor for the BBC "mitch" for London Weekend, then back at Elstree for ATV on a show called "pictures." This took me up to Sunday 29th October, when I reported for rehearsals to play my part of Sparky Bright in "The Gaffer," for Yorkshire T.V. The first read through was at 2.00pm at the Hyde Park Recreation Club, Headingley in Leeds. I had about five pages of dialogue, and felt very grateful to Bill Maynard for his continued confidence in me.

When I looked around the rehearsal room I knew that I was in good company, apart from Bill there was Russell Hunter, Pat Ashton and Chris Langham, and the Producer/Director was Alan Tarrant. The rehearsals were great fun, and it was a joy to see the actors deliver their lines, and then fall about laughing. Of course I had seen that before with Bill when I worked with him on "Selwyn Froggitt" and the director on that occasion was Ronnie Baxter.

We were in the rehearsal room for four days, then on the Thursday we were in the studio where you could really get the feel of things.

The show was recorded in front of a live audience on Friday 4th December. It was a great night, and I enjoyed every minute of it.

Sparky Bright was a great character to play, he was chirpy with a sharp wit. Unfortunately for me, it was the last episode of the series so Sparky Bright was just a "one off." I only wish that I could have had a run with him, as I'm certain that I could have developed that character and made Sparky Bright real special. - Well I guess it wasn't to be, and as the saying goes "that's the way the cookie crumbles."

The following week I was back as a stand in on "The Generation Game" with Larry Grayson for the BBC. The "Gen Game" was always recorded at the old Shepherds Bush Empire. I remember saying to Larry Grayson, "did you ever play here?" to which he replied "No did you" - thought 'I wish.'

On stage with Ken Dodd.

Miss Ladbroke finals, 1982.

The cockney in me, for "The Sing-a-long Show", 1990.

The Dallas Boys, give me a bottle of Champagne on my birthday, June 1990.

My "Havenmate Show" of 1993.

Late Night Cabaret with Tom O'Connor and my dancers, Tracy and Jo.

I always enjoyed playing the Chairman in "Old Time Music Hall".

The Flanagan and Allen routine. with band leader Mick Urry.

Late Night Cabaret at Caister.

With the General Manager, Mike John, presenting a prize to a Miss Haven winner. Hastings 1990.

With Kathy Staff and King Rat, in "Dick Whittington". My very last panto 1993.

With ex corrie star Chris Quinton and singer Keily Hampson. Panto 1993.

DAVE THOMAS

Publicity photo's, 1980's.

It's a tough job but somebody has to do it. Compereing the finals of the "Miss Haven". Presthaven Sands 1997.

Performing days almost over. Busy at my job as Entertainment Manager, 1997.

One of my last performances.

Me and my mate Crumble take a stroll on Broadway, New York.

CHAPTER FIFTEEN

A Randy Bass Player, An iffy Beauty Queen and a Bum Competition. The Big Red Book, Santa Claus Is Missing

It was now the 21st December and I was on my way to Ladbrokes Caister Holiday Centre for my second Christmas Season.

When I arrived back on the site, it was like coming home. It seemed like all the punters were the same as the previous year I can remember standing outside Neptune's Palace speaking to a member of staff, and as the cars drove past on their way to reception they would toot their horns, wave their arms and call out my name. They would all have big smiles on their faces, and it was a wonderful feeling to know that they were so pleased to see me.

When you get adulation of that nature, you always feel pressure, as you know that you have to be on top of your game, and deliver the goods. After the first night I soon realised that there was no need to worry as the response I got from the audience was truly amazing. Like I have already mentioned, if an audience knows you, and likes you, it's a walk in the park. But by the same rule, you must never take an audience for granted, and always show them the same respect that they show you.

It was on this second Christmas at Caister that my running gag of the handbag check, went down so well and as previously mentioned I used big Jean as a plant. Having said that there were many genuine cases that I didn't know about that had their handbags stuffed with all kinds of goodies.

Once again it was a wonderful week, and the atmosphere was terrific, we made so many friends at Caister, and it was just like one big happy family. The last night finished on a high, and as we made our way home the following morning I thought to myself what a great year it had been, and was wondering what the New Year would bring.

Big Ben chimed at midnight and it was 1982. My first job in January was for the BBC, on a show called "Goodbye Mr Kent" it was filmed at the old Golders Green Hippodrome. As I looked around at the old building I would once again think how wonderful it must have been to have played in all these old Theatres. If only I had been born thirty years before I actually was, that would have been the right era for me. I always felt that was real showbiz. Anyway I knew that I must be thankful for the showbiz that I am in today, and lets face it, it's a lot better than a proper job.

I was continuing with my T.V. extra work, with the odd line here and there, and also a few T.V. Commercials that came my way. By the end of February I decided to audition for the Tavistock Rep Company, who were based at the Tower Theatre Canonbury, in Islington. It was an amateur company, but it was such a professional set up that you would never know. Of course they would not take anybody, and would hold auditions every now and again. I figured if I could do a few plays with them it would give me the acting experience that I needed.

The auditions were held at the Tower Theatre, and I had prepared two contrasting pieces. The first was a piece from Bill Naughton's "Alfie" and that was just up my street. For my second piece I did the man from the Foreign Office, Richard, from "Rogers Last Stand" by Dimitri Frenkel Frank. I was very happy with the way things had gone, and was even happier when I was told that I had passed the audition and was now a member of the Tavistock rep company.

The first meeting that I attended at the Tower Theatre, I did not feel too comfortable, and it seemed a bit cliquey, and I felt like an outsider. I recall speaking to one girl who had seen my audition, and was quite friendly. I asked her how many new members they took each year, and if there were anymore new ones with me. She then said "we get quite a lot of actors who pass an audition, and then we never see them again." That did surprise me, but I thought 'I'll just see how it goes.' One thing did concern me, and that was the fact that I would be away for seven months doing Summer seasons, and if I had any decent T.V. jobs coming in, I could not commit myself one hundred percent to the company.

After a couple of weeks they began casting for a couple of new plays, and you would have to audition again for the parts. I was invited to audition for one of the parts in a two hander. They sent me the book, and as I began to read it, I found that it was quite heavy stuff, in fact to be honest I couldn't even understand it. - How the hell could I give a good performance in a play that even I didn't know what I was talking about. I tried to learn the part as best I could before the audition, and after about a week the director rang me to let me know the time and details.

On my way to the audition, I was thinking that I don't really want this part, and I wasn't at all happy with it. The lines that I had learned I couldn't remember, so it was more or less a reading, and I am what I would describe as a real lousy reader. Anyway I did the audition, it wasn't good, and it's the only audition that I have attended in all my life that I was hoping I would fail. - Well I know that if I had been the Director, I wouldn't have given it to me, but you never can tell, it's a funny old game, and strange things happen.

The Director was a woman, and what if she fancied me, - I was now beginning to get worried, I could end up on that stage with a Theatre full of people, spluttering out words that I had no idea what they meant it would be a complete disaster, and all because the Director wanted her wicked way with me. All kinds of things were going through my head, but before I had time to say - "Walter Mitty," I got the news. - I didn't get the part. - result!!

Soon afterwards I started getting busy with T.V. work, and I didn't go back to the Tavistock Rep Company, as I couldn't seem to fit in the time. It was a pity, as I would have loved to have been part of the set up, as they really did put on some wonderful productions.

At the end of March I worked a day on a thing called "Radio Phoenix" at the T.V. Centre Southampton. This was followed by two more days on "The Gentle Touch" for LWT, and then on Saturday 3rd April I drove up to Birmingham to Villa Park where Spurs were playing Leicester City, in the Semi-Final of the F.A. Cup. I didn't have a ticket, and it was the first and only time that I have bought a ticket from a tout. He was a young black lad, who only looked about 14. I took him with me to the turn style to check that the ticket was genuine, before I gave him his money. It was, I paid him, and I was in. It was worth every penny, as Spurs won the match 2.0 and went on to Wembley to win the F.A. Cup for the seventh time in the clubs centenary year 1982.

When I got back to London, the work was quite steady, and apart from the usual T.V. shows that I worked on quite regularly, I was fortunate enough to work on a number of commercials including "Worthington bitter, "Nat West Bank" the "Post Office," "Halifax Building Society and "Guinness" to name a few. I then did a day on "not the nine O'clock news" and "Love Story" for the BBC.

This took me up to the beginning of May, and on the 3rd May we set off once again for Gt Yarmouth for my forth season at Caister Holiday Centre, and my second as Ents Manager. That first week was a five day seminar for all the Ladbroke Entertainments Managers. They were quite interesting and most of the presenters doing a presentation were very good. But there were also a few that were boring and would send you to sleep. All in all though it was quite a social gathering, and a good opportunity to meet other Entertainment Managers from other sites. At that time most of them were experienced performers in their own right, unlike today of course, where you would be hard pushed to find an Entertainment Manager who has ever walked on a stage before, apart from one on a Holiday Camp.

I would always be pleased when the seminar was over, and all the other Ents Managers had left my site, as it would enable me to get on with the job, and train my own staff in my own way.

Each year you would have different Bluecoats, and there would always be a few that you would have back from the previous year, and that would give you a good start. Over the years there were many characters, and you could fill a book about them alone, I only wish I had kept notes on them. Of course I can remember some of them very well, and we will go into that later.

The season soon got under way, and it soon seemed like we had never been away from the place. To think when I first came here in 1979 as compere in the Holiday Inn I only intended to do the one season, and here I was now into my fourth.

Of course now that I was the Entertainments Manager, and was doing less entertaining myself I guess it didn't matter anymore how many seasons I came back, so I guess I may do it as long as the Management keep asking me. I was well into the job now, and enjoying it. Each day was different, and of course there were the odd problems to solve. Handling the cabaret artistes, and musicians was a walk in the park, as I was on their wave length and they were all Pro's. The funny thing was, the hardest part of the job was looking after the Bluecoats. Some of them couldn't get out of bed in the mornings, and others thought they were on holiday, and were only interested in how many conquests they could make in a week. I didn't have a problem with that, as long as they did the job first, but I guess that's the difference between amateur and a pro.

Over all the Entertainment Staff were very good, but as I have said before you always get the odd bad apples. It always reminded me of the time years before with a Butlins Ents Manager. He would employ two extra Redcoats that he did not need, and then after two weeks, he would sack a couple that were not shaping up. "It keeps the others on their toes" he would say. I could not do that as I didn't employ the Bluecoats personally, but a few years later I did attend recruitment, and was able to pick my own staff and that was so much better, in fact the years that I picked my own, I didn't lose anybody, except on just one occasion, - well I guess we all make mistakes.

I remember one season I had to get rid of a Bluecoat, and I was awaiting for a girl replacement that was being arranged from Head Office.

In one of the bands that year we had a bass player that was a ladies man of the first order. I don't know how he kept it up, but he always had a different girl coming out of his chalet every morning.

Word got round that apart from the punters, he was making his way through all the girls on the Bluecoat Team. I didn't mind as it kept a smile on their faces, it didn't effect their work, and what people do in their own time, is their business.

Anyway the new girl arrived, and after a few days it was clear to me that she would be no good for the job. It may not have been her fault, as she should never have been employed in the first place, she could not do anything right, and apart from that, she had a very bad attitude. One night I walked into the club that she was on duty in, and I was in despair to see how she was conducting herself.

I then went into the dressing room to see the band who were on a break. After we had a bit of a chat, and I was about to leave, the ladies man bass player said to me "How's the new girl getting on?" to which I replied "Don't ask, - I think she will have to go" as I went to open the door he called me back, "Dave - give 'us a week will 'yer," and the rest of the band burst out laughing.

Within a week, she was gone, but I never did find out if it was long enough for our amorous bass player.

That year I worked for the first time with Peter Collins who had won "New Faces" with Pete Collins and Style, I remember the night they won, as they certainly did have style, and were a class act. Peter was working solo now, and was quite a regular at Caister over the years, and of course he was a local boy.

I will never forget the first time I saw him work, he was on stage doing his thing, and I must say he was a good looking guy. I was stood at the bar watching his act, when one of the Bluecoat boys came up to me and said "doesn't he look good for his age? - I tell you what, I hope I look like that when I'm 41 don't you?" - "I sure do" I said. At that time I was 43.

By now Caister was not only staging their site finals, but we were also hosting the National Finals as well at the beginning of the season for the previous year. No expense was spared and they were wonderful events. On my second year I did however have a minor problem with the "Miss Ladbrokes competition national final."

All of the finalists were the winners of site Finals from their respective sites around the country. At the first meeting we discovered that one of the smaller sites in Devon had sent two winners. As if that wasn't complicated enough when I saw the two winners, what a shock that was. One of them was a non-starter, she was in her late forties, her dyed blonde hair had gone frizzy, and to be quite honest she looked an absolute mess. The other woman wasn't much better, she looked about 35, but would look totally out of place on a cat walk with eighteen and twenty year olds.

Jack Pound told me what I had to do. I had two options. One was to talk to them and see if one would stand down, and the second was to run an extra heat with just the two of them in it. I did not fancy the second, as with just two in a heat, and knowing what they looked like, it would be a complete farce. I thought the first option was the only one, and I was confident that I would be able to get one of them to stand down.

She would still be able to have the free holiday, and enjoy the week. I figured that the one that looked a bit 'iffy, surely she knows she looks 'iffy and will stand down. I then arranged to see the two women in my office, and explained the situation to them. The first one to say anything was the iffy one, - well they were both iffy but she was by far the iffier of the two. "I'm not standing down" she said "why should I?" - "and neither am I" said the other. "But you do realise that you will have to compete against each other in a heat of two." - "That's okay by me" - "and me."

I could not believe what I was hearing, I was gobsmacked, - these two - thought they were beautiful, I could just not understand how these two women could have such a big opinion of themselves. I know that age does not come into it, as there are lots of beautiful women in their fifties and beyond, but this was not the case here, I only wished that it was. It soon became clear that neither of them would change their minds, and I arranged for an extra Heat.

We run the heat in a morning, it was an embarrassing event, and when they both turned up wearing swim suits, it really did put me off my lunch, it was even worse than I expected it to be. Thankfully it didn't last too long, and the inevitable happened. – The 'iffy' one lost.

It was in 1982 that prior to the season opening they had given the Holiday Inn a complete makeover. They also changed the name to The Old Bull N Bush. It looked really good, and had a Victorian flavour. I decided to stage an Old Tyme Music Hall in there once a week, I used the tried and trusted format of my Butlin days, and I played the chairman.

It was a great success and once again proved to be a winner. The Welsh comedian Phil Jones was back in his second year as compere, and of course by now he had a great following. It was great to see, and I was delighted that the old Holiday Inn, now known as the Bull N Bush was in its fourth successful year of packed houses.

It was sadly to be its last. I didn't know then, but after that year and for the years to follow it slowly went into decline. Phil was a funny man, and as I have already mentioned he would get away with murder. What I liked about him though was that he was never offensive, he never used four letter words and you could take your old mother to see him. Having said that, there are other comics I know that could use the same material and make it sound crude and very offensive indeed.

If I walked into the room and Phil was on he would say to the audience "I was going to tell you a really rude joke, but Dave Thomas has just come in, and if I do, he will give me the sack." You can imagine the reaction that he would get from that, I was cast as the villain, and a real spoil sport, but it was great fun.

One night about mid season he announced to the audience "Ladies and Gentlemen, on Friday night we are going to do The 'airey 'arse competition." I could hardly believe my ears, but the audience roared with laughter. Then on Friday night with the audience waiting in anticipation, he would hold one hand up to his ear, as if he were on the phone and say "Ladies and Gentlemen, I've got some bad news for you, - I've got Dave Thomas on the phone, and he tells me that we 'Can't do the 'airey 'arse competition - what's that Dave, yes I've told them all, and they all agree with you, that we shouldn't do it, - that's right, you all agree don't you?" With that he would then hold his outstretched arm to the audience as if he had a telephone in his hand and in one voice the audience would shout out "No" - he would then put his hand back to his ear "Did you here that Dave? They all agree with you, the 'airey 'arse competition's off." He did this as a running gag every week, and it worked very well for him. Then on the very last week of the season he asked me if he could do it for real. I told him that I had no objection, but I didn't think he would get anybody to enter.

On the Friday night he got a white sheet strung across the Archway at the back of the stage with four big round holes cut out. It was all set up, there was a drum roll, and he announced "its now time for the 'airey 'arse competition would all male contestants who would like to take part please make their way back stage through that side door."

What followed next was quite unbelievable, it was a stampede of blokes rushing to get back stage. He even had a judges table set up, and when he asked for three lady judges, that was another stampede of women to get to the table. When the event eventually got under way, it was an hilarious site to see their bare bums through the holes in the sheet.

I can't remember who won, or why, but I do remember it was a memorable finish to the season in the Old Bull N Bush.

Phil Jones was a real character and on my birthday in June he even did a "This is your life" on me complete with a big red book. At very short notice he got all the details from Livvy, and as I was sat on a chair on stage he would have different Bluecoats coming on from the back of the stage in various states of dress. It was so funny when he announced "and now Dave, here is your Mum and Dad all the way from Cloudsley Square - John and Harriet, and two Bluecoats came on dressed as an old man and an old lady. - He even had my old mate Roger. The whole thing only lasted about fifteen minutes, but it was a great tribute, and I enjoyed it as much as if it were the real thing.

The season finished on a high, and well before that I was invited back to do another season and I was very happy to accept. After a couple of weeks break I was back at Caister for a "Special Function" week. It was known as the "Jazz Bands Week."

When I first heard of it I thought 'great' being a jazz fan I was really looking forward to it. However I soon found out that they were not jazz bands as we know them. It was children's bands of baton twirlers, and Bazooka blowers. They came from all over the country, and even as far as Scotland. They arrived in these clapped out old buses, I don't know how many of them made it.

I must say they were very good, and their costumes were very colourful. They were all in competition against each other, and the Finals were at the Marina Centre in Great Yarmouth. The only problem was that they rehearsed all day, and all night. They could be seen marching in different formations all around the site. As soon as you awoke in the morning you would hear them. They had taken over almost every venue in the place, and wherever you went you could not get away from these marching bands, and the biggest problem was they all sounded the same, and I can tell you after about three days, it did do your head in.

I did get on very well with the organisers, they arranged their own Entertainment programme and I did give them a lot of advice on many things, and I must say they were a joy to entertain in the evenings, and the atmosphere in Neptune's Palace was electric and when the DJ played "Starmaker" from the "Kids From Fame," it was a truly amazing site. The kids jazz bands at Caister was an experience that I was so pleased to be part of, and I was happy that the organisers asked me back many more times.

At the end of the week when their clapped out old buses were chugging out of the main gate, with steam coming out from under their bonnets, black smoke from their exhaust pipes and the kids playing their Bazooka's and waving out of the windows. You could see the mothers sitting on the back seats sowing new sequins on the costumes no doubt in preparation for next year.

On the Sunday night that followed, the Norwich Brewery had hired Neptune's Palace for their Special Function. I had done the

Cabaret Spot for them two years earlier at the Hotel Norwich. They had asked me to do it again for them, and paid me £150. So it finished off a nice week.

It was nice to get home again, and I had three weeks rest before my next job that was a commercial for Guinness. That was soon followed by a day on a show for Thames Television called "Tom, Dick, and Harriet." The day after that I was off to the Bray Studio in Windsor for another beer commercial.

The T.V. work kept me going, and it was soon December, after a couple of days for London Weekend T.V. on "A Fine Romance" and a show called "A Married Man", I had one more job for Central T.V. at Elstree on "Forever Young" before I was back at Caister Holiday Centre to do my Christmas Stint.

Christmas at Caister did become like a family Christmas, only it was a very big family. It would seem like I knew everybody that was there. The punters would come back year after year, and were always delighted to see me they would give you hugs and kisses just like real family. Many of them would make friends, and keep in touch with each other throughout the year, and then get together again at Christmas. It was always a wonderful atmosphere, and after the first day you just knew that it was going to be a fantastic week.

However I was soon informed of my first problem to be solved. The man who had played Father Christmas for the past few years, was not well and did not feel up to it, so I had to get a replacement asap. I only had two days before he was due to make his big appearance on his sleigh in Neptune's Palace. Over the past couple of years I had built this up to be a big major event, with the Bluecoats dressed as Toy Town figures, and Santa's little helpers, the big band on stage, full lighting effects, and I would do a little warm-up with the kids, and get them in the mood before I introduced Santa Claus. The only problem we had this time though, was the fact that we didn't have a Santa Claus.

I didn't have anybody in my department that would be suitable, and I had to make enquires and ask if there was a suitable gentleman from another department. This was proving to be a hard job, as nobody was interested, time was moving on and it seemed to me that I had asked almost everybody on the staff. I then came out of reception, looked down towards the football field, and I spotted a guy driving a tractor. As I got closer to him I could see that he was the right age group and build, and would make an ideal Santa. I soon recognised him as JIM one of the maintenance men. He brought the tractor to a halt. "Hello Dave, you look like your looking for somebody he said with a big smile on his face, - "Not anymore I'm not Jim" I replied with an equally big smile on my face "I've been looking for you, and you are going to be the Main Man this Christmas." - "What do you mean?" he said, as his smile changed to a puzzled look. "I've been looking everywhere for somebody to be Santa Claus" I said "and you are without a doubt the best candidate I have seen so far" - "you want me to play Santa Claus, - don't be daft, I don't even like kids" - "Well I expect they get on the real Santa's nerves at times, but he still does it every year, - come on, you'd be great at it." After about ten minutes of persuasion, he finally, decided to do it, and boy was I relieved "Okay then I'll do it, but just this once mind" - "Thanks Jim, you won't regret it, and you will be well rewarded, come and see me in the morning and you can try the Santa Costume on, and I'll give you all the details."

The only thing I didn't tell him was that giving out the presents was a long job, and it could take up to two hours.

Christmas Morning came, and the whole presentation went down fantastic. Jim really looked the part, and appeared to be enjoying himself. After the event as he took off his beard and costume backstage he said to me "Dave that was great, I really enjoyed it, do you want me to do it again next year?" I thought to myself 'what do you know, even Santa Claus is Stage Struck" "You sure can Jim, the jobs yours, and many thanks." It was indeed another terrific Christmas, but it could have been dodgy without a good Santa, but I was delighted that our maintenance man "Jim Fixed It.'

We headed back home and it wasn't long before the New Year was with us, and it was 1983. It was the year that Spurs finished fourth in the league and qualified for the UEFA cup for the first time since the season 1973/74, and once again us Spurs fans had something to look forward to.

My first job of the year was two days at Lee International Studios, Wembley, on a commercial for Tennants Bitter. I was very well featured on the ad, and had a funny bit that I did eating a bag of crisps in close up. I even made the crew laugh, but I never did see the advert as it was for up North.

The next week I had another two days filming an advert for John Smiths Bitter, then a further two days working for the BBC, on "Cheers Before Breakfast," and the "Kenny Everitt Show." I guess that I was lucky to be getting this type of work on a regular basis, but I would get a bit frustrated, as I felt that I should be getting better work, and it would annoy me when the extras working on a television show would not be given the respect that they deserved. It was this lack of respect that did creep in over the years, and by the late eighties it was almost gone altogether.

I remember when I first started doing extra work you had to be in the Actors Union Equity, and everybody was a performer of some sort in their own right, and many of the extras were resting actors. Today you do not have to be an Equity member and the TV Companies employ anybody that will do the job. Some film companies would take anybody off the street, and they never pay the full rate. In more recent years I worked on a film that was on location, and the agent that sent me asked if I knew anybody else I could take with me. When I got there I found that people from the same agency had been asked the same thing. One bloke had brought his wife with him, his mother-in-law, and a dog.

Another guy had never done it before, it was his first job, and he'd got the day off from Sainsbury's. - I thought 'no wonder they don't show the extras any respect anymore, as they were not professionals, but even so they still deserved to be treated better than they were, as it was not their fault. The call boys with their clip boards would often talk to people like dirt, and most of them would stand for it. One guy up at Yorkshire Television tried it with me once, but I soon put him right, and he was very polite for the rest of the day.

After another day on "Murphys Mob" at Elstree, I worked on "Jeremiah Shaw" for Thames T.V. and I had a few days on "Give Us A Break" for the B.B.C. I then had a quiet spell and was resting for four weeks, but I wasn't too concerned as it was now into April and I would soon be starting the Summer season again for Ladbrokes on the 26th April, when the Entertainment Managers Seminar would be starting. At the seminar we were all informed of a few changes that would be put into place for the '83 season. During the evenings it was the usual "Jolly," and many of the Managers would swap stories, and tell of their past experiences that happened the previous year. It was soon over, and all of the Ents Managers were soon in their cars and setting off to their different sites.

At Caister we were soon up and running and it wasn't long before we were back in the old routine, and everything was ring-a-ding ding. After two great years in Neptune's Palace, the Christy Lee Showband, moved on, and in their place Jack Pound had contracted The Mick Urry Showband. I knew Mick, as he had appeared for the previous two seasons at one of Ladbrokes other Great Yarmouth sites Seashore Holiday Park.

Chapter Sixteen

"He's a Good Musician - But the Suit Wont Fit Him" A Bathtime Meeting. A Funeral With Laughter and Tears of Joy. "What's My Line"

Mick Urry was a great character, and we got on very well together. He was very professional, his band were always well turned out, and immaculate in appearance, he was always on time, and like myself he was a great one for discipline. He also did his own band show once a week, and one item was a Flanagan an Allen routine. He asked me if I would play Bud Flanagan with him doing Chesney Allen. Of course I was delighted to do so, and I even had my own fur coat that I have already mentioned when it made an appearance in the pantomime, when Jimmy Page wore it climbing through the window in "Babes In The Wood." I also had my own Bud Flanagan style straw hat, and once Mick had taught me the routine, it was a walk in the park.

I must say that I did enjoy doing the routine each week with Mick, as the spot light followed us strolling along in front of the band as we sang "Underneath The Arches" and many more of their hits. The audience loved it, and it would always go down very well. We both had a great respect for each other, but of course we didn't always see eye to eye. If ever we did have a disagreement we were always able to sort it out, and there were never any hard feelings.

In the two seasons that I worked with Mick Urry I only ever had one bad fall out with him, and to tell you the truth I cannot even remember what it was all about. What I can remember though is that it was quite a big row. We were backstage and he was just about due to go on. We both lost our tempers and were shouting and swearing at each other having a right old ding dong. If he wasn't about to go on, we may have even come to blows. The band were not going on to play a dance set, they were about to start the "Mick Urry Band Show." The row fizzled out, and the show began. Thirty minutes into the show, and its time for the Flanagan an Allen routine.

The intro music played, on I go to meet up with Mick in the middle of the stage, he puts his arm around my shoulder, and off we go singing "Strollin," the band could hardly play for laughing. We both had a good laugh about it afterwards, and became good mates.

Mick was a true pro, but I don't think all of his band liked him, especially a trombone player that he had. The trombone player was a nice guy, but unfortunately for him, it was his birthday and he had a bit of a Shindig in his chalet. I heard that there was quite a lot of noise and it went on till the early hours of the morning. A number of guests then complained to the General Manager who in turn spoke to me and then Mick Urry was informed about it.

Mick saw red, he went round to see his trombone player, and sacked him on the spot. He then came to see me in my office to let me know what he had done. I personally thought he had been a bit harsh, but he said to me "you see Dave, I've got to maintain discipline, he had to go, otherwise they will all be having bloody parties, and where would we be then 'ay?" - "But don't worry I'm on the case, I expect to have a new trombone player in a couple of days, I will be auditioning a few guys late this afternoon and tomorrow." He was full of apologies, and assured me that the band would be on top form. I didn't doubt him for a minute, as indeed they were.

About an hour later I went into Neptune's Palace, and I bumped into the Trombone Player with his bags all packed, he looked at me and said "Its my birthday today, and the 'Bastard has given me the sack, what kind of a present is that?" - "a unique one" I said "Happy Birthday."

The next day, it was around tea time, and I walked into the venue, and Mick was talking to this very big guy who was about 15 stone. A short time later Mick came up to me and said "I've just seen a great Trombone player, he's really good and I want to take him on, but I don't know what to do" - "What do you mean" I said. "I've got a problem" - "what's the problem". He looked me straight in the eye, with a serious look on his face and said "the suit wont fit him." - I burst out laughing, and then he started to laugh and could see the funny side of it. "Look" I said "the trombone player sits on the back row, right" - "that's right" - "well if he slits the jacket up the back, nobody will notice." He didn't really fancy that idea, and the very next night he had somebody else, and the suit was a perfect fit.

I have conducted business meetings in a number of various different places. In my office, in somebody else's office, in a bar, in a club, in the front stalls of a theatre, to name but a few. However the most unusual place I ever had a meeting was the time when I was having a bath. There I was enjoying a nice relaxing soak in the soap suds, when I hear Livvy's voice "you've got a visitor," and before I had time to squeeze my sponge, in walks Mick Urry. - "Sorry to disturb you Dave, I didn't realise you were in the bath" - "That's okay Mick, I'd offer you a seat but we haven't got one, but you can sit down on the toilet if you like." I was only joking and was quite surprised when he said "Thanks" and put the toilet seat lid down and sat on it.

"Something's come up" he said "I thought I'd better let you know" - "what is it" - "It's my drummer, he's had on accident and he's in hospital, they reckon he will be off for a week. - but don't worry I have arranged for a dep (deputy) to cover for him." He then continued to discuss a few other matters with me, and all in all he must have been with me for about fifteen minutes "That will be fine Mick, and thanks for letting me know about the drummer, give him my best wishes, and I hope he is back on his feet soon". He then got up off the toilet seat and said "right I'd better go, I'll keep you informed, and I'll see you tonight. - Oh by the way, enjoy your bath." - By this time of course it had gone cold.

A week later the drummer was out of hospital and back on the bandstand. I went backstage to ask him how he was, and he said "I'm fine thanks, but when it happened I was feeling a bit low. The first night in hospital, I'm lying in my bed with my arm strapped up, and my leg up in the air on straps all bandaged up feeling really sorry for myself, when Mick Urry comes in to see me and the first words he says to me is - "You've Right Let Me Down You 'Ave."

It was typical of Mick Urry, but he was, as I have already said, a great character and a real pro, and unfortunately there are not many left. The season flew by, as they all did, and before we knew it we were into the very last night, followed by the usual sad faces and tears from the girls.

After about ten days rest I did a TV job for Channel 4 called "Lady Is A Tramp" that was filmed at Wandsworth, then two days later I was back at Caister for another Jazz Bands Week experience. It was once again a very enjoyable time. When it was over I had a quiet couple of weeks, then I got two TV Commercials on the trot. One was for Springfield Bitter, and that was shot at Isleworth Studio's, and the other one was for an American Rainwear company and it was filmed at night outside the Tower of London. I was playing a City of London Policeman, and when they turned on the rain machines I felt like Gene Kelly In "Singing In The Rain." Fortunately over my P.C.s uniform I was wearing a police cape, and as I was patrolling along the pavement in the pouring rain along the embankment of the Thames with the tower at night lit up in all its glory. I passed two young lovers in their American rainwear, they only had eyes for each other, and didn't even notice the pouring rain. Of course they were kept dry by their American rainwear.

I never did see the finished product as it was for the American market. Well I guess at least I can say that I appeared on American T.V. I still had an ambition to go to America, and to go to New York, and walk down Broadway to Time Square, and to jump in a Yellow Taxi and say "follow that cab" -'well maybe one day.'

A week later starting on Monday 21st November I had the lead role in a Training Film for Bass. It was four days work, filmed at the Cavalcade Pub at Willenhall, Walsall. I played the pub manager, and it was all about saving energy. There were quite a few different scenes that I was involved in. Bar scenes, cellar scenes, a bedroom scene, and a dream sequence when I wake up in bed in the middle of a building site. I was quite pleased with the outcome, and I understand that Bass used the film at their Training Seminars for a few years afterwards.

My next T.V. Commercial was for Johnsons Wax Polish. It was filmed on a railway carriage that was supposed to be the Orient Express. I had to go for a costume fitting at Burnham an Natham, and was told that the suit I was given was one worn by Albert Finney in the film "Murder On The Orient Express." I was quite thrilled as Albert Finney has always been my favourite actor.

I then had a good run with the BBC on the series "Bleak House," with at least two days each week that took me up to Christmas. It was Christmas 1983 that I first worked with a young children's entertainer known as Captain Crumble. I had met him on a number of occasions before, as he had done a couple of seasons at the Ladbroke site Silver Sands, which was directly next door to Caister, with just a narrow road between them. I always called him 'The Crumble, and it was the first time that he had actually worked for me. After the Christmas I was determined to make sure that he worked for me in the summer. He was the best kids entertainer that I had ever seen, and I had seen a lot of them over the years. Most children's entertainers, would do magic tricks, dress as clowns and use a lot of props. Not Crumble, he didn't do magic, he didn't wear funny clothes, he didn't use props. He was entirely different from the conventional children's entertainer. He would just turn up in smart clothes, talk to the kids, and within minutes they would be eating out of his hands. He only looked about seventeen when I first knew him, in fact he looked like one of the kids, but they loved him.

It was the beginning of a long association between us, and he is now one of my closest friends, who also happens to be a Spurs Supporter. It was soon the New Year of 1984, and it was a good year for us Spurs fans as Tottenham won the UEFA cup for the second time.

My first job of the year was a T.V. Commercial for McCain Chips, then I did a couple of photographic jobs. The photo shoots were always good money, and only took a couple of hours, but you never got your money until about three months after the job. Many a time I had forgotten about it, but it was always nice to receive a cheque that you weren't expecting.

Over the past couple of years we had a few family problems. Mums' sight had been getting worse, and she was now almost blind. Dad was suffering from senile dementia, and he also had been getting worse over the years. He would move things and Mum couldn't find anything that she wanted, as it wasn't where she expected it to be. Things went from bad to worse, and he ended up by setting the house on fire. The fire brigade had to be called, and one of the bedrooms was completely gutted. It wasn't the first fire that he had caused, and it became clear that he was a danger to both himself, Mum, and to anybody else in the house upstairs.

Dad was taken into hospital, and Mum who did not feel safe on her own moved into a Sheltered Accommodation with a warden, just around the corner to where we live, so in the winter when I was at home I could pop in and see her regularly. I guess it was an end of an era, as Pleasant Place had been the family home for so many years, and it was always a meeting place for other members of the family, aunts, uncles, and cousins. Over the years ever since I left home to go to Manchester I would always phone my Mum, and when I was away in summer season I would phone her every Sunday, and I knew that she would look forward to it.

My brother Tony and I would visit our Dad in hospital, and it was not a nice experience. Each visit we could see him deteriorate and he didn't even know who we were. One day we took him for a walk in the grounds, and he never said a word to either of us. When we took him back we found that we couldn't get in as the door was locked, and we could see a male nurse through the glass. Our Father then banged on the door and in his best "officers" voice shouted "I say - open this door will you." - It was said with great authority, and the nurse came and opened the door, they were the only words he had spoken during the whole visit.

He was very proud of his family, I remember a few years before he said that somebody had asked him about his family, and he said "yes I've got a daughter and two sons, one's a Policeman, and ones A Star."

Mum had a wonderful sense of humour, and would make everybody laugh, but she did get fed up at times and frustrated that she could not get out on her own. Even though she was a good laugh to everybody she would moan at us and tell us all her frustration, and sometimes she would seem really down. She once said to me "If you 'cant moan at your own family - who can you moan at."

She had a point of course, but even when she was down she made me laugh. I recall one time when Tony and I were taking her out for a walk one day. She was in the middle of us both, and we were all linking arms. I then said to her "Mum, you are really lucky, not many people have two sons taking them out for a walk," to which she replied "Some people got four." - We both burst out laughing, and from having a dead pan face, a wicked grin would slowly creep up on one side of her face. She had great comic timing, and milked every moment of it.

January was quite a good month for me, I went on a couple of auditions, and got them both, one was for a beer commercial and the other was a photographic job. I then did a thing for Yorkshire T.V. called the "Glory Boys," that was followed by three days working on a film at Pinewood Studio's called "Blood Royal". It was a costume drama, and we were all wallowing about ankle deep in mud, in the freezing cold, with horses galloping all around us, I was glad when that job was over. I had a few more bits and pieces coming in, then in February I did a couple of days for the B.B.C. on "Life of John" and a show called "King." The following week I drove up to Leeds where I had three more days on "The Glory Boys" for Yorkshire T.V.

When I got back to London I had nothing at all for a week, then I got a day on "What's My Line" as a stand in for Thames T.V. I really enjoyed it, sitting on the celebrities panel, and asking the contestants questions, it was good fun, and it really was a walk in the park, I remember thinking to myself that 'the celebrities that do this show, for them it really is "money for jam."

When I got back home that evening on Thursday 16th February, I had a phone call from the hospital to tell me that our Father had just died. It was a shock of course, but in a way it was also a great relief. It was awful to see him in a place like that, and to see how he had deteriorated over the past months. He didn't even know who we were, it was very sad to see. He hated being in there, and every time I went to see him he asked me if I had come to take him home. But in the last few months he didn't say anything to me at all, it was so very sad knowing how he had been so full of life in his hey day.

I phoned Tony straight away, and I could tell he was upset. our Dad hadn't been the Father that we wanted him to be, but he was still our Dad, he was one of life's great characters, and everybody that knew him had their own favourite story of him. Over the years I must say that many times, he was a real pain in the 'arse, but I'm happy to say that I only remember the good times. He brought so much joy and laughter to a lot of people's lives, but he did cause Mum a lot of anxiety.

I remember many years before when we were all living at home in Pleasant Place he once said to us "when I'm dead and gone you will miss me," and Tony said "I won't, when your gone I'm 'gonna have a party." - Dad roared with laughter with that wonderful loud laugh that he had, - "I hope you do" he said "1 don't want anybody crying at my funeral, I want everyone to have a good time."

We buried Dad on Friday 24th February, and he certainly got his wish. Now as we all know funerals are very sad occasions and no doubt we would all wish that we didn't have to go to any. I've been to quite a number of them over the years, but I can honestly say, and this may sound very strange to some people, but our Fathers funeral was the best funeral that I have ever been to. All those years before when he said. "I want everybody to have a good time," I'm sure that he would have been absolutely delighted when he saw that everybody did. There was laughter and tears of joy, and the laughter was coming from the younger members of the family being told stories by older members of the family about our Dads colourful life.

Aunt Carrie who was Dads older sister was riding in the same car as us on the way to the cemetery and she recalled the time when she wasn't feeling very well, and her next door neighbour said that she should see a doctor. "I don't need a doctor" she said "my brother is coming to see me tomorrow, and he makes me laugh and when I've had a laugh I always feel better."

We gave him a good send off, he will always be remembered, and we speak of him almost everyday.

In late February I had two days filming a commercial for Beneficial Finance. It was a football theme and shot at Fulham F.C. at Craven Cottage. They used quite a number of fans to fill up part of the stand, and myself and a number of professional artistes were placed in the crowd with the two principals Zoot Money and Jimmy Greaves. It was a most enjoyable two days with Jimmy keeping the crowd laughing with his quick wit.

It was ironic that Jimmy's son was down on the pitch with a number of other players. He was the one that was banging in the goals, and each time it hit the back of the net we would all be on our feet jumping for joy. They did a lot of takes, and after seeing the ball go into the back of the net for the umpteenth time, Jimmy Greaves turned to the crowd of Fulham fans and quipped "I bet it's the first time you lot have seen so many goals over 'ere" - the moans and jeers that followed could be heard at Stamford Bridge, but it was all in good fun, and everybody enjoyed the moment.

After doing a few more T.V. extra jobs I was asked back to Thames T.V. at Teddington to do another "What's My Line" as a celebrity stand in. I really enjoyed doing those, and I was pleased when I was given another five over the next five weeks.

I then got two days as a stand in on Cilla Black's "Surprise! Surprise," but I didn't enjoy that half as much.

I did one more "What's My Line" on 30th April, and the very next day on 1st May we were off to Caister for the Summer Season with the first week being the Ents Managers Seminar.

Just before I left my agent Ivor Kimmel rang me to say that Thames T.V. wanted me to do six more "What's My Lines" every Monday starting on the 7th May. I was delighted, and gave myself Monday as my day off so I was able to travel down to Teddington each week to do the show and drive back to Great Yarmouth the same night.

It was about this time that Ladbrokes decided to amalgamate Caister Holiday Centre with the site next door Silver Sands Holiday Park. They did a lot of alterations, and it was now one big site called Caister Holiday Centre. I now had another club under my control the Carousel Club. It was quite an exciting time taking over another site, but we all soon got used to it.

We also had a new General Manager, and I must say that I was sorry to see Colin Wright go as he was the Top Man.

I now had Captain Crumble working on the team, and the children's entertainment had never been better. I would always say that if the kids are happy then the Mums and Dads will be happy, and we all had a great season. It was the end of September when the season ended, and five days later I was off to Bristol for a days filming on another Bass training film for Spafax T.V. The following week back in London I did a T.V. Commercial for Tennants Larger, and then played a postman on the cop show "Bulman" for Granada T.V. Two days later I was back at Caister for 10 days for the Jazz Bands week, and once again a good time was had by all. By now of course I was well used to the fact that I was not performing in the clubs anymore, and I must say that I did not miss it for one second. I did miss performing though especially when we went to see a West End Show like "Me and My Girl" I would have loved to have been in that kind of show.

I was still keeping my hand in of course during the summer seasons, but not half as much as what I used to do, but I was happy with that, and it was always a joy to help young performers.

If ever I saw anybody on the Bluecoat Team that had talent, and showed promise, I would give them all the encouragement that I could, and give them every opportunity to perform in front of a live audience. It was always good to see how they would improve over a season, and get better every performance. On a few occasions if I thought a girl or boy were exceptional I would put them on the bill for the Star Late Night Cabarets.

I recall many years later I had a boy working for me on the team when I was with Haven Holidays. He was tall, dark, and a good looking lad, and had a really good voice. He had the right attitude and was showbiz mad. I gave him a cabaret spot in both of the clubs, and he was doing very well. I spoke to our head office about him, and they even offered to help with his progress and paid for a new stage suit for him. It wasn't long after that, he sold the suit, and done a runner. 'Ah well, that's showbiz I guess. I think I was right about him though, as the last I heard of him he was doing well in a band, and as far as I know he is still earning a living in the business.

Next I did a thing called "Who Sir, Me Sir," for the BBC, then I was back in police uniform for "Hilary" also for the B.B.C., before working on a show called "Dutch Girls" for London Weekend. On Friday 30th Nov. 1984 I was down at Elstree Studios for the B.B.C. on a new soap they were doing called "Eastenders."

It was the very first episode where they find a body in one of the houses. The only faces that I recognised were Bill Treacher who I had seen in many films and Wendy Richards who we all knew from "Are You Being Served."

I remember sitting in one of the cabin dressing rooms with the actress that was playing Angle the pub landlady. She was quite excited at the prospect, and said how she did not want to be compared with Bet Lynch from "Coronation Street."

Three weeks later I was booked for two days on "Eastenders" again, when I got on the set the landlady behind the bar in the Vic was a different actress. I asked one of the other actors "what happened to the girl that played the landlady that was here two weeks ago?" And he replied "she wasn't up to it, so they got somebody else." That somebody else was Anita Dobson.

Soon after that I had three days on "Magnox" for the BBC. Then I did a day on a show for Tyne Tees T.V. called "Operation Julie" that was filmed at the Nova Hotel, Hammersmith.

This was followed by a T.V. commercial for London Transport, then I was back on "What's My Line" and that took me right up to Christmas, where I started my stint at Caister. It was once again a terrific Christmas, and I enjoyed it as I always did, with the audience being just like old friends..

When we got back to London the old year was almost out, and we were all saying hello to 1985. It was at the beginning of this year that Ladbrokes asked me if I would be interested in going on the road for two weeks delivering brochures to Travel Agents. I thought 'why not, it would be two weeks work, and it would be another experiences to see what it would be like as a delivery man.

I picked up the Ladbroke Van at Beesons Holiday Centre, at Newton Abbott. It was loaded up with Holiday brochures, and off I went heading for the North West, and my first port of call was at Leyland. I stayed over night at the Ladbroke Mercury Hotel. After a few Travel Agent drops I then moved on to a few more towns including, Blackpool, Fallowfield, Liverpool, Manchester, and Chester. I stayed in some very nice hotels, and it was quite a nice change, in fact it was like having a proper job.

For the second week I had to go to this Industrial Estate to a warehouse, and be reloaded with more holiday brochures. The van was fully loaded, when the guy that was loading up with me said "There's only eight more packs, you might as well take 'em." - "I can't take anymore, its down on its springs" I said "Just squeeze them in, it'll be alright, be a shame to leave 'em." He stuffed them in, and the van was absolutely chocka block. As I looked at the van, the springs were that low you could only see half of the wheels. Before I could say anything the guy had disappeared back into the warehouse. I knew that I had a couple of drops not too far away, and I figured if I got them off quickly it would ease the load.

I got in the cab, and as soon as I pulled away I knew that I was over loaded, and it must have been against the law.

My first thought was to drive with great care, and not put anybody in any danger. I made my way off the Estate, and did not go over 20 miles an hour. If I came to a bump I would almost be at a stand still, I was very concerned, but I kept going, and once I got back onto the main road, I was able to get in the inside lane and stay there. Lucky for me, the Travel Agent that I was going to was on this Main Road, and I was so relieved when I came to a stop outside. They only wanted two packs but I gave them five. When I got back in the van, it did make a difference, but I was still over-loaded.

Twenty minutes later I got to my next stop, and this time I got rid of four packs. This time the van had gone up a bit more and I could see more of the wheels, and feel the springs, and I did feel a lot more comfortable. I was now in between towns, and going along a country road at a steady speed, when suddenly the back of the van went out of control, I gently braked and pulled in to the side of the road. I then got out to find that I had a puncture in the near side back tyre. I thought 'great, that's all I need.' I looked up at the sky and it was getting a bit cloudy with very dark clouds. My next thought was to change the wheel before it started to rain. I undid the spare wheel from under the van, but when I tried to jack it up, it wouldn't go up enough as there was too much weight in the van. I then had to take out some of the packs of brochures and put them on the side of the road. The next thing I knew there was a cloud burst, the heavens opened, and it poured down with rain. I had to take out twenty packs before it would move up and the back wheel cleared the floor. By now I was absolutely drenched to the skin, I worked as quickly as I could, and once the spare wheel was on, I loaded the packs back into the van, and fortunately they were covered in plastic wrappings, I only wish that I had been. I can tell you I was not in a good mood, and when I put the last pack in and closed the back door, I was in an even worse mood. - It stopped raining. At the end of the two weeks I returned the van to Beesons Centre at Newton Abbott, and was soon on a train heading back to London. It had been quite an experience, and I had quite enjoyed it, as it had been a nice change, and I always enjoyed driving.

My first job when I got back home was a day for Thames T.V. on a show called "Who's Baby." The following week I was back on "Eastenders," and of course at this time it had still not hit the screens, and nobody would have guessed what a run away success it would become.

Soon after that I was given another eight "What's My Lines" for Thames T.V. at Teddington, and that pleased me, as I guess they must have been happy with my work on the show, or they would not have had me back so many times. Next I had a nice little run on the cop show "Dempsey And Makepeace" over a period of five weeks. A couple of the days we were filming on a river boat up and down the Thames.

I recall one stunt that was quite exciting to see. The actor playing a villain, was sat at a dining table with his back to a glass panel having a meal with some friends. They are engaging in conversation, when suddenly a gunman appears and shoots the villain in the chest at point blank range. He is thrown backwards through the plate glass partition, and finishes up lying dead on the floor with his legs in the air, and the splattered glass all over the place.

At the beginning of the take, they were doing the dialogue, and at the point where the villain bends his head forward, the director stops the action, the actor playing the villain comes out of the set, and the Stunt Man wearing identical clothes sits in the same position with his head bent forward in the seat that the actor has just vacated. The director then sits in the seat directly opposite the Stunt Man, and points a finger at him as if it were a gun. He then instructs the Stunt Man and tells him when he fires the gun he will say "bang" and the Stunt Man will then throw himself backwards through the glass pane.

The clapper boy had marked it, the camera was rolling - "Action" - the director pointed his finger, and in a very soft voice he said - "Bang." The Stunt Man threw himself back as if he had been shot, straight through the glass partition, and landed on his back with his legs in the air. The director then shouted "Cut" and all the cast and crew on the boat burst into applause. It was so realistic but the glass panel was not real glass of course, it was sugar glass.

When the Stunt Man got up, the actor that was playing the part, then got in the same position as the dead body, and he was sprinkled with blood and glass. All in all they did three takes using three different sugar glass panels, and the Stunt Man got applause each time.

After a couple more T.V. jobs, and a commercial for Albright Bitter, we decided to take a holiday just before we were due to start the summer season.

We flew to Portugal and spent a wonderful week on the Algarve. It was unspoiled at the time, and you could see that they were just starting the building of the many hotels that are there today.

It was a really peaceful holiday away from all the hustle, and bustle. The weather was wonderful, and it was great just sitting in a deck chair on the beach sipping ice cold beers, and watching the local fishermen mend their nets.

We did however spend an amazing day in Lisbon seeing the sights, and we both enjoyed it very much.

On our return to England we both felt rested and relaxed, and ready to start the summer season. During the one week that we were at home beforehand, I did a day on "What's My Line," and a few days after that we were off to Great Yarmouth and I attended another Ents Managers Seminar.

I was now in my fifth year as entertainments manager at Caister, and this was the seventh seminar that I had been to, needles to say I was finding them quite boring.

I guess you could say they were an occupational hazard, a thing that went with the job at the beginning of every new season. Of course I could understand they were necessary, especially for any new managers that had not worked for the company before, but as the years went on, the Seminars just seemed to get longer and longer.

When Ladbrokes were taken over by Warners, and Warners were taken over by Haven and became Haven/Warner Holidays, we were all under the Rank Organisation including Butlins.

It did become quite confusing. Then Haven and Warners, split and went their own ways, and I was then working for Haven Holidays. Now a Haven Seminar, that was boring. The Entertainment Managers were getting younger every year, and they looked like they were all being cloned. I remember once one of the other more experienced managers came up to me one day, and said "I had a dream last night that I was at a Haven Seminar, - and when I woke up I was!"

CHAPTER SEVENTEEN

A Spot of Lunch with the Prince of Wales. Bruce Forsyth Does My Line. A Sad Loss Mum Gets Her Wish. The Comedians Midnight Gala

After the 1985 season, I did three more years at Caister, the last one being in 1988. It was three glorious years and I have many happy memories. The Jazz Bands Week, soon became the Baton Twirlers week. It was exactly the same as the Jazz Bands, with their clapped out old Buses, with painted logo's on the sides, and all the colourful costumes, the only difference they were twirling batons, and it was so funny to see so many kids with black eyes where the baton had hit them, or one of the other kids had accidentally given them a wack.

The end of season finals was always a great week, and over the years we had some really good curtain raisers for the events. I would use a different presenter every night to compere each event, and I would present the last night myself. It would give the audience a chance to see a different face each night in Neptune's Palace, and I would use the comperes from the other clubs.

The first time I gave "the Crumble" the chance to compere the Finals of the Junior Talent, he was thrilled, I knew he wouldn't let me down, and he didn't. He made his entrance in a Scottish outfit complete with kilt, sporran, jacket, the works. I don't know why he chose a Scots outfit, but he got a great reaction when he walked on.

The show was a great success, and Crumble did a first class professional job. He had hired the outfit, and didn't take it off, and wore it to the after show bash that was always hosted by the General Manager in the "House."

It was always a very nice buffet that was laid on, that would not look out of place in a five star hotel. The booze was flowing freely, and towards the end of the night, or maybe I should say the wee small hours, the bars manager would produce a couple of bottles of his finest brandy.

Crumble was really enjoying himself, but a short time later I noticed that he had disappeared. I did not know at the time, but apparently he had wandered upstairs to go to the bathroom, and on his way out of there, he noticed the bedroom door was open. On seeing the large double bed, he fancied a kip. He then laid on the top of the bed in his full Scottish regalia, and fell fast asleep, where he remained until the morning.

He did not realise how lucky he had been, as the Managing Director was down for a few days to make the presentations at the finals. Whenever he and his wife were on a visit, they would always stay overnight in the "House". On this occasion he stayed at an Hotel in Great Yarmouth. I just cannot imagine what he would have said when he and his wife were about to go to bed and found what appeared to be a drunken Scotsman fast asleep in their bed.

That winter I continued with the T.V. jobs and the odd commercials one of which was for British Telecom. I then had a couple of days at Ealing Studios for the B.B.C on a show called "Look What They've Done," followed by "Yes Prime Minister," and "Slip Up."

After my Christmas stint at Caister, before we knew it, Big Ben was chiming and it was 1986. It was to be a great year for me. It would be the year when I met royalty, and Bruce Forsyth used one of my lines. After a couple of photographic jobs, and a thing called "Cats Eyes" that I did for T.V.S. at Chatham we were now into March, and Livvy and I decided to go on holiday to Malta for eleven days.

We flew out on the 14th March, and found Malta to be a wonderful place especially the people who were really pro British. It is a country that is very big on churches, but they were all beautiful. We went to see the "Malta Experience" and that was really special, they love the Brits, and I love them, I was indeed a proud Englishman in Malta.

When we got back home my next job was as a police driver on a show called "Call Me Mister" but I have no record of what company it was for. We had only been back home just over a couple of weeks, and we were off to Paris for a long weekend. This was a trip arranged by Ladbrokes for all their Entertainment Managers. I had never been to Paris before and it was one of the great cities of the world.

We all had a great time, but found it to be far more expensive than London, I don't know whether we went to the wrong places, or whether we were being ripped off, but we didn't mind as it was a really wonderful weekend.

The very next weekend I was off to Caister, for what was to be a very special week for all of us. It was the week that Caister was to play host to "The Princes Trust" and H.R.H. Prince Charles would be making a visit. I had known about this since last November when I attended a meeting in London with two of the Ladbroke Bosses and officials from "The Prince's Trust." It was to be a holiday for hundreds of unemployed youngsters from all over the country, who would be attending training workshops in a number of different venues on the Caister site. I would be responsible for organising the entertainment in the evening, and The "P. Trust had arranged for Phil Collins to do a couple of performances and also run a music workshop.

It was a very exciting time, and I had never known security like it before, every nook and cranny was checked. When I saw Prince Charles bodyguards, they were all big guys in smart dark suits, and some of them had what looked like a bulge in their jackets. They all looked like James Bond type characters, and as the week went on we got used to seeing them on various balconies, and strategic places.

Many of the young people that attended, had the punk rocker look dressed in black leather, with spikey hair dyed in various bright colours, with studs in their ears, noses, and I would imagine other places that you wouldn't want to hear about.

It was a real mixed bag, but they all attended the various workshops, and looked like they were working really hard. They were a pleasure to entertain in the evenings, and I even put on a few competitions for them that they could enter, and we all had some great fun with them. The Talent Contest was a great success, and there was some very good talent among them.

The beauty contest for the girls got a good response, and some of the raunchy remarks they gave me to my questions got some real howlers from the boys. Phil Collins proved to be a real superstar working with a bunch of guys who had got together as a band. In the evening they performed a concert and Phil sat in with them on the drums.

The day that Prince Charles arrived the atmosphere was electric. He toured all the workshops, showed a very keen interest in all the projects, and spoke to as many people as he could.

One of the Trust organisers then asked me to contact the girl that had won the Disco Dancing Competition during the week. The plan was for the girl to go up to Prince Charles when he was in Neptune's Palace that afternoon and ask him for a dance. When we told the girl about it, she almost went white "I can't do that" she said "it wouldn't be right." The man from the Trust who was very close to HRH replied "I can assure you it will be perfectly alright, and he will be absolutely delighted to dance with you."

Neptune's Palace was packed to the rafters, it was quiet, and we all awaited the entrance of HRH. The press were there in abundance, and were all positioned in one corner near the entrance.

Everybody was waiting in anticipation, then suddenly he walked in the front entrance ahead of his entourage, and from being a strange quiet, the place erupted into cheers and applause. He walked round Neptunes shaking hands and talking to the youngsters as he went by.

What happened next is a bit of a blur, but the bodyguards were beginning to look a bit edgy. By now the DJ was playing some music, and a few people were on the dance floor. The young girl that had won the Disco Dance competition, had gone with the Prince's Trust organiser. I did not see her go up to Prince Charles, and I don't know what she said, but the next thing I remember this terrific reaction from the crowd, and the prince is on the dance floor with this young girl, before you could say "Pump up the Action" everybody floods onto the floor, its absolutely packed and Prince Charles is in the middle of it.

The Bodyguards were now looking very concerned, as he disappeared in the crowd. They were all about six feet four, but now they seemed to have stretched themselves to about seven foot as they peered into the mass of dancers. It seemed a long time that he was out of sight, but it was only a matter of seconds before he came into view again, and the bodyguards necks went back into their bodies like a family of tortoise, and you could see the relief come over their faces.

The Prince of Wales was not a great dancer, but he was having a go, and the crowd loved it. When the time came for him to leave, he walked out of the venue, waved to the crowd, and was given a standing ovation. He went for a freshen up in a specially prepared chalet, just before his final port of call to the restaurant where a buffet had been laid on.

I remember I had just moved away from the buffet table, having just helped myself to a few tiny sandwiches and the odd sausage roll. I was just about to get stuck in when the Trust organiser took me by the arm and officially introduced me to Prince Charles, who incidentally was also holding a plate with a couple of sandwiches on it.

We shook hands, and had a short chat together. He asked me how long I had worked for Ladbroke Holidays. After telling him, I then said how I had worked for Butlins before that, he then told me that when he was young he and his sister always wanted to go to Butlins but they never could.

During the conversation he took a bite of his sandwich and I did the same. It was a wonderful moment, and I could hardly believe it was happening, here was 1, having a sandwich with the future King Of England. It was a Royal Command Performance, without doing a performance, the only performing I was doing was having a chat and eating a sandwich. Lots of performers meet

Royalty in a line-up and shake hands, but this was a real meeting, it was something really special, and one of the greatest moments of my career.

Outside the restaurant, the roadway had been roped off, and the crowd were behind the barriers. Three limos were in the middle of the road with the engines running, and the doors open on the middle car.

The security men in suits were stood by the cars with their eyes looking everywhere. As H.R.H. came out of the restaurant, the crowd cheered, he made his way to the middle car, and the crowd continued to cheer. He then walked round the back of the car, and made his way over to the crowd. The security men looked disappointed as they were anxious to get him into the car. He shook hands and chatted to the crowd as he walked along the line. It seemed ages, and the engines were still running. It was almost ten minutes when he finally walked to the car, turned and waved to the crowd before climbing in. The security men got in the cars, the doors slammed, and they drove off. Everybody that was there, and that was involved will never forget that wonderful day, Friday 25th April 1986.

He was friendly had lots of time for everybody, showed great interest, and made it a day to remember for all of us, the day HRH Prince Charles came to Caister.

That summer we were really set up for another great season, and by now of course I was not only doing the summer season, I was also doing all the special events that were before and after.

Another great event that we staged at Caister was a European Sporting Event. They had teams from all over Europe, the place was full of Germans, French, Belgians, and many others. I will never forget the first night when I stepped out on stage in Neptune's Palace the place was packed, and they all looked friendly but I soon found there was only one small problem. None of them could speak English. I stepped out onto the floor, and went up to the ringsiders, and was soon able to sort out the Germans from the French, and the various other nationalities. It was quite unreal, but I did manage to communicate. At one point I found myself talking like Tarzan "Me David, You Frenchie," and I was even getting laughs.

They loved a song where they could clap their hands, and tap the ashtrays on the tables, and make a noise. As the week went on, I built up a great relationship with them, they called me Daveee, and even if they saw me outside during the day they would shout "AY Daveee, Daveee you Good, OK." We had arranged cabarets for them each night, and it was always a speciality act, that would be musical and visual, and they all did very well.

Toward the end of the week, a comedian was booked, I had never heard of him, but when he walked in you would have thought he was a superstar. I was unable to get a word in, and I took an instant dislike to him as he was so full of himself. He told me what he had done, and what he had lined up, and how much in demand he was, and that he was one of the top five comics in Britain. I was then about to tell him that the audience could not understand English as they were all foreigners, when he cut me off, and told me what a big house he had just bought in the country, and that he had two cars.

It had been my intention to advise him to adjust his act, cut out the gags, do visual comedy if he could, or stick in a few extra songs. I then thought to myself, no, this guy is so far up his own backside, he needs bringing down a peg, so I never said a word. I walked on stage and did my usual warm up, and the audience gave me their usual "Hello, Daveee" routine. I then settled them all down, and introduced the comic. He walked on full of confidence, and died on his arse.

When he came off he wasn't so talkative I said to him. "Your number five ranking must have gone down a bit.." I never did tell him that the audience couldn't understand him, but I reckoned it would do him good. I know that it isn't right to see a fellow artiste die on stage and be pleased, but in his case, he was such a nasty piece of work, I must admit it brought a big smile to my face.

At the end of the season in mid October I did a couple of days as a stand in for Bruce Forsyth on the sit com "Slingers Day." I was told by the agent that the guy that had been doing it was taken sick.

That was followed by a day on "Bread." For the B.B.C. and then I did a "Rumpole" for Thames T.V.

Soon afterwards my agent rang to say that they wanted me back for "Slingers Day" for two more Thursday and Fridays. The four dates over-lapped the "Baton Twirler's" week at Caister, but the organisers were okay about it, and I was able to drive back from great Yarmouth and do them.

The following week I did three days on "Duty Free" for Yorkshire T.V., and the very next day I started an eight day run on "Slingers Day" as Bruce Forsyth's stand-in. When we had finished rehearsing in the rehearsal room, we would then be in the studio for the last two days. I would work with the book, and do Brucie's part as Mr Slinger, so that they could get the camera angles, and then I would come out of the set, and Bruce would go in and take over.

In one scene the Managing Director of the store is on a visit, and his bowler hat gets damaged, and the rim comes away from the top. During rehearsals Bruce would place the top of the bowler that now looked like a pudding bowl, on the MDs head, and each time would say "Goodnight your worship." When he had the top of the hat on his head, I thought that he looked like a Rabbi. Each time I rehearsed it I would say "Goodnight Rabbi" When we came to the last day on the dress run, Bruce was doing the scene, and he said "Goodnight Rabbi." When he finished the scene, he came out of the set, sat next to me and said "that was a better line." I must say that I was quite flattered that Bruce Forsyth (who was one of my heroes) had taken my line.

Apart from being Brucie's stand-in, I also had a small part in the episode, playing the MD's chauffeur, and I got a laugh on one line that was a laugh line, and that did please me. Speaking of laughs, there were not many laughs during rehearsals on "Slingers Day," unlike working with Bill Maynard on his sit-coms, it was a laugh a minute, and they were much more fun to work on.

I was sorry Thames T.V. did not do anymore "Slingers Day" as it would have been a nice little earner for me, but I wasn't surprised.

I did just one more TV job for the BBC on a show called "Our Geoff' before I started my usual stint at Caister for Christmas. Jim the maintenance man, was still playing Father Christmas, and by now of course he was a real pro. Time went by so quickly that before we knew it, we were back home and saying hello to 1987. It would not be a happy year for the family, as right at the beginning of the year, we lost our Mum.

When I was at home in the winter I would pop in to see Mum at least twice a week, and we would enjoy our little chats over a cup of tea and a biscuit. Sometimes she would talk about when she would not be with us anymore, and that old people that went into hospital, never came out again. She would often say "I don't want to hang about." Of course I did not dwell on the conversation, and would change the subject to something a bit more jolly. It was a Sunday afternoon, and I was on a visit, and we'd had a few laughs, and were talking about Tony and Maria. As I was about to leave, I gave Mum a kiss on the cheek, and she said to me "I love you David." "I love you too" I said, then with that lovely smile that she had she said "that's good, we all love each other."

The next day I had a days filming for the B.B.C. on "A Perfect Spy." The very next morning I had a phone call to say that Mum had a fall in her flat. I got to the flat within ten minutes, and Mum was on the floor with the warden and a helper. They had not moved her, and were waiting for the ambulance. Mum was quite chatty, and seemed in good spirits. I had only been there for a couple of minutes when the ambulance men arrived. Just as they were about to take her out, one of them asked "is there anything else you'd like to take Hetty?" to which she replied "yes a bottle of Whisky." They all laughed, and that wicked smile crept up one side of her face as they carried her out on the stretcher. We followed the ambulance in my car, and then were in the waiting room while they attended to Mum.

It was about two hours later when a nurse appeared and came up to me, I could see from the look on her face that it was not good news, and when her first words were "I'm sorry" I knew. She then told me that Mum had died.

I went to see her, the curtains were pulled round her bed, and I stayed with her for quite a long time, she looked very peaceful and at rest. I said a few words to her, then said a prayer. I then thanked God for giving her, her wish, and I know that she would have been pleased as she did not "hang about.".

I miss my Mum, even today, and I will always remember the last words that I heard her say to the ambulance men. If it had been a sit-com it would have been a laugh line, and her last line got a laugh.

A week later I had two days at London Weekend T.V. on a thing called "Running Wild," and that was followed by a weekend on a special event for Ladbrokes at the Sussex Coast Country Club.

I then had a few T.V. jobs including one more for LWT on "Bust," and "A Perfect Spy" for the B.B.C.

On the 2nd April we were off to Amsterdam on another Ladbroke Managers Trip, for a long weekend. It was my first visit to Amsterdam, and it was a real eye opener, especially when we all went with our wives and girl friends on a visit to the "red light" district. It was like a trip to Madame Tussauds with all the girls posing in their windows, with whips and chains. It looked like rows of them, I must say they were very well presented, and it was a sight worth seeing.

Once we had walked through the area, we then had a boat trip and finished up in a nice bar. All in all it was a great weekend, and we all enjoyed ourselves. When we got back to England I had three days at Elstree working on a T.V. commercial for Barclays Bank.

For all of us long suffering Spurs supporters 1987 brought us all joy when Tottenham reached the F.A. Cup Final at Wembley for the eighth time, and Clive Allen set a new club record with 49 goals in a single season. I had a ticket for Wembley, and I was there, but sadly it ended in tears and we were beaten by Coventry.

After the summer season and the special events that followed, we were soon into November, and I got three "walk-on" jobs for the B.B.C. on the shows "Rockcliffs Babies" "Cop Out" and "Radical Chambers." Five days later I had three days on "The Birmingham Bombings" for Channel 4.

1 then did a day on the BBCs "Yes Prime Minister" that was recorded in front of a live audience before doing a couple of days on "London's Burning" for LWT, and that took me up to the Christ-

mas period. All in all it had not been a bad year, even though it had been a very sad start. We were now into 1988, and even though I was to have a really great year at Caister it was to be my last, but I did not know that until the end of the year in December.

Jack Pound the Entertainment Executive was about to retire, and the new man to take over was an ex band-leader and General Manager from one of the other sites. There was a lot of talk about takeovers, and the whisper was that Ladbrokes were about to be taken over by Warner's.

During my time at Caister I had worked for four different General Managers, and I am happy to say that I got on very well with all of them. Colin Wright for me will always be "the Guvnor" but it was Alan Castledine that I worked for longer than anybody else, four years in fact Alan and I had a first class working relationship and I think we only had about three occasions when we did not agree. We both had great respect for each other, and we both wanted to be the best. Caister Holiday Centre was indeed the number one site across the whole Ladbroke group, and in three out of the four years Alan Castledine won the General Manager of the Year Award.

In early February we went on the Ladbroke Managers Trip to Majacar in Spain, and once again it was a great time. On our return I had a few T.V. jobs, and after a day on "Eastenders" for the BBC, Livvy and I decided on a holiday before the summer season started so we went for a week to Majorca. We both enjoyed it, but have never been back, and have no intention of doing so.

Every Ladbroke summer season the Managing Director was very keen to raise money for the Variety Club Sunshine Coaches, and various raffles were made each week.

I mentioned to Alan Castledine that I would like to stage a midnight gala show in Neptune's Palace for six weeks every Wednesday with a star name, and proceeds from the ticket sales would go to the Variety Club. He agreed and then left me to organise it. (This was in 1987). The first show would be a "Comedians Gala" featuring the comedians from the seaside shows in Great Yarmouth and from the Cromer Pier Theatre. I spent many hours on the phone contacting performers, and asking them if they would give their services for the Variety Club Charity. I offered them all expenses of £50, as I was keen to get it off the ground.

Eventually I got a great line up of comics including Mike Osman, Bradley Walsh, Jeff Stevenson, Mike Lancaster, Maxie Mann, Syd Wright who was also a musical act that I put in the middle, and a very young Darren Day who was about sixteen, but I could tell at that age he was on his way up.

Not everybody agreed. I got turned down by Freddie Starr, Brian Connelly, and Bobby Davro who incidentally turned up on the night in Neptune's Palace and was drinking at the bar. Once I had set things up I got some posters made up, from a sign writer in Great Yarmouth, and tickets were put on sale in reception. I had not put anybody's name on the posters it was just billed as a Midnight Matinee "Comedians Gala" in aid of the Variety Club Sunshine Coaches. I was absolutely delighted when the tickets sold out on the first day.

I compered the night, and had the full band in, with my two girl dancers doing the opening. Each comic did about 10 minutes and it was the best night I had seen in Neptunes, it was truly a fantastic success, I had even arranged for a walk-down finale, and the audience gave them a standing ovation. When I did the running order, it was a problem for me who to close the show with, and I figured that none of them would want the closing spot, and I was right.

I decided that Mike Lancaster who was very strong, would be ideal for it. When I asked him he didn't fancy the idea, but I took him to one side and told him that in my opinion he was the only one who could do the job. I talked him into it, he closed the show, and did a brilliant job. Bradley Walsh who was unknown at the time, was outstanding, and I always remember he wore this great suit.

The following year I did it again with a few different comics, and Bradley who was doing another reason at the Pier Pavilion Cromer, also came back. He had been so outstanding the first year that I decided to close the show this time with him. It was indeed another great success, but this time another performer stood out above the rest it was comedian Maxie Mann. I must admit he was a bit "blue," but he wasn't offensive, Brad wasn't too happy about following him.

As we all know Bradley Walsh went on to become a big name, and rightly so, but it looks like Maxie Mann ended up in the box with the rest of us labelled "Not Everybody Makes It." After I had paid out the expenses I still had over £800 for the Variety Club, the punters had a great night, the General Manager was happy, everyone was a winner. In Alan Castledine's office the next morning, he said that he was amazed that the place was still packed out at 2am in the morning. He of course at that time, had only been used to keeping the late venue open until 1 a.m. With my experience with L.N.C. at Butlins, I knew that keeping the bar open until 2am would not be a problem.

The following week I got the Dallas Boys who were old mates, and they agreed to come for a lot less than their usual fee, as did the rock band The Dooleys. They were all fantastic memorable nights, and always a sell out.

After that I got the hypnotist Hugh Lennon, who was a big success, and with just one artiste to pay expenses we made a lot more money for the charity. That of course appealed to Alan Castledine more as he thought that I paid out too much money on the other shows. He then said that I should book Hugh Lennon every week, and on my last two years at Caister we had Hugh on the "Variety Club" nights more times than any other performer. Right across the Ladbroke Holiday Group a lot of money was raised for the Variety Club, and when I saw the Chairman on T.V. handing over a brand new Sunshine Coach it was nice to know that we had played our part.

As we came to the end of the season we all knew that the days of Ladbrokes had come to an end as the Holiday Division was taken over by Warners. I finished my last stint with the Baton Twirlers on the 29th October, and then did a few T.V. walk-on jobs for the B.B.C., Thames, and LWT, on shows "The Country Boy," "The Bill," and "London's Burning."

On the 8th December we flew out to Spain once more for five days on what was to be the very last Ladbroke Managers Trip. It was on this trip that the new Entertainment Executive told me that I would not be going back to Caister anymore, and that he wanted me to go to the Warner site Puckpool St Clare, on the Isle of Wight.

After telling me what a fantastic place it was, I agreed to go, in fact I was quite looking forward to a new and exciting challenge, but little did I know that it was not half as cracked up to be to what he had told me. Back in England after a few T.V. extra jobs, I was soon into what I thought would be my last Christmas season at Caister. It was now of course under the Warner banner, and Warner's were the new paymasters.

When 1989 came in, it was a quiet start for me. I had a job for Thames T.V. on a thing called "Storyboard," a few days on "The Bill" and a TV Commercial for United Biscuits. On the 12th March I was off to Sinah Warren Holiday Park at Hayling Island to attend my first Warners Seminar, for Entertainment Managers.

CHAPTER EIGHTEEN

"What Have I Let Myself in For?" Disaster On The Isle Of Wight It's Heaven In Haven

The company now controlled over 50 Holiday sites, with a mix between Warners and the old Ladbroke sites. At the seminar it was soon plain to see that it would be a managers meeting of two companies, Ladbrokes and Warners.

The Warner people were not too happy, as the Entertainment Executive and his Team were all Ladbroke People. As the meetings went on, you could feel the resentment. I never was a big fan of seminars but this was the worst that I had attended so far. We were instructed to put on a "Welcome Show' with our Team of "Coats" for the staff before the site actually opened. It was not a good show that we were given to do, but I thought with some talented coats we might get away with it.

On the very last night of the seminar I was informed that I would be going to the Isle of Wight that weekend, as it was open, and then prepare for Easter the following weekend. I had never worked on a site at Easter before, and was not expecting to do so at this Easter. Of course I would be happy to do so, but to just have it sprung on me at the last minute I felt was totally out of order. When you go away for seven months you take almost everything with you bar the kitchen sink, and of course I had only gone down to Hayling Island prepared for a week. Fortunately I did not have any other commitments, but the company did not know that. It then dawned on me that this could be the start of something bad, and I was beginning to wonder 'what have I let myself in for.'

I asked the main man if I could leave early on the Friday morning as I had to drive back to London before going to I.O.W. and it would give me a little more time. He said, No as they would be taking a group photograph at lunchtime. A group photo of 50 people - well maybe I would have been missed.

We got back home early evening on the Friday, and just had the Saturday to sort out our usual arrangements, packing up, and then we set of for the Isle of Wight on the Sunday.

Puckpool St Clare on the IOW were two Warner sites put together. On arrival it was plain to see that the site was run down, it had a well worn feel about it. The accommodation we were given was a punters chalet that was full board, so we would have to eat in the dining room. We were told that this would only be temporary until the staff accommodation was ready in the big house.

Now I had always been used to first class accommodation at Caister, self catering with fully equipped kitchen, and nice furniture with colour T.V. I also had full use of the dinning room if I wished to do so.

The big house was a magnificent looking old stone built mansion from the outside, but inside was the pits. It was converted into different rooms, with shared bathrooms, and it was nothing short of a disgrace. We were given a large downstairs room, that I suppose I could describe as a bedsit. We had a kettle so we were able to make tea and coffee. Once we had got our own bits and pieces in it, we did manage to make it look quite comfortable, and were also able to make sandwiches, and I managed to acquire a fridge.

At the top of the house were a lot of catering staff, cooks and waitress's, and of course they would always be up early at 6.30am, and when you don't finish work until 1 a.m. that does not go down too well. The bottom line is that it was lousy accommodation, and I felt that I should have been given better. I had met my Greencoat Team at the Seminar, but you don't really get to know them until you get on site, and start working with them.

We had our first meeting in the Green Coat room, and I was keen to find out what kind of talent they had. That was to be my next shock. Not one of them was able to do, an act, I had brought two girls with me from Caister, they were excellent Bluecoats, and very good movers, but they were not trained dancers, and the rest had no talent whatsoever.

The next evening the general manager had a meeting of all staff and his senior Departmental Managers, where we were all introduced to the staff. It was at this meeting that I and the rest of my staff had to perform a "Welcome Show" that had been devised for us by "Head Office," who in turn had told the G.M. that this would happen. About 45 minutes before we were due to start, I went up to the club Manager and asked him where the microphones were so that we could set up. "We don't have any microphones here" he said "we never have." - "What are you talking about" I said in disbelief, "how can we do a show in a venue this size without mics." He then said "Look, we do not have any equipment like that the show people always bring their own." It was then that I learned the real truth about the set up at Puckpool St Clare.

Warner's Greencoats were all talented entertainers, where as Ladbroke Blue Coat staff were taken on mainly for their personality, and if they had any talent that was a bonus. For the previous two years at Puckpool they had the same Entertainment Team that had been together even before that.

They worked for Warners all the year round, and over the years had built up a first class wardrobe of costumes. I heard that over the past two years they had presented excellent production shows, with stunning costumes. They even had their own scenic artist that built them wonderful stage sets and back drops. And not forgetting of course they supplied their own P.A. system, and microphones.

Now I was expected to follow that with no talent, no costumes, no scenery. No money and no microphones. I then made a big mistake by saying we would do the "Welcome Show" without a microphone. I knew it was rubbish before we even started it, but being the professional that I was, I thought we must do our best and see what happens.

The outcome was an out and out disaster, it was the worst thing that I have ever been involved in, I just wanted the ground to open and swallow us up. It was a total embarrassment, and I felt utterly humiliated.

The General Manager was a nice guy, and he could see what I was up against. The next day he bought some brand new microphones. On the night time I decided to hold some auditions with a keyboard player just to see if any of them could do anything. One girl said she could sing and dance. By this time the G.M had been in watching what was going on and he sat a few seats away from me. The girl started to sing, she was flat, out of tune, and sounded like a scalded cat. She then put the mic back in its stand, and skipped around the floor like a demented traffic warden that was trying to dodge traffic. The G.M. put his head in his hands, then before she had finished he came over to me tapped me on the shoulder and said "Good Luck," he then left.

Next morning it was time to kit out the team with their uniforms, and what a fiasco that turned out to be. A lot of Greencoat uniforms were delivered from the stores, they were not new, and were all in dry cleaning bags.

As we tried to fix up each member of the team, we found that there was not one of them that was able to find a complete uniform. They all got a Green jacket but some of them did not fit properly. There were no shirts for the boys, and no blouses for the girls, so they had to wear their own. They had different colour trousers, and the skirts looked a mess. All in all when they finally got dressed they looked like a bunch of renegades that had looted a Warner Holiday Camp. After a day or so we eventually got the uniforms sorted out to a reasonable standard, but before that I was in for another shock. When I went back stage the filth and mess that I found was unbelievable. Every nook and cranny was stuffed with empty bottles beer cans, half eaten burger in boxes, and underneath the stage area was heaps of rubbish, that you could tell by the cob webs had been there for years. I thought to myself that 'my predecessor's may have been able to put on great production shows, but they were lousy house keepers. The place was an out and out filthy tip.

I put on some old clothes and with the rest of my staff we cleaned the place out. We actually filled up twenty two black bin liners with rubbish. It took us all a long time, but when we had finished it looked real ship shape, and smelt as sweet as a nut, and I was very pleased with the outcome. The backstage area, and the stage looked great, even though I didn't have anything to put on it.

When I came to look into the games room and equipment, that was the same. A complete mess. I could find no darts, the dart boards looked thirty years old with big lumps sticking out of them. table tennis bats with the rubbers hanging off. The pool tables did not have a complete set of balls between them, it was a joke. When I spoke to the games room attendant, who had worked there for a few years, he told me that he was sick of asking for stuff, and that nobody was interested. "Make me a list of what you need" I said to him "I'm interested, and I'll get it sorted out." You cannot run an Entertainment Department, by just doing shows, the holiday makers pay good money. And they want to use all the facilities.

The next day I got a list of stuff from the games room attendant, and after I had spoken to the G.M. he okayed it for me to order all the games equipment that I needed. The games room attendant was a nice old boy, and he was delighted, he said it's the best this place has looked in five years. We did the Easter, and all went quite well, it was not perfect but I knew that it could get better. I had a young lad of about eighteen who was doing well as the children's Entertainer he was never going to be a "Crumble" but he was getting better every performance, and I felt he would be a big success.

The team was now bonding well, and they knew what I expected of them, and we all got on very well together. I did put on a mini Variety Show with what talent I had, it wasn't great, but it was passable. Of course I was getting comments from punters of how good the shows were last year "but your Greencoats are much more friendlier" they would say.

That was good to hear, because if they liked them as people, they could get away with it, and at least the audience would know they were doing their best.

Prior to Easter, and for three weeks after Easter we did Special Weekends with some Star Cabarets with Marty Wilde, Frank Carson, and Mike Read. All was going well, until the week before the full season was about to start when we had what was called the Mecca Bingo Week. The site was taken over by the Managers, staff, and families of the Mecca Bingo Clubs from ail over the country.

As always on all of these type of special events they always have a committee of people who are in charge. It was these people who gave me a really hard time. It was not long before they were complaining about the entertainment, or lack of it. I think we only had one cabaret booked for the whole week. Our Entertainment Executive at Head Office was expecting me to put on shows for this Bingo week, with the Team that I had. Now the Greencoat team were lovely people and were doing a first class job as Greencoats, but they were not entertainers. It was not their fault that they had been put in this position. The Bingo Committee would keep on about the production shows of previous years, and that by comparison this years Greencoat Show was rubbish. - Well I guess it took a big brain to work that out.

As the week went on there was a lot of nasty stage whispers, and back-stabbing. They were not your typical holiday makers, and I knew that once they had gone and the season was up and running properly, things would work out fine and we would have a great season. However, I did not realise at the time but the committee chief had been on the phone to Head Office with his complaints. H.Q. in their wisdom, decided then to send down another Entertainments Manager, and did not even tell me.

He was a Warner man and just turned up out of the blue. He was not a stranger to me, and I knew him quite well. "What are you doing here?" I asked him, "I don't know" he said "Head Office just asked me to come down. He was there for three days, did not make one scrap of difference, and did a 25 minute comedy spot on the last night. I had nothing against the guy, as I knew it was not his idea to come down, and I always got on very well with him. But I was angry and felt humiliated, and I knew that first thing in the morning I would be on the phone to Head Office myself, as there were a few questions I wanted answers to.

In the morning after a good nights sleep, I felt quite cool and relaxed, the Mecca Bingo crowd were on their way, the team had all worked well, I was confident that things would work out fine, and I was really looking forward to the season. You could say that I was feeling good, but as I picked up the phone, to call Head Office all those feelings were about to change in a matter of minutes.

I got through to the Entertainment Executive, and of course he was aware of the troubles we had been having. I asked him what was the idea of sending somebody else down without even telling me. I could not believe it when he went on the offensive saying that it was all my fault. Things then started to get a bit heated, and we were both raising our voice. I then said to him "How the hell do you expect me to put on two production shows in one week with no costumes or props and above all no talent." He seemed to think that it was easy, and it could be done. "Alright then" I said "If you think its easy, you come down and do it." His reply was quick "That's your job" he said. It was for me like a red rag to a bull.

"Not anymore it isn't - I resign," I then quickly added "but I won't walk out on the job, and leave you in the lurch, I will stay on until you find a replacement." Without any thought he came back with "That's ok, you can go today."

My next job was to tell the team. It was to be one of the hardest tasks I had ever had to do. They were a great young bunch of people I had grown fond of them all, and I felt awful as I was letting them all down. I called a meeting in the Green room, and I was not a bit prepared for their reaction. The girls burst into tears, and even some of the boys were crying. It was a very sad occasion, but I guess it was nice to know that they liked, and had a lot of respect for me as their boss. Over the years I had built up a reputation, and was very well known in the Holiday Centre industry in all the big companies. But though a reputation takes years to build, it can be knocked down in a matter of minutes, and I felt that I had taken a fair bit of damage to it during my time at Puckpool St Clare. It would have been restored of course had I stayed, but it was not to be, and I have always been a firm believer of the old cliché "when one door closes another opens."

As I drove onto the ferry, and then watched the Isle of Wight disappear, I wondered how long it would be before that next door would open. Well I'm pleased to say that it wasn't that long, in fact it was five weeks.

Back in London, I must say I was very concerned, and was beginning to wander if I had acted a bit hasty. I had put myself out of work, we were coming up to the beginning of May, and for the first time in twenty six years it looked like I would not have a summer season.

I was soon on the phone to my T.V. Agents, and the first week I got a couple of days work, one on "Eastenders" for the B.B.C. and a day on "The Bill" for Thames. The following week I did two days filming on location on a T.V. commercial for the Halifax Building Society. In the mean time I was writing various letters for seasons that I had seen advertised in the "Stage" trade paper, but I wasn't very confident, as none of them looked that good and I didn't think the money would be that good either.

I also rang around various contacts that I had, one of which was my old mate Ken Hopson, who I knew from my Butlin days. When I left Butlins he was at that time the assistant to the Entertainment Chief Executive Frank Mansell. I rang him at home, and he was now working as a Booker for Haven Holidays, it was a company that I had never heard of at that time.

He told me that he had nowhere he could place me for the summer, as he had already set up all the Holiday Parks under his control. However if anything came up that would be suitable for me, he would let me know. I then did another T.V. job, and a commercial for Nat West Bank.

I was now into the fifth week since I left the I.O.W., and I was not feeling too upbeat as we were almost into June. The phone rang, it was Ken Hopson "Dave, a vacancy for an Entertainment Manager has come up at Hastings, I wonder would you be interested?" - It was like music to my ears, as I was beginning to wander if it was too late in the year for me to get fixed up. "I sure would" -

"Great" he said "its at Combehaven Holiday Park, it's a nice site, and we have fixed some great late Night Cabarets, including Bob Monkhouse, Little An Large, The Rockin Berries, Kenny Ball and the Jazzmen, and the Dallas Boys." I thought "Ring-A-Ding-Ding, if its good enough for them its good enough for me.'

Ken then arranged for me to go down to Hastings to meet him on the Sunday, and he would introduce me to the General Manager. I did not know at the time but the G.M. was new to Combehaven, he had come from another Haven Park and had only been there for a few months. In the short time that he had been there, he had made quite a few considerable changes. In fact he was quite an axe man, having already sacked his Catering Manager, his Club/Bars Manager, his Head of Security, and his Entertainment Manager, (who I was going to replace).

Anyway like I have just said, I was completely unaware of all that had been going on, and I guess it was just as well as it could have been a bit off-putting. I met up with Ken Hopson at 11 am outside reception, and we soon headed for the G.M's. office.

As we walked in the G.M. was sat behind his desk. He stood up to greet us, and walked around to the front of the desk. He was of stocky build, about five feet nine, had fair hair, with a short Perry Como style haircut. He looked very smart wearing a light grey suit, with matching tie. Ken then started the introduction "Dave I'd like you to meet the General Manager, Mike John. It was to be the beginning of a long and happy association between the two of us. I have always said that Colin Wright at Caister was the Daddy of all General Managers, but Mike John was a close second. For the first few weeks that I worked for him I thought he was a bit harsh with many people, and if he said jump, they really jumped. Many described him as a tyrant, and those that did not know him too well would not disagree with that.

The bottom line was, that he was a great G.M., and looked after his staff. The staff accommodation was the best that I had ever seen, and they all had colour T.Vs. He did say that if ever they were short of a T.V. for a guest caravan then it would have to come out of a staff caravan, but I never recalled that ever happening.

If you were doing a good job to his high standards you had no problems, but if you were a slacker, and not doing your job, it would be "see you later" and you were gone. I once said to him "I don't suffer fools gladly," he looked at me in the eye and said "I don't suffer fools at all."

I worked for Mike for three years, we had great respect for each other, became good friends, had a lot of laughs, and drunk a lot of booze, but more of that later. After I had agreed terms, the contract was signed, and I was back the next day on the Monday to take up my position as the new Entertainment Manager at Combehaven Holiday Park.

My first job was to call a meeting of the Entertainment Staff. They were not called coats, they were called Havenmates. I decided for the first week to let them carry on with what they had been doing and I would observe, and see how they had been operating. It did not take me long to see why the previous Entertainments Manager was no longer there, the Entertainment Department was on absolute shambles.

It was the most undisciplined team I had ever come across, and it was quite clear to me that I would have to make changes, a lot of changes.

When I got into my second week I knew that I would have to get rid of everybody and start from scratch. It would not be easy, as I could not get rid of all the Havenmates in one sweep, as it would be impossible to replace them.

I made inquires about replacements, and it became gradual. I started by getting rid of the odd one or two, with new ones coming in, and after about four weeks I had completely changed the team bar one.

The one that I kept was a nice young man, who had been a bit wild, but once he knew how I liked things to be done, he buckled down to the job, and at the end of it all he became a very good Havenmate.

We now had a reasonably good Entertainment Team, and the department was looking in good shape. It was when I joined Haven Holidays that I first became aware of Caravan Owners.

Unlike Butlins, Ladbrokes, and Warners, Haven were a selling company. They would sell caravans for up to £25,000, and they had no shortage of takers. Once the owners caravan was sited on a plot, they would then pay the company an annual rent for the plot. It was good business, and when I first started at Combehaven I would say that just over half of the caravans on the site were owners.

The only trouble was that many of the people who owned a caravan, thought they owned the whole park. Unlike the normal holiday maker who would be there for a week, the owner would be there every weekend, and many of them for six weeks during the school holidays.

As the weeks went on I got on very well with most of them, but there was always the odd pain in the 'arse, that done nothing but moan about everything. They were very demanding, and at that time the company would bend over backwards to keep them happy, and they always seemed to get what they wanted. Even if the DJ was not playing what they wanted, and they would want "Sixties Music" it would not mater if the floor was packed, the D.J. would have to play sixties. I was still new to the company so I went along with the owners demands, but after a couple of years that did change.

At the beginning and the end of each season we would put on an "Owners Party." They would be quite swell affairs with a big star name cabaret, and a lavish buffet, and the room would be decorated in flowers and balloons, and I must say that Mike John really knew how to put on a party, they were great nights, and of course it was good for business, with the caravan sales manager always about to get owners to up-grade their caravan to the very latest model.

My first season at Haven was a great success, and though it was a shambles when I started, and I found Haven to be well behind in expertise compared to the other companies that I had worked for, I was soon able to bring it up to a good standard with my experience and ideas that I had gained over the years. I could see that Mike John was well impressed and he gave me every support. When we got to the Finals week, it really knocked 'em bandy, as they had never seen anything like it, but I always staged these events, the only way I knew.

It was always a joy to compere the Late Night Cabarets, and I felt completely at home working with such quality performers. I have already spoken about the class of Bob Monkhouse, he really did stand out from the rest. I would always be amazed at his outstanding memory. Every time he came he would ask me the names of various people that worked on the site, or if anything unusual had happened. He would then use it in his act, and of course it would bring the house down.

I worked with Bob many times over the years on the L.N.Cs, it was always a great pleasure, and he made me laugh each time I saw him. The only regret that I had was the time we were talking in the dressing room after his performance, and he was telling me some stories of the old Variety days, I could have listened to him all night, and I told him so, but unfortunately it was getting late, (the early hours of the morning in fact) and he had to go. I wished that it had been earlier and he could have stayed longer. He was such an interesting man and was so knowledgeable about my favourite subject.

It was the very last night of the season, and it was one hell of a party. No sooner had I emptied my glass of whisky, Mike John was there to put another in my hand. About half way through the evening he came up to me and asked if I would like to come back and work for him again next year. He then said "there are four reasons I want you to come back next year. First, I have learned a lot from you, over this past season second - you are very professional in everything you do. Third, you have got a lot of class. And the fourth is the most important of all - I like you." With that he gave me a kiss on the cheek. How could I say no. All in all as I have already mentioned, I did three seasons at Combehaven with Mike John, and I had a fantastic time on all of them.

Mike was a great family man with two children, and his wife Lynn was the admin manager on the site. During the winter a lot of money was put into Combehaven, it had a complete refit, and a brand new club was built. It was called The Conqueror Club. At the start of the new season in 1990 it looked like a new site, everywhere was spotless, and the place had a great buzz about it.

When Mike had said that he had learned a lot from me, I did not doubt that, but in turn I also learned from him, I guess that was maybe one of the reasons that we got on so well together. That of course is one of the fascinating things about our business, you can never stop learning. If ever the time comes when you feel that you do know it all, that's the time to give up. I recall one time when I didn't have a lot of talent to put on a show Mike suggested to me to "put on a sing song." I said "a sing song?, that's so old hat." I hadn't done a sing song since my days at Butlins in the old Pig and Whistle. We spoke about it for a while, and then I thought well I haven't got anything else at the moment, so I'll give it a try for a couple of weeks until I can sort out something better. Anyway I got a few medleys together of old songs, and the band leader had a few medleys of his own. I got the Havenmates dressed in fancy dress, and it was a big success. I then knew that I could build this up, and developed certain characters and before I knew it, we had a real show. We did a Bride and Groom routine, together with guests and a photographer as I sang

"Flash Bang Wallop, What a Picture" as they all changed pose's to match up with the lyric. We did many different numbers, and each one was well staged and choreographed. I had posters made up and it was billed "The Sing-A-Long Show." We did it every Friday night, and it was the smash hit of the week.

The owners that came down every Friday, would come in especially to see it, and that did please me.

The "Sing-A-Long Show" was a great success, and word spread to Head Office, but if Mike John had not asked me to do a sing song, it would never have happened.

On that very last night of the 1989 season before Mike John had asked me to come back, he was on stage handing out gifts, presents, and champagne as only he could, to members of his staff as a thank you for all their hard work. He was the only G.M, that I ever saw do that. It brought back memories of my very first summer season at the Coliseum Theatre Rhyl on that last night.

The seasons were now getting longer, and I guess that was down to the owners, as they wanted to get into their caravans as soon as they could in March, and stayed as long as they could till the end of October, and that was soon to become the beginning of November. It seemed that the winters were now getting shorter for me, and with my T.V. work I did not have a lot of dates to fill before I was back for the summer season again.

Christmas 1989 was the first Christmas that I had spent at home for that many years I couldn't remember the last time. It was just Livvy and me, and it was fantastic after all the excitement at Caister over the years, and we enjoyed every minute of it. To be in your own home with home cooking was really special. We went to Midnight Mass, and it was a really wonderful peaceful Christmas, there was nowhere else in the world that I would rather have been, just Livvy and me, and all the usual goodies.

It was the end of a decade, we were into 1990, and we had hardly finished wishing everybody a Happy New Year when I was thinking about the start of the new season. I had a few T.V. jobs including four days on "Eastenders, and some photographic work, and before I knew it the date was 2nd April and I was back at Combehaven at Hastings.

We had some Special Event weeks before the main season started on 4th May. I went into the new season feeling very confident and up - beat, as I knew that I did not have to prove myself to anybody having done that the previous year. The owners welcomed me with open arms, and I felt that I was now really a part of Combehaven.

As I have said before, it is so much easier to entertain an audience that knows you. I had quite a good Haven Mate team, some of whom I had asked back from last year, and things were looking really good, in fact it was unrecognisable from when I first walked into Haven last June, to find unorganised chaos.

I was still not happy with certain areas, and knew that they could be improved upon. The most important thing on a holiday park of course is the children's entertainment. If the children are happy, then the parents are happy.

Havens children's entertainment is called the Tiger Club. When I first arrived last year, this comprised of a Sunday morning meeting with about a dozen kiddies, and two Havenmates they took them for a ride on the swings, it was a joke. I did change that on my second week, and got them to open the club, so that we could take the children inside, and organise a few more activities for them, and as the weeks went on it did get better.

However we were lacking a quality children's Entertainer. I spoke to Mike John about this and for the 1990 season, he got a guy that he knew and assured me that he was top drawer. I must say that he did do a good job, but he was not in the same league as the guy that I had in mind. It was then that I made up my mind that next year I must get the one person that will really get this family room buzzing, - my old mate Captain Crumble.

The season went by very quickly and once again it was a great success. As always I always enjoyed the L.N.Cs, and we had some top quality acts. It was quite funny the night we had Tom O'Connor, as I walked out at the beginning to do my usual warm-up and introduce the show, a section of the audience shouted out "Hi ya Tom" - they thought I was him, but they soon realised their mistake. We both did look a bit alike from a distance, I guess it was the grey hair.

The night my old mates The Dallas Boys came it was my birthday, and before they finished their act, they called me onstage and presented me with a bottle of champagne courtesy of Mike John, I then of course had to suffer the embarrassment of the happy birthday song, but it was a really nice moment, and I enjoyed the champagne. As we came towards the end of the season, and various acts would be making their last appearance, Mike would come on at the end of their act as I was calling them back to take a final bow, and present them with a bottle of champagne. I used to call him "Champagne Charlie" he didn't know that, - until now of course. It was a nice gesture on Mikes part, but any acts that hadn't done so well over the season, they got nothing.

Towards the end of the season there was another takeover, and this time Haven Holidays were about to takeover Warner Holidays.

It was quite ironic, when I left Puckpool on the I.O.W. at the beginning of 1989, I thought that would be the last I would see of the Warner's crowd, and now it looked like at the beginning of 1991 they would all be back on board again, I did have mixed feelings about it, but it looked like Haven would be the Masters, as the new company was to be called Haven/Warner.

CHAPTER NINETEEN

An MFI Stool For A Superstar, Back To Beer Stains And Chewing Gum, Fighting A War On Two Fronts At Presthaven

It was during my time at Combehaven that I experienced one of my most exciting showbiz moments.

It was a Country and Western Music Festival, that was staged over a week. The place was packed out with country music fans, and many of the top names in country music had been booked for this event. It was a self contained package, and they had their own M.Cs that would introduce the various bands.

When I looked at the list of artistes that would be appearing, I was quite excited to see that one of my boy-hood all time favourites was on the list. It was the big American star of the fifties Guy Mitchell, who had so many big hits including "Singing The Blues" "Pretty Little Blackeyed Susie," "She Wears Red Feathers," and many many more. In fact when I was fifteen the first record I ever bought was his hit "Look At That Girl."

I had seen him live twice, once at the London Palladium, and once of the Finsbury Park Empire, and I must say that I was quite looking forward to seeing him again after so many years.

You can imagine how thrilled I was when the Haven Booker, that had arranged the festival, Al Harris, who used to be a Butlin man, asked me to compere the show. I had not introduced any of the bands up to that point, and said to AL that I did not want to tread on anybody's toes. He then said "It's a special night, and I don't want anything to go wrong." The day before Guy Mitchell was due to appear, we got a message from his management that he required a stool. The only stools we had were not suitable, and the one back-stage was too tatty, so I said to Mike John "can we get one from another site?" He said "no, we will buy a new one, I'll send somebody out to MFI." I said "MFI?, I hope it doesn't collapse when he sits on it." Anyway when we got the stool and put it together it did not look too bad, and was quite sturdy.

The night came, and it was such a thrill for me to stand on stage and introduce one of the biggest American star of the fifties, Guy Mitchell.

I went out front to watch his performance, and was surprised how good he looked for his age, and the voice was almost the same. It was a real nostalgia trip, and I remembered all the songs from all those years ago. He gave a very good performance even though he did forget the words a few times, but a girl on guitar just behind him soon helped him out with that. The audience loved him, and it was a most memorable night, especially for me.

In the dressing room afterwards we had a chat, and I told him that his record of "Look At That Girl" was the first record that I ever bought, and that I still had it in my collection of 78s. He seemed quite pleased to hear that, and I was pleased to find that Guy Mitchell was a really nice Guy.

The trips abroad with Ladbrokes were long gone, but Mike John would look after his Management team at the end of a season. It was to show his appreciation for their hard work.

I recall one occasion when he arranged for the ladies to have a night out in a fancy restaurant, and for us guys it would be a night out in the West End. He laid on a stretch limo, champagne in ice buckets were placed in the boot together with glasses, and off we set to Stringfellows London Hippodrome.

We pulled up outside the Hippodrome, and the driver was given a time to come back to pick us up. A table was laid on and we had quite a nice meal.

With hindsight, I guess it wasn't the best of venues for our night out, as it was so noisy and you couldn't hear yourself speak. We did however all have a good time, and it was worth suffering the noise to experience the wonderful Disco lighting rig, it was quite amazing to see. I did however notice that Mike was getting rather agitated about the volume, as he was always keen to keep the volume at a decent level in our own venues.

By now we had all had quite a few drinks and you could feel the vibration from the sheer noise under your feet, and I must say the volume was quite unbearable, but it didn't seem to bother the regular punters, and the dance floor was packed. Suddenly Mike turned to me, pointed to the DJ, and at the top of his voice shouted "Dave, tell that DJ to turn the fucking volume down."

I did no such thing of course, but for a moment he must have felt that he was the governor of the Hippodrome. As we drove back in the stretch limo to Hastings, sipping champagne, and Mike and a couple of the others puffing on their cigars, it was a wonderful end to a very pleasant evening.

They were really great times in those early days at Haven, and Mike was an excellent G.M. and was well in control of Combehaven, but now that it was Haven/Warner, I feared that he may lose some of his power.

When the season ended Mike asked me to do a few special event weekends, and then for the first time they were going to open the site for New Years Eve. Mikes wife Lynn would always put me in the top of the range accommodation, with fruit on the table, a bottle of wine in the fridge, and all the little nick nacks that you get in a first class hotel.

Of course I know that I would not have got this kind of treatment, if I had not been doing a good job, but I was always very grateful.

New Years Eve was a great triumph for me, and I did some material that I had not done before, and a mime routine that I had not done for a couple of years brought the house down.

The booze was flowing freely, and it was a wonderful night, we rang in the New Year, the balloons came down, streamers were flying and champagne corks were popping. As the night ended Mike invited me round to his house in the morning for a "late breakfast." When I got out of bed the next morning, before I went round to Mikes' house I must admit that I had to walk around the site first of all to get my head together. When I got to his house, I had a cup of coffee, but I could not face a breakfast.

We were now into 1991 and it was the year that us long suffering Spurs supporters were pleased that the year ended in one, and we reached the F.A. Cup Final at Wembley. I was there, to see us win the F.A. Cup for the eighth time by beating Nottingham Forest, and were now back in European Competition.

As the year began I did a few T.V. jobs on shows like "Desmond" for Channel 4 "Collision Course" for the B.B.C., and "The Bill" for Thames. The seasons were now getting longer, starting in March and going right through to the beginning of November.

By now of course with the new company Haven/Warner there had been a lot of changes in top management. The Entertainment Executive that I had words with over the Low. fiasco, had been replaced by a new younger man. He did appear to have a lot of good ideas, and things were looking good.

The Entertainment Managers were now given a new title and were now known as the Head Of Entertainment. The first Haven/Warner H.O.E. Seminar was held at Combehaven At Hastings, commencing on Sunday 17th March. There were lots of people that I knew, and many Warner people that I thought I would never see again. The week was a real drag, and the meetings would go on from 9am until 10pm. Of course we had meal breaks, but it was far too long. As I have already said many of the ideas put across were very good and once they were put into operation worked very well. However, I felt that most of the stuff had nothing to do with entertainment, and it was a complete bore.

When the week came to an end I was more than pleased, and could get on with training my own staff, and running my own site. It was to be my best season so far, my Havenmate team were the best I had ever had, they had pride, they all wanted to be the best, and they were. The icing on the cake for me was that I had my old mate on board Captain Crumble. At Caister he had always worked in the Childrens' Club, but at Combehaven I put him in the new Conquerer Club as compere . It was a family room, and it proved a great success, as indeed he is the complete family Entertainer. The place would fill up at 6.30 every evening so that people could get a seat.

It was indeed the best season that I had at Combehaven, and it was a joy. I was very proud of my Havenmate team, they worked together like a well oiled machine.

1991 was the year that I won the Haven/Warner Head of Entertainment of The Year Award. Mike John said I should have won it the year before, but it was just Haven then. The following year Warner's broke away from Haven, and it became just Haven once more, so I guess in a way it was quite unique to be the only one to win the award when the two brand names Haven/Warner were together.

As the season was going into its last few weeks Mike John came into my office one day and sat down for a chat. After about five minutes or so he asked "Have you ever thought about going back to Caister?" - "No I haven't, why do you ask?" He paused for a moment looking up at the wall, then he said "They want me to go to Caister next year." I then said to him "I have had no inclination whatsoever to go back to Caister, but if you go, then I'll go." - "great that's exactly what I hoped you'd say." - "Sounds good to me," I said "and we'll take the whole team with us."

The season finished on Friday 25th October, and on the Saturday it was the Owners Party. The Pantomime producer David Lee was based in St Leonards, and he was eager to get a footing in with Haven Holidays. I had known him for a couple of years and seen some of his production shows. I spoke to David and said I may be able to fix it for him to put in a production show for the owners Party Night, if he could keep the cost down, he was dead keen and he gave me a price. All I had to do now was to sell it to Mike John. Mike was not too sure at first, but when I pointed out to him what a good deal it was, and what a great night it would be, he agreed.

On these Owners Party Nights, we always had a star name Top

of the Bill. It was always a secret who the star would be, and they never knew until it was announced on stage.

David Lees production show would be an hour show during the first half of the evening, and the star attraction was to be comedian Mike Read (East Enders Frank Butcher). The production show was a great success and when the time came for me to introduce Mike Read, the audience still had no idea who it was, and I just said to them "I'll give you a clue" with that the band struck up the theme tune of "Eastenders and the buzz around the room was fantastic ………."and if you don't know here he is - Mike Read." The audience erupted with excitement, and Mike tore the roof off, it was a really wonderful night.

I was pleased that it went so well because when Mike Read arrived he wasn't too pleased to learn that he had an hour production show in front of him. He said had he known he would not have arrived so early, as he likes to get on as soon as possible, and not hang around too long. I knew exactly what he meant as I was the same when I was doing cabaret, the more you hang about the more nervous you get. He was given a nice caravan to rest up in while he waited, and Mike John gave him a bottle of whisky, I was only pleased that he didn't drink it.

It was nice to get back home for a few days break, and then the following weekend I was involved with the Disco Dancing Championship Finals.

In the next few weeks I had signed a contract to return to Caister for the summer, and also for the Christmas Season. I had just got used to spending Christmas at home, but I soon got used to the idea, and I was more than happy, as I had arranged for my Combehaven Mate team to all come with me. I also took all my props and costumes, so we moved into Caister "Lock stock and barrel." The General Manager at Caister (who I had never met before) gave me the impression that he was not too happy that I was there. He was quite a young G.M, and maybe he would have preferred a young H.O.E.

However, I think he soon changed his opinion, and when we did the "Havenmate Show" I was really proud. Neptune's Palace of course had great facilities, and the costumes looked fantastic the performers were on top of their game, and we tore the roof off, the audience loved it. In all fairness to the G.M. he made the effort to find me afterwards, and said it was the best show he had seen.

I was surprised then to hear him talking about next year, as it was clear that he did not know that Mike John would be taking over after Christmas, and of course I did not enlighten him. It was all a bit hush, hush, but there were a few rumours going around. Just before we opened for Christmas, Mike and his wife Lynn came on to Caister to look the place over, and I broke off from rehearsals to speak to them. I thought that everything was in order. - But was it? I knew that the young GMs days were numbered. But I did not expect them to sack him on Boxing Day, but that was what happened. I thought the company was out of order in their timing, but of course I did not know all the details, but I do know that when the axe falls, it falls fast.

Christmas was soon over and it was a great success, but before I left Caister I was in for another shock. Mike John would not be going to Caister after all. The only reason that I agreed to go back to Caister was because Mike was going as G.M. now he's staying at Hastings and I'm here. I can tell you I was bitterly disappointed. I would have loved to have seen M.J. at Caister, and I know that he would have loved it.

Mike did book me again at Combehaven for New Years Eve, it was to be my very last appearance there. He told me his reasons for turning down the Caister job, and they were personal, and I fully understood. We saw in the New Year of 1992 together, and it was the last time that I worked for Mike John. It would not however be the last time that I would have a drink with him, that would be another major event in London's West End.

I was back at Combehaven at the end of March for the Entertainments Seminar, and by now the new Regime had over 300 Havenmates in attendance apart from the H.O.E.s, it was like a Jamboree.

At the end of the week clutching my folder that had been daily filled up with paper work, and by now was about 12 inches thick. I set off for the road to Great Yarmouth, and my second stint at Caister Holiday Centre.

I must say that Caister had always been very special to me, as I had so many fantastic times there, and of course I could never forget my triumphs in the Holiday Inn.

Of course there were lots of changes since the Ladbroke days. Many of the old chalets had been knocked down, and replaced with caravans. The Haven Sales Office had been busy, and there were now lots of Owners on the site. I was very used to owners by now with my experiences at Combehaven, but a lot of the old Caister Staff some of which had been there for a number of years found the Owners to be very demanding (as they were,) and a pain in the 'arse, (as they were) but not all of them I hasten to ad. I was sorry to see that the football field had now gone, and was full of caravans, so that put an end to my organising a football team as I had done in the past.

I soon got back into the swing of things at Caister, and after a few weeks it was as if, I had never been away. It was to be the first of three more great years at Caister, and over the years I do have some wonderful memories. One of the regular punters over the years was a very large lady called Nellie. I would say she must have been at least 16 stone. She was very bad on her feet, and would use a couple of walking sticks. For the whole week she would wear the same clothes, a pair of big baggy shorts, a T-shirt an old green cardigan, a woolly hat, white socks and trainers on her feet. We always knew when Nellie was approaching, as the smell would arrive two minutes before she did. She did put on a lot of talcum powder, but that only made it worse. One day she came into my office and asked me if I could arrange transport to take her over the other side of the site to the Carousel Club for the afternoon Bingo session. "My legs have been playing me up all day, and I'll never make it" she said. "Of course I can Nellie, I'll arrange a van, and two of my lads will take you over there." I then told her to go to a pick up point half an hour before the Bingo session, to meet the boys with the van.

When the time came I thought I would just take a walk up to the pick up point to see that she got picked up okay. I was one hundred percent sure that all would be okay, as the two boys that I asked to do the job were very reliable but I must say that when I first told them what I wanted them to do, neither of them fancied it one bit.

Suddenly I saw a Transit van being driven by one of my lads, as it passed me, I could see both the back doors were open, a pair of chubby legs in shorts, with white socks and trainers were hanging out of the back, as it turned round a bend and disappeared.

I heard some time later that when the boys met Nellie with the van, they could not get her up into the passenger seat, and had to put her in the back. They then found they could not lift her up into the back of the van, as she was too big and heavy. They then got her to put her back side up against the back entrance of the van, go up on her tip toes, and one of the boys pulled her shoulders slowly back while the other lifted her legs up, and they both tried to push her up into the van. They then found that she got stuck half way and decided that one would hold onto her, while the other one drove the van. They did get her to the bingo session quite safely, and Nellie was very happy, but I can tell you, it was not a pretty sight.

We had some great, big name acts in Neptune's Palace, with Edwin Starr, and Jimmy James and the vagabonds pure class, but I guess the best night of all was Cannon And Ball.

The night they came, they put rows of chairs on the dance floor, closed the bar when they were on, and turned Neptune's Palace into a Theatre, and of course it made such a difference.

Another double act that was a big hit were Little and Large, but they played the Carousel Club on the night of the Owners Party. I must say that Haven really did look after their owners well, I had seen it at Combehaven, and now it was at Caister.

It was early in the season that I was offered pantomime by David Lee of Pantoni Productions, to play Alderman Fitzwarren at the Civic Theatre, Halifax in "Dick Whittington." I was happy to accept the part as it was a good cast with Kathy Staff (of Nora Batty fame) Chris Quinten (who had made his name in "Coronation Street," and Paul Henry (Benny In "Crossroads.") To top all that, Halifax was not too far from Rochdale, and I was able to stay with my daughter Bernadette and her family. We would also be able to spend Christmas together.

When the season finished on the 10th October, I went home for five days for a nice break, and the Entertainment Executive gave me five more weeks work at Caister to work on the out of season special events.

They included the Keyboards Cavalcade, that included a week of keyboard players giving concerts, and a number of different companies setting up mini shops to sell their instruments. It was a very popular week, and it was full of keyboard enthusiasts. That week was followed by the Baton Twirlers, and their broken down old coaches that I have already told you about.

We then had a Ladies Keep Fit Weekend, now that was a sight to see. They all enjoyed themselves, and had a wonderful time. The dance floor in Neptune's Palace, would be packed and not a man in sight, except of course those in the Band. I never thought that women could have such a great time without any men, but they can, and they did.

During the day they would all attend various keep-fit sessions in their leotards and tights. They were all different shapes and sizes, and it would amuse me to see a group of these very large ladies, that had just come from a keep-fit session. You would see them an hour later at the servery in the restaurant, piling their plates as high as they could with chips, sausages, pies, the lot, and when they sat down, they would really get stuck in, they may have been keeping fit, but they were also keeping fat.

We then had an Accordion Festival for a week, that was similar to the keyboards, followed by a week of Majorettes, who were not unlike the Jazz Bands, except that their transport looked a lot more safer, as all of their coaches looked quite new.

I eventually finished at Caister on 22nd November, and after a few days at home, it was great to sit in my own armchair, catching up on a bit of telly, and sipping my own favourite Malt Whisky.

The first week in December we went down to Exeter to spend a few days with my eldest step daughter Sonia and her family. It was a very nice visit and we all enjoyed ourselves.

When we got back home, we were not there for very long before I was off to Yorkshire to start rehearsals for the panto at the Halifax Civic Theatre. I was pleased to be doing pantomime again, and it was a joy to be back working in a theatre again (Proper Showbusiness). It was only a four week run, but it seemed a lot longer, as unfortunately it was not what I would call a happy show.

It was an excellent pantomime, well dressed, and well produced, but there were quite a few "fall outs" backstage. I did not regret doing it, but I must admit I was happy when the final curtain came down as were quite a number of the cast.

It was now the middle of January 1993, and Haven Head Office asked me to join their Recruitment Team. I was delighted to do so, as I thought I would be able to pick my own Havenmate Team for Caister, as indeed I was. It was a recruitment road show, spread over three weeks starting with two days in Newcastle. We then did two days in Manchester, followed by two days in Bristol.

The interviews and auditions were held in various hotels, and we must have seen hundreds of people. Applicants would be interviewed in one room, then go into another for an audition with our keyboard player that travelled with us. We would of course fill in forms on each applicant, and at the end of the day the team would meet to access everybody. We saw some very good people, but you can imagine we also saw quite a lot of odd-balls. Many had just walked in off the street to see what was going on. I asked one guy why he wanted to be a Havenmate and he replied "I've heard you can pull a bird every night." I didn't think he would have had his mind on the job, and he didn't get it.

Another time a scruffy character walked in, I think he was a tramp, he even had a piece of string tied round his dirty old raincoat. He sat down with a group of applicants that were waiting, and a couple of them moved away. He then got up went over to the coffee urn, poured' himself a coffee in one of the paper cups, stuffed a few biscuits in his pockets, walked out of the door, and we've never seen him since.

From Bristol we went to Birmingham for two days, and we finished the tour with three days in London. I picked some excellent boys and girls, and with team members that I had from the previous year coming back with me again, some of which were with me at Combehaven, my 1993 Havenmate team was to be my very best team ever. They were "simply the best," and we were like a family. Week in and week out, punters would come up to me and compliment me on the boys and girls, and say what a wonderful hard working Havenmate team they were, and I was very proud of them.

The season was a great success most of the cabarets did very well, and the Late Night Cabarets were always a big hit and with my two dancers Jo and Tracy opening the show we couldn't miss. Having said that Roger De Corcey and his Nookie Bear was never a happy man on the L.N.Cs. I had worked with Roger many times and make no mistake he's a great act, and he always makes me laugh. At Combehaven he would tear the roof off, as it was adults only. Roger was never happy at Caister as Neptune's Palace is a family room with children in, and it is no secret as he has said on T.V. that he does not like kids in the audience.

For a show or a cabaret I would always get the children to come down and sit on the floor in front of the stage. It worked very well, and they were well behaved, and the parents could enjoy the show without being disturbed by their children. Roger De Corcey was not happy with the kids on the floor, but I told him that it would be worse for him if they went back to the tables with their parents, as they would be pestering their parents for drinks, crisps, and God knows what else, some would be running around, and the room would get really noisy. I must say that his act did not go as well as it normally would with an adult audience, but he did not die, and it was ok.

Of course as a performer I know that "ok" is not good enough, especially when you know how good it can be. Anyway after a couple of visits Roger was still not happy, and he complained to Head Office. In turn they got in touch with me, and I was "ordered" to clear the kids off the floor for Rogers next visit.

When he turned up for his next visit I was surprised that he had brought his agent with him, to make sure that there would be no kids on the dance floor. I gave him his wish, there were no kids on the floor, they were sat on their mums laps, many of them were running about, the audience were getting noisier and noisier, and the bottom line is Roger De Corcey died on his arse. If I had been him I would have settled for ok anytime.

Before we knew it we were into October, and the main season ended on the 9th I stayed on with a few selected members of the team to do the special event weeks, and my contract at Caister finally finished on the 21st November.

Last Christmas we had spent with our daughter Bernadette and her family up in Rochdale, and this Christmas we were invited to spend Christmas with our other daughter Sonia and her family at Exeter, where again we all had a very nice time.

We were back home in London to see in the New Year 1994, and after doing a few T.V. walk-on jobs it was soon March, and I was off to the Entertainments Seminar at the Haven Blue Dolphin Holiday Park, Filey. Most of the old Entertainment Managers that I knew, were now gone and been replaced with new younger Head of Entertainments. It was also noticeable that half of them were now female. There was nothing wrong with that of course, but they all seemed very inexperienced. However it suited the company as one member of the Head Office staff said to me that the girls were better at the paper work. In my opinion the paperwork was getting out of control, each year we were getting more and more

At the end of the Seminar I packed up the car and headed down to Great Yarmouth for what was to be my very last season at Caister. It was during this season that I received a letter out of the blue, from a guy who had worked for me as a Bluecoat in the old Ladbroke days. His name was Joe Wembourne who incidentally was one of the boys who took Nancy in the van across the site to the Bingo Session a few years beforehand.

Joe was now a partner in the Pantomime Company Chaplin's Pantos. It would specialise in children's Touring Pantomimes putting out tours at schools, clubs, and Civic Centres all over the country. At that time they were doing sixteen different tours, but today they are producing twice that amount. The reason that Joe had written to me was to ask if I would be interested in working for the company as a Pantomime Director. It would only be for two weeks but I was happy to accept his offer. My last season at Caister was another great one, but I did not know that it was my last until we were well into the New Year. The Accordion Festival was the last special event week that I did and finished on Friday 18th November. It all fell into place nicely as the following Monday 21st November I started rehearsals for the Chaplin Pantomime "Red Riding Hood."

Each panto had a cast of six, and of the sixteen shows that were in production I was directing four. Two in the first week, and two in the second. The company had hired quite a number of rehearsal rooms, and six Directors. It was assembly line production of pantomimes, but it did work very well.

It was hard work to split yourself between two groups of actors. But I soon worked out a system. I would work with all of them together on the first day, and on the second day when I had set things up, I would separate them in two different rehearsal rooms, and work with one group in the morning, and the other in the afternoon. The group that I would not be working with would then rehearse on their own.

I did enjoy working with young actors and it was nice to be able to help them, and give them the benefit of my experience as a pantomime performer. Many of them were young actors that had just come out of Drama School, and in many cases it was their first professional job. A few were ex-coats from the Holiday Parks, and indeed the very best of those were better suited for Pantomime than the drama students as they were not afraid to adlib and talk to the audience.

It was a very enjoyable experience, and very rewarding, it was also the first of many pantomimes that I would be directing for Chaplins. A Chaplin Pantomime was totally self contained, and after the final dress rehearsal each group of actors would load up their mini buses with costumes, scenery, PA system, lights, tool box, first aid kit, and everything that they would possibly need on an eight week tour.

The tour buses would then pull away in different directions heading for their accommodation base all over the country. I can tell you if I had been their age, I would have loved to have been with them. It was really a wonderful way for a young performer to be starting out in the business.

After a two week break I was off to Caister for Christmas and the New Year. I had not done a Christmas for a couple of years or so, and I was looking forward to it. It would also be the very first time that Caister had stayed open for New Year, and that would be another "first" that I would be involved in.

It was as always a blinding Christmas, and everybody had a fantastic time. It was difficult to imagine anything better. But when New Years' Eve came, it was out of this world, without a doubt it was the best New Year that I had ever had, the atmosphere in Neptune's Palace was out of this world. I had experienced some wonderful nights in this venue, some really great moments, but when the chimes of Big Ben rang out to welcome in 1995, that was a truly magic moment.

It was the very first time that it had happened at Caister, and I was so pleased to be part of it. It was about a week later that Haven Head Office informed me that I would not be going back to Caister. At one point it looked like they did not know where they wanted me to go. About three different locations were mentioned but nothing definite.

A couple of days later the Entertainments Chief Executive rang me and said "I'll tell you where I'd like you to go, - Presthaven Sands." He then told me that it did need a strong Head of Entertainment, and that I would be the right man for the job. He sold it to me, and I agreed to go, although the other two places that had been mentioned did not leave me with much choice, and he made it sound that Presthaven Sands was by far the best choice.

I had no idea at the time when I signed the contract but P.S. had a very bad reputation of being the roughest site in the whole Haven Group. It may have been a big mistake on my part over the years, but I was always so fully focused on what I was doing where I was, that I had no interest of what was going on elsewhere, as it was none of my business.

NOT EVERYBODAY MAKES IT

When I got to the Entertainments Seminar up in Scarborough on the last week in April, the idea that I was going to Presthaven Sands in North Wales was of great interest, and causing much amusement to the other H.O.Es.

After a couple of days I felt like I was going into a War-Zone. I was getting comments like "I hear you're going to Beirut for the season" and "don't forget to pack your crash-helmet."

During the meeting every time Presthaven Sands was mentioned a big jeer went up from everybody. I must say that I did not take too much notice of their comments, and felt that they were exaggerated. However it was not long before I realised they were not. I then began to wonder if the company wanted to get rid of me, and had sent me to P.S. thinking I would quit. We arrived at P.S. on Monday 3rd April, and by Tuesday I knew it was going to be tough, and a big challenge.

Unfortunately my super team from Caister had now broken up, and all gone on to do their own thing. From having a premier league Team of Havenmates, Head Office had sent me a group of Havenmates that were not even good enough for the conference league with the exception of three. However it was not all bad, as fortunately I was able to get my old mate the Crumble back on the team as the Presenter in the Dunes Club which was the main family room.

One of "the three" was a young man called Danny Fletcher, and Danny was a real diamond, was mister reliability, was like one of the family and to this day is a great friend. When we first arrived at P.S. we found a pig-sty, with muck and rubbish from the previous years. We had a week to prepare before the site opened for Easter. We all had to get stuck in, to shift the rubbish, but many of the team were not too happy about that, and thought it was beneath them. In between I also tried to get some kind of a show together, but again that was a near impossibility as the majority of the team had no talent whatsoever.

After a few days it became clear that many of the team were working against me. I had never experienced this before as I had always tried to build a family spirit in my teams, and we all worked for each other.

The day before we opened for Easter I knew, and I had to admit, that this was a real lousy team. The main Entertainment Complex was at the end of a long straight road that went from the main entrance right through the site. The road came to an end with a large car park in front of the complex.

It was nice and compact as it was all under one roof. The three clubs were the Sands, adult only room, the Carousel, a family club, and the Dunes another family room that was nicknamed "the Animal House" as the chaos and order in there was so bad. Every room looked like it could do with a make-over, but the Dunes was by far the worst of all.

The carpets were thread-bear and full of beer stains and chewing gum. The upholstery on the seating was also stained with big slash marks everywhere, exposing dirty foam rubber. All of the chairs were either stained, ripped, or broken, everywhere you looked was a real mess, I remember thinking when I first saw it, 'I don't know about Animal House, I think its more like a 'Shit House.'

Having said that once the place was open, it was jam packed. When the house lights went down, and the stage lights went up, you couldn't see the muck and tatty furniture and it looked quite good. It did not take the Crumble long to get into his stride, and he soon had the room rocking, as I knew he would.

The first night appeared to be fine in all three clubs, but trouble really started on the Saturday night. I was compering the night in the Carousel Club. At one point I came off stage and was greeted by a guy with a face like thunder. He was one of the caravan owners, his eyes were almost coming out of his head "That cabaret act in the sands was a load of crap, what are you going to do about it" he asked. Before I had time to answer three more owner's appeared, and all started shouting at me at the same time, complaining about the standard of the act in the sands. I managed to calm them all down, but that was not the end of it, the worst was still to come. These were the most unpleasant owner's that I had ever come across, and they were very hostile towards me.

It was like fighting a war on two fronts. I had the back-stabbers in my own team on the one side, and the hostile owners on the other side, it was not a nice situation, and I knew that it could blow up into a very bad scene. It was very frustrating with regard to the cabaret acts, as I had no say in the booking of them, as they were all booked from Head Office via Havens agency L.S.A

I must admit that many of the acts were miss-placed, and were not good enough for P.S. That does not mean they were bad acts, some acts will go down very well in certain rooms, and in other rooms like we had at P.S., where the audience are very hard to please, they would die a death. It was clear to me that the bookers at Head Office that were agreeing acts with L.S.A. had no idea what would, and would not go in the club rooms at P.S.

Easter was going ok, the Friday and Saturday had gone well apart from the incident over the cabaret act in the adult room. Then I walked into the sands and it was like world war three. I was literally pushed against the wall, and surrounded by four guys that again were all shouting at the same time, and I was blocked from being able to move away.

It was very intimidating, and this time they were complaining about the entertainment, or lack of it in the carousel club. It was Easter Sunday, and No cabaret had been booked in that room. Of course there was a band, a disco, a compere that did an audience participation competition in the middle of the evening, in fact it was quite a full night, but no cabaret.

The funny thing was, when they did have a cabaret, nine times out of ten, they took no notice of it, and the room would be very noisy, but if they didn't have a cabaret they felt cheated. Being as it was Easter Sunday a Cabaret act should have been booked, it was quite disgraceful to think that one hadn't been. I was very annoyed that I was put in this position, and I had to stand and take all this abuse from these four angry men, and I was unable to give them any answers. 'Why? I thought' should I be humiliated and insulted for other peoples mistakes.

I would estimate about 25 high profile owners who would cause so much trouble, and thought they owned the place, and would interfere, especially in the running of the Entertainment Department, at least that is what they had been doing over recent years. It was my intention to change all that, but I knew that it would not be an easy job.

These owners would always be in the Sands Adult Room, and in their eyes that was "their club." I remember the very first night in that room a woman in her sixties introduced herself to me, then said "I'm the Chairman of the Owner's Committee, we have a meeting in the pub at the top of the camp every Sunday lunchtime, - I hope the entertainment is better this year as last year it was crap." She had a strong Liverpool accent, and didn't even smile, I knew that she would be a tough nut to crack. "And by the way" she said "this is my seat, I sit here every weekend," - and sure enough she did, every Friday, Saturday, and Sunday.

The General Manager at P.S. was David Fisher, he was a nice guy and we got on very well together. He knew that a hard core of owners were "a pain in the arse" and was on my side, nobody had stood up to them before, and he liked the idea that I intended to do so, and gave me his full support. Over the weeks a few went to see him in his office to make a complaint about me, but they got no joy as he told them "Dave Thomas is running the Entertainment Department at Presthaven Sands, and I am very happy with what he is doing."

The next three weeks were pretty tough, and by now the bad apples in my team had been making phone calls to Head Office to cause trouble, and they were a bad influence on the other members of the team. There was only one thing for it, they had to go, so I requested they be transferred to another site, and they were. I was sent replacements, who soon settled in, and with the "bad apples" gone it was a much more relaxed atmosphere, and the team began working as a team.

One day a smart well spoken lady came up to me in the Dunes Family Room, and said to me "Hello, I saw you at Caister last year, what are you doing in a terrible place like this?" - I guess that summed up P.S., and I was beginning to wonder myself. I was so glad that my mate Crumble was with me, not just because he was a great family Entertainer but he was a true friend, and we could talk about the problems we were having.

I would still cover the comperes nights off in the three clubs, and always enjoyed my nights in the Sands Adult Room. When I was not performing there was still a lot of hassle, and at times it got me down. It was now the middle of May, and I felt this will be my last season, I'm not enjoying it anymore.' It was a real 'yo 'yo season then on the 6th June it was our first Late Night Cabaret. Topping the bill was comedy impressionist David Copperfield. I compered the night, and did the warm-up, and it was a great night, the best night I had enjoyed so far doing what I do best, proper show business.

The next couple of weeks, were much the same, and I was feeling up and down, by the middle of June I was even counting the weeks to the end, and that really is bad news, I have never done that before ever. Once the fun goes out of things it is time to give up, and I was now seriously thinking about making this my last season.

The next L.N.C was Tom O'Connor, it was another great night, and I was back on a high. The rest of the week went along very well, and I was feeling pretty good. When the American singer Sheila Ferguson came with her three backing singers, it was real class. I so much enjoyed working with class performers as I know that a little always rubs off on you. The following week was the complete opposite as we had Bucks Fizz, but I'm sorry to say there was no Fizz in their performance. Some of the comments that I received from the owner's were quite unprintable.

Funny enough the whole week went down hill after that, and from being on a high for a couple of weeks I was feeling very down again. It didn't last long, and the following week we had my old mates Brother Lee's who I had worked with many times over the years. Working with the Lees boys was always a joy, and the atmosphere backstage was just as it should be, we had so many laughs together, and I would always still be laughing as I walked on stage to introduce them. That is just how it should be in this business, and they always gave a great performance.

The whole week was a great week, its now the third week in July, its Friday night, I'm having a drink at the bar with Crumble, and I can hardly believe what I am saying. - I'm talking about doing next year again at Presthaven Sands. "I'll drink to that" said Crumble, "We've Cracked It." He drunk up and put his empty glass down on the bar. "Hey, don't get too excited" I said "I'm only talking about it."

It wasn't too long before the talking became a reality, the following Wednesday the G.M. David Fisher was having a chat with me in his office, when he said that he would like me to come back next year. I said that I would be happy to, and I felt really good about it. As I came out of his office, and walked into the sunshine, I felt really relaxed, and I knew that I had Presthaven Sands licked.

Three weeks passed by, and all was well, when two members of the band from the Sands Club came into my office. "Can we have a quick word" one of them asked. "Sure, - sit down, what is it?" - "We've got a small problem." It then went quiet for a few moments, and then again I asked "What is it?" then both together they said "we want to sack the band leader." I was quite amused to hear this, and then I explained to them that I did not think they could, as they were self-employed musicians, and the band-leader was the holder of the contract, and he employed them.

Apparently they were not happy with his leadership, he was never on time, and they felt that they were always carrying the can for him. I suggested that I would have a meeting with all of them to sort things out, and they were happy with that. We had the meeting, the air was cleared, and they all finished the season.

It was not unusual to see police cars outside the Club Complex at P.S. It was down to the fact that there was often trouble, with fights breaking out between local yobs that would try to get into the clubs and the security doorman, that did in fact look like a load of bouncers in dinner suits. I have seen as many as six standing across the main entrance, and they always looked intimidating, especially to the many decent holiday makers.

The man in charge of the security had been there for some time, and he also thought he owned the place. On my first week there I recall that he said to me that the song "You'll Never Walk Alone" is banned from all the clubs. "It would 'cause riot" he said.

It was absolute nonsense of course, and about halfway through the season I did get the band in one of the clubs to play it, and it was a great success, especially with all the Liverpudlians that we had each week on the site. From then on we did it every Friday night, it was a good way to finish the week off.

I must say that first season, there were a lot of fights breaking out, and I saw more police at P.S. than I ever see on the streets of London. It was during my second season at P.S., I remember an incident where one of the doorman was quite badly hurt, in fact a knife was involved.

The very next night I could not believe it, when I saw the same doorman on duty at the door, with a black eye, scratch's on his face, his arm in a sling, and a couple of fingers on his other hand bandaged. When I asked his boss what the hell was he doing on duty? He replied "I'm short of staff." As I was quite well established at that time I said "I don't care if you are short of staff, no way is he working in that condition, send him home now." - Nothing more was said, and he was sent home.

As my first season at P.S. was coming to a close, we were soon to be doing the finals week, and that was not going to be an easy ride. I had been planning it for a few weeks, and it was all set up. I had arranged for different Judges to come in each night for the different events, and the programmes were back from the printers. The week before it was all due to start, a few of the owners called me over and asked what time the Adult Talent Final would be starting on the Friday night. "Its not on the Friday night" I said "The Miss Haven Final is on the Friday, the talent is on the Thursday and it starts at 8pm."

"You 'cant do that" they shouted "Its always on a Friday, and you better get it changed." They all looked so angry and wound up about it, and at one point as was always the case, were shouting and screaming out at the same time, one of them looked as if she was about to burst a blood vessel in her neck. I waited until they had calmed down a bit, then I said to them, "Look, its too late for me to change anything now,' the programmes are printed and its all set up. I'm sorry if you are not happy with it, but that's the way it is, and that's the way its going to be ." - "we'll see about this" said the woman with the veins in her neck at almost bursting point, "we will be off to see David Fisher, and if he doesn't change it, we will be onto Head Office."

I know that a deputation went up to see David Fisher, and they got no joy, I don't know if they phoned Head Office, but I do know that nothing was changed, and all went to plan. I had no idea how hostile things could be at these Finals until we actually came to do them. I should however have had an inclination when David Fisher said to me "straight after the event get the Judges out of the venue by the back door."

I then heard from various different people that when the Result was announced, especially after the children's events, like the "Junior Talent," and the "Junior Disco Dancing Competition" the Judges would be abused and pelted with any bits of rubbish they could lay their hands on. One local Theatrical agent who I had contacted said that he would never judge again at Presthaven Sands, as the last time he had done it, he had been spat upon.

The build up to the events all went very well, from the first meetings of contestants, to all of the rehearsals. Everybody involved working on them did a great job, and I was very pleased when we were getting comments of how well organised it all was, and even some of the owners were saying that the organisation was the "best it had ever been."

As always I would have a different presenter for each event with the exception of Crumble who did both the Junior Talent, and Junior Disco. They were both fantastic nights with some really talented youngsters, but when the results were announced, I must say that the reaction was very hostile, but thankfully no objects were thrown at the judges, and I was delighted with the way the events went.

Rumours were now going around about what was going to happen on the last two nights, especially the Friday night. It was said that a hard core of Owners were going to cause disruption, and sabotage the "Miss Haven Final." I did not take a great deal of notice about these rumours, but of course I knew that it could be a possibility, but I tried to put it at the back of my mind.

Come the Thursday and the Sands Club was packed. The Adult Talent Final was an excellent show, the audience loved it, and it went by without any incidents. All was well until the winners were announced, and you could feel the hostile atmosphere over the result. Who would be a judge 'ay?, I must admit that I did not agree with their result, but it was nothing to do with me, and the Judges result is the final one.

It was the last night, and it was all down to me, as I was to compere the very last event. The "Miss Haven Final." It was at the back of my mind about the threat of sabotage, but I did my utmost to keep it there, at the very back, and stay focused. We opened with the curtain raiser that I had first done at Caister, "Standing on the Corner, watching all the girls go by" complete with lamp post and dimmer light. As the girls came on, the reaction from the audience was terrific, and I knew it would be a winner.

I had compered this event many times over the years, but this was the first time I had done it in a room for Adults Only. The place was packed, and it was like playing to a theatre audience. As I interviewed the girls, they were giving me the right answers to all of my questions, and I was able to come back with some great "one liners," and getting some great belly laughs. I was really on form, and I knew that it was my night.

At the end of the event, there were no hostile feelings from anywhere, it was truly a great finish to what had been a great week. Even some of the Owners that had been moaners, came up to me, shook me by the hand and said how much they had enjoyed the night. I must admit that first season at Presthaven Sands, was very hard, and I had lots of ups and downs, and some of my down moments were very down indeed. It never crossed my mind to quit, but as I have said I was seriously thinking of making it my last season.

My good friend Crumble was a great help of course, and I had no worries whatsoever about the Dunes Family Room that he was running, and that year they had record bar takings. Of course I was glad I stuck with it, and once I had turned things around I really enjoyed it.

I'm now looking forward to next season, and I am delighted to hear that they are going to spend many thousands of pounds giving the whole Entertainment Complex a re-fit.

CHAPTER TWENTY

From A First Class Dump, To A Touch Of Class, Stabbed In The Back

Two weeks after I had finished the season I was back working for Chaplins Pantos as a Director for their touring pantomimes, "Aladdin." Once again it was a very enjoyable couple of weeks, and all went very well.

Soon after that I did two days filming a T.V. commercial for the Woolwich Building Society, at Tunbridge Wells. That year Livvy and I had a marvellous Christmas at home, just the two of us, it was wonderful. Before we knew it, old Big Ben was at it again with those familiar chimes, and it was 1996. My first job of the year was on location at the Woolwich Arsenal as a walk-on, in "The Bill."

Before anybody had time to say "Your Nicked" we were into March, and were off to start my second season at Presthaven Sands. When I arrived it was great to see what had been done to the place. From what was a first class dump it now looked quite classy with new carpets and fittings everywhere. The adult room was now the "Sands Showbar," complete with electric plush velvet curtains, and the stage also moved out, and raised up electronically over the dance floor. The furniture and decor were excellent, it was indeed a class room. What was called the "Animal House" the "Dunes Family Room," was also unrecognisable with new fittings, carpets and furniture, and Crumble said to me "I wonder how long it will stay like this?"

Well it was only a matter of weeks before there was chewing gum all over the dance floor, beer stains on the carpets, slash marks

NOT EVERYBODAY MAKES IT

in the upholstery, and broken tables and chairs. - Well come on, we are back at Presthaven Sands after all. I remember one night I saw a woman change a baby's nappy on one of the tables. It wasn't an empty table, there were pints of beer each side of the baby. As she lifted the baby's legs to remove the dirty nappy, she picked up a pint of beer, and moved it, placing it at the top of the baby's head. I don't know what she did with the dirty nappy, I didn't hang around to find out, but I do know that the early morning cleaners used to find all kinds of unmentionables behind radiators, and in the weirdest of places.

Having said that, I don't think the management were too concerned if they wrecked the place, as the P.S. punters really knew how to enjoy themselves, and the place was always packed. It would sometimes take me ten minutes to walk from one side of the room to the other to get backstage, as there were so many people standing, that could not get a seat. A family of owners complained to me one night that they did not have a seat, a woman said to me "we've always had a seat" I said to her unfortunately we are victims of our own success, due to the entertainment this room is the most popular that it has ever been." I then told her, and her family that I would get them some chairs from the backstage dressing room. I then got one of the Havenmates to help me take four chairs out to this family. We carried two each, halfway round the room, gave them to the family, - and never even got a thank you.

The Carousel Club for the first time was staging a Resident Revue type show. It was a well produced show, and the dancers and their routines were very good, but the principal artistes were given a rough time by the very critical P.S. audiences. It didn't help matters with the kids that would continually try to get onto the stage. I saw one kid once in that room reach up, and try to pull the leg off a chair that was containing the cabaret acts props, he was stopped by a Havenmate just in time, otherwise the props would have been scattered all over the stage, and that no doubt would have started a stampede of kids nicking them.

The girl who operated the follow spot would wear these thick industrial gloves, as the spot light would get very hot. One particular night we were short of staff and the kids were getting out of control at the front of the stage. The girl on the spotlight still wearing her gloves goes down onto the floor to shift the kids. When asked afterwards why she had kept her gloves on? She replied in a rather posh accent "I don't like touching them."

The year before, a boy with a toy sword, reached over onto the stage just as the dancers were coming to the end of a routine. He caught one of the girls on the ankle causing her to trip and fall over with her shoe coming off. The boy then tried to pull the shoe towards him with his sword. The dancer jumped up, and as she grabbed back her shoe she yelled "give me that shoe, and piss off!"

Most of the caravan owners were very nice people, especially the new buyers, and I would get on very well with them. It was just the hard core that thought they owned the place, that could cause so much trouble. They would have their Sunday lunchtime meetings, and would forever be complaining.

One night quite a big name act was on during the late night cabaret, when somebody tapped me on the shoulder, I turned round to see who it was, and soon recognised him as one of the owners. He said "This act is crap," then turned and walked away without saying another word. Another time a guy came up to me and said "I don't pay ground rent to watch this crap." It was one of their favourite words.

It was not until my second season at P.S. that I realised that many of these owners, actually owned about four caravans, and would let them off. It was like they were running a mini holiday camp of their own inside a big one.

I remember one time, a guy came up to me, who I recognised as one of the four who had pushed me up against the wall, when no cabaret had been booked over the Easter Sunday on my first season. He said "I've got four caravans that I let out, and one of my punters has asked for his money back, because the cabaret was crap."

I can tell you it took a hell'ava lot for me to keep a straight face on that occasion. As I have already said some of the cabaret acts were mis-placed on that first season, and I requested certain acts for my second season, and in all fairness to Head Office, the booker gave me what I wanted and my second season was so much better. The first season I recall I was on the phone once to head office, and I said "One of the owners said to me, and I quote "The cabaret is crap, and its Bank Holiday weekend" - and a quick reply came back to me down the phone line "He can't be crap, he was in the Talent Competition last week, and he came second." - It was one occasion when I agreed with the owner.

The Caravan hire fleet were always situated in a different part of the park than the owners caravans. You knew when you were in the owner's section, as they were top quality vans and most of them were keen gardeners with some wonderful flower displays, with white painted fencing around the outside. At Combehaven they even had a competition every year, with a trophy for the "Garden of the Year," but no such competition at P.S.

I was in the caravan sales office one day when a guy came in, went up to the sales manager and said "I've been an owner for sixteen years, and never complained, - but I'm going to complain now."- "what's the problem?" said the Sales Manager. "The Rabbits have eaten my flowers." I didn't wait to hear his reply.

During the bank holiday weekend the caravan sales team would put on a promotion for owners and prospective buyers. The sales team would show people around the new models, and they would lay on a buffet outside the sales office.

I saw an amusing incident at one of these promotions, when an owner pulled up in her car, filled up four plates of food, put them in her boot, and drove off. The Caravan Sales Manager always had some good stories to tell, like the time when a guy went into his office put a carrier bag on his desk, and inside it was twenty grand in notes. He sold him a very nice caravan.

Another time he was showing a prospective buyer around the park, and took him to a plot. "This is a very nice plot" he said "as you can see, it has a wonderful view, and it's nice and quiet." At that moment a bottle came smashing through the window of a nearby caravan splattering glass everywhere. That was followed by a man and woman screaming at each other, 'effing and blinding at the top of their voices. The buyer then turned to him and said "we'll give it some thought."

My second season at P.S. was indeed a great season, unlike the "yo yo" season of the previous year. I had a very good team, I certainly had the measure of the place, and felt that I had completely turned things around.

We also had a lot of laughs, which is very important, like the time when the Crumble was organising a Treasure Hunt for the kids, and on the list of objects that he wanted the kids to collect he put on "A grain of rice." Soon afterwards I had a telephone call from the Reception Manager. She said "Could you have a word with Captain Crumble about his Treasure Hunt, the shop manager is going bananas, as the kids are opening up his rice packets."

One night in the Sands Showbar, the doorman handed a note up to the compere and he read out, "would Michael Barnes please go back to his caravan, as his mother cannot cope with the kids." - I think it got the biggest laugh of the night.

The G.M. David Fisher was now talking to me about next year. Who would have thought I would be at P.S. for three years. I would pick my own team and write up a list of cabaret acts that I would request.

During the summer young Danny Fletcher had been showing a lot of promise, and I had used him as a stand-in compere in the Carousel Club on the resident comperes night off. He had done very well over the weeks, and I decided to put his name forward for the compere's job next year.

My plan was, Crumble in the Dunes Family Room, Danny in the Carousel Club that would be for families with teenagers, and a new experienced compere in the Sands Showbar. I was thinking ahead, and was confident that we could make it even better than it had been this year. I then asked Crumble and Danny how they felt about the idea, and they were both up for it. I then bought around of drinks, we chinked our glasses, and all together said "1997, lets do it."

The season ended on a high on the 2nd Nov, and eight days later I started work once again for Chaplins directing their pantomimes "Humpty Dumpty" for three weeks, and that took me up to the end of November.

After a couple of T.V. jobs, I arranged to go and see my old G.M. from Combehaven, Mike John. Mike was no longer working on the sites, and had been given the job as Area Manager looking after the West End venues in London. Under his control were the New London night spot at Drury Lane, The Cockney in Tottenham Court Road, and the Butlin Grand Hotel.

After a couple of drinks at the New London, we watched part of the show before grabbing a cab, to the "Cockney." It was there that we had a few more drinks, had a very nice meal, then saw a terrific floor show. I was very impressed with both venues, they were top quality, that you would expect in the West End.

They were the quality venues that I would have loved to have worked in. It reminded me of my time at the Showboat Theatre Restaurant in the Strand all those years before. At the end of the night we got another cab to the Butlin Grand Hotel. My glass was never empty, no sooner had I finished one whisky, another one was there. If you go for a drink with Mike John, you never remember the last one. He laid on a chauffeur driven limo to take me back to Islington. I don't remember much of the journey home but I do remember it was three days before I felt sober again.

The early part of 1997 went by quickly, and on the 5th March we attended the Entertainments Seminar at Lyme Bay in Devon. At the Gala Dinner I won the Award for H.O.E. "Best All Action Park 96." I can tell you there were no funny remarks about Presthaven Sands on this occasion. After the seminar, we drove straight to North Wales, and arrived at P.S. on 14th March. It was great to see everything was ship shape and exactly how we had left it. We were soon into Easter, and the weekend had gone so very well, I remember thinking to myself, 'this season will be a Doddle'. I also felt that I would go out on a high, and probably make it my last season. Over the years I could never understand why so many musicians would get upset if the DJ happened to play a record that they would be playing in one of their sets.

It would cause many arguments between band - Leader and DJ, if there was a clash of numbers. The way I looked at it, was if you go to a party very often the same record would be played over and over, and everybody would enjoy it no matter how many times it was played. In fact a certain record would always be a nice memory of a great night. Some of these band-leaders that get so up tight about it, should listen to the recording of "The Ratpack live in St Louis 1965," with Frank Sinatra, Dean Martin And Sammy Davis Jnr.

Half way into his act Sammy sings "I've Got You Under My Skin" with just drums accompaniment. Soon afterwards Sinatra follows Sammy, and after about four numbers he says to the audience "We have a slight duplication here, but I don't think you'll mind" - he then goes into "I've got you under my skin." - Are you band-leaders taking note?

One night we had a big name band on the L.N.C. The place was packed with about fifteen hundred people. I opened the show and did the warm-up, and the Sands Showbar audience were really in a good mood, and I knew they were really looking forward to seeing the star band. I introduced a solo singer who would just do three numbers before they went on. We were all back-stage and the band were getting dressed and tuning up, when suddenly the drummer went ballistic because the singer was singing one of their songs.

He then did a moody and said "I'm not going on." With that he starts to take his stage clothes off, and pack his bag. He then walks up and down the corridor back-stage swearing and cursing every step he takes. The other members of the band took no notice of him whatsoever, and continued to get dressed, comb their hair, and tune their guitars. It was as if they had seen it all before. I had of course already spoken to him, but the time was getting on. I had by now taken the singer off, and told the audience that we will now re-set the stage and be back with the top of the bill in five minutes. The drummer was now having a row with the singer over him singing their song, the singer retaliates, and now we have a row going on back-stage, a packed audience waiting, and the drummer by now with his hat and coat on and bag in his hand.

In the meantime the other members of the band have not said a word, and are now ready to go on. I then put my arm around the drummers shoulder and said "look, there are fifteen hundred people out there waiting to see you, we 'cant let them down now can we?" he said "alright Dave, I'll do it for you, - but keep that fucker away from me". They went on, did a great show, and I'm sure that nobody noticed the duplication.

As the season went on, I was still wondering whether to make it my last, but it was proving to be my best season so far out of the three I had done at P.S. I must admit I was enjoying it very much, and when I went with the G.M. David Fisher on a trip to Scarborough for a couple of days, we visited a few of the Haven Parks on that coast. I was pleased to find that none of them could hold a candle to P.S. and I was pleased to get back. In fact we both felt very proud of our park.

I spoke to Livvy about making it my last season, and she felt that I still had a lot to offer, and should do one more at P.S. Both Crumble and Danny who were like family also said we could all do another one, but make it the last. We were all now used to the idea and G.M. David Fisher was very happy with the prospect of another season.

I did not know at the time, but knives were being sharpened at Head Office. It was a fantastic season, and everything went as sweet as a nut. On the last night even the chairperson of the Owners Committee, who was very hostile towards me on my first season, bought me a bottle of whisky.

The season finished on Friday 31st October, and we set off to return home the next day. It was less than two weeks later, that I had a phone call from the Entertainment Executives P.A. She told me that there was now a new pay structure, and all Heads of Entertainment would be on the same salary. The salary would depend on the size of the park. The biggest parks were known as Red Parks (it was a red park that I had always worked on) and the H.O.E.s on Red Parks would be on the top money. She then told me that my salary was well above the rest, and that if I wanted a job I would have to take a pay cut of £100 per week.

I could not believe what I was hearing down the phone, and the way the conversation was going I could see that she would not budge. The next day I spoke to the Entertainment Executive who I had known for many years, and he told me that there was nothing he could do, as it was all down to his P.A. (what kind of Govnor is that?). After giving it some thought, I did not want to let Crumble and Danny down, and I reckoned I could afford to take £100 cut. I then rang the P.A. two days later and said reluctantly that I would go back to Presthaven Sands for that money. I was stunned when she told me that she had offered Presthaven Sands to somebody else.

I then knew that they wanted to get rid of me, and I felt that I had been stabbed in the back. After all the service and good work that I had done over the years for Haven Holidays I felt I was treated really badly. If they had given me a years notice about the new wage structure, and told me that I could only be on that salary for one more season, I would have been happy with that. And as I have said it was my intention to only do one more season anyway, but to treat me like this, it was abominable.

I knew of course that over the years the H.O.Es were getting younger, and when Head Office said "jump" they would say "how high." They wanted to control everything from H.Q. and pull the strings. Maybe that was one of the reasons that they wanted me out. They knew that I was nobody's' puppet, and liked to make my own decisions, and do things my way. You have to be at the sharp end to know what works, and what doesn't work.

To give you an example, a few years ago at Combehaven, Hastings, there was a big mix up over a cabaret booking. It was in fact a treble booking, and I had three magic acts turn up. I knew it would be too much to play the three of them, as most magic acts do the same tricks anyway, so I decided to play the first one to arrive, and give the other two an early bath? I said to the other two "don't worry, its not your fault, and you will still be paid." Of course they were delighted with that. An inexperienced young H.O.E. would have played all three of them, because they thought they had to, and bored their audience to death. In fact I had heard of a couple of occasions on different parks when that did happen. If I had been able to fit two of the acts in the other two rooms I would have done, but they were both overloaded.

At the end of my second season at P.S. I was contacted by a boy band from Manchester. The boy who spoke to me over the phone had heard about the finals of the "Disco Dancing Championships" and asked if they could perform on that night as a guest band. I told him that I did not think I could fit them in. He was very persistent and said they would not charge a large fee. I stuck my ground, and I was very sorry, but I could not find a slot for them. The next day, he rang me again, and boy could this young man sell himself. It reminded me of when I was his age, and trying to get started, and I did admire his persistence. He then said, that they would do the show for free, with a view for next year. I then asked them to come down and do an audition for me first.

A couple of days latter in the afternoon they turned up to do their audition. Four black guys and a white guy, they were all dressed the same in track suits, looked very professional, and were friendly and polite. They did the audition, and I knew they were not the finished article, but they would be just right for me, and with a few more performances under their belts, they could be very good.

I gave them the curtain raiser spot for the final of the "Disco Dancing" Championships." On the afternoon they were setting up doing sound checks, and rehearsing a few numbers, when the Entertainment Executive arrived unannounced. He did not seem too happy and looking back now, I think he objected to the fact that I had booked a boy band without the permission of Head Office albeit the fact that it was not costing any money and was free. But he never said a word, and at the time it never even crossed my mind, that he did not like the idea.

Come the night time, and the boy band tore the roof off they were a tremendous success, and at the end of the evening the young teenage girls were queuing up for autographs. It was then my plan to arrange to get the boys booked as the resident band in the "Carousel Club" for the 1997 season. I knew that club was good for teenagers and with this boy band it would be packed out every night.

I put in a request to the booker at Head Office, but unfortunately it never happened, I wonder why that was, looking back now, I think I know. It was a great pity the way my long association with Haven Holidays came to an end. I left under a cloud, and I must admit that I did feel bitter about it.

It would have been nice to have done one more season, and announced that it would be my last, and left on a high, but it was not to be. Once I got used to the idea, I was not too fussed, and as I have always been a complete optimist, I knew that when a door closes, another one opens, as indeed it did.

Chapter Twenty-One

Its Not Good, But Think Positive. From Ents Manager To Casting Director, I Live The Dream

I was back directing panto for Chaplins once again, this time it was "Dick Whittington." After that I had a few T.V. walk-on parts, and by mid March 1998 I went for an audition for a T.V. commercial for Kellogg's. I was delighted when I got the job, and we filmed the advert at a car showroom in Mayfair.

There were a few of us who had to sample the Kelloggs Bite Size, and say how nice it was. However I could not figure out why it was shot in an expensive car showroom. After a couple of actors had done a few takes, it was my turn. The Director said to me that I did not have to eat the Kelloggs, but to make it look as if I was eating. I said that I would eat them, as it would feel more natural.

I was then given a bowl of the Bite Size but there was no milk on them. "Can I have some milk on them?" I asked "you want milk" I heard a voice say "somebody get some milk." One of the crew then rushed out of the showroom, to a shop a few doors away to buy a pint of milk.

When he came back he poured some milk over the Kelloggs bite size, and we were ready to do the take. I was then told to ad-lib the whole thing. As soon as I heard the Directors instruction "Action" I was into it. I cannot remember exactly what I was saying, but in between mouthfuls, I was giving it some, and saying how good it tasted, but one thing I do remember saying was "this tastes really great, Ring-A-Ding, Ding."

I did about three takes, and after I had finished, the crew all looked like they had really enjoyed it, then the guy who had gone out for the milk, came up to me and said "would you like a cold drink, - coke" "thanks that would be nice" - I then went over to where the other actors were standing, and the guy came up to me and gave me a coke. "He never got me a coke" said one of the other actors. Then with tongue firmly in cheek I said "1 know - they only do that to the star."

A couple of weeks later when the advert was shown on television, there I was, with the line "Ring-A-Ding, Ding," they kept it in, and I was pleased that they liked it. Soon after that I had a days filming at Windsor on a river boat in a series called "Brokers Man." It was on this show that I became very disillusioned with "extra work" as you got the feeling they were dragging people off the street to do the job. Over the past recent years it had been happening, but on this show it was really noticeable.

My next T.V. Commercial was an ad for Pringles Crisps that was filmed at Millwall Football Club, it was only as one of the crowd, and once you have had a good feature like the Kelloggs ad, you are never really satisfied doing this kind of work.

We were now well into the Summer, and I must say how wonderful it was to be in London at this time of year. I just could not remember the last time I spent the summer in the capital. I had been away doing summer seasons every year since 1963 without a break and that's a lot of summers.

I guess most Londoners take it for granted, as indeed I did, but London in the summer is a great place to be. You can see why so many well travelled people say it is the greatest city in the world, and indeed it is. The parks and the open spaces are out of this world, there are so many places to go and see, and to stand in the middle of Waterloo Bridge, or any of the others for that matter and just to look up the Thames is a sight to behold. And like the old Sinatra song "London by Night" it truly is a wonderful sight. Being at home in London in the summer of 98 I really enjoyed, and of course it was World Cup year, and I was able to see all the games on T.V. for the first time ever. It was also that year that Chaplins were to put out a Summer Pantomime Theatre Tour for the first time. They asked me to direct the show and the panto was "Humpty Dumpty." It was one week rehearsal, and all went very well.

It was soon after that, the other door opened that I mentioned when the Haven Holiday Door closed. Chaplins asked if I would like to take up the position of Casting Director and work in the office on a five months contract. Naturally I was happy to accept. This all happened in July, but it was on the 19th June in 1998, that I had that special birthday and reached the big Six-0. I must say that I did not feel like sixty, whatever sixty is supposed to feel like.

I was only grateful that I had remained fit and healthy, all of these years, and was looking forward to many more fit and healthy years. Unfortunately come the end of August, and it all went pear shaped. Well it wasn't so much a pear, more like a small plumb. I notice this quite large lump appear on the left side of my neck. I went to see my G.P. and she sent me to the Whittington Hospital the very next day. After having tests, I was diagnosed with having Non-Hodgkin's Lymphoma.

The only reason that I am writing about this, is that I hope that it may help any other cancer sufferers with the same disease. When you are first told about it, I cannot deny that it is a hell of a shock, and of course at that time you do not know anything about it, and all you think about is that it is the Big C. Well I can tell you that it is not like that, and that you are not going to die.

There are two types of Lymphomas, the low grade, and the high grade. I guess I was lucky in a way that I had the Low Grade Lymphomas that often grow very slowly. The high grade is faster growing and need more intensive treatment. Initially you go for quite a lot of tests, that when you first hear about them, you don't feel that cool about it. But nothing is ever as bad as it seems, and if you think positive it's a walk in the park. Over the next week or so I had blood tests, chest x-ray, a biopsy on my tonsils, that wasn't a walk in the park, but I didn't know anything about it until I woke up after the operation. Some time after that I had to give a bone marrow sample. My consultant told me that it would be the worst thing that was going to happen to me. I was expecting a rough time but in actual fact it was fine, that was, a walk in the park.

The very worst test for me was the CT scan where you lie on a couch inside a metal cylinder, it is quite painless but you have to lie very still, and hold your breath every now and again. If you are anxious about most of the tests they will give you a mild sedative. I didn't realise this when I had the scan, but I did have to have another scan, and the second time I asked for a sedative, and the second one was a good result.

It is now five years since I was first diagnosed, I go for my regular check-ups every four months, and I am delighted to say that I am on no treatment whatsoever. I eat porridge every morning, and plenty of fruit and veg. My plan is stay positive, and do not show the Big C any respect, he doesn't deserve it, put him out of your mind, he is so unimportant that he is not worth a thought.

Of course I understand that we are all different, and that not everybody can think like I do, but if you worry about it, then it will be like the dog and the postman, it will jump up and bite you on the 'arse. We must not let that happen, I'm certainly not going to, and if there are any new patients that are reading this that have just been told they have N.H. Lymphoma, I would say to you, its not as bad as you think, be positive and you can beat it.

It was about his time when all of these hospital visits were going on that I was due to start work in the office for Chaplins, of course I told them the situation, and they were very good and understanding about it, and I started working my first day in the Chaplin office on the 7th September.

I was kept very busy, as at that time they were producing 23 different tours, and were now down to a cast of five. That was 115 actors to find, plus 6 under studies. I was never off the phone talking to actors that were known to me, and arranging rehearsal rooms where I could hold auditions. By the end of the month we were well into the auditions at a venue in Forest Gate East London. I would receive sacks full of post in response to our advertisement in "The Stage," and that alone would take me many hours to sort through. I held auditions for a period of nine days, spread over three weeks. It was hard work, and very frustrating at times when people would let you down at the very last minute, but I did enjoy it, when the casting was complete, and that last name would go down on the chart it was very rewarding.

It would give me quite a buzz when we went into production, and I could see the finished product at a dress-rehearsal. To watch a pantomime and know that it all started with a blank piece of paper and see it grow. There are a lot of people involved of course, from the scenic artists painting the scenery, the dress maker making the costumes, the music and backing tracks being recorded in a studio, the props, the lights, the script, and then the Director makes it all come to life - I can tell you when you see that first dress-run it's a magic moment.

With all 23 productions now out on the road all over the country we were now into 1999. It was the year us long suffering Spurs fans had something to cheer about when we won the "League Cup" for the third time. It was the first time we had won a trophy since winning the "FA Cup" in 1991. It did put a smile on all our faces, but sadly it was not to last for long.

My contract with Chaplins came to a finish in February, but the last week in March they asked me to direct their production of "Humpty Dumpty" that was to go out on a Theatre tour in the summer. A short time after that I did a T.V. commercial that was filmed at Kilburn for Macdonalds. The following week I was sat in a tube train for two hours at East Finchley doing an advert for the "Millennium Bug." A short time later I went for an audition for a T.V. commercial at the Camelot Studios in Kensal Road W10, but on this occasion I was not what they were looking for, and was unsuccessful.

A short time after that I got three days filming at Pinewood Studios on the P.C. World advert. I then did a few T.V. extra jobs, and then by the beginning of July I was back directing once again for Chaplins other summer tour. Apart from "Humpty Dumpty" they were also touring "Dick Whittington." Before I knew it we were into September and I was back as the Casting Director in the Chaplin office.

Even though I did enjoy doing the casting, I must admit that an office job was not really me. My first stint in the office was a novelty especially after what I had been used to doing, but this second stint I was not so happy. Once I was out of the office and doing auditions it was great, I needed to be at the sharp end, working with performers, and it was always nice to be able to pass on advice and help young performers. That was my bag, not stuck in an office.

By now of course all the talk was about the Millennium, and we were rapidly approaching that historic moment when we went into the 21st Century. There was only one place to be at the stroke of midnight on New Years Eve, down by the Thames, near Big Ben. Livvy and I were there, and it was a fantastic sight. I have never seen so many people in one place, and everybody, was in good spirits. When the fireworks went off from the barges on the river, the sky lit up, and it was absolutely wonderful. It was now the year 2000 and London was rocking, I was so glad that we were there. You can watch these things on T.V. but to be there, that really is special.

It was the same for the Queens Golden Jubilee, when Concorde flew up The Mall and over Buckingham Palace with the Red Arrows. That was also great on T.V. but we were there, outside the palace, and that was "Extra Special." The many thousands in the crowd were singing "Land of Hope and Glory," I can remember I was standing tall, my chest was puffed out, and I was so proud to be British.

Indeed since I had no longer been going away for summer seasons, I was enjoying life to the full, and visiting places in London that I had never even thought about before. In our Capital City there are so many things to do, and places to see, that you can never get bored. Incidentally bored is a word that has never been in my vocabulary, as I can honestly say that I have never been bored in my whole life.

It was 2000 that Spurs reached the League Cup Final for the 5' time and made their first appearance at Cardiff's millennium stadium at the end of the match we were still suffering as we were beaten by Blackburn.

In April 2000 I went for an audition in S.W. London for a training film. On this occasion I did have the right look, and got the job.

It was a training film for the Home Office, and I was playing an MP. At least I think I was playing an MP.

We all had a wonderful weekend, as it was filmed over three days at the beautiful Wiston House, Steyning, W. Sussex. It was more like a weekend break, and the food was excellent. The summer flew by, work wise I had a few bits and pieces, and we had a couple of holidays. We did not go abroad, we had one week in Devon and a few weeks later we had a week in Cornwall, and both places are out of this world. There was one place of course that I had never been to and it had always been a burning ambition to go to since I was a teenager, in fact it had always been one of my dreams - New York. Livvy did not want to fly anymore, and I felt the dream was beginning to fade away.

A date that will always stand out not only for me, but for every true Englishman, is Monday 8th December 2003.

It was the day that the England Rugby Team brought the World Cup home on a parade through London. Livvy and I were there, and I would not have missed it for the world. I had never been a rugby fan, as being a long suffering Spurs Fan was quite enough. However I did watch all of the England games on T.V. during the Rugby World Cup, and was hooked, even though I didn't quite understand the rules.

We were in a good position at the top of Regents Street, near Oxford Circus. As the opened top buses turned the corner into Regent Street the crowd went wild. The players looked terrific in their light grey suits, and even though you could see they were enjoying the day, they all looked so very humble.

The affection and gratitude wafted up to the players from thousands of ecstatic fans. The roads were transformed into a sea of smiles. There were people on the roofs of bus stops, and some had climbed up traffic lights. They were in trees, anywhere they could climb to get a better view of their heroes.

From above, red and white tissue paper rained down, while the sound of "Swing Low Sweet Chariot" was ringing in our ears. The England Rugby team had put the pride back in England, and we were so proud of each and every one of them. In the summer at the

Golden Jubilee celebration I was proud to be British, (as I always have been of course) but now I really was proud to be English. It was a wonderful day, and I was so happy to be part of it.

It was round about November of 2002 when I was having a drink with my very good friends Crumble and Danny. We were in the Tramshed Bar near Highbury Corner in Islington. They also are long suffering Spurs Fans, and when it was possible we would see the odd match together at White Hart Lane. Two or three times a year they would come and visit Livvy and I, and then in the evening us lads would go out for a drink and put the world to rights. On this occasion New York came up in the conversation, and we decided that the three of us would go. Livvy was quite happy for me to go with the lads, and "live the dream". It was all set, and we booked a five day break. For so many years I had wanted to make this trip, and now at last it was really on, and it was going to happen. - New York here we come.

We were all set to fly out from Heathrow Airport on the 20th February 2003, when suddenly a dark cloud was cast over the operation. The week before, Heathrow was put on a high security alert, and a ring of tanks were placed around the airport. There was talk of a possible terrorist attack, with the aim of firing, a missile at an aircraft on take off.

Livvy was quite nervous about the situation, and suggested that we should postpone the trip. After waiting so long for this trip I did not want to do that, and I had no intention of letting a bunch of terrorists stop me now. No the trip was on, and we were all up for it, and agreed it was probably the safest time ever to travel anywhere, but we weren't going anywhere, we were going to NYC.

When we arrived at Heathrow it was indeed the tightest security that I had ever seen with armed police everywhere you looked. We were happy about this and so was everybody else, even though it did take a long time to get checked in. As we boarded the airliner I could swear that I heard Sinatra singing "Come fly with Me," and before we knew it we were up, up, and away.

On the flight out from Heathrow, a girl two seats up stood in the gangway talking to her friend. She had a London accent and was very loud, and did not stop talking for the entire flight. When we touched down at JFK airport, it was quite a relief to get away from the sounds of her voice.

We then got on the end of a queue to go through customs, and to our dismay there she was again, with her friends just a few yards up, her jaw was still going up and down ten to the dozen, and hers was the only voice you could hear. When we eventually got through customs we were told to go to exit 24. When we got there, you've guessed it, there they were again.

After getting our luggage, we came out of the airport and made our way to a Taxi rank. There were rows and rows of Yellow Cabs. I thought back to when I was about fifteen and was a regular film goer, somebody always jumped into a yellow Taxi and said to the driver "follow that cab."

As I have already mentioned many pages back, it was one of my early ambitions to do just that, maybe my time has come. In the old movies the cab drivers were full of chat with strong New York accents. It was not too long before I realised that I was in for a disappointment in that department. As we made our way to the end of the queue, we could see the yellow cabs coming up in a long line, and every driver was either Asian or Indian, they were wearing Turbans. Some had long beards, and many could not speak English too well. It looked like my New Yorker taxi driver would have to stay in the movies.

It was a minor disappointment, but there was worse to come. - As we got to the end of the line (as they say in New York) we could not believe our eyes. The loud mouthed London girl was at the end of it with her friends. As we moved up closer to them we noticed that she had a paper in her hand. Crumble was very close to her, then he turned round to us and said "They are going to the same Hotel as us." - "your kidding" - "I wish I was - the heading on her letter says the Ramada Hotel". I thought 'that's all we need, I know we are in a city that never sleeps, but what if she is in the next room to me, I won't get any sleep at all.'

A cab pulled up, the driver got out, he was sporting a big bushy beard and wore an orange turban. He loaded the girls' luggage into the boot, they all climbed into the cab, but none of us could hear where they told him to take them. As they pulled away another cab pulled up immediately, and loaded our stuff in the boot.

As we jumped in the taxi I was about to say "follow that cab" but the cab that was carrying the girls was now out of sight, and the moment was gone. However we were lucky with the driver. He was a Cuban with a Bronx accent. A stocky guy, with a bald head, he never stopped talking, but he kept us entertained for the whole trip, and gave us quite a few good tips. He had lived in New York for twenty years, and was very good with the oneliners, one of which was "Try not to get in an Indian cab, they stink of fuckin' currie."

We stayed at the New Yorker Ramada Plaza Hotel, it could not have been in a better location. Just around the corner to the Empire State Building, and almost opposite Madison Square Garden, it was perfect. As we walked into the foyer I said to the lads "well there's no sign of the noisy women" to which Crumble replied "there won't be, - I lied, " - I thought 'what a nice porky from the 'Crumble.

The next five days would prove to be absolutely fantastic. New York was everything that I imagined it to be, 'and then some. We took in as much as we could. The boat trip up the Hudson River was real special, we were all knocked out with the view of Manhattan from the river it was awesome. And when the boat went up close to the Statue of Liberty I knew that my dream all these years was now a reality.

As we walked up Broadway to Times Square, what a buzz that was especially at night, the lights were quite breath taking, to see for the first time. It was indeed the capital of the entertainment world.

We found some great places to eat. For breakfast we just had to try the pancakes with bacon and eggs, and boy was that some breakfast. One lunchtime we had the omelettes and fried potatoes, it was terrific, and the coffee cups were as big as a chamber pot. Next on our list, we just had to see a Broadway show. Danny had organised the trip and arranged the bookings so we figured it would only be fair that he picked the show. He fancied seeing the

Musical Rent, so "rent" it was. I never did fancy "rent" when it was in the West End, but this was Broadway, and I was really up for it.

We saw the show. Danny liked it, Crumble liked it but didn't understand it, and I didn't like it at all, but I must say that there were some very fine performances from some great singers. The next day we saw a Real Broadway show, - "42nd Street," and that was magic, but the lads still pull my leg about "Rent."

A ride in the elevator to the top of the Empire State Building was like a rocket to the moon, we were at the top in no time at all, and the view was awesome. We did all the usual tourist stuff and found some great bars, we even spent one night in an Irish Pub. The most memorable night though was in Greenwich Village at a Jazz Club that claimed to be "The Worlds Finest Jazz Club and Restaurant" on West 3rd Street, it was the "Blue Note Club."

When we sat at our table, straight away I knew that this was my kind of place. It was just wonderful to watch these jazz musicians at work, they were making great music, and were also great showmen. Top of the bill was a black girl singer called Regina Belle, and what a great voice she had, she did an hour show, and was truly outstanding.

The five days we spent in New York were absolutely amazing, I had lived the dream with my two great friends Crumble and Danny and we had so many laughs together, it was a laugh a minute, and that's just how life should be. We all felt very comfortable and safe in NYC, and there was a big police presence, in fact there were cops on every block, we were falling over them. In London you never see any police on the streets. When we got back to the UK I wrote a letter to the Metropolitan Police Commissioner Sir John Stevens and asked him when he was going to make the streets of London as safe as the streets of New York, and put the police back on the beat. I never even had a reply.

I love New York, it's a great place, and I would say that it is the second best City in the world. - As for the best, well I live in it, and I wouldn't want to be anywhere else but London. My life in show business has been a real roller coaster, but the ups and downs are all part of it. The downs are not very nice, but the ups are out of this world and well worth having a few downs for. From the early years at the Islington Town Hall, where I became quite well known, packing a suitcase and going up to Manchester and into the world of Clubland. The summer seasons in theatres where I really wanted to be, the class cabaret clubs that I enjoyed, the rough W.M.Clubs where I didn't want to be. The big Butlin Gaiety Theatres where I felt so much love and warmth from the audiences. The pantomimes that were always a joy, my London Palladium appearance where I knew I could have given a better performance than I did. Sunderland where I got paid off three times in one week, the Sunderland Empire where I gave my best performance ever, and knew that if I had lived in the time of the Moss Empires, they were the places where I was born to be.

I feel really grateful to have been able to do what I have done, and not once over the years have I felt like I should pack it in and get a "proper job" I always knew I would be able to work in this business, and I also knew that I would not become an old pro and I haven't. I have always loved show biz, and I still do, I have had a wonderful life in the business and enjoyed every minute of it. There are a lot of us out there who entertain, and bring great joy to a lot of people.

Not everybody makes it. BUT ITS FUN TRYING.

THE END

Printed in the United Kingdom
by Lightning Source UK Ltd.
125695UK00001B/326/A

9 781906 210526